LINDA SIMON has taught writing at Fordham University at Lincoln Center. She is the editor of a previous book, GERTRUDE STEIN: A COMPOSITE PORTRAIT, and is at work on a biography of Thornton Wilder, who, along with Max White, provided many of the intimate recollections that form the heart of her present book.

THE BIOGRAPHY OF ALICE B. TOKLAS

LINDA SIMON

 A DISCUS BOOK/PUBLISHED BY AVON BOOKS

AVON BOOKS
A division of
The Hearst Corporation
959 Eighth Avenue
New York, New York 10019

Copyright © 1977, 1978 by Linda Simon
Published by arrangement with Doubleday and Company, Inc.
Library of Congress Catalog Card Number: 76-23798
ISBN: 0-380-39073-6

First Discus Printing, July, 1978
Second Printing
DISCUS TRADEMARK REG. U.S. PAT. OFF. AND IN
OTHER COUNTRIES, MARCA REGISTRADA, HECHO EN
U.S.A.

Printed in the U.S.A.

Acknowledgments

For their assistance in the research for this book, my thanks go to Alma Compton, Irene Moran, William Roberts, and the staff of the Bancroft Library, University of California at Berkeley; and to Donald Gallup, Peter Dzwonkoski, Anne Whelpley, and the staff of the Beinecke Library, Yale University. And to Joan Brewer, Indiana University; Harry Mulford, the San Francisco Art Institute; Mary Ashe, the San Francisco Public Library; Phoebe Harris, Seattle Public Library; Nell Ezequelle, the Stockbridge Library; Ruth A. McLendon, American Consul, U. S. Embassy, Paris; Horace Robinson and Martin Schmitt, University of Oregon; David Farmer, University of Texas; Andrew Johnson, University of Washington.

For their kind responses to letters and questions, I am grateful to Carlos Baker, Joseph Barry, Alice Beer, Sylvia Bennett, Simon Michael Bessie, Martha Boaz, Dorothy Bowen, John Malcolm Brinnin, Melville Bruml, Vern L. Bullough, Fleur Cowles, Tess Crager, Neil Fabian, Bernard Faÿ, Paul S. Friedlander, Frederick Hard, H. L. Kirk, Calman A. Levin, Robert Levinson, James Mellow, Lois Rather, Herbert H. Salinger, John Schaffner, George Wickes; and most especially to the late Thornton Wilder, for his interest in the book and his warm recollections of Alice Toklas.

For their encouragement and many efforts on behalf of

ACKNOWLEDGMENTS

this book, sincere thanks to Anne de Gruchy Low-Beer, Paul Padgette, and Samuel Steward.

For the privilege of his friendship, above all, my deep gratitude to Max White.

For his cheerful assistance and continued enthusiasm, a special thank you to Fred Cabrera.

The most profound debts cannot be repaid in public acknowledgment; still, I am thankful to have shared the realization of this book with my husband.

Contents

In Memory of
Helen Pacula

1

The Years of the Lark

. . . The girl had never attempted to write a book and had no desire for the laurels of authorship. She had no talent for expression and too little of the consciousness of genius; she only had a general idea that people were right when they treated her as if she were rather superior. Whether or no she were superior, people were right in admiring her if they thought her so; for it seemed to her often that her mind moved more quickly than theirs, and this encouraged her impatience that might easily be confounded with superiority.

Henry James,
The Portrait of a Lady

One

SHE WAS BORN in San Francisco, California, on Monday, April 30, 1877, in her grandfather's house at 922 O'Farrell Street. In the next day's *Chronicle*, Ferdinand and Emma Levinsky Toklas placed a modest announcement of the birth of their first child, a daughter. They named her Alice Babette.

She began life in the optimism of the nineteenth century, when imagined order lent a certain security to everyday existence and rules nicely regulated hopes. She would grow up in "the Paris of the West," a city celebrated for its bounce, its gaiety, and its raucous innocence. And, it was assumed, she would glide quietly into the coming century, comfortable in the Jewish middle class, a well-trained flower of pale Victorian womanhood.

As a proper young lady, tightly corseted and weighted with six layers of petticoats, she could indulge in such temperate diversions as a stroll through Golden Gate Park. Only by walking pigeon-toed might she lengthen her strides without tripping on her skirts. Thus safely restricted, she could go as far as her legs could take her, or gain a kind of upward mobility by riding the cable cars.

By her late teens, the bicycle would offer some measure of liberation: she could, after all, go farther faster—but there was no transport beyond the strictures of her class and kind. After a suitably brief period as a dutiful daughter, silent and invisible, it was expected that she would marry a man of the same stock as she—German-Jewish on her mother's side, Polish-Jewish on her father's—and put into practice the niceties of household management, all her mother would teach her.

She would live her life in San Francisco, considered locally to be the finest city in the world. Its climate alone

3

aroused a chauvinism undaunted by experience. "There is no thunder and lightning,"[1] one resident asserted, only gentle September rains and mellow spring days; only blue skies and tawny hills; only gray-green fog settling over the city in the early morning and big bright roses blooming on a January afternoon.

Except in the central Chinese ghetto—an area of somewhat murky intrigue to those who did not live there—prosperity was everywhere. The city was built, and built quickly, with money from the gold rush, the silver lodes, the transcontinental railroad. Asphalt from the La Brea pits, thousands of tons, had already been used on new roofs and roads by 1875, when fossil remains were first discovered. By the mid-1870s, burgeoning middle-class neighborhoods climbed the hills, each house with its protruding bay window to catch whatever sun filtered through the thick morning haze.

All that glittered by the bay was imbued with the dreams of the Argonauts. Their daring for adventure, their lust for quick success, their insatiable longing for freedom inspired a glistening vision. Despite hard-binding family ties, despite an ill-fitting ideal of womanhood, the infant girl born in 1877 would know their strength and their special willfulness. She inherited their legacy of hope and spirit and color. And the color was gold.

In 1848, Louis Levinsky, twenty-one, and his brothers John and Mark, left their native town of Exin, in Prussia. Maps of the United States with mining towns gilded across California were being circulated in the villages of Eastern Europe, but the lure of wealth was not reason alone for the Levinsky brothers' departure. Inspired by a slogan scrawled on billboards and heralded in the local papers, they joined the thousands of Jews in Catholic Silesia who were "Up and to America!" "Can one live on freedom?" one editorial asked. "Only on freedom—it is the real elixir of life!"

They went first to New Orleans, where a building boom promised immigrants quick money, but after their newly acquired partner died of cholera they decided to seek prosperity elsewhere. Unsure of the future of the construction industry, enticed by rumors of the California mines, the Levinsky brothers booked their passage, crossed the isthmus, and landed in San Francisco in time to be forty-niners.

The mine they had heard about was near Mokelumne Hill between Happy Valley, Chili Gulch, and Big Bar on the Mokelumne River. They settled in nearby Botellas, nicknamed by some Chilean miners for the heaps of empty bottles littering the town. Botellas, it seemed, was "just one bottle full" from the surrounding mines.

Strategically located on the "Immigrant Trail," Botellas had already attracted a sizable community of Jewish ped-dlers who set up makeshift general stores. The Levinsky brothers joined them in a tiny "slop shop" offering such indispensables as red flannel shirts, thick boots, and bowie knives. Their first shop was next to the blacksmith's—a profitable, if somewhat noisy, location. Later, they opened three others at Sutter Creek, Dry Town, and Rancheria. With the income from the stores, added to the profit from their mine, they found they could live comfortably.

But life in Botellas, by then renamed Jackson, was less than satisfactory. There were few unmarried women and fewer unmarried Jewish women. Though prostitution flour-ished and San Francisco was not far, Louis and John de-cided, in 1854, to return to Europe for wives. They quickly found suitable brides: Louis married his cousin Hanchen Lewig; John, her sister Mathilda. In 1855 they returned to America, taking with them Lena Levinsky, their younger sister.

Louis and Hanchen, expecting their first child, remained in Brooklyn while the others went directly to Jackson. Though John had warned the two women that the town was small and rustic, Lena thought it "first class" and was puzzled by her sister-in-law's tearful homesickness. "How could I cry after all the boys have done for me and the amount of money they spent on me?" she asked the incon-solable Mathilda.[2]

By 1856, the Louis Levinskys, with their infant daughter Emma, headed for San Francisco via Panama. But Louis, unlike John, had not prepared his wife for the wild West.

On May 14, James Casey, irate editor of the *Sunday Times*, shot and killed his rival in publishing, James King of the *Bulletin*, who had recently denounced him for ballot stuffing. A vigilance committee was formed immediately and claimed 2,500 members by the next morning. Though Governor J. Neely Johnson called for the group to disband, the mob ruled, marched on the jail in which Casey and another political prisoner, Charles Cora, were held, and on May 19 tried, convicted, and sentenced the two. On May 22, the same day King was buried, Casey and Cora were hanged from gallows crudely constructed on Sacramento Street. That afternoon, as bells tolled throughout the city, Hanchen and Louis Levinsky disembarked.

Wondering at the ominous welcome, Hanchen asked her husband what it all meant. He told her that it was a mistake, but the temper of San Francisco had not eluded Mrs. Levinsky. Like her sister Mathilda, she thought that she had come, indeed, into the wilderness.

Life in Jackson was comparatively peaceful, though a hanging tree stood in the center of town and once, at sunrise, one of the Levinsky brothers served as an interpreter for a Swede on trial for having stolen a horse. Ignoring a bill of sale which the defendant produced, the judge swiftly condemned him to death, and his body remained hanging from the tree until noon.[3] In 1861, floods washed away twenty buildings. The next summer, the town was ravaged by a fire that cost Mark Levinsky twenty thousand dollars in goods. But the mines still flourished and business was booming.[4]

By the time Louis and Hanchen arrived, John and Mathilda had had a son, Arthur, and Mark had brought a third Lewig sister, Fanny, as his wife. Lena, too, was married. Society centered around the families and sometimes extended to a simple frame building completed in the fall of 1857, the first synagogue in Jackson, of which John Levinsky was president and the three brothers were on the board of trustees. The Jewish community—numbering about thirty—disregarded most observances and kept their shops open on Saturdays. Still, having a synagogue at the mother lode meant avoiding the trip to Sacramento's temple for marriages.

In the next ten years, Louis found himself more successful as a merchant than a miner. The lode on Mokelumne Hill began to run dry, and in 1868 he bought a tract of land in the San Joaquin Valley, left Jackson, and opened a store in Ellis. He loved his land and would have preferred to live on it if Hanchen had not objected. She missed the city's concert halls and theaters, claimed there were no good schools for her daughters—Laura was born in 1869 —and finally convinced Louis to go to San Francisco.

Louis installed his family in the Nucleus Hotel while a block of houses on O'Farrell was being built, one after the other, on the planked, even street. Soon 922 was ready, and Hanchen Levinsky took up her position behind her own bay window, her feet dangling above the floor as she sat watching her world go by.

O'Farrell displayed a milder scene than she had known in Jackson. The middle-class neighborhood often rang with the sound of strolling peddlers, junkmen, and amiable beggars. "Rags, bottles, and sacks" was yodeled in the early morning. One beggar serenaded with *"Die Wacht am Rhein"* or cajoled softly with *"Lieb Vaterland, magst ruhig sein."* Each Monday morning an old Frenchman made his way down the street collecting pennies for his hearty rendition of *"La Marseillaise."* And the knife sharpener, with his tinkling bell, called for "Any old knives to grind," in a soft singsong. On Sunday, the melodies brightened with the addition of the organ grinder who cranked out an Italian repertoire in front of the Levinsky's house. For Hanchen, city life brought her closer to her youth in Hamburg.

Like her sisters, Hanchen Levinsky was a short, dark-haired woman, with high cheekbones, heavy features, and dour expression. Better educated than her neighbors, she held herself aloof in their company, drumming her fingertips on her armchair and ruminating on what were taken to be higher thoughts. She read German and French, and even the London *Times*. But her greatest accomplishment was playing one of her two large square pianos, whose pedals had been raised to accommodate her short legs.

Family legend had it that she and her sisters had been pupils of Frederick Wieck, the austere music master and father of Clara Schumann. One sister went so far as to become a concert pianist, inciting her parents' wrath and causing them to disinherit her. Hanchen, however, took the more moderate course of performing for friends and family, occasionally hosting a chamber group in her large parlor.

7

In his own way, Louis was as formidable as his wife, with a somber appearance and unwavering opinions, aired to his neighbors as he walked to work or to his family as he presided over the dinner table. He was a stubborn Republican, a strict patriarch: a Victorian gentleman.

Emma took on her parents' seriousness without their willfulness. Quiet, gentle, she took pleasure in gardening and flower arranging. She was small, like her mother, but dressed with taste. Her hair was dark, her eyes blue— sometimes appearing violet or periwinkle—deep, liquid, and most memorable. When she was nineteen, she met Ferdinand Toklas.

Ferdinand was twenty when he left Poland and came to America in 1865. His first job was as a bookkeeper at the Oregon Woolen Mills in New York, but after a few years he went west, stopped in San Francisco long enough to meet and marry Emma Levinsky, and, in 1875, began his own mercantile firm in a ramshackle wooden building in Seattle. Auerbach, Toklas & Singerman, though stocked with only two thousand dollars' worth of goods, quickly gained a reputation for excellence and honesty. He and his partners were so successful that they were able to sell their business profitably within two years in the hope of establishing a similar firm in San Francisco, where Ferdinand and Emma would live at 922 O'Farrell, the Levinsky homestead, with the child they were expecting on April 29, 1877.

Alice was born a day late and, Ferdinand often reminded her, never found a way to catch up. He saw little of his daughter in her first years. Trying to re-establish his firm in Seattle, he shuttled back and forth from San Francisco, where Emma and Alice remained. As she grew up, Alice knew her father as someone remote, quiet, and reserved. Her grandfather was always an awesome, unfathomable presence. She was raised by women—her mother, grandmother, and aunts—and always felt more comfortable and secure with them than with any of her male relatives.

Fragrances and flavors were among her first impressions. There were gardens, especially one at a house on Post Street near Van Ness, where she often played with another child in his grandmother's backyard.[5] There were her mother's flower beds—Homer roses, dwarf yellow pansies, periwinkles, sweet peas—and delicately arranged bouquets that perfumed the house. Years after, she treasured a basket of sweet grass which evoked memories of her mother.[6]

She would climb into the lilac trees to pick the blossoms; her grandfather forbade her to pick any other flower. He was a tyrant, she decided. And lilacs became the favorite fragrance of her childhood.

Cracked wheat topped with sugar and cream, corn meal with molasses, or farina with honey for breakfast; sugared soufflé fritters, homemade raspberry ice cream . . . Emma's automatic ice-cream freezer, requiring no cranking, was one of the many new gadgets she collected. Her mother's handwritten cookbook, which Alice found years later, included recipes for melon marinated in liqueurs and a fragile vanilla wafer known as "Alice's cookies." Though fond of desserts, cookies, and candies, Alice could not forget a meal of capon braised in port, which always evoked for her the memory of one special birthday luncheon. But as a child, she was less interested in cooking than in spending hours poring over her button collection.

She led, as she was apt to repeat later, a gently bred existence. When she was old enough, the Toklases sought a suitable private school where Alice could profit by kindergarten.

Emma Jacobina Christiana Marwedel was a dreamer. "Her feet never trod the solid earth," one of her student teachers commented. She dressed in long, unfashionable smocks, wound scarves around her head like turbans, and delighted little children with her heavy German accent and strange lessons. She would sit across from a single child, manipulating cylinders, cubes and blocks of wood, bright and intricately graded objects. The exercises she devised were more rigidly patterned than those of Maria Montessori, and Froebel's theories, on which they were based, were attractive to many parents dissatisfied with the dull offerings of early education in America.

Miss Marwedel had been invited to America by Elizabeth Peabody, Nathaniel Hawthorne's sister-in-law and the alleged prototype for Henry James's Miss Birdseye, the indefatigable clubwoman of *The Bostonians*. After a few years in New England and Washington, D.C., Marwedel went to Oakland, Berkeley, and, in 1880, to San Francisco, where Felix Adler's Society for Ethical Culture had sprouted the San Francisco Public Kindergarten Society. Emma Marwedel was made director, training teachers—among whom was the author Kate Douglas Wiggin—and setting up classes for children throughout the city. It was to one of these that the Toklases sent Alice, paying the monthly tuition of six dollars so that their daughter could play with dolls and dishes, seeds and shells, minerals and insects, beads and cubes and learn German, English, geography, and a bit of arithmetic besides.

Her formal education begun, Alice was given over to her grandmother for piano lessons. But the task proved too arduous, and a music teacher, a Frenchwoman, was hired to come each Saturday morning for a session with her unwilling student. There was only one consolation: Saturday morning was the time each week's *Argonaut* arrived, a newspaper to which her grandfather had subscribed since it began in 1877. Though the reading matter was sophisticated for any child, Alice read it regularly.

Her grandmother was determined to instill in her a love of music. She took her to the Tivoli Opera House, known by San Franciscans as "the Tiv," where, for twenty-five or fifty cents, the audience was treated to performances which ranged from Gilbert and Sullivan to *Cavalleria Rusticana* and *Aïda*. At intermission, ushers circulated among the two thousand patrons, serving beer for the gentlemen and Queen Charlottes—raspberry sodas—for the ladies and children. There was a new opera every week, year round. Alice remembered hearing *Lohengrin* there for the first time and a startling performance by Luisa Tetrazzini, singing Violetta. Gradually, her aversion to music turned to an appreciation which deepened as she matured.

Two

EARLY IN 1885, Emma and Ferdinand departed for New York with their eight-year-old daughter, en route to Poland for the golden wedding anniversary of Ferdinand's parents. Alice's dislike for New York was not mitigated by sledding in Central Park. The city was cold and snowy, icy and bleak. The family took the ferry to Hoboken, where the steamer had to be cut from the ice to embark on its twelve-day voyage. Once the trip began, the sun shone and Alice happily played on deck.

When they landed in Hamburg, her parents took Alice to the Rentz circus, with its performing horses, dancing elephants, and brass band. Then they went on to Kempen, where the Toklas family was gathered for the celebration. Alice found her grandmother tall, elegant, and poised, and her grandfather quiet and gentle, despite family stories of his escapades during the Paris uprisings in 1848. Determined to see the battles from the barricades, he had left his wife and gone off to France. But when Paris banks refused to cash his checks, on his wife's orders, he was forced home. From then on, he contented himself with excessive patriotic doggerel and with the painting of fierce battle scenes, one of which he bestowed on his son Ferdinand. To Alice he read *Grimm's Fairy Tales*, frightening to the child brought up on Hans Christian Andersen.

The Toklases hired an English-speaking governess for their daughter and continued on to Stettin, where Alice drank champagne to toast her homeland; to Pest, where Alice danced the cachucha and waltzed until she was dizzy; to Vienna, Dresden, and Paris.

By then spring had come, and Alice rolled a hoop with bells in the Luxembourg Gardens while the Arc de Triomphe and all the streetlights of Paris were being draped in black crepe. She and her governess sat in armchairs on the Champs-Élysées while a seemingly endless procession made its way to the simple coffin which bore the body of Victor Hugo. But, having seen so many flag-draped caskets borne down Van Ness Avenue, Alice was not impressed by another cortege.[7] Much more exciting, thought Alice, was the house of Monsieur Worth.

Her mother quickly proceeded to the designer for dresses, coats, and suits to be taken back to San Francisco. "They opened my eyes," Alice remembered, "fired my imagination, and formed a standard for creative dressmaking."[8] She was fascinated by a certain dress of Spanish lace, draped by Monsieur Worth himself, and plunging equally deeply in back and front. Its suitability, her mother told her, depended on one's anatomy.

England was next, where her grandmother's brother lived with his Scottish wife and two young daughters, Violet and Adela. Alice and her governess remained with them while Emma and Ferdinand traveled alone for a while. One night Alice witnessed Adela's sleepwalking, both frightening and romantic, she thought, since it took place on a balcony without a railing. They were "sweet companions," she said, and they gave her a gift of a family of guinea pigs. With them, she visited an Indian officer who served elephant-tusk jelly, an exotic delicacy to the children.

From England they returned to Hamburg, where the Toklases spent some days with relatives of Emma. Alice was amazed at the regal treatment shown the family's two black poodles: coffee and milk were served them by a valet, a tray at a time. Later, when she had a dog of her own, she realized that the owners were trying only to control the dogs' greed.

Soon they left Hamburg to board the boat home, and Alice tearfully parted from her governess. On the return trip, she encountered former ambassador to Turkey and Civil War general Lew Wallace, who gave her an inscribed copy of his *Ben Hur*.

When they arrived back in San Francisco, it was necessary to find a school for Alice, and the Toklases decided upon Miss West's School for Girls on Van Ness, one of the city's outstanding academies. Geared for graduates who would go on to Vassar, Smith, and Wellesley—or at the least, the University of California—Miss West's curriculum was rigorous. The primary department, in which Alice was enrolled, included map drawing, daily mental arithmetic, recitation of poems, French or German, and featured Johonnot's series of Natural History Readers. Alice developed the facility of reading German aloud without knowing what she saying.

Mary West, a beautiful blue-eyed blonde, was a congenial headmistress. But Alice's classmates snubbed the little girl whose father was neither a millionaire nor a yachtsman, and Emma decided to find another school for her daughter.

Mary Lake, a distinguished fifty-year-old woman, had recently opened her school, attracting girls from San Francisco's upper-middle-class families. There was a fine library, bequeathed by Miss Lake's father, a judge. Though Alice was a day student, she boarded with the other girls when there was a special event. Kalakaua, the last Hawaiian king, appeared at the school's charity bazaar; Harvard's president Charles William Eliot once visited. Alice remembered his beautiful head—a head like a Greek sculpture.

With none of the pretensions of Miss West's, Miss Lake's was bright and happy,[9] and some friendships Alice began there were to last until her death.

Immediately, she formed a close attachment to a "radiant, resilient, brilliant little girl," Clare Moore, who lived in the house directly in back of the Toklases. With only a small backyard separating the two homes, the girls found that they could easily communicate with each other by a system of pulleys which carried a small basket. Though they saw each other every day in school, and often spent the afternoon reading books they enjoyed in common, the basket was in frequent use.

Alice felt warmly toward the three Moore children—Paula, Clare, and Jeannie. As they grew older and traveled with their mother—their father died when Clare was in her early teens—Alice kept up a regular correspondence with Clare. Though Clare was sometimes away for as long as two years, her friendship with Alice resumed with mutual affection when she returned to San Francisco.

Through Clare, Alice met Eleanor Joseph, a bright,

witty girl whom Alice nicknamed California Nell and called Nellie. Nellie and her sister Ada were exuberant and high-spirited, adventure-loving and independent.

Alice would recall with amusement some giddy moments of their childish escapades. On the cable cars, she and her three friends often sat on the four seats in front, the part known as "the dummy." As the car started, the dummy would jerk, cuing Ada to cry out, "I almost fell off the dummy!" "Who almost fell off the dummy?" the other three would chorus. "I almost fell off the dummy," Ada would reply.[10] Even years later, the nonsense question caused nostalgic laughter for Alice.

The Toklases took no major trips after their voyage to Europe except for a summer vacation to Alaska, a month's journey from Seattle on the large side-wheel steamer *Ancon*. Alice and her mother were rowed out to the Taku iceberg, where they posed for a photograph, and the Toklas family was taken to an Indian ceremony by John Green Brady, later to be appointed Alaska's governor, an important merchant in Sitka and a friend of Ferdinand. The forests and wildflowers, more vivid and beautiful than any Alice knew in California, were rivaled in her memory only by the Russian-Greek church in Juneau.

They bought a small totem carved in slate, some masks, two slate platters; such souvenirs of the exotic Indian communities were popular with West Coast tourists even ten years before Alaska's gold rush.

The pleasant existence as an only child was soon to come to an end. Alice, however, had not been indulged. She was required to meet her responsibilities cheerfully; goodness, she soon found, was to be its own reward.[11] She was a precocious little girl who spurned childish diversions. Once, given a jack-in-the-box, she watched calmly as the puppet popped, his face frozen in an astonishment she did not share.[12] But she was given to restlessness, again and again pestering her mother for activities.[13]

By 1887, the Toklases had moved out of the Levinsky home and into a furnished house nearby. One August evening, Ferdinand brought Alice to her grandparents for an overnight visit. When he came for her in the morning, he told her that he had a surprise for her—a baby brother. "Is it Tommie?" she asked, hoping to be given a small marble Renaissance head which belonged to her mother. "No, I don't think so," Ferdinand replied, and brought her to see the "small red-faced thing" who was not Tommie, but Clarence.

Alice, on the verge of tears, was horrified. "He is red like a lobster," she told her mother. "Are you going to love him?"

"Not like you, darling," Emma said, holding her daughter in her arms. "You will always come first."[14]

After the initial shock, Alice came to change her opinion of her brother. He was, she decided, a beautiful child, with Emma's eyes fringed by long lashes and the high coloring of his Polish ancestry.

The life to which Alice and her mother had by now become accustomed was, if not extravagant, certainly expensive. In Seattle, Toklas & Singerman, thriving under the management of J. B. McDougal, was among the Northwest's major businesses. In Olympia, Toklas & Kaufman's elegant two floors of showrooms stocked "dry goods, fancy goods, clothing, carpets, boots, shoes, hats, gents' furnishings goods, notions, trunks and valises. . . ." Ferdinand Toklas, a business review noted, was "one of the prominent and successful merchants on the coast."[15]

But on June 6, 1889, sixty-five acres of Seattle's commercial district went up in flames, destroying six hundred thousand dollars' worth of the Toklas & Singerman stock. Ferdinand felt he could no longer remain so far from his business and decided to settle his family in the north.

The move was delayed only by the last illness of Hanchen Levinsky. On June 16, 1890, she died, and shortly after, the Ferdinand Toklases took up residence in the gracious First Hill area of Seattle, where their neighbors were among the city's socially distinguished and affluent families and their view encompassed Elliott Bay and the distant Olympic Mountains. Alice was sent to the Mt. Rainier Seminary, a few blocks away, where the sisters Mary and Nina Cochrane taught their girls what little they knew. "They were from the Shenandoah Valley and remembered the Civil War, which was the occasion of considerable bitterness between the Misses Cochrane and their

Northern pupils," Alice commented.[16] The seminary left Alice too weak in algebra and trigonometry to be able to enter the University of Washington.

While in San Francisco visiting her grandfather, she contacted a local teacher, Sarah Dix Hamlin, one of the first women to graduate from the University of Michigan and a forthright suffragette. All through the summer vacation, each morning from eight o'clock, she reluctantly sat through lessons, and in the fall of 1893 entered the music conservatory at the University of Washington.

It was a dull summer compared with the previous year, when Louis Levinsky had taken his granddaughter to southern California when he visited old friends. They traveled by horse, mule, and buggy and even crossed into Tijuana. Mexico, Alice thought, offered little except souvenirs.[17] But the trip brought her closer to her grandfather and his "cronies," and inspired an affection for "things Spanish" that would never die.

At the university, still lacking confidence in mathematics, she became friendly with the first person she sat beside in her geometry class, a twenty-three-year-old woman far ahead of the other students. Viola Startup, Alice thought, was exceedingly lovely—a striking dark-eyed blonde.[18]

Viola was the daughter of a wealthy farmer, but since she had many siblings, it was necessary for her to work her way through normal school, and she supported herself as a teacher. Because she wanted to get a position at the high school, she was now at the university. She was bright, vivacious, and, above all, independent. It was her independence, especially, that Alice envied. Unfortunately, Emma did not fully approve of Alice's choice of friend.[19]

Mathematics was something to be endured, taught perfunctorily by John Hayden, a lieutenant stationed in Seattle, who imparted his knowledge to the often bewildered freshmen for very low wages. Music was Alice's consuming passion—her grandmother's influence had finally taken effect—and she found it shared by John's sister, Louise, a scatterbrained young woman who could barely concentrate on anything else.[20]

Even if Louise were somewhat flighty, Emma must have thought her a more suitable companion for Alice than

Viola was. Louise's father, Major James R. Hayden, occupied a prestigious place in Seattle society as a former member of the governor's staff, a bank officer, and president of the board of regents of the university.

While Alice enjoyed a diverting first year at college—dances, outings on Puget Sound, new friends—Emma Toklas divided her time between her flowers and the many women's clubs to which she belonged. On the hill surrounding their house, she planted small beds of different blossoms. The house was always filled with her beautiful arrangements, which were, Alice remembered, quite imaginative.

Though the depression which struck the country in 1893 was felt in Seattle, Ferdinand saw to it that his business recovered fully. He was active, too, in dealing with local reaction to Coxey's Army.[21]

On Easter Sunday, 1894, Jacob S. Coxey, a mild-mannered, bespectacled Ohioan, led a parade of unemployed men to Washington, D.C. They arrived at the Capitol on May 1, when Coxey, intending only to read a petition, was nevertheless arrested for walking on the grass "with the intent to commit a demonstration." His arrest spurred scenes of discontent throughout the country, and in Seattle farmers were especially disgruntled. Ferdinand joined a small committee of men who channeled tools and implements to the farmers and tried to maintain good prices for their harvests.

At the same time, his own firm, Toklas & Singerman, moved to larger and more sumptuous quarters with a more extensive stock. His five-story yellow brick building was fireproof; he employed over one hundred "hand-picked" salesmen; and, unlike many of his competitors, he hired an advertising manager to boost his image and his sales. "It is undoubtedly the busiest and most profitable acre and one-third in the Northwest," a trade journal noted and, in keeping with Ferdinand's temperament, it was run "quietly and methodically . . . like the stroke of a perfect engine. . . ."[22]

But the family was to be uprooted once again. The next spring, Emma became ill; cancer was diagnosed, and an operation performed. She was slow in regaining her strength, more doctors were consulted, and Ferdinand decided to return to San Francisco, where surgeons would determine if still another operation was necessary. The furniture was packed, and Alice and her eight-year-old brother moved into a house at 2300 California Street.

Several more operations left Emma so weak that even a drive through Golden Gate Park proved too great an exertion for her. Alice was required to keep house, caring for her father and brother and tending her mother. At eighteen, the age when she would have made her entrance into the social world, she was forced to remain at home.[23]

The new friends she had made in Seattle were left behind, and she returned to Clare Moore and the Joseph sisters. But now, she could no longer partake in their lively adventures. When they called for her, they often found her busy making soup, cleaning the house, taking on her mother's duties. They wondered why she never thought to put aside her chores for some diversion, but Alice took her responsibilities seriously. For many years, she dropped out of the foursome.

Instead, she renewed a friendship with a quiet young woman, Lily Anna Elizabeth Hansen, four years younger and still a student at Miss West's. Lilyanna, as Alice called her, was the eldest child of Danish parents, a quiet and gracious person who shared Alice's interest in music. Alice soon became close friends with her and frequently called for her to go on walks. Sometimes accompanying them was Lily's younger sister, Agnes Camilla, or her brother Frederic. Frederic was doted on by the girls. The charming young man, Alice remembered, refused to eat pancakes because he was afraid it would ruin his complexion. The Hansens were a gentle, reserved family, though on request Lily taught Alice some useful Danish expletives.

Another of her few friends was Annette Rosenshine, related to her on her father's side. Annette, then fifteen, had known Alice since she was six and had admired her even then. Alice had been sophisticated in a way that other children weren't, didn't play with dolls, and treated the withdrawn Annette as an adult. The admiration grew, nurtured by Annette's own insecurity. She had been born with a harelip and cleft palate, and no operation had yet been performed to correct the deformity or relieve her nasal speech. Once, trying on hats in a department store, she caught sight of her face in a three-way mirror and drew back, startled and repulsed.[24] To Annette, Alice was a princess—poised, confident, strong.

Annette found Alice changed after her few years in Seattle. She had evidently met people unlike those she was used to in San Francisco. She had a worldliness she did not have before, an air that seemed the sole possession of those enviable Gibson girls.

"The Gibson girl was the rage at the time," Annette wrote later. "Our clothes were replicas of the styles and gowns he depicted and whatever we might have imagined about the girls' behavior."[25] Alice, to her mother's astonishment and her father's horror, had framed a Gibson girl illustration and hung it in the sitting room.[26] Gibson's pen had created a queen, a long-limbed, athletic goddess, the quintessential American girl. She was tall because, according to one commentator, "It is the fashion for girls to be tall. . . . This is much more than saying that tall girls are the fashion. It means not only that the tall girl has come in but that girls are really becoming tall, because it is the fashion and because there is a demand for that sort of girl." She was bright and independent, with a condescending grace that made men, women, and especially her parents defer to her. And to plump Alice, barely five feet tall, and Annette, with her distressing harelip, she was the essence of womanhood.

Three

On March 10, 1897, Emma died. There were now two households bereft of a woman to run them as quietly and efficiently as Ferdinand conducted his business. Louis Levinsky decided that everyone would benefit if Alice took over 922 O'Farrell Street, moving there with Ferdinand and Clarence. Alice balked, but Louis insisted; and Ferdinand decided to vacate the house at 2300 California.

She became, as she put it, "the responsible granddaughter" in a house filled with male relatives—not only her grandfather, father, and brother, but uncles and cousins from neighboring cities. "When I went to dine," Annette remembered, "I felt most keenly the stultifying pall that hung over the dining room; the stale smell from the chain of after-dinner cigars that were smoked during these discussions clung tenaciously to drapes and carpet, and seemed to saturate the wooden frames of the chairs. Alice and I sat meekly swallowing our food, never attempting to venture an opinion, nor were we encouraged to do so; quickly we fled at the first opportunity to Alice's room to reestablish our lost identities."[27]

The discussions centered on politics and economics, often dominated by John's son Arthur, a rising young attorney from Stockton. Even Louis deferred to his nephew's unshakable opinions. Alice's ideas were ignored or dismissed with a laugh. Arthur, it was acknowledged, was a "crackerjack."

But even Arthur's domineering views could not dissuade Alice from her own political opinions. In a house of stalwart Republicans, she considered herself a "good democrat." In a city which relegated the Chinese to the most demeaning existence, she was ardently pro-Chinese. She read the *Argonaut*, she said, because Frank Pixley's editorials expressed her own feelings.

Colonel Frank Pixley, a former U.S. district attorney, began his weekly because he wanted to run the Irish Catholics out of San Francisco politics. Concerned with that personal mission, he paid little attention to the literary quality of the paper; those editorial tasks were given to such writers as Ambrose Bierce. Its literary standards, therefore, were so high and so exacting that the *Argonaut* became the one paper read by the journalists, artists, sculptors, architects, and poets of "Bohemia." Its stance was uniformly irreverent. "The most universally popular act of the President," it reported once, "was when he gave his arm to his wife and walked to Foundry Church. His best friend did not expect him to do anything quite so good as this."

The paper was supported by advertisements from the San Francisco Establishment, but eschewed its domination. "We advertise the Bank of Nevada, the Hibernia Bank, and some other of our money institutions," they announced. "Whether our advertisement is of any service to them or not we do not know, and if we thought we returned them no equivalent in this way, we should still take their money without any feeling of embarrassment."

Alice described herself then as intensely political, and her concerns transcended the local scene. In 1898, David Starr Jordan, a noted ichthyologist, turned his investigations to the biological aspects of war. While his previous lectures had taken place at the Academy of Sciences and dealt with the nature of fishes, he now began to speak at clubs and schools about disarmament, international arbitration, and peace.

Tall, handsome, personable, Jordan, who had lost an older brother in the Civil War, was a convincing and attractive speaker. Alice attended his lectures on the Napoleonic Wars and was greatly moved. It was from Jordan, she told Alfred North Whitehead years later, that she learned her pacifism.[28] Jordan's was a pacifism based on eugenics, on Darwin's theories turned to sociology, on science as the great hope of the new century. Jordan told his audiences,

In a picture gallery in Brussels, there is a painting by Wiertz, most cynical of artists, representing the man of the Future and the things of the Past. A naturalist holds in his right hand a magnifying glass, and in the other a handful of Napoleon and his marshals, guns and battle-flags—tiny objects swelling with meaningless glory. He examines these intensely, while a child at his side looks on in open-eyed wonder. She cannot understand what a grown man can find in these curious trifles that he should take the trouble to study them.

This painting is a parable designed to show Napoleon's real place in history. It was painted within a dozen miles of the field of Waterloo, and not many years after the noise of its cannon had died away. It shows the point of view of the man of the future. Save in the degradation of France, through the impoverishment of its life-blood, there is little in human civilization to recall the disastrous incident of Napoleon's existence.[29]

But the Levinsky dinner table was not the place for talk of pacifism. It was, Annette said, "a world of decrepit Victorian gentlemen," from which the two young women were glad to escape. Even in her own room, Alice had little to reflect her personality—only, perched on a black writing desk, a life-size plaster sculpture, Alice's own, the head and shoulders of a woman, which she called "the Unknown."[30] In this refuge, she and Annette would smoke, once unexpectedly caught by Ferdinand, who sarcastically remarked, "Very commendable"; or they would discuss Henry James, Alice's passion.

Annette read some of James's novels to please Alice, but Alice read them with the devouring spirit of many young women in raunchy, glittering, boisterous San Francisco. James created a Europe of dreams, a Paris more a state of mind than a city, a London veiled by a benign but alluring mystery. His women, though sometimes undone by circumstance, were nevertheless mistresses of their fate. And his sharp sarcasm about his native land was understood by his American readers. "I don't believe it!" his Christopher Newman says in complete seriousness. "I don't believe that, in America, girls are ever subjected to compulsion. I don't believe there have been a dozen cases of it since the country began."[31]

In James's books, which she would read and reread throughout her life, Alice found refined company and cultivated society. The genteel world he so gravely etched was a world whose existence she did not doubt. And the life which he presented was infinitely more attractive than the life she led. As one critic later recognized, James understood "the art of the kind of life in which one can do what one wants."[32] And Alice would live it.

She was twenty when she took over the Levinsky household, and whatever vague plans she had about her future, she needed a dream to endure the present. With the equivalent of an associate degree in music, she decided to continue studying piano with the hope of becoming a concert pianist. She attended as many concerts as she could, she recalled, and for a time her whole life centered on music.[33] Her teachers were two of the best that San Francisco offered.

Otto Bendix was a Danish pianist who had studied with Liszt and taught at the New England Conservatory before coming to San Francisco in 1890. Young and enthusiastic, he would salute his students with "Hats off to you" when they pleased him. Through him, Alice found Bach. Nothing she ever learned, she admitted later to Lilyanna Hansen, also a student of Bendix, proved as vital to her life as Bach, and she felt forever thankful to Otto Bendix.[34]

Oscar Weil, with whom Alice studied theory, was "a pedagogue of the old school, believing in thoroughness and educating young musicians according to the rules of absolute efficiency without arousing false hopes or making his lessons merely commercial propositions. When you studied with Weil," one of his students said, "you were sure to know your business."

Weil, a slim, energetic man with sparkling blue eyes, conveyed to his students a personal aesthetic that they respected and revered. He talked with them of books, painting, poetry. Music, he told them, must somehow spur "some degree of growth of the better self." Technical proficiency alone was meaningless; music must come from the heart: art could not be reduced to arithmetic. To Weil, there was no understanding more significant than the deepest personal response. "One may dilate on the technique or methods of the painter and have said nothing at all. . . . There is no printed word that will describe the beauty of a line, no cunningly contrived phrase that will convey the charm of a tint." The bell that rang for Alice when she encountered genius was a sounding that Weil would recognize.

Music gave her access to a world outside her family. She often joined the gatherings which Bendix hosted at a local café, and found she could participate easily in the bright conversation. Merely by reading the reviews of books, she told Annette, she could discuss them with authority.[35] Her friends were musicians and students who shared her enthusiasm.

The young woman who existed outside the Levinsky household was different in spirit and appearance from the submissive granddaughter who planned menus and cooked meals and watched over her younger brother. At home, she wore a long gray dress, reminding Annette of a Quaker. On the street, she buttoned herself into a severe gray suit and wore a gray cloth turban, seeming, one friend thought, like a nun. She darted past her neighbors with lowered eyes, and kept her passive demeanor even when she went out with her family.

On Saturday evenings, Ferdinand and Alice would sometimes join Annette and her father at one of the local taverns which featured an orchestra. Ferdinand invariably requested a Hungarian czardas, complimenting the conductor with a stein of beer. Alice and Annette, wary of their chaperons, would dare only to "cast modest sheep's eyes at the attractive young men" and, at most, raise their glasses to one of them.[36]

She was a lively, curious, adventure-loving young woman forced to be an onlooker to the spirited art world that would make its notoriety as San Francisco Bohemia.[37] Among her friends was Gelett Burgess, a former instructor of topographical drawing at the University of California, whose *Lark* soared euphorically for two years. The journal was inspired by the *Yellow Book*, published in

London, which Alice had read with amusement when it was first published in 1894. The *Yellow Book*, its editors said, looked "backward to the waning age of Victoria and forward to the age of the artist's alienation," just as the *Lark*'s founders saw themselves as protesters of emancipation from the narrow literary dicta of the nineteenth century. The *Lark*, Burgess wrote, "protested the joy of life, the gladness of youth and love, and the belief that those shall endure." The gaiety of the nineties, the exuberance and the innocence, are hardly expressed better than in the silly Goops cartoons which Burgess invented, the ticklish nonsense rhymes that found their way onto the ecru bamboo paper, the literary pranks which characterized the *Lark*.

Alice thought Burgess' drawings were definitely ahead of their time,[38] and admired the *Lark* for its animation and the skepticism with which its writers examined their culture.[39]

But her own forays into Bohemia were rare. With Annette, who had left school to study art at the Mark Hopkins Institute, she attended the annual Mardi Gras, one of the major social events of the winter season. Each February, the spacious Hopkins mansion on Nob Hill was opened to socialites, artists, and a few students for a masquerade and dinner.

Alice and Annette quickly fled from the eyes of their fathers and immersed themselves in the festive atmosphere. At once, Annette saw the change in her friend. Alice, her dark hair and gray-green eyes bright, had come as Carmen and immediately attracted the attention of a tableful of artists who asked her to join them. Annette was forsaken for more attractive company and, watching from the side, was surprised at Alice's boldness and regretful of her own "childish nibbling at the edges of Bohemia." The evening, Alice told Annette later, had been "most hilarious."[40]

Annette's company, not only at the Hopkins frolic, was beginning to irritate Alice. She thought Annette was using her deformity as a defense, and was stifled by the younger woman's dependence on her.[41] Ferdinand urged her to be more understanding, but the friendship was clearly growing cooler. Even Annette's devotion and desire to please her did not inspire compassion. Alice was interested in more mature friends—friends who led a wider life. Gradually, Annette was replaced by Harriet Levy, the woman who lived next door to the Levinskys.

Harriet was a writer, the drama critic of the *Wave*, a new weekly that vied with the *Argonaut* for its readership among the art circles. She was intelligent and intuitive, Alice thought, and the two shared an interest in theater.[42] John O'Hara Cosgrave, the journal's editor, had created a paper filled with lively stories and thoughtful essays; in accordance with its name, it was intended for those in the social swim. Of all his staff, Cosgrave considered Harriet Levy and novelist Frank Norris to be his rising stars.

Though Harriet was rarely invited to the Levinsky home, her window faced Alice's and long conversations could be conducted in privacy. Sometimes a tapping at the pane caught Harriet's attention, and she would raise her window to receive a bouquet. The excursions that Alice once took with Annette were now taken with Harriet.

Annette had discovered the small artists' colony at Monterey on a sketching outing and loved it at once. The village was built in a crescent around the bay, with white, red-roofed houses and fragrant rose gardens. It was the quiet, peaceful town in which Robert Louis Stevenson had made his home. "The population of Monterey," he wrote, "is about that of a dissenting chapel on a wet Sunday in a strong church neighborhood." Its Main Street was bordered by adobe houses, whose window boxes sprouted geraniums or trailed fuchsia. For Alice and Annette, and later for Alice and Harriet, Monterey was a refuge.

Alice stabled a horse there, which she would saddle in the early morning and ride madly along the then-rustic seventeen-mile drive toward the point at Tres Pinos. The flight to Monterey became an annual event. Before her departure in the spring, Alice would gather together all her old clothes and sell them to the junkman. Sometimes she would throw in a household utensil or one of her grandfather's sets of woolen underwear. Then, with the proceeds, she took a room at Señorita Bonifacio's adobe inn, known romantically as Sherman's Rose.

Maria Ygnacia Bonifacio, legend had it, was once beloved of General W. T. Sherman. He planted a rosebush in her garden, promising to come back to marry her when the roses bloomed. Thirty years later, with a twinkle in her eye, Señorita Bonifacio nurtured the rosebush as carefully as she did the tale, attracting visitors and tourists who would buy a bouquet of the gold-of-Ophir roses.

The inn was popular with artists and writers, who seemed not to mind its lack of conveniences. Francis McComas, a watercolorist, had managed to build a shower in the center of the patio, which he blockaded with gunnysacks and fed by a hose. But the faucet was inaccessible to the bather, and Señorita Bonifacio had to stand by to turn the water on and off. The other plumbing was correspondingly inadequate.

Though Alice speculated that the rosebush was not the gift of the wayward general, she agreed to promote the innkeeper's story. She would stand in the garden, draped in a fringed Spanish shawl, and pretend to be the daughter of the house. Tourists were as much delighted as Señorita Bonifacio herself, who would, with a wink and a smile, encourage the deception.[43]

But though Alice was charmed by the story, she thwarted any romance in her own life. If one of the guests began to pay too much attention to her, Harriet noticed, "a romance budded but did not blossom, for Alice fled before the pressure of a wooing."[44]

The highlight of the stay at Monterey was a dinner at the elegant, towering Del Monte Hotel. Wearing her most distinguished clothes and her customary white gloves, Alice would hire a carriage to take her through the pine forests to the hotel, generously tip the groom, dine in rare splendor—and return to the modest Sherman's Rose on foot.

She left her dull gray clothing in San Francisco and brought to Sherman's Rose stunning silk robes that she had bought in Chinatown, batik dresses, a long blue brocaded merchant's coat. Going to Monterey was always refreshing, she said, and once, on their last night of a vacation, she and Harriet aired their disgust at "grandfathers, uncles, German cousins, and all the impedimenta of life, liberty and the pursuit of happiness." Harriet asked for a toast, and Alice, swinging herself onto the table, raised her glass to the ceiling. "To the eternal damnation of the Crackerjack of San Joaquin Valley!" she cried, and she and Harriet downed their drink, choking with laughter. But the following day, Harriet said, "she returned to San Francisco, re-entered her monastic livery, and gave faultless service . . . for another year."[45]

At home, Harriet observed, Alice was looked upon "only as a housekeeper, provider of food and of general comfort." Annette was amazed at the efficiency with which the household was run. Alice had learned everything on her own, managing with a meager food allowance. The merchants at the California Street market tried amiably to dissuade her from economy.[46] But she learned then how to stretch a meal, come to an understanding with the grocers, plan a menu, and ration her supplies.

Moreover, she accepted full responsibility for raising her brother. She helped him with his schoolwork, made sure he attended classes, tutored him so diligently that he was able to skip two grades in grammar school despite a six-month illness. Clarence became close to his father, which pleased Alice, but she was doubtful that he should have been given so much freedom. Once, when he was ten years old, he went off by himself, ostensibly visiting Louis Levinsky's land in the San Joaquin Valley but really, as Alice knew, riding the Southern Pacific with indulgent drivers. He came back after a week, unwashed, with a ring of soot around his eyes.

Alice, of course, did not lack her own idea of adventure. One New Year's Eve, she decided that she and Annette would accompany the milkman on his rounds to their neighbors. Annette took the seat next to the milkman, Alice was perched beside her, gay with amusement as the carriage rattled up and down the hills. The driver allowed Annette to take the reins, but Alice never had a chance herself. Once Annette felt his arm encircle her waist, she became frightened, and the two jumped from the wagon at the next stop.[47]

She also contrived two pranks, jesting in a role she would someday enact seriously. When she learned that a well-known lecturer was to visit San Francisco, she invited him to tea and persuaded Annette to take over as hostess. A few friends would come as guests, but Alice would spend the afternoon pretending to be the maid.

With Harriet, she once proposed a similar plan. Harriet belonged to a small literary group which called themselves

"The Spinners" and met for meals and talks. For one of their gatherings, Alice offered to prepare the meal—provided she could again surprise her friends by appearing as the maid.[48]

By the time she was twenty-six, her passion for music had been all but extinguished. Though she had performed in two recitals—one in Seattle with her friend Lilyanna Hansen, and one in San Francisco—she determined for herself that she was actually commonplace. When Otto Bendix died suddenly in 1904, Alice decided not to seek another teacher. Even music was no longer enough to shape and fill her life.[49]

Her grandfather died at about the same time,[50] and her father took a smaller house on Clay Street, overlooking the Presidio. Clarence, now seventeen, needed less of her attention. More and more, Alice could spend time with friends, becoming closer to the San Francisco art world. Her first steps, however, were tentative and self-conscious.

She once attended a matinee performance of a play which she thought convincing and well-constructed. But there was a definite point, she was sure, where both the acting and the script itself failed. The next Sunday afternoon, she was taken to a gathering at the home of a local drama critic, a woman she admired. Alice remained diffident and silent throughout the afternoon, daring only to speak up concerning the one point in the play about which she felt so strongly. To her amazement, the critic agreed with her and, as Alice was leaving, invited her to visit again.[51]

She began to look at paintings with some discernment. Some friends, after all, had Corots hanging in their homes, and Alice frequently browsed through Vickery, Atkins and Torrey, a gallery of high repute. What she found, she remembered, could not be called "modern"; but it taught her, nevertheless, to know a fine painting when she saw one.[52]

Friends introduced her to their friends, many of them students at the Hopkins art school, many working artists: painter Maynard Dixon, later well-known for his murals and paintings of the western landscape; photographer Arnold Genthe, who counted Alice among his subjects for portraits; sculptors Ralph Stackpole and Arthur Putnam. Putnam introduced her to Jack London, but Alice found the writer's façade uncongenial. His stylish clothes and his affected manner offended her. And, she decided, she didn't even like his work.[53]

With Nellie Joseph or Harriet Levy she frequented the exotic restaurants in Chinatown with their delicate green-lined bowls, bird's nest soup, water chestnuts. And she even managed a few invitations to the elite Bohemian Club.

The Bohemian Club, since its founding in rooms above the California Street market which were pervaded by the odor of fish, had grown into a special fraternity of some seven hundred freewheeling artists, writers, and a few businessmen. Their new quarters were elegant, with velvety oriental rugs, leather armchairs, marble sculptures, tapestries, and a paneled library which boasted its rejection of Hearst's papers.

On the last Saturday of each month, ladies were allowed to penetrate the famous rooms, and on rare occasions each summer they were admitted to observe the Jinks—High and Low—featured at their Bohemian Grove in what is now Muir Woods.

The Jinks were theatricals not unlike collegiate revues, and the club's ambiance bordered on the giddy. Their redwood grove, sixty miles north of San Francisco on the Russian River, was depicted by one member as a midsummer night's dream. "Tents are pitched in a portion of the grove where the shade is less dense, where the sweet-smelling bay, the oak, and the California laurel sweep their feathery branches in fairy arches." Alice referred to the country place as their "summer camp" and seemed unimpressed, except for the time she hoped to meet Henry James who was traveling through the West in the spring of 1905. He agreed to appear at the club, but, to Alice's disappointment, wasn't there when she was.

She was associating with people who lived well—often better than they could afford on the little that artists and writers earned. They were, as she described them later, "*dans le monde*," and with them Alice enjoyed a sufficiently pleasurable existence. "We went to theatres, we went automobiling, we went to the Little Palace Café and Hotel which had become a fashionable shopping district where one could buy Paris clothes and perfume if one could afford it, and even if one could not."[54] She had been left some money by her grandparents and now began to spend it freely. Nellie Joseph's boyfriend, Frank Jacott, called Alice, Clare, and Nellie "The Necessary Luxury Company." And Alice's desires often exceeded her funds.[55] Soon she was deeply in debt.

For one occasion, she felt the necessity of buying a set of silver fox—gone were the days of drab gray—which was clearly beyond her means. But she wanted it, and she had it. She took a liking to Aztec objects sold in a certain shop in Santa Barbara which featured Mexican imports, and spent a great deal of money there.[56] Immediate indulgences were some compensation for an amorphous reality.

She had been brought up to be a lady, a perfect hostess, an excellent housekeeper. She would have made an efficient housewife, but she knew she would not marry. Her father had taught her, "If you must do a thing, do it graciously." He had told her that "a hostess should never apologise for any failure in her household arrangements, if there is a hostess there is insofar as there is a hostess no failure."[57] But among the useful knowledge imparted to her, there was no clue about what the future would be for an unmarried twenty-eight-year-old woman, born when the West was adolescent, chaperoned through youth by middle-class Victorians, grown into womanhood in the shadows of the gaslit nineties—when she is a Lesbian.

Though Alice had danced with young men at the Mardi Gras, though she had kissed the boys good-by as they went off as soldiers to the Spanish-American War, her romantic attachments were with women: Nellie Joseph, whom she had known throughout her adolescence, and Lilyanna Hansen. Like many young girls, she had treasured a few close friendships among her classmates, and had promised unending friendship with Clare Moore when they were still in grade school.[58] But her feelings for Nellie and Lilyanna troubled and confused her. There were few, however, in whom she could confide. Before her mother died, Alice tried to talk with her, but Emma was already too ill to deal with a subject so emotional and difficult. When she became visibly upset, Alice broke off abruptly and never spoke of her feelings again.

"Sex," Annette Rosenshine wrote later, "was an uncharted sea in the lives of the Victorian woman. . . . Marriage was considered the most important step in her life. When this was accomplished, one 'lived happily ever after.' The difficulties of adjustment either psychologically or sexually were unknown in the tragic confusion of both women and men."[59] Heterosexuality was fraught with misconceptions, but there were a few gynecologists who offered a sympathetic ear to a woman's problems, and many of those returning from training in Germany had been enlightened by the work of Krafft-Ebing, Albert Moll, Iwan Bloch, and Magnus Hirschfeld. For a female homosexual, there was hardly a physician to whom she could turn for understanding and reassurance. At the turn of the century, homosexuality was thought to be caused by physical degeneration, classified with onanism or masturbation as "self-abuse."

One of the more advanced gynecologists at the time was Dr. Oscar Mayer, who set up his practice in 1892 when he returned from studying at the University of Berlin. His treatment of young women who reluctantly came to him about the problem of self-abuse consisted of moral lectures and some strong drug which apparently dulled the sensations. He conveyed to his patients the widely accepted fear that if masturbation went on for an extended length of time, aversion to the opposite sex would be the sure result. His most drastic solution was threat of removal of the ovaries. But his usual advice was early marriage and intercourse.[60]

Despite the severity of his counsel, Mayer was sympathetic to the plight of his young female patients. And in his willingness to deal with the problem at all he was a pioneer. Lesbianism, however, was a subject rarely spoken about openly.

In 1902, the publication of *The Story of Mary MacLane* shocked the country. The author became infamous for her splash of lurid color against a uniformly gray background. Mary MacLane's confession of Lesbianism gave full bent to her sexual fantasies. The only comparable revelation of a woman's sexuality was the journal of the young artist Marie Bashkirtseff, who disclosed her aversion to men, though she did not blatantly confess a love of women. She longed for the freedom which masculinity would give her, and felt encumbered by society's limitations. "To marry and have children? Any washerwoman can do that," Marie declared. "What then do I desire? Ah, you know well what I desire—I desire glory! . . . If I had been born a man, I would have conquered Europe. As I was born a woman, I exhausted my energy in tirades against fate, and in eccentricities."

Alice read both books, but no author, however passionate, could sufficiently console. Nellie Joseph in time became engaged to Frank Jacott and eventually married him. Lilyanna returned to her family in Seattle. In the righteous temper of the time, there was no one to whom Alice could turn. Unable to fulfill the expectations of marriage and children, limited to those very few friends who understood her, Alice looked forward to a lonely future; and luxuries were indeed a necessary solace.

She wanted to leave home; but she was unable to go until she saved enough money.[61] Harriet had gone to Europe and returned with descriptions of a world that Alice knew only from Henry James. She would go to Europe too, she told Harriet, and Harriet would go with her. "At worst," she told her friend, "it would be more diverting to sit behind a window in Paris and see life go by than to observe it from an apartment in San Francisco."[62]

Four

On April 18, 1906, at 5:13 a.m. the city of San Francisco shuddered with a violence that tumbled its buildings and caused its sidewalks to undulate like the waves of the Pacific. For forty-eight seconds, the earth shook in a quake that was only one degree from complete destruction on a seismological scale. Alice, in her house of steel and Vermont stone, was awakened by the smell of gas. She felt no shocks, but immediately noticed the chandeliers dangling about and swaying. She looked out of the window onto an incomprehensible sight. The sky, she thought at first, was filled with dust. But as she looked, she suddenly knew the thick haze was caused by smoke.[63]

She immediately went to her father's room, drew open the curtains, and raised the windows. Ferdinand, apparently a heavy sleeper, had not yet awakened. She urged him to wake up. And, looking over the city once again, she decided that San Francisco was on fire. This conclusion she conveyed to her father, who, noticing the swinging chandeliers, astutely surmised there had been an earthquake.[64]

Merely commenting that the quake would "give us a black eye in the East," Ferdinand rose, dressed, and coolly departed to the business district to check on the bank vaults. Alice, in like manner, knowing she would have to forgo her bath that day, took some coffee prepared on an alcohol burner. Then she left the house to see how her friends were faring.

By nine o'clock she arrived at the Rosenshines'. She and Annette, both having had little damage done to their homes, decided to hire a cab to go to Annette's art studio to see about her clay sculptures. "The livery-stable man was aghast at our request," Annette recalled, "telling us that all cabs had been commandeered for hospitals and casualties. This was our first inkling of how grave the situation was in other parts of the city."[65]

She and Alice returned to the Rosenshine home, where they found parked outside a wagon piled with bundles. A friend of the family, it seemed, had been staying at the Palace Hotel in the center of the city and had been evacuated by the threat of fire. Now smoke was seen billowing closer, and passersby carried rumors of death and injury. The water mains, broken by the quake, left firemen helpless. Both Annette and Alice were frightened, and Alice decided to hurry home.

She packed the family silver in a Chinese chest and had Clarence dig a hole in the back garden to bury it.[66] Though the Presidio was farthest from the fires, Alice planned to go to Berkeley, where she would stay overnight with friends. Ferdinand and Clarence would remain in the city. A makeshift wharf had been set up at the Presidio, with boats that stopped at the Ferry Building before going to Oakland, where passengers would take a train to Berkeley.

Alice's friends took the event with legendary California calm. Harriet Levy picnicked with Alice before departing to Oakland, and related the scene she had witnessed at the St. Francis Hotel, where members of the Metropolitan Opera were staying during their tour in the City. "Muhlman, the baritone, asked me, his voice strained with fear and amazement, 'Gott in Himmel was ist denn!' and looked up at the sky as a plausible place from which such a catastrophe might be expected at any time."[67] Enrico Caruso, after a performance of *Carmen*, rushed to the street in his pajamas and fur coat. As soon as he had awakened he had tried his voice but failed to produce any sound. Muttering aloud, he swore never to return to San Francisco. For the displaced singers and other homeless visitors, the hotel was offering free breakfast and temporary refuge.

Nellie Joseph secluded herself in her darkened library with some novels. Clare Moore went off to Sausalito. Ferdinand sauntered home with four hundred cigarettes for his daughter and any unexpected guests. "With these," he told Alice, "one might . . . not only exist but be able to be hospitable."[68]

By noon, San Francisco was in ruins. Associated Press-man Paul Cowles, a friend of Alice, held a news conference at the Fairmont Hotel and was asked by reporters if they should meet him tomorrow. "If there is a tomorrow," he replied.[69] Fire had spread, unchecked by a failed water supply. The fire chief himself had been killed under a collapsing building. The blaze, and the looting that followed, was far out of control. The gas and lighting companies were ordered to turn off their facilities; the police were instructed to kill all looters; a curfew was imposed. The National Guard was called in, and by evening the city was in a full state of crisis. Seventeen hundred federal troops, summoned to control the lawlessness, in fact promulgated it. It was a military patrol who looted Delmonico's Restaurant at the corner of O'Farrell Street and, to cover up the crime, set a blaze which quickly swept up the block.[70] With no water available, the only way to halt the spread of fire was to dynamite burning buildings. Whatever remained of O'Farrell Street was blown up, as were Jackson and many of the surrounding blocks. For four days the explosions continued. On April 21, the flames were finally brought under control.

Alice's composed recounting of the city's virtual destruction can be matched only by one other observer's optimistic perception. William James, rushing excitedly to the city from Stanford University, where he had been lecturing, saw no crime and found that Californians were behaving laudably. "Intact skyscrapers dominated the smoking level majestically and superbly," he wrote. "I heard not a single really pathetic or sentimental word in California expressed by anyone."[71] The conflagration, he thought, brought out the best of the Western spirit.

But others saw the quake as the end of a world, "the end of San Francisco's splendid, impetuous, undisciplined youth. . . . The curtain fell on a city swept and ravaged, on a blackened outline, on skeleton walls against the sky. It fell on a period, cut off, ended; it set the seal of finality on an epoch. . . ." It was the death, one journalist lamented, of "something rich and untamable and brilliant."[72]

When Alice returned from Berkeley the city was still burning. She stopped in at the flower shop run by her cousin Annie Fabian and found the woman overcome with budding carnations. The heat of the flames, she explained, had created a hothouse, and thousands of carnations had been forced into bloom. Alice took a large bouquet to bring to Nellie.

Even in the first chaotic days after the quake, the Josephs' Chinese cook had reported to their house and prepared what Alice remembered as an excellent lunch. Several weeks later, Nellie told Alice that the cook was feeding not only her family but a horde of relatives for whom he had provided refuge in Nellie's basement. They managed to stay there for weeks, quietly existing on rice and dried Chinese provisions.

Clare Moore had also returned from Sausalito, bringing back a few packs of Venus de Milo cigarettes, which supplemented Ferdinand's contribution.

Slowly, daily life regained its normal pace. Nearly five square miles had been burned. More than twenty-eight thousand buildings had fallen, but the Toklas residence was not among them. Chimneys and water mains were not yet fully repaired, but Alice had already set to work washing the soot from the walls and putting the house in order. Two weeks after the earthquake, she was cleaning out a drawer when she came upon two tickets for Sarah Bernhardt's performance of *Phèdre* at the famous Greek Theater. She would go with Harriet's niece, she decided, and have a bath before at Harriet's sister's house in Oakland— the bath as attractive a prospect as the play.

Bernhardt's performance on the streets of the devastated city prior to the play attracted nearly as much press attention as her enactment of the heroine's part. By her own request, she was taken on a tour of San Francisco, stopping in front of the Palace Hotel to survey the catastrophe. She rose in the carriage, nearly overcome with tears. "Heaving with sobs and arms extended, in her golden voice she delivered an apostrophe to the city that had been, the city that next to Paris was the 'darling of her heart.'" And after her performance, stirred by her appreciative audience, she admitted, "I never have played Phèdre like this. . . . How marvelous to think they could come here to me today, after all they have been through, and respond with such sympathy. . . . They felt that I had something to give them to make them forget the loss of their material possessions."[73]

Alice concurred that Bernhardt's voice was exciting, especially at the end of the first act, when Phèdre gives a mournful cry as she leaves the stage. "Evidently," Alice thought, "Bernhardt had had no rehearsals, nor had she studied the large stage. Her arms outstretched, with her piercing cry she backed forever towards the curtained door. She prolonged her cry, the golden voice continued. The audience was breathless. Finally she reached the curtain and disappeared. I had seen her in many of her poignant roles," she added, "but was never more moved than then." Afterward, however, catching a glimpse of the actress as she was drawn from the theater, Alice noticed "her visibly large teeth."[74]

Though Alice and her friends tried to settle back into their former way of life, they realized that the changes to come were more than external.[75] Newspaper reports following the quake read as obituaries. "The gayest, lightest hearted, most pleasure loving city of the western continent, and in many ways the most interesting and romantic, is a horde of refugees among the ruins," the *Sun* declared. "It may rebuild; it probably will; but those who have known that peculiar city by the Golden Gate, have caught its flavor of the Arabian Nights, feel that it can never be the same. It is as though a pretty, frivolous woman had passed through a great tragedy. She survives, but she is sobered and different. If it rises out of the ashes it must be a modern city, much like other cities and without its old atmosphere."

When the elegies subsided, bright plans for reconstruction began to be published. The city would have parks and plazas—its character would be totally changed, and that, Alice decided, would be decidedly unfortunate.[76] James Phelan, the city's former mayor, detailed the improvements. "The San Francisco of the future will be . . . a more carefully constructed city . . . remedying for all time the defects of its early plan."

Though for Alice part of the city's charm was in its narrow, winding streets, its steep hills, Phelan disclosed that streets were to be widened, graded, extended. "San Francisco," he proclaimed, "shall come out of its crucible better and stronger. The ravages of time have been simply anticipated in a fateful night." The horrifying damage and uncontrollable fires were just the prodding needed to build a bigger and better city. To facilitate the "architecturally impressive" municipal improvements, Phelan called upon the residents to show their pioneering spirit and latent patriotism. "Even the most obdurate are willing to see their city rise so long as they will rise with it," he was sure. But Alice would have none of it. If ever she would leave, now was the time to go. Still, she needed money.

Five

SOME YEARS BEFORE, Harriet Levy had visited a fortune-teller with her friend Sarah Samuels. The woman had revealed to Sarah that she would meet a man from Baltimore who would be "in wheels" and marry him. It was hardly a surprise to Harriet, then, when Sarah met and married Michael Stein, who, though born in Pennsylvania, had attended Johns Hopkins before he came to Oakland to join the rest of his family. At twenty-eight, as assistant superintendent of the Omnibus Cable Company, he had given Collis Huntington the idea of a consolidated street railway in San Francisco. Huntington made Michael director of the railway, a position he did not want, but one which certainly made him a man "in wheels."

Michael, born in 1865, was the eldest of five children and head of the family after both parents died—his mother in 1888 and his father in 1891. In his new position, he was able to support his brothers and sisters, Simon, Bertha, Leo, and Gertrude, and to live comfortably with his wife Sarah and their son Allan Daniel, who was born in 1896.

Michael, however, disliked everything required by his participation in business. When a man was sent to him to be disciplined, he never knew quite what to say, and could only stand uncomfortably avoiding the other man's eyes, muttering and looking solemn. More than once, he threatened, "I'll throw up the whole damn business," but he stayed on, knowing he was the sole support of two families. By 1903, however, Michael decided to part with the establishment. The demands of the railway unions seemed to him just, and he could not maintain the expected opposition. He preferred to stay out of politics, Alice found out later, and his compassion was for the workers.[77] His investments in San Francisco—several duplex apartment

41

buildings on Lyon Street—would provide enough income, he thought, to allow him to live simply and economically in Europe.

In December 1903, the Michael Steins left San Francisco for France. When they arrived in Cherbourg, they were met by Michael's youngest brother, Leo, thirty-one, who had already settled in Paris's residential Montparnasse.

Leo arrived in Paris in December 1902, and on the recommendation of his uncle, a sculptor, found an apartment at 27, rue de Fleurus. He had already been abroad for two years: in Florence, where he had met Bernard Berenson and studied *quattrocento* Italian art; and in London, where for several months he was joined by his sister Gertrude. Though he had not intended to settle in Paris, once there he succumbed to the atmosphere, and at dinner one evening with Pablo Casals, he was suddenly struck with the determination to become an artist.

Casals had met Michael and Sarah in San Francisco when he toured with the company of singer Emma Nevada earlier in the year. The Steins' neighbor, Isadora Duncan's brother Raymond, who served as a combination advance man and publicity agent for the tour, called on Sarah for help after Casals had injured his hand during an outing. Sarah offered the cellist warm hospitality and arranged for friends to keep him company and help with the prescribed therapy of constant massage. From Sarah and Michael, Casals heard about Leo and Gertrude, though he did not meet Leo until he came to Paris.

Once they met, Leo and Pablo Casals saw each other often at dinner and for walks. Apparently Leo felt that their meeting was the coming together of like minds, since in January 1903 he gave Casals a portrait of himself as a token of their "permanent friendship."[78] After one of their dinners, at which they discussed, as usual, aesthetics, Leo returned to his rooms, built a fire, took off all his clothes, and began to draw himself. Pleased with the experience, he then enrolled in the Académie Julian, one of the finer art studios, and diligently browsed in galleries for paintings.

When Sarah, Michael, and Allan arrived late in 1903, Leo was still in pursuit of a career as an artist and was enthusiastic about introducing his family to his own Paris. He brought them to the Hôtel Foyot, near his apartment, and in a short time the Michael Steins found permanent quarters at 58, rue Madame—a neighboring street to the rue de Fleurus.

Early in her marriage, Sarah wrote to her sister-in-law Gertrude that Michael was finally asserting himself and was "no longer Mrs. Stein's husband, but a very decided Mr. Stein."[79] If her perception was correct, the behavior was short-lived. Settled in Paris, Michael seems to have retired into a comfortable position as Mrs. Stein's husband, the Stein family financial adviser, a quiet and unobtrusive manager. Given his reserved temperament, it was a position he probably enjoyed. For Sarah, too, Paris was the place where, finally, she would be herself.

Even in San Francisco, Sarah was not bound to domesticity, though she wrote glowingly of her young son and even urged Gertrude to get married and experience the joys of having a baby. By the time Allan was three, Sarah had returned to school, taking courses in art and comparative literature, attending lectures, going to the theater and concerts, keeping up her friendships with like-minded young women. But in San Francisco, the most she could be in the eyes of her world was a bright, outgoing matron, with a few ideas questionable even to Californians. In Paris, Sarah Stein was the center of her own salon.

Her lofty living room—forty by forty-five feet—was a perfect setting for the heavy Renaissance furniture that she and Michael bought and had restored. On the high white walls, they began to assemble their newly purchased paintings—by Cézanne, by Renoir, and, in growing number, by Matisse.

At thirty-five, a year older than Sarah, Matisse already had the air of a grand master. "Except for his eyes, which are blue," one gallery owner described, "everything about him is yellow: his overcoat as well as his complexion, his boots and his lovingly trimmed beard. As he wears spectacles, they are, naturally, golden."[80] An imperious demeanor earned him a nickname, "the German Professor,"[81] which lasted only until the war. Most thought of him by a more fitting and enduring appellation, *cher maître*.

Sarah and Michael were taken to his studio by Leo, after

the Steins had seen and purchased Matisse's *Woman with a Hat* at the 1905 Salon d'Automne. If Matisse was the archetypal Painter for Sarah, Sarah was no less than the Patron around whom artists' dreams are spun. Though she briefly attended the Hopkins Institute, Sarah managed to overcome that aesthetic provincialism to be able to respond to the bold, liquid, sensuous color and form of Matisse's recent work. Her strong personality was a match for Matisse's own opinionated nature. "My school doesn't explain," he once retorted to a timid young art dealer.[82] But the artist soon found himself explaining at length at Sarah's Saturday gatherings.

The sale of the *Woman with a Hat* was the stroke of good fortune for which Matisse had long waited. The Steins—there is still debate about which one actually bought the painting—readily paid the five hundred francs asked by the artist. For years supported by his wife's millinery shop, derided by the reigning critics, Matisse found in the strange Americans an enthusiastic and vital audience. They were direct. They said what they thought. They were enlivened by a good argument. They knew what they liked with a hearty approval. And they liked Matisse.

By the time the Steins met Matisse, Gertrude had joined Leo in Paris. She had visited him before, in the fall of 1903, but sailed back to America the following spring, only to return to Europe in June 1904, meeting Leo in Florence. From Florence, the two came back to Paris, where Gertrude decided to share Leo's home in the rue de Fleurus.

Both Gertrude and Leo had been students at Johns Hopkins—he in biology, she in medicine—when Leo left for Europe in 1900. A year later, Gertrude gave up her medical studies, claiming to be bored, after having failed obstetrics and several other courses in her final year. She had intended to become a specialist in what she described to one friend as the "nervous diseases of women," and in another instance as "pathological psychology."[83] Her choice of specialty seems to have been influenced both by her undergraduate work with William James at Harvard and by her own predilection for character analysis. Perhaps, too, like many beginning psychology students, she was attempting to understand herself, an effort which often sent her plummeting into what she called "the Red Deeps."

At thirty, Gertrude was still suffering from the repercussions of a stifling and unhappy adolescence. She had yet to find a direction for her obvious talents and her bright mind; she had been frustrated in love; and she felt herself an outcast from her society. In appearance—an uncorseted two hundred pounds—she was clearly outside the expected image of femininity.

The London winter with Leo in 1902 had been dismal. Staying with her brother at 20 Bloomsbury Square, she spent long days in the nearby British Museum but found little comfort there against the damp, gray city. ". . . The drunken women and children and the gloom and the lonesomeness brought back all the melancholy of . . . adolescence . . . ,"[84] she said later. Finally, she sailed back to New York, where she shared an apartment on Riverside Drive with some friends. There she began to write.

Her early pieces—those written as assignments for an English course at Radcliffe—then the Harvard Annex—frequently dealt with her own search for identity and for a place in a society where she felt alien and uncomfortable. "Sometimes I fiercely and defiantly declare that I won't believe neither now nor in the future," she had written in 1894.

> "Be still you fool," then says my mocking other self, "why struggle, you must submit sooner or later to be ground in the same mill with your fellows. The path is straight before you can but choose to follow. Why waste your strength in useless cries? Be still, it is inevitable."[85]

But she could not be still, nor accept as inevitable the fate of "a sheltered life, domestic tastes, maternity and faith," that one friend urged her to realize.[86] She had been irrevocably disillusioned and deeply hurt by a rejection from a fellow student at Johns Hopkins, a woman she loved. Suddenly, she knew "the complete realization that no one can believe as you do about anything," and the realization was at once shocking and saddening. She had come of age. But she knew she was outside her own time and even her own culture. She was marked with the "strain of singularity" that set her apart from other women.

45

To a bourgeois mind that has within it a little of the fervor for diversity there can be nothing more attractive than a strain of singularity that yet keeps within the limits of conventional respectability; a singularity that is so to speak well dressed and well set up. This is the nearest approach the middle class young woman can hope to find to the indifference and distinction of the really noble. When singularity goes beyond this point the danger is apparent, the danger of being taken for the lowest of them all simply bad or poor and from such danger the young ones in the middle class peculiarly shrink.

Singularity that is neither crazy, faddist or low class is as yet an unknown product within ourselves. It takes time to make queer people time and certainty of place and means. Custom, passion and a feel for mother earth are needed to breed vital singularity in any man and alas how poor we are in all these three.[87]

Singular in her sexual preferences, singular in her creative aspirations, she felt increasingly separate from her friends, and withdrew more and more into her own mind, where her problems festered.

Brothers Singular [she cried in her first novel] we are misplaced into a generation that knows not Joseph. We flee before the disapproval of our cousins, the courageous condescension of our friends who gallantly agree to sometimes walk the streets with us, we fly to the kindly comfort of an older world accustomed to take all manner of strange forms into its bosom. . . .[88]

In Paris, she tried to find a home. Still depressed and unsure of herself, she joined her brothers and sister-in-law in their quest after art, and even began to voice her opinions in the purchase of paintings. With them she met Matisse, and later a young Spaniard, Pablo Picasso.

Picasso was twenty-three when, in 1904, he took a studio at 13, rue Ravignan, the cradle of what his friend Max Jacob later called "the heroic age of cubism." Icy in winter, steamy in summer, the dilapidated building was hardly bearable even for the poor young artists who lived and worked there. But the building itself, more a stage set than a home, encouraged an intimacy that bolstered its inhabitants both in their personal lives and in their work. It was an artists' commune whose surfaces had been enriched by the patina of those who passed through. The studios seemed alive, each a reflection of the spirit within. Picasso's was exciting in its multihued disorder, cluttered with paints and canvases and piles of books he would buy at a small bookshop on the rue des Martyrs. There was little real furniture—especially for seating—but there was one large broken chair, large enough even for Gertrude.

Shortly after they met, Picasso asked Gertrude to pose for her portrait. The request indicated a sharp break from the work he was doing: he had not used a model for years, and though he admitted that it was useful for an artist to observe nature, he cautioned that one should never overly concern oneself with attempting a resemblance to reality.[89] Nevertheless, though Gertrude never knew why and never asked, he invited her to model for him. She immediately accepted.

Strikingly different in their appearance and the expression of their personalities, Gertrude and Picasso became friends at once, admiring in each other a powerful ego and a hard brilliance. Each was a fighter, resigned to living in an absurd world, but determined to fulfill a belief in genius. "When I was a child," Picasso once related, "my mother said to me, 'If you become a soldier you'll be a general. If you become a monk you'll end up as the Pope.' Instead I became a painter and wound up as Picasso."[90]

But in the winter of 1905–6, when their friendship was solidified during Gertrude's weeks of sitting, Picasso was not yet the legend he wanted to become. He was a young man who came to dinner, though certainly more vibrant and attractive than the other guests. He was, as Gertrude described, "small, quick moving, but not restless. . . . He had the isolation and movement of the head of a bull-fighter. . . ."[91] To his Spanish heritage—he was born in Málaga on October 25, 1881—she attributed his innate cynicism and skepticism. "The Spaniards," she decided, "are perhaps the only Europeans who really never have the feeling that things seen are real, that the truths of science make for progress. Spaniards did not mistrust science they only never recognised the existence of progress."[92]

Whatever the portrait would mean for Picasso's artistic development, for Gertrude it was the image she would one day assume: the rich-toned maternal presence, calmly witnessing the birth of cubism, her own face a powerful mask intimating the future of art. With that portrait, critics were later to decide, Picasso took a new path, showing increasingly the influence of the African masks that hung on his walls and the African sculpture with which he was fascinated. The portrait was done in two stages: the body completed first, but the head blacked out; and then, after some months, a new, stark, bold head painted in. When it was finished, Picasso gave the portrait to Gertrude, a gesture which later amazed her friends. But even as late as 1914, when Picasso's apartment was burglarized, only his linen was stolen. In 1906, the portrait was a gift to a dear friend. And at the time, Gertrude explained, "the difference between a sale and a gift was negligible."[93]

But except for her friendship with Picasso, Gertrude's first years in Paris were somewhat lonely. Many who knew her then remember an unusually quiet woman, large, placid, reserved, sitting by while Leo entertained their guests. The photographer Alfred Stieglitz remarked to her later that he had never known anyone to sit still so long without saying a word. She was more Leo's sister than Gertrude Stein.

The Steins were leading their life not quite of *luxe*, but certainly of comparative *calme* and *volupté* when the news of the earthquake reached Paris. Unable to assess the damage to their buildings, Michael and Sarah decided to return to California to inspect the scene themselves. Determined, perhaps, to make a grand entrance into her friends' lives, Sarah packed two Matisse paintings and one drawing in her luggage.

As Sarah might have foreseen, her friends were shocked at what was supposedly a portrait of the artist's wife, *The Green Line*, and at the other painting, *Nude Before a Screen*. "The wild color and curious design," Annette Rosenshine noted with excitement, were far removed from what she had been seeing at the Mark Hopkins Institute of Art.

For the few months she spent in San Francisco, Sarah enjoyed being the center of her friends' attention. She renewed what had been a casual friendship with Harriet Levy. Harriet, Sarah had thought before she left for France, did not take her seriously enough. Besides, she had seemed to enjoy the company of people whom Sarah deemed "inferior," and was not really living up to her potential as a writer. Sarah advised her to go east, but in 1899 Harriet had no desire to leave a good position and pleasurable life in San Francisco. "Harriet is right in with the literary set and is apparently very well satisfied with life at present," Sarah reported to Gertrude.[94]

But by 1906 the situation had changed. Harriet generously entertained Sarah, spent a good deal of time with her, and divulged that she would soon be returning to Europe. The prospect delighted Sarah, and she immediately suggested that Harriet return with her and Michael. When Harriet disclosed that Alice wanted to travel with her, Sarah saw no obstacle. Harriet's friend would go too, she decided.

Alice, however, had no desire to leave home under the wing of Sarah Stein. Sarah, as Harriet described her, was extremely opinionated, with "an unbreakable wall that kept her vanity intact."[95] Her domineering personality was softened only by a maternal exterior which drew out confidences and revelations from normally unwilling subjects. Annette, meeting her for the first time in 1906, described her as "medium height with a rather flabby stoutness. Her features were undistinguished, but her expression was keenly alert. Her frizzly light brown hair was arranged in a pompadour and gathered in a knot on the back of her head. Her appearance suggested comfort—a good San Francisco bourgeoise. . . ."[96]

Alice and Harriet, probably to distract Sarah from her determination to take them with her when she returned to Paris in the winter, tried to interest her in Annette instead. Annette, they confided, longed to go to France. Sarah, though, was wary. She thought Annette fairly intelligent— Annette, after all, had recognized Matisse's special qualities as soon as she saw the paintings—but she knew that Annette would be a responsibility rather than a companion. Annette, unaware at the time that she was being manipulated, confirmed to Sarah that she very much wanted to go to Europe but had not been able to convince her parents.

Somewhat softened by Annette's eagerness, Sarah did

not immediately refuse to take her, but agreed to go to dinner at the Rosenshines', where she tried to paint a dismal picture of life in a Paris pension—"a kerosene lamp, wash bowl and pitcher, no bath tub, and crude plumbing facilities."[97] But Annette told Sarah that she had lived with worse inconveniences in her parents' country home, and once again declared that she wanted to go. Her parents finally agreed, Michael was sympathetic to the young woman, and Sarah found herself outnumbered. ". . . I don't love *any* extra responsibility these days," she wrote to Gertrude in October,[98] but in two months, Annette was sailing with her on the *Ryndam*, bound for France.

Sarah Stein's description of Parisian life, hardly the gloomy scenario she presented to Annette, further fueled Alice's own desire to leave. But she was living on borrowed funds already and saw no way to pay her passage. Throughout the winter she kept her plans for leaving secret from her father, growing more and more frustrated by her captivity in San Francisco. Annette's letters painted a vivid picture of a better life. Sarah had found a room for her at Madame Vernot's pension, in the same building as her own apartment, and on her first night in Paris, Annette had dinner with Leo and Gertrude. Gertrude, she thought, was unlike anyone she had known before.

"It is difficult to convey the total impression Gertrude Stein made upon me," she wrote later. "I was aware of a dynamic magnetism, an inner distinction which, while quite sensible, remained indefinable. There was power in the beauty of her splendid head with its heavy coil of brown hair which dominated her squat, rotund body. Not one feature was outstanding, but an intellectual luminous quality shone in her face. Her hands were the only adult hands I had ever seen that resembled those of a small child— dimpled with the bony structure well concealed."[99]

Leo, Annette thought, "acted as Gertrude's mentor, dictionary and encyclopedia, supplying on demand any information she required."[100] He was well-read, though his choice of books usually related to his own psychological self-explorations. On her first morning in Paris, he escorted Annette through the Louvre.

In her letters to Alice, Annette related the pleasanter aspects of her new life, trying to omit the shocking changes she was undergoing, and keeping silent about the details of her real relationship with the Steins—especially Sarah and Gertrude. Alice, on her side, had not ceased trying to manipulate Annette, and once suggested that she strike up a flirtation with Leo.

Meanwhile, life in San Francisco was continuing in predictable post-catastrophe confusion. In July, the city found itself with three mayors, each claiming official sanctity, and each conducting business as usual. It was not until the end of August that the courts designated one to take over the seals, and he inherited the task of dealing with an outbreak of bubonic plague.

Middle-class San Franciscans, convinced that bubonic plague existed nowhere in their city, were shocked when cases were reported with such rapidity that federal aid had to be sought to exterminate the rats. Safe within the pipes and walls of Chinatown, the rats had been loosed by the quake and fled unchecked into the comfortable residential neighborhoods where they could breed freely. The plague, which for so long had been successfully denied, now felled citizens who would not die silently and be buried invisibly. There ensued, therefore, the largest, quickest, and most efficient rat hunt in the country's history, and the broadest and most intensive sanitation campaign devised by the Public Health Department. The plague was quickly eradicated, but not without turmoil in its wake.

Plague had stuck a medieval terror in the hearts of San Francisans. The city was in an uproar; hospitals were unprepared to handle the contagious disease. Proper isolation facilities were lacking. Few could be found to handle the dead. Tents were resorted to when there was no other place available for the patients' treatment. As the September rainy season approached, fear augmented and physical conditions worsened.

Alice, of course, had her own more personal problems. She had finally arranged with Harriet to borrow a thousand dollars, a sum which would enable her to act immediately. She had finally disclosed to her father that she was going to Europe, a decision Ferdinand accepted without comment, merely emitting a noncommittal sigh. She was finally, at the ago of thirty, leaving home.

There was no feeling of nostalgia for what she was leaving, she admitted later. She thought of nothing but the future.[101] And there was only one reason she ever gave for her departure. When she left with Harriet at the end of August 1907, she fled to freedom.[102]

2

Two Are One

O Lord, Lord! it is a hard matter for friends to meet; but mountains may be removed with earthquakes and so encounter.

Shakespeare,
As You Like It
(Act III, Scene ii)

Six

AFTER A HOT TRIP across the country, Alice and Harriet stopped briefly in New York. One evening at dinner, they excitedly noticed the glamorous Lillian Russell—one of "the heroines" of Alice's youth—at a nearby table. The actress had returned to New York on August 31 for the fall theater season. Nellie Jacott, then living in the city, took Alice to a matinee at the Bijou where Alla Nazimova was performing in an Ibsen play. The next day, on the way to the ship, they passed the excavation for Grand Central Terminal, a sight Alice described as "quite biblical."

On board, she found flowers, fruit, and books—all gifts from Nellie—and began reading her own copy of Flaubert's letters. Her only distraction was "a distinguished oldish man, a commodore," who engaged her in conversation day after day. Harriet, Alice noted, thought she was being indiscreet, and the commodore was apparently encouraged by Alice's attention. Several days after she arrived in Paris, she received "a most compromising letter" from him among her mail at her bank in the Place Vendôme. "There was no question of my answering it," she knew. She took it to the Tuileries, tore it up, and surreptitiously dropped it in the lake.

They had arrived in France on Sunday, September 8, 1907.[1] It was a fête day, the celebration of the Virgin Mary's birth, and on their first night, in Cherbourg, from beneath the window of the hotel Alice heard "French voices . . . singing French songs in the mild French air."[2] It was a lovely sound. She and Harriet went to Caen, where the town was celebrating in regional costume, the women in long black velvet dresses and high starched hats. The next morning the two boarded a train which would take them through Normandy and to Paris. The scenery

55

was thoroughly delightful, Alice thought, with poppies and cornflowers, tiny villages, fields and cows. "I was so grateful for it all,"[3] she remembered.

The French themselves were a surprise to her. So many wore black that Alice at first thought they were in mourning. She asked if there had been recent fighting in one of the colonies which had cost families a son or brother, but found that the drab dress was merely the customary style. The French in San Francisco, she thought, had been more stylish, more distinguished, more elegant. Still, there was an intelligence in the faces of Parisians that struck her as exceptional.[4]

She and Harriet took two fiacres from the train station to the Hôtel Magellan, which had been recommended by Nellie. They passed luxurious shops, beautiful wide avenues, and parks that Alice vaguely remembered from her childhood trip. Each neighborhood, she saw, had its own character, with its own flower shops, bakeries, groceries. And the trees, she thought, were especially lovely, flanking the boulevards and diffusing the city's special light. September would always seem to her one of the finest months, when the air was as crisp and fresh as a fine white wine.

By afternoon they had settled into their rooms at the Magellan, and Harriet promptly contacted her friends the Michael Steins, telling them that she and Alice were on their way to the rue Madame. Their fiacre brought them to a narrow, quiet street in Montparnasse, one block from the Luxembourg Gardens, and stopped before an imposing building, formerly a Protestant church. The interior had been transformed into a comfortable residence, lighted by high windows. Richly toned Persian rugs and runners covered the old wooden floors, and on the dark, massive furniture Sarah displayed some Chinese and Japanese figurines and objects which she and Michael had brought from San Francisco. There were paintings everywhere, sumptuously framed, hanging on pillars, above doorways, and one above the other on the walls. It was a striking setting. And it was there that Alice met Gertrude.

"She was a golden brown presence, burned by the Tuscan sun and with a golden glint in her warm brown hair. She was dressed in a warm brown corduroy suit. She wore a large round coral brooch and when she talked, very little, or laughed, a good deal, I thought her voice came from this brooch. It was unlike anyone else's voice—deep, full, velvety like a great contralto's, like two voices. She was large and heavy with delicate small hands and a beautifully modeled and unique head."[5]

Gertrude sat, quiet and composed. She hardly spoke but at times smiled slightly. Her presence, especially her eyes, reflected the richness of her inner life, Alice thought. Gertrude's experiences, Alice knew at once, must have been far deeper than her own. Though only a few years younger, Alice felt almost like a child with Gertrude.[6]

At dinner Leo joined them, and at once Alice could see the contrast with his sister's personality as Leo gave his customary eccentric performance. "Are you a Monist?" he suddenly asked Harriet. Harriet, not knowing what the word meant, was puzzled by the outburst. Alice, she recalled, merely looked into space.[7]

Leo, thought Alice, was amiable, with a bright, springing step and a physical grace. Like his sister, he was a golden presence, but with a golden beard. But it was Gertrude who impressed her, who held her attention, who, she would reveal later, rang the bell in her that signified encounter with genius.

In Gertrude, Alice piqued a curiosity not caused by this first meeting alone. Gertrude knew a great deal about her. For nearly a year, Annette had been regularly showing Alice's letters to Gertrude, and Gertrude read them with keen interest. The letters, Annette saw, were Gertrude's "first closeup to Alice's psychological makeup, so much so that it finally brought forth the peculiar remark that the chief difference between Alice and [Annette] was that Alice had 'a higher nature but a lower ideal.' "[8]

By the time Annette came, Gertrude had settled into a pleasant existence with Leo—more satisfying, at least, than any she had known before. Though she still wavered at times in her conviction of her talent as a writer, she worked diligently at her craft, keeping notebook after notebook of character analyses. Her considerable strength and self-assurance impressed Annette, who began to confide in Gertrude as she had before in Alice.

Annette's revealing of Alice's letters, while she realized it was a breach of confidence, was done to help Gertrude deal with Annette's psychological problems, which Gertrude deemed many. When Annette first arrived, both Gertrude and Sarah found her uncongenial. Gertrude, especially, "seemed to fear something," and to think that Annette "might be a disturbing factor in their family group. . . ."[9] Sarah first suggested that Annette live with friends in Neuilly, but Annette remained firm even under this rejection and told Sarah that she was determined to stay at Madame Vernot's pension. Drastic measures were needed, Gertrude decided, and Sarah was instructed to give Annette an inventory of her many failings. Sarah, Annette related, vented a crude attack, pointing to her egotism, self-centeredness, and neuroses. "I was crushed and startled . . . ," Annette wrote. "Her words were unheard, meaningless as I took refuge behind my wall."[10] But still, she determined to stay.

Finally, Gertrude herself decided that Annette might be an interesting subject for observation. "A human guinea pig had fallen into her lap that she could control," Annette saw, "instead of my being a disturbing element in their midst."[11]

Though she had been deeply hurt by Sarah's tirade, and could have been justly suspicious of Gertrude's interest in her, Annette "immediately had faith in her. . . . I turned myself over to her as years later I learned one turns oneself over to an analyst."[12] Hungry for the security that any close relationship would offer, Annette readily acquiesced to Gertrude's requests, among them the disclosure of all letters she received.

Gertrude's probing was not limited to an analysis of correspondence. Each afternoon at four, Annette would arrive at 27, rue de Fleurus, when Gertrude would be finished writing and free to engage in long, intimate talks. "Leo," Annette rememberd, "was usually in the atelier when I arrived, pacing the floor, expounding some philosophical theory. He was a striking figure with a distinguished face. The full, reddish beard which he affected was unusual and startling."[13] Leo, too, was admitted to the psychological sessions. He had, after all, read Freud's *Interpretation of Dreams* and was even more interested in a book by Otto Weininger, a Viennese psychologist who had killed himself three years before *Sex and Character* was published.

Weininger had evolved a mathematical system to calculate the maleness and femaleness in each individual. He believed that "the male and female are merely abstract concepts which never appear in the real world"[14] and that each individual is to some degree bisexual. Femaleness is uniformly disparaged; a woman can never have genius, nor even a conscious life—certainly, "women are devoid of imagination."[15] "All those who are striving for this real emancipation," he declared, "all women who are truly famous and are of conspicuous mental ability, to the first glance of an expert reveal some of the anatomical characters of the male, some external bodily resemblance to a man."[16]

"The genius," he continued, "is a man who knows everything without having learned it,"[17] is "not a critic of language but its creator,"[18] and is "outside and unconditioned by history."[19] A female genius, he concluded, "is a contradiction in terms, for genius is simply intensified, perfectly developed, universally conscious maleness."[20]

Leo was in agreement with Weininger, Annette found. Once when she was talking to Gertrude about women, Leo interjected, "If you can take their minds off their wombs, you can help them to some kind of intellectual development."[21] For the moment, Leo was, by his own estimation and Gertrude's outward concurrence, the genius of the Stein family.

But Weininger's theses were attractive to Gertrude also, and she recommended the book to a college friend as one which embodied her own views.[22] Perhaps Weininger's discussion of homosexuality mitigated for Gertrude his diatribe against women and against Jews. He postulated that ". . . the woman who attracts and is attracted by other women is herself half male," and included in his roster of famous women who exhibited maleness in their characters such notables as George Sand, George Eliot, and Madame Blavatsky.[23] Gertrude, trying to understand what she considered "maleness" in her own character, must have found Weininger's ideas in keeping with some of her own. A few years earlier, writing about the value of college education for women, she pointed to the "over-sexing" of children by society. Difference between the sexes was enforced when children were still infants, at an age when the difference should be meaningless.[24]

When she discovered Weininger, she was deep into the writing of *The Making of Americans*, her involved, convoluted study of one family as Every Family, which dealt in part with the nature of women. Various patterns of womanhood are described, most having as basis an essential weakness. There is, however, a certain type of woman who manages to succeed. "Some women . . . are to themselves like men in their living there are many women who are always vigorous young women energetic and getting information and busy every moment in their living. . . ."[25]

About genius, Gertrude must not have agreed with the psychologist. Though later she would write that a genius is "some one who does not have to remember the two hundred years that everybody else has to remember," and someone who exists "without any internal recognition of time . . . ,"[26] for Gertrude genius was not incongruous with her own sexuality. ". . . There is no such thing as a person who is physically female and psychically male," Weininger asserted, "not withstanding the extreme maleness of their outward appearance and the unwomanliness of their expression."[27] Nevertheless, Gertrude Stein would be a genius.

Annette, though knowing she was under Gertrude's domination, showed no will to free herself. She came to Gertrude with all her problems, and she tried to follow Gertrude's counsel. In discussions of sex, however, Gertrude was less than helpful. "She glossed over the matter," Annette wrote, "by saying that sex was an individual problem that each one had to solve for herself or himself."[28] When Annette tried to speak of her feelings when she first realized she had met a homosexual, she found Gertrude amused that her shock had been so great she could hardly remember the details of the experience. "I remember most vividly Gertrude that day, hugging herself, saying in glee, 'No memory, no consciousness.' "[29] But in other ways, Gertrude offered some help. She suggested that each night before going to sleep Annette reflect about the day, her meetings with people, and attempt to understand her own responses. She was, Annette admitted, "of greatest psychological help to me at that moment."[30]

At the same time, Annette was useful to Gertrude. "Ger-

trude made no bones about the fact that I was a trial.
Once, in a moment of exasperation, she said, 'Well, any-
how, you are worth the price of admission.' "[31] She was
worth the effort to analyze, Gertrude saw, because her
difficulties could be so easily brought to the surface and
her particular characteristics could be added to the analyses that were going into *The Making of Americans*. What
Gertrude did not see, however, was that it was merely upon
superficialities that she was basing her understanding of
Annette, and that deeper problems were hidden within.

In 1904, Annette had undergone several operations to
correct her disfigurement. As Gertrude knew, her harelip
and cleft palate were the source of many of her psychological problems. There were other reasons, besides. She had
long suffered with the knowledge that her parents had
hoped for a son instead of a daughter when she was born.
She had suffered, also, in knowing of her mother's guilt
about bearing a deformed child. Never having had so eager
a confidante, Annette allowed herself to be a specimen for
investigation. But her problems were intensifying rather
than becoming ameliorated. After her first four months in
Paris, her mother and younger sister came to Europe for a
vacation. They were appalled at the change in Annette and
wanted her to return home with them after a few weeks of
traveling. Annette would not break her relationship with
Gertrude, though she admitted confusion. She wrote to her
father, begging for permission to stay. He granted her another year.[32]

Annette continued as Gertrude's main interest, her
primary experiment in amateur psychoanalysis, until the
September day she met Alice. Then, it seemed, a more
interesting subject had appeared. When Alice left the Steins'
home after her first day in Paris, she left with an invitation from Gertrude to visit the rue de Fleurus and go for a
walk the next day.

Seven

SHE WAS LATE. That morning, Harriet suggested that they have lunch in the Bois de Boulogne, and Alice courteously sent a *petit bleu* to Gertrude informing her that her arrival might be slightly delayed. She came half an hour later than she was expected, unprepared for the "vengeful goddess" who met her at the door.

Gertrude's rage was incomprehensible. "I did not know what had happened or what was going to happen," Alice said. Gertrude took Alice's tardiness as a personal affront, a breach of manners, a lack of consideration. "I am not accustomed to wait," she told her, as she raged and paced around the Florentine tables in the atelier.[33] Then, she suddenly stopped, stood in front of Alice, and declared that it was over. She was through. "It is not too late to go for a walk," she told Alice. "You can look at the pictures while I change my clothes."

Alice was astounded, but Gertrude's heated performance only added to her attraction. While Gertrude was changing, she did as she was told. The walls were covered with pictures, and the furniture and objects were fascinating. There was a big Tuscan table, and octagonal Tuscan table with clawed legs, a Henry IV buffet with three carved eagles on top, some seventeenth-century terra-cotta figures of women, and several pieces of Italian pottery. She hardly had time to notice the paintings.

Soon Gertrude returned, smiling and jovial, began an innocuous conversation about Harriet, and as they walked pointed out some shrubbery to her companion. "Alice," she said, "look at the autumn herbaceous border." But, Alice recalled, "I did not propose to reciprocate the familiarity." They walked through the Luxembourg Gardens, where the sight of children rolling their hoops and sailing their boats in the lake brought Alice memories of her childhood visit. "The nurses," she noticed, "were still wearing their long capes and starched white caps with long broad streamers."[34] As they walked, Gertrude asked her what she had been reading; when Alice mentioned Flaubert's letters, she wondered if they had been translated, since she herself enjoyed reading only in English.

They walked toward Boulevard Saint-Michel, where Gertrude knew of a pastry shop where they might have excellent cakes and ices. Alice ordered a praline ice, "just like San Francisco." At the café, Gertrude invited her and Harriet to dinner on September 28, the Saturday before the opening of the Salon d'Automne.

When Alice returned to the hotel, Harriet was curious about her walk and asked if she had enjoyed it. "I told her only of the walk," Alice said, "and nothing of what had occurred before." And Harriet was pleased.

In the intervening mornings and afternoons, Alice explored what she knew was to become her hometown and found Paris increasingly enchanting. On Saturdays, she attended another salon—Sarah's.

Sarah's gatherings were centered around Matisse, whether or not the artist himself was present. Sarah reclined on a couch in the corner of her huge living room, elegantly gowned and adorned with antique jewelry. From that languid position, she set forth explaining "the paintings on the walls, the greatness of Matisse, his unique position in the world of art."[35] Her loyalty was unwavering. "Having accepted Matisse," Harriet saw, "he . . . remained for her the one great artist."[36]

Alice and Harriet found themselves treated as curiosities. The earthquake, they discovered, was extremely interesting to the Steins' friends. Their stories were told in factual detail until, after a while, Harriet thought they had better embellish them to keep their listeners' interest. "We may even have to be burned with the house," was Alice's suggestion.[37]

There was no rivalry between the two Saturday salons. Sarah's attracted much the same group as Gertrude's and Leo's; sometimes guests divided their evening between the two. The painters Hans Purrmann, in Paris from Munich, and Patrick Henry Bruce, like Matisse sporting a golden beard, were strong supporters of Sarah's artistic tastes. Others were not as kind about her dogmatic views, presented bluntly and permitting no argument. Though neither Harriet nor Alice spoke French fluently enough for real conversation, they often found Americans amid the European artists. Annette was still at Madame Vernot's and so was a fellow Californian, Lawrence Strauss, who was studying voice. The evenings were an initiation for the livelier doings around the corner.

Leo greeted Harriet and Alice on the appointed date, as usual wearing sandals, the only European shoes, he and Gertrude maintained, that would fit them properly. He took them through a small passageway and then into the book-lined dining room. Alfred Maurer, another of the dinner guests, was already there. He had, Alice would remember, "dancing" eyes, an expressive face, and lightning wit.[38] The forty-year-old American painter, however, was soon eclipsed by the entrance of a young man, "very dark with black hair, a lock hanging over one of his marvellous all-seeing brilliant black eyes. . . ." Picasso, with his mistress Fernande Olivier, had arrived late, but the misdemeanor was overlooked by his hostess. Fernande, it was explained, had to wait for the delivery of her new dress, ordered for the *vernissage*. Fernande, tall, dark, "an oriental odalisque," apologized to Gertrude, and dinner was served. Too soon—for the conversation was lively, Alice said, and the meal, prepared by Gertrude's servant, Hélène, was excellent—guests began arriving and the party joined them in the studio.

At first, Alice paid less attention to the guests than to the paintings on the walls: Cézannes, Renoirs, Matisses, Picassos, Gauguins. ". . . I looked and looked and I was confused,"[39] she admitted.

> . . . On all the walls right up to the ceiling were pictures. At one end of the room was a big cast iron stove that Helene came in and filled with a rattle, and in one corner of the room was a large table on which were horseshoe nails and pebbles and little pipe cigarette holders which one looked at curiously but did not touch, but which turned out later to be accumulations from the pockets of Picasso and Gertrude Stein. . . .

The pictures were so strange that one quite instinctively looked at anything rather than at them just at first. . . . The chairs in the room were also all italian renaissance, not very comfortable for short-legged people and one got the habit of sitting on one's legs. . . .[40]

It was difficult to focus full attention on the kaleidoscope of pictures.

There were two Gauguins, there were Manguins, there was a big nude by Valloton that felt like only it was not like the Odalisque of Manet, there was a Toulouse-Lautrec. . . . There was a portrait of Gertrude Stein by Valloton that might have been a David but was not, there was a Maurice Denis, a little Daumier, many Cezanne water colors, there was in short everything, there was even a little Delacroix and a moderate sized Greco. There were enormous Picassos of the Harlequin period, there were two rows of Matisses, there was a big portrait of a woman by Cezanne and some little Cezannes. . . .[41]

But gradually Alice's attention shifted to the guests, and she and Harriet were engaged in conversations, including a discussion with Gertrude's friend Ethel Mars about makeup, a subject all three found fascinating. In San Francisco, rouged lips and tinted cheeks were effected only by "painted ladies," but in Paris, it seemed, artful *maquillage* was accepted. It makes you feel cheerful, an artist's wife told Harriet. Mars, with her hair dyed purple and lips colored orange, had definite opinions on the subject.

Harriet, gregarious as always, acquainted herself with many of the guests, among them Georges Braque, Guillaume Apollinaire, Ramon Pichot, and Henri-Pierre Roche. Most would be seen again at Tuesday's *vernissage*.

The paintings exhibited at the Fifth Salon d'Automne were as bewildering as those on Gertrude's walls. Alice and Harriet could not discriminate "art" from the renderings of Sunday painters, but they were able to recognize a Matisse when they saw one, a discovery which made Alice joyful.

The people were as exciting as the paintings. ". . . It was

indeed the vie de Boheme just as one had seen it in the opera and they were very wonderful to look at," Alice thought.[42] She was especially surprised to see the number of men who came to the exhibit. In San Francisco, art was a pastime for women.

They sat to rest for a while, when suddenly they felt a hand on their shoulders and a burst of laughter. Gertrude had found them, admirably situated in front of a Braque and a Derain. ". . . Right here in front of you is the whole story," she told them. But the two were puzzled at the strange paintings, similar but not identical, of "strangely formed rather wooden blocked figures. . . ."[43]

With another laugh Gertrude departed, and as they looked after her, they recognized many faces from "the Saturday evening crowd"—and one forefinger, Fernande's, memorable for its length. By the time they left, they had an agreement with Fernande to give them French lessons at fifty cents an hour, and an invitation from Picasso to visit his studio with Gertrude.[44]

Planning a long stay, Alice and Harriet decided to look for a furnished apartment and found an alluring advertisement in *Le Figaro*. Alice went alone to the small stone house on the rue de la Faisanderie, not far from the Bois de Boulogne, where a certain Monsieur de Courcy was leasing one floor. The rent for three rooms, he told her, was one-third less than whatever she was paying at the Hôtel Magellan, and the cuisine, he assured her, would be excellent. Harriet, skeptical at first, was delighted by Alice's description. Seeing the apartment the next day confirmed her opinions: they would move immediately.

The suave young man, with his Oxford English accent, was an accommodating landlord. He entertained them with Chopin études, played, Alice thought, "with a good technique and interesting interpretation," filled their rooms with flowers, and invited them to the Folies Bergères. The show, Alice remembered, "was elaborately staged, and what was not understood was happily not understood."[45]

Alice could not wait to write to Gertrude about her fortunate news. But Gertrude, when she came to lunch the next day, promptly ended their idyllic existence. Though the young man had told Alice and Harriet that his mother, who owned the house, would be returning imminently, Gertrude decided that her absence could mean only one thing. Warning her friends against being compromised, she told them they must move as soon as possible. Monsieur de Courcy was astounded at the sudden change, but Alice and Harriet hardly took time to explain their hasty departure.

This time they moved to a hotel, L'Universe, on Boulevard Saint-Michel, closer to Gertrude and farther from disgrace. Gertrude came with flowers and candy, inspected Alice's small room, which faced the garden of the Institut des Sourds-Muets, and Harriet's, which faced the Petit Luxembourg.

Now, it was decided, since Gertrude's home was a mere twenty-minute stroll across the Luxembourg, she and Alice could see each other more frequently. "It was the beginning of my friendship with Gertrude Stein," Alice wrote, "and I was to call her Gertrude."

Walking with Gertrude, Alice soon found, was not unlike striding beside Ferdinand. Alice lengthened her steps and quickened her pace to keep up. Their wanderings soon brought them to Montmartre. It was Alice's first visit to the quarter, and it gave her an inexplicable "tender expectant feeling" that recurred each time she went there. It was time, Gertrude thought, for Alice to visit Picasso.

When Gertrude had brought Annette to see the artist at work, they found Fernande lying between Picasso and another man, recovering, Annette believed, "from a Bohemian revelry the night before. . . ."[46] None of the three rose for the guests. Gertrude expected Annette to be shocked, but her most lasting impression of the scene was of the "luminous penetrating quality" of Picasso's eyes.

On the day Gertrude brought Alice, however, Picasso, currently at odds with Fernande, was alone. The studio, with its "general smell of dog and paint," was furnished with a motley assortment of objects varying in usefulness— a rusty iron stove, some broken chairs, one large dog. Canvases, paint tubes, and brushes were scattered everywhere. To Alice, the paintings were dazzling. "Against the wall was an enormous picture, a strange picture of light and dark colors, that is all I can say, of a group, an enormous group and next to it another in a sort of red brown, of three women, square and posturing, all of it rather frightening."[47] There were smaller pictures, one "a rather unfinished thing that could not finish, very pale almost white, two figures, they were all there but very unfinished and not finishable. . . . I cannot say I realized anything," she admitted, "but I felt that there was something painful and beautiful there and oppressive but imprisoned."

Silently watching Picasso and Gertrude talk together, Alice began to understand the depth of their friendship. Gertrude's special way of saying Pablo and Picasso's way of pronouncing Gertrude were almost proof in themselves of the quality of the bond between them. Each was solitary, strong, yet emotional—and each approached the other with the wariness of the disillusioned. "Is there anything more dangerous than sympathetic understanding?" Picasso once remarked. "Especially as it doesn't exist. It's almost always wrong. You think you aren't alone. And really you're more alone than you were before."[48]

Alice did not intrude on their low-toned conversation, and in a short while Gertrude ended it by announcing that she and Alice were off to see Fernande, with whom Alice had begun French lessons. "Ah, the Miss Toklas," Picasso said, "with small feet like a Spanish woman and earrings like a gypsy and a father who is king of Poland like the Poniatowskis, of course she will take lessons."[49] He told her, though, that Fernande was very likely to be bored and warned against its becoming contagious.

Alice and Harriet had studied French briefly in San Francisco with a charming Berkeley professor, Robert Dupris, who introduced them to early-nineteenth-century French plays but failed to give them a mastery of general conversation. Alice, Harriet recalled, spoke the language quickly but poorly. "She talked fast. The greater her ignorance of a language the faster she talked."[50] She had a strong American accent, which she never lost, and a carelessness about such grammatical details as the agreement of nouns and adjectives. With Fernande, the conversation never reached a deeper vein than clothes, perfumes, or poodles—subjects, Harriet said, which seemed sufficiently stimulating to Alice.[51]

Fernande, raised in the provinces, where her parents made artificial flowers, discovered art in the Luxembourg Museum and artists in Montmartre. Shortly after moving into 13 rue Ravignan, she noticed "a rather curious person." She had been living with Picasso for several years by the time Alice arrived. As the first "wife" of the first genius Alice met, Fernande seemed unimpressive except for her beauty, which Alice admitted was astonishing. Her interests, as Alice recorded them, were trivial; her petty jealousies flared too often; and her apartment, when she wasn't living with Picasso, was in "wretched taste." "It was elaborately furnished with rented objects, an upright piano, Turkish covers for bed and table, opaque glass bowls and ash trays."[52] Fernande shared Picasso's love of the Katzenjammer Kids—comics given to them by Leo or Gertrude—and she shared, too, the hardship of the painter's early poverty. She understood the man, she claimed, as well as his work. Of her apparent superficiality, she offered a brief defense: "There is a tendency in France," she wrote, "particularly amongst intellectuals, to regard women as incapable of serious thought. I sensed this, and it paralysed me. So I contented myself with listening. I believed in the profundity of the ideas I heard exchanged. I listened, passionately attentive, but I never dared utter an opinion of my own."

Even Alice, not usually reticent, had difficulty uttering opinions about what she was hearing and seeing. When Gertrude asked for her thoughts about what she saw in Picasso's studio, her reply was, "Well I did see something." When pressed, she admitted that what she saw was "rather awful" compared with the paintings at the *vernissage*.

"Sure," Gertrude told her, "as Pablo once remarked, when you make a thing, it is so complicated making it that it is bound to be ugly. . . ."[53] Inventiveness, she said, inevitably produced an ugliness born from the struggle of creation. Gertrude herself, Leo divulged later, had been repulsed by the first Picasso he bought, the *Young Girl with a Basket of Flowers*, and that painting was hardly as sensually violent as the attenuated harlequins and shattered nudes which Alice saw.

Alice, as always, was able to maintain a peaceable calm, even if she was confused. She was content to await the understanding that would focus her vision. Harriet, on the other hand, conjured up a vision to spark her understanding. More easily shaken than her friend, she was not satisfied with Gertrude's explanations of Picasso, nor Sarah's of Matisse, nor Leo's of art in general. Her sensibilities jolted, she needed no less than a talk with God.

The night when I discovered God, I asked him. And He told me, as he told me everything else. I asked Him about this strange life I was seeing. Of the world of artists who talked a language of which I understood nothing. What was it all about? I asked God what they meant by all the strange words: the "realismus," the "idealismus." What was the realismus? For answer I beheld a drawing. A drawing in black and white. A segment of light so brilliant that it was beyond all light, the shadow segment beside it was unreality. . . . I asked: What about all these people who are flocking to the new visions offered in Paris? All these excited young people who ask burning questions of Leo and Sarah?

I did not know much, but it was enough to make me ask "What was it that makes a man willing to surrender his own convictions?"[54]

God's explanation seemed to have consoled the troubled Harriet, and the next morning she awakened Alice and said in a hushed voice, "I have seen God. . . . He came to me in a drop of water from Heaven." Alice, about to offer her congratulations, was stopped. "Go over to Gertrude," Harriet said, "and bring her over at once."[55]

Gertrude was heartily amused, but Harriet, of course, was not. It was necessary, Gertrude thought, to find someone to deal with the problem, and the family's current expert on religion was Sarah.

Early in January 1908, Sarah, with the help of Hans Purrmann and Patrick Henry Bruce, had finally realized her dream of establishing an art school taught by Matisse. Annette was among the first students; Leo attended occasionally. Each Saturday morning, Matisse would come by the rue de Sèvres studio to criticize the work accomplished during the week. His comments, carefully noted by Sarah, reflect the discipline, care, and forethought that he gave to his own work. "No lines can go wild; every line must have its function," he told his students. "Order above all, in color." He tempered the young artists' quest for the new and the modern with his own feelings about construction and composition.

The school was a success but Sarah was not. She determined for herself that she would never be a first-rate artist, and quickly sought something which would make full use of her talents. Though she continued her warm patronage of Matisse, she now put her daily efforts not into art but Christian Science.

Sarah's fervent embrace of Christian Science took her friends by surprise. More than thirty years after Mary Baker Eddy first published her tract, Christian Science was gaining notoriety—and engendering a good deal of derision —in Paris. The word was being spread partly through the efforts of Cora Downer, a Boston practitioner who claimed to have had her sight restored by a Christian Scientist when she was a child. Witty, intelligent, well-spoken, she soon attracted active followers. Sarah was one, and a friend of the Steins, Swedish sculptor David Edstrom, was another.

Edstrom had met Gertrude and Leo in Fiesole, near Florence, in 1904 and saw the Steins frequently in Paris. Gertrude, Edstrom thought, "was the only out-and-out fat woman whose every ounce of avoirdupois seemed precious and lovable." But, he was quick to add, "Do not misunderstand me—I did not have any feeling of romantic love for her. One did not fall in love with Gertrude Stein; at least I never heard of any one doing so."[56]

Edstrom, when he first met the Steins, was a lonely, unstable, frightened young man, harboring within him "a core of terror and foretaste of doom."[57] He was, as he later realized, close to madness. Gertrude was fascinated. She thought Edstrom had multiple personalities and observed with interest to see which facet would emerge at any time. One never knew. Even his physical appearance could alter perceptibly from one meeting to the next. Edstrom, when cherubic, was a gentle, slender, handsome blond. Edstrom, demonic, was wild-eyed, with lids that drooped at the corners, hair that fell madly across his brow, and a cold, inhuman expression of "almost fiendish joy."[58] Sometimes he would appear trim and fit, sometimes bloated to an enormous girth.

Marital difficulties compounded his other problems. In 1902, he had wed a wealthy Swedish woman. Two years later, he found out that she had taken a lover. The blow to his inflated ego ignited an already well-established hatred of women. "Woman," he decided, "with her crooked, illogical ways, was for the propagation of the species, an instrument of pleasure at best, but a creature anyone who wanted to reach the heights must evade like death itself."[59] Civilization in general, and American civilization in particular, owed its problems to the emancipation of women. "No despot in history has fought more bitterly to suppress the truth about himself than the women of America have fought to suppress the truth about woman, her psychology, her abilities and limitations, physically and spiritually."[60]

His heart breaking from the wrongs perpetrated on him by his wife, he sought solace at the feet of Leo and Gertrude, Michael and Sarah. But other friends, too, came to know of his woes. The writer Hutchins Hapgood, in Fiesole with his redheaded wife, Neith Boyce, turned a sympathetic ear. A self-proclaimed "intellectual anarchist," Hapgood had gained recent attention as the author of *The Autobiography of a Thief*. When Edstrom visited him and proposed that he work with him on his own autobiography, Hapgood agreed without hesitation. As the sessions progressed, however, Hapgood saw that Edstrom was reveling in his own past, embellishing his exploits and venting ruthless anger at his wife. He wondered that Gertrude and Leo were able to maintain sympathy for the man, and arrived at his own conclusion about the relationship. "It is a very striking thing, in both Leo and Gertrude Stein," he decided, "that they are capable of absolute aesthetic and moral condemnation of human beings, and are also incapable of close human association. Coming in contact with only a few elements of personality, which fit into their a priori ideas, they never get the full personality of anyone."[61] Interested in Edstrom as a subject, they nurtured his dependence on them to ensure their continuing observation.

Leo, especially, Hapgood thought, seemed "almost always mentally irritated. The slightest flaw, real or imaginary, in his companion's statements, caused in him intellectual indignation of the most intense kind. And there seemed to be something in him which took it for granted that anything said by anybody except himself needed immediate denial or at least substantial modification. He seemed to need constant reinforcement of his ego. . . ."[62] Gertrude, immensely devoted to her brother, furnished the reinforcement. Powerful, brilliant, self-possessed, she adored Leo, Hapgood wrote, "in a way a man is seldom admired and loved. . . ."[63] The magnitude of her personality was matched by her physical appearance; she loved to sit in the hot, noonday sun, perspiring profusely, Hapgood remembered. She hardly spoke, but he felt her warmth "in her handclasp, her look, and her rich laughter."[64]

Hapgood kept Gertrude and Leo informed of the progress of Edstrom's life story, confiding to them his own feelings about Edstrom's malicious glee in exposing the women he had known. The working sessions, he told them, consisted in Edstrom's narrating his adventures and Hapgood's recording the dictated work. The finished manuscript, however, would show Hapgood's own view. While the book was still in progress, Hapgood showed his notes to Gertrude.

"In a few days," David Edstrom recalled, "I was told by Gertrude that he [Hapgood] had written a book about me. She had read the manuscript. I do not remember her comment on it, but I do remember that she told me she had persuaded him not to publish it. In a way it acted like a terrible whiplash on me. I felt just as I did over my first marriage, a sense of shame and self-condemnation for being a fool."[65] Pretending that he wanted to look over the notes, he managed to get the manuscript from Hapgood and then, Hapgood revealed, absconded with it to Paris. Horrified by what he read, he vowed that he would kill Hapgood, who he was convinced was "a vampire, a bloodsucker, a leech who pumped him dry. . . ."[66]

Nearly at the point of self-destruction, he met Cora Downer. It was, Edstrom admitted, love at first sight. "She was . . . a wonderful listener, and those who had sensitiveness and intelligence expanded and were at their best with her. She was to me the incarnation of Pallas Athene."[67] Christian Science, he decided, would heal his body and his weary soul.

His instant and dramatic conversion so impressed Sarah

Stein that when Harriet presented herself with her problem, David Edstrom was called in as an aide. When Sarah took Harriet in hand, she demanded exclusive rights, and Harriet's formerly carefree days with Alice and Gertrude were put to an end. Sarah devoted her time to instructing Harriet in Science, and Edstrom, as he grew more interested, decided that Harriet should visit his studio each morning to sit for her portrait.

Edstrom, Alice said, "had not known anything like Harriet before." Though he was ardently infatuated with Cora, he firmly believed in polygamy, and could find no reason to quash a blossoming friendship with Harriet. In the few days of sitting for him. Harriet found him a charming young man. Gradually, however, his submerged selves began to surface. One morning he appeared distraught and upset. She had an awful effect on him, he told her. He began each day by reading a portion of St. John. Then she arrived and immediately dragged him from the heights to which he had risen. Another day, he was cold and angry. His wife had been just like her, he said. She, too, was Jewish, had exalted her parents, had kept her girlhood friends—all of which he found repulsive.[68] Harriet began to feel frightened.

One day she met him as she was leaving a café. "Did you know my wife was in town?" he blurted out as soon as he saw her. He said he was afraid of her and pleaded with Harriet to let him walk with her. His wife, he confessed, had once beaten him up and he was sure she would do it again if she knew he wanted to divorce her. Humoring the worried man, Harriet consented to let him walk beside her. But it seemed odd to her that a Christian Science practitioner, teaching Harriet not to be afraid, should be cowering in anticipation of meeting his wife.[69]

Harriet's relationship with Sarah was no better. The woman was so dogmatic, so impatient, that Harriet began to feel intimidated. Nevertheless, Christian Science held its attraction, and Harriet attended all the local meetings, befriending the lovely Miss Downer. Her friendship with Alice and Gertrude continued to be warm, but with her new consuming passion, she rarely saw them. She was present, however, at one momentous occasion.

"Picasso squeezed my hand under the table," Alice reported matter-of-factly. At this, Gertrude dropped her fork. "Ah," she said, looking at Alice, "and what else?"

"Nothing," Alice replied. "He just squeezed my hand."

Still looking hard at her friend, Gertrude tried to analyze the gesture. "It might have been a mere transient casual act," she mused. "But it may have been a more important sign. If in squeezing her hand he experienced an emotion that entered into his imagination, that would be entirely different. That might be the beginning of a permanent feeling. . . ."

At these words, Alice began to pale.

"Might be love," Gertrude continued.

Alice, Harriet thought, looked terrified.

"Might even be love."[70]

Eight

ANNETTE, LIKE HARRIET, was seeing less of Gertrude now that Alice had come. The probing sessions had all but ceased. She was studying art at the Académie Matisse, working at her sculpture, attempting to direct her own life. But her conscience was bothering her, and she promised herself that she must tell Alice that she had shown her letters to Gertrude.

One afternoon, when the two went walking in the Luxembourg Gardens, she confessed. Stammering and nervous, she told Alice that she felt she had broken a trust. She said that she had violated their friendship and could feel no peace of mind while Alice was unaware of what had happened. Alice's reaction did little to help the distraught young woman. She merely continued walking, accepting the revelation without comment. Annette felt no better for having disclosed her secret. For Alice, the confession only confirmed her own feelings about Annette and made more apt the nickname by which she privately called her: "the Stinker."[71]

Alice felt no regret at the loss of Annette's friendship, nor did she try to bring Harriet closer to her. Gertrude, she knew immediately, was and always would be enough. The two began to spend more and more time together—on long walks, in talks at the rue de Fleurus, on visits to Gertrude's friends. Except for Picasso, with whom Gertrude engaged in discussions on art which Alice could only witness silently, there was just one rival for Gertrude's attentions: Leo. And Alice sensed that the bond between Leo and his sister was straining. Two causes were splitting the "closed corporation": Leo didn't understand Gertrude's writing, and Leo no longer approved of Picasso.

Picasso, Leo thought, was artistically inventive, technically adept, and personally attractive. "His comment on persons and things was commonly humorous and satirical, and he smoked his pipe and twinkled while others speculated and disputed. . . . His dark, brilliant eyes were the most absorptive that I have ever seen," Leo wrote, "and I wondered at times, when he was looking at a drawing or an engraving, that anything should be left upon the paper."[72] But as for his work, Leo was not convinced of its greatness. It was ingenious—that he would concede—but it was trivial. By 1907, Picasso's leap to cubism was more than Leo could bear. He defected to Matisse.

Gertrude, on the other hand, grew stronger in her support of Picasso. They understood each other, she felt, and what she wanted to do with words he wanted to do with shape and color. In long knee-to-knee conversations they shared their thoughts about painting and writing, and found that they had in common the realization that they were both creating the twentieth century. Her understanding of the artist, she thought, went deeper than aesthetics. She understood his egotism. She understood his defiance. She understood the light that emanated from those striking black eyes. She likened him to Turgenev's Bazarov: Picasso, too, flaunted his independence. He stood outside convention—even outside art.

" 'So,' " says Turgenev's Pavel, "barely raising his eyebrows as though he were falling asleep. 'You, therefore, don't acknowledge art?'

" 'Art is just a means of making money, as sure as hemorrhoids exist,' Bazarov exclaimed with a contemptuous smile.' " For true genius, life itself was art, and individuality alone worthy of exaltation. " '. . . As for the times,' Bazarov declared, 'why should I be influenced by them? Rather let them be influenced by me.' "

Picasso's attraction for Gertrude was, Alice said, that of an older sister toward an audacious and charming younger brother. If there were rumors they were lovers, Alice wrote to a friend once, then incest would have to be part of the scandal.[73] Picasso was the first of Gertrude's young men— and there would be many—with whom she would show her greatest brilliance. Youth and masculine vigor fired Gertrude's own incisive mind. The conversations she had with Picasso would never be captured—not even in her lucid, witty essays. She herself was buoyed by his hopes. She took strength from his strength. She confirmed her own potential creativity from his avowal of genius. And above all, she admired his independence—from his fellow artists, from would-be patrons, from women. " '. . . A man should be fierce, as the excellent Spanish proverb says!' " exclaimed Bazarov.

Of this friendship, Leo understood little. He was disturbed because he was sure that Picasso was not realizing his powers. One evening, Leo caught Picasso in his studio and proceeded to lecture him. It was some time before he let him go, and when Picasso emerged he was furious. "He does not leave me alone," he told Gertrude. "It was he who said my drawings were more important than Raphael's. Why can he not leave me alone then with what I am doing now?" Leo was equally angry. He slammed the door to his room and remained cloistered until Picasso left. Then he came out and tried to explain to Gertrude why he had said what he said. He could not restrain himself from criticizing Gertrude's writing at the same time. But Gertrude was not interested. It was the first of many clashes, but this one was quickly ended by the thud of Gertrude's books on the floor as she succeeded in overpowering Leo's antipathies.[74]

Gertrude was thirty-four years old and always had followed Leo. As a child she had trailed him up and down the hills of San Francisco and Oakland. Later she had followed him to Cambridge, Baltimore, and then to Paris. She nodded in silent agreement as he expounded his many theories on a wide range of subjects. Leo had taken care of her, which she needed and appreciated; and she had idolized him, which he came to expect. Now, with difficulty, she was trying to determine her own identity and pursue a career. She still sometimes became darkly depressed and often felt isolated and alone. Now, when she needed Leo, he was not there. He listened but seemed not to hear what she was really saying. He had always been the one "compelling" and "deciding"; she, "accepting" and "asking."[75] She loved him, but now she was not sure that the love was returned. She had felt that they were so much alike all these years. Suddenly, she discovered how essentially different they really were.

He simply could not say yes. To deny Gertrude her

independence would have been inconsistent with his concern for any individual's inner life and would have contradicted everything he knew about psychology. But still, he could not permit Gertrude to declare herself—either as a fully separate being or, even more dangerous to Leo, as an artist. Her success would only point starkly to his own failure. At thirty-six, he had already turned away from many disciplines which might have resulted in a career. He had decided for himself that he never would be a painter. He was closest to art history but in no way approached the erudition or achievement of someone like Bernard Berenson, whom he respected, already well-known at Leo's age. Even those who derided him for his impatience and obstinacy could not fail to notice his quick intelligence and his marked intuition about art. But he had produced nothing.

He was willing to admit Gertrude's need to express herself in her own way. He had no desire, really, to stifle her ambitions as a writer. But his theoretical understanding of another's needs was undermined by an obsessive penchant for honesty and by his own need to dominate. Once, he saw Gertrude go to bed in tears because he refused to admit that her writing contained any art at all. But no matter how distressed Gertrude seemed, no matter how desperately she needed his approval at the crucial beginning of her much-desired career, he could not yield.

After her first novel, *Q.E.D.*, which she wrote in New York and then buried among her books, she completed *Three Lives*, the histories of three women. *Three Lives*, which was inspired in part by Flaubert's *Trois Contes*, was written in a direct, bare, and intelligible style, very different from her next work, *The Making of Americans*. She showed this new manuscript to Leo. Though he had offered no praise of *Three Lives*, Leo could not allow Gertrude's latest effort to continue without comment. It meant nothing, he told her. Though he knew in theory that "life is a monstrous fugue," he could not praise Gertrude's work for its interweaving repetition of word and phrase. *The Making of Americans*, a rumbling, rhythmic unfolding of a family's progress, meant nothing to him. Perhaps it meant something to Gertrude, but he believed any artist must turn "outward and not inward, unless he turns himself inward outward."[76]

He began explaining the shortcomings of the book but, strangely for Gertrude, the more he explained the surer she was that he was wrong. Yet she lacked the strength to assert her convictions to Leo. ". . . My brother led in everything," she wrote later. "He had always been my brother two years older and a brother. I had always been following."[77] She needed support. She needed encouragement. She needed approval. And she found everything she needed in Alice.

Throughout her life, Alice's own literary tastes remained conventional. She liked a well-wrought tale, written in a masterly style, preferably Henry James's. As a child, she had been fed the bland outpourings of Juliana Horatia Ewing, whose Brownie stories inspired Lord and Lady Baden-Powell's name for their girls' clubs. She was unmoved by Louisa Alcott, and of Dickens preferred *A Tale of Two Cities* and *Great Expectations* to *David Copperfield*. In Seattle, in her late teens, she read Howells' *April Hopes*, a tale of the jealousy and reconciliation that marked young love, Sarah Orne Jewett's *King of Folly Island*, and a Scottish historian's rendering of *The Reign of Emperor Charles V*.

James, of course, was her one great and abiding passion. *The Awkward Age*, in fact, so impressed her that she conceived of the fairly obvious idea of dramatizing the novel, and suggested the plan to James in a letter. James, she said, responded with a "delightful letter" concurring with her notion of turning the novel—which is to a large extent dialogue—into a play. But Alice was so embarrassed at suggesting herself as a playwright that she destroyed the letter. Nevertheless, the candid, articulate, outspoken Nanda Brookenham stood as her favorite heroine.

Unlike Gertrude, Alice enjoyed reading French as well as English. When she arrived in Paris, she found the many-volumed memoirs of George Sand at a bookseller's along the quai.[78] She once read Nietzsche—incurring her father's disapproval—but admitted that it was only affectation that drew her to the philosopher.

A few months before leaving San Francisco, she had read with interest Alfred Jarry's bold, wild play *Ubu Roi*. Jarry, later hailed as a precursor by the surrealists, offered a succinct explanation of his work. "Talking about things that are understandable," he wrote, "only weighs down the mind and falsifies the memory, but the absurd exercises the mind and makes the memory work." When it was first performed in Paris in 1896, the play caused a riot among the audience, which included W. B. Yeats. "After us the savage gods," Yeats was moved to declare. For its early readers, *Ubu Roi* was a lightning flash illuminating a glimpse of the future of literature.

When Gertrude gave her some pages of *The Making of Americans*, Alice was immediately fascinated not so much by the style but by Gertrude's intent. Her search for the psychological "bottom nature" of each individual was the kind of analysis that Alice herself tried to perform on her various friends and acquaintances. Gertrude asked her to explain what she had found out, and was impressed by Alice's insights. She was convinced that Alice understood.

Alice's admiration of *The Making of Americans* came at precisely the right moment in Gertrude's career. The book, Alice told her, "was very exciting, more exciting than anything else had ever been. Even," she said to her, "more exciting than Picasso's pictures promise to be."[79] There could be no higher praise for Gertrude.

Alice was neither a literary critic nor an art critic. Though she would later offer perceptive remarks about Gertrude's writing and Picasso's painting, it is difficult to separate her own opinions from those gleaned from Gertrude. But she did have an immediate and powerful response to personalities. She did acknowledge a real jolt— the ringing of a bell—when she confronted genius. Whatever she thought privately about *The Making of Americans*, there was no doubt in her mind that the writer herself was unique. Her San Francisco friends—though some had been interesting, some amusing—were inconsequential by comparison. From the powerful first impression which Gertrude made on her, Alice knew Gertrude was worthy of her devotion. She would give her what Gertrude said every writer needed: "praise, praise, praise." And she would give her what Gertrude needed even more: love.

They had grown closer, their walks longer, their talks more fruitful. In winter, Gertrude dubbed her "an old maid mermaid," an evaluation that Alice found unbearable; but by spring, the nickname "had gone into oblivion," Alice said, "and I had been gathering wild violets."[80] Still, they were just good friends.

Though Alice would have spent all her time with Gertrude, old friends visited her during that first winter in Paris. Ada Joseph, now Mrs. Harry Brackett, arrived unexpectedly. Gertrude, unfortunately, was bored with Harry, but Alice felt obligated to entertain them. "Ada wanted to take me to all the restaurants and theatres she knew and we went gaily from one to another, starting with the restaurant Lapérouse." Besides dining at fine restaurants, they attended "the most questionable of the comedies." Alice, shocked by Ada's choice of entertainment, suggested that they leave after the first act. "Nonsense," her friend replied. "This is mild."[81] After a week, Ada returned with her husband to London.

One evening at the rue de Fleurus, Alice was surprised to see her Seattle friend Louise Hayden. Louise, she learned, was in Paris studying piano with the renowned teacher Philippe. Since she lived near Gertrude, on the Boulevard Raspail, Alice was able to see Louise frequently. But she did not see less of Gertrude.

Only Lilyanna Hansen, who visited in the early spring, competed for Alice's attention. Together, Lilyanna and Alice walked through the city, lingering in the Luxembourg Gardens, where the chestnuts were budding. But Lilyanna left before the trees were in full bloom, and Alice resumed her walks with Gertrude.

As summer approached, the Steins, as in previous years, made plans to rent a villa in Fiesole. This year they would take the Villa Bardi, and Gertrude suggested that Alice and Harriet leave Paris and rent the smaller Casa Ricci, where the Steins had stayed the year before.

The train trip to Milan was hot and uncomfortable; the trip to Florence almost torrid. In the train's dressing room, Alice removed her cerise girdle and flung it out of the window with rare abandon. "What a strange coincidence," Harriet remarked when she returned to the car. "I just saw your cherry-colored corset pass by the window."[82] That evening, they drove from Florence to Fiesole, where the Steins had already arrived.

The ancient town of Fiesole, with its steep hills, charming gardens and piazzas, and Roman ruins, was a suitably romantic setting. Gertrude took Alice on long walks, especially in midday, when she loved to stride along under the hot sun. Alice's favorites were what she called "pilgrimage walks." On the first, they climbed to the mountaintop where St. Francis was said to have met St. Dominic. The dry earth was so slippery that both Gertrude and Alice took off their sandals and completed the steep climb with bare feet. From the summit, the view of the valley was magnificent; in the clouds, they picnicked on sandwiches which Alice had brought along.

For Alice, Fiesole would forever evoke "so many happy memories"—above all of one special afternoon. While climbing the hill from Settignano to Fiesole, Gertrude and Alice found themselves in the midst of a lovely garden. Here, finally, Gertrude summoned enough courage to ask Alice what she long wanted to know.

The conversation began with a banal discussion of weather, the comparative heat of the places in which they had lived. Cautiously, Gertrude admitted, "I have been very happy to-day." Then, abruptly, she asked, "Didn't Nelly and Lilly love you?" There was no need for Alice to confirm what Gertrude already knew from her letters to Annette. But the question was prerequisite to their continuing relationship. The question, for Gertrude, was an expression of her deepest wish, her intention, she proclaimed, "to win my bride." Alice's response showed that her wish had been "guessed expressed and gratified."

"Care for me," Gertrude implored. "I care for you in every possible way." She wanted no one else. ". . . There was really no need of men and women. Sisters. What are sisters, and sisters and brothers."

What she proposed to Alice was nothing less than marriage. They would live together, Alice as wife, Gertrude as husband. "When all is said one is wedded to bed." She needed Alice to care for her. "Pet me tenderly and save me from alarm," she pleaded. "I hear you praise me and I say thanks for yesterday and to-day," she told her, adding, "And tomorrow we do not doubt." She needed a wife: "A wife hangs on her husband that is what Shakespeare says a loving wife hangs on her husband that is what she does." She needed a protector. "I love my love and she loves me. . . . She can be responsible for me and I can see this responsibility."

Alice cried, her tears drying on her cheeks under the hot Tuscan sun. But her answer was definite and firm. "She came and saw and seeing cried I am your bride." And Gertrude said, "I understand the language."[83]

Alice had not stopped crying by the time they returned to the Casa Ricci. Harriet counted thirty handkerchiefs a day as her friend continued intermittent outbursts. "Day after day she wept because of the new love that had come into her life," Harriet recalled.

But Gertrude and Alice were well-bred ladies, and Queen Victoria had died a mere seven years before. They both fully realized that outsiders would view their liaison with derision, and they had no desire to flaunt what should remain a private relationship. Though they knew "our future would be for ourselves alone," they decided to proceed slowly.

Alice remained at the Casa Ricci with Harriet, Gertrude with her family at the Villa Bardi. They met each morning, going first to the Gabinetto Vieusseaux, a bookstore and rental library, and then shopping and visiting friends. Michael Stein, who had taken Alice under his wing as financial adviser, permitted her to have boots made to order—her one luxury, she claimed.

Gertrude took Alice to I Tatti, Bernard Berenson's villa in Settignano, which struck some as a museum and others as a mausoleum, and to the nearby Villa Gamberaia on the Via Rossellino, where Florence Blood lived with Princess Ghika. The princess, as the notorious Liane de Pougy, had worn emerald rings on her toes—but only in bed—and counted among her conquests as a courtesan Napoleon III and Natalie Barney. Now, at forty-two, she had settled down to domesticity with Miss Blood and lived in a sumptuous villa amid elegant gardens.

They stopped at a small villa on the Via San Leonardo where the Von Heiroths lived—she, a beautiful thirty-year-old blond Finn, and he, a Russian artist with a pointed beard and red, protruding lips who played the piano, Alice thought, "in a masterly manner."

They visited the Algar Thorolds at their Villa Fontanelle, Algar being the son of the Bishop of Winchester and his wife Theresa the daughter of another Church of England cleric. Both were recent converts to Catholicism, which accounted for their daughter's concern over having committed a blasphemy by allowing her cat to have kittens in their chapel.

In Florence they lunched with two old friends of Gertrude, Claribel and Etta Cone. Claribel, a physician, had known Gertrude since 1897, when Gertrude entered the Johns Hopkins Medical School. Alice thought Claribel "handsome and distinguished," but immediately disliked her sister Etta, finding her stubborn, opinionated, and too fond of flattery. She and Gertrude nicknamed her "Pomposa." Ill-feeling began when Alice and Etta disagreed about who should pay the luncheon bill, and when Etta confided that she could forgive but never forget, Alice rejoined with, "As for myself, I can forget but not forgive," which endured as her personal motto.

But often Gertrude and Alice were alone. They visited Assisi via Perugia, staying overnight in a hotel that had been a sixteenth-century palace, and making the climb on foot to the shrine of one of Gertrude's favorite saints. Assisi was torrid, Alice remembered, and during their long climb to the church, Alice ducked behind some bushes to remove some of her silk underwear and her stockings. She became only imperceptibly cooler, but, she said, "It was all I could do."

Though Gertrude was very fond of St. Francis, Alice had a weakness for St. Anthony of Padua, who helped find lost objects. As Michael Stein once commented about Alice, if she had been a general she would never lose a battle, only mislay it. Her donations to St. Anthony were in the manner of insurance.

Harriet joined them in Assisi, staying at the same inn, and the three returned to Florence. Florence and the surrounding countryside were, Alice thought, not unlike the loveliest parts of France or England.[84] She was intrigued by the antique shops, choosing from among "the most tempting treasures" a Tuscan table and some chairs, intended for the apartment she and Harriet would look for when they returned to Paris.

In September, Alice and Harriet stayed at the Hôtel des Saints-Pères, small, quiet, and woody, on the rue des Saints-Pères, until they found four rooms on the rue Notre Dame des Champs, a few blocks from the rue de Fleurus. The low rent included a kitchen but no private bathroom. But the apartment was sunny and suited to the furniture which Alice and Harriet had acquired in Florence. Alice set to work making mesh curtains, buying cushions for their chairs, and overseeing their Swiss maid, Marie Enz. Most of her time was spent with Gertrude.

Each morning she arrived early at the rue de Fleurus to type the pages of *The Making of Americans* which Gertrude had left for her the night before. The typewriter was an old Blickensdorfer, which Gertrude soon deemed unsatisfactory. She decided to invest in a new Smith Premier, which was delivered with a great many accompanying appliances. But the "imposing personage" who brought the machine surprisingly placed the gadgets in his bags, and Alice wondered why they were not deducted from the bill. With her new instrument, she began to type more efficiently, gradually taking on "a Gertrude Stein technique, like playing Bach."

Gertrude was usually asleep when Alice arrived, but Leo was frequently present and sometimes gave her his own work to be typed. They remained cool but amiable toward each other except for one incident.

Nellie Jacott and her husband were visiting in Paris, and Alice still maintained a possessiveness toward Nellie despite her having married. Leo found her attractive and tried to strike up a flirtation with her. Alice, resentful of his intrusion into their friendship, lashed out harshly, but Leo laughed at her, and Nellie never took him seriously. Leo's ability to flirt seems to have been a new-found talent. Only a few years before, he had confronted Neith Boyce, Hutchins Hapgood's wife, with the whole question of flirtation, wanting to know in detail "the technique of this art . . . the reasons and use of it, and . . . all the methods, with their various ramifications."[85]

Gertrude would join Alice at about one, having her breakfast coffee while Alice had lunch. They would talk about Gertrude's writing, then Alice would return home while Gertrude worked, and come again to the rue de Fleurus in the evening.

Harriet was concerned that Alice be home by midnight —she thought it was dangerous to walk the streets after that—especially when Alice related an unexpected encounter. One evening, on the narrow rue Vavin, she found herself face to face with a stranger. *"Eh, bien,"* said the man, "do you not intend to give me the right of way?" Courageously Alice replied, "Never!" Apparently her tone convinced him. "How difficult the Creoles are," he muttered, as he stepped aside.[86] Alice found the story humorous; but Harriet was not amused.

Harriet was one obstacle to Gertrude's and Alice's living together. Alice, having come to Paris with Harriet, felt an obligation to keep her company especially since she was apt to get lonely and fearful when she was not with her friends. Her involvement in Christian Science had waned somewhat, and her desire for Alice's company correspondingly increased. As it was, she found herself alone more and more often, though she was included in the Saturday-evening gatherings and in a few interesting escapades.

Picasso's banquet in honor of Henri Rousseau was outstanding in Harriet's memory. According to Harriet, Gertrude had come wearing a brown and yellow felt sailor hat, and she, a hat with velvet roses. Alice remembered wearing a new hat with a yellow feather trim. The hats assumed such extraordinary importance in their minds because André Salmon, drunk, allegedly devoured the trim from both Alice's and Harriet's. In general, dress was eclectic, as was the food.

Fernande Olivier intended to supply a dinner from the grocer Félix Potin, but the food had not yet arrived by the time the party was to begin. Alice, with her never-failing good sense, suggested that Fernande phone to ask about the order. But by the time a phone was found, it was too late—Potin's was closed. Since a large quantity of Fernande's *riz à la valencienne* was already cooked, however, Fernande thought she could make do by buying some dishes in neighboring Montmartre shops. The party began as scheduled, centered around a huge dish of excellent rice.

Entertainment consisted in the guests' singing and dancing, Apollinaire's reciting a poem to Rousseau, and Rousseau's performing on his violin. Picasso asked Harriet to sing a song from America. Apollinaire requested the hymn of the Indian Territory, and Harriet responded enthusiastically with a Berkeley cheer:

TWO ARE ONE

Give them Oski!
Oski wow wow
Whisky wee wee
Ole Muck I
Ole Berk-keley
California
Wow![87]

The guests, besides Leo, Gertrude, Harriet, and Alice, included Apollinaire's mistress, Marie Laurencin, Georges Braque, Ramon and Germaine Pichot, and Maurice Raynal, all assembled to honor the sixty-four-year-old Henri Rousseau, the gentle painter much loved by his fellow artists. They doted on him, Alice thought, as if he were a favorite little brother, and she shared their affection, perhaps because Rousseau told her that she reminded him of his late wife.

"Le Douanier" Rousseau had begun painting at forty, a year before he retired from the municipal toll service in 1885. At his first public exhibition, his works were slashed with knives and finally had to be removed from the show. Nevertheless he persevered, translating dreams to canvas. Generally modest and quiet, he once told Picasso, "We are the two greatest painters of our epoch, you in the Egyptian style, I in the modern style." His explanations of his work were as ingenuous as his technique. Of *Le Rêve*, he told André Salmon, "You shouldn't be surprised to find a sofa out in a virgin forest. It means nothing except for the richness of the red. You understand, the sofa is in a room; the rest is Yadwigha's dream."

The small, round-cheeked man affected his friends with his impish quality. They adored him, and Guillaume Apollinaire even created for him a fantastic past, filled with exploits in Mexico and adventures as colorful as Rousseau's own paintings. Soon the myth became inseparable from the man, and the stories were told and retold with delight. The denial of a history and the fabrication of myths to replace it were intrinsic to the spirit of the time and of the place. Apollinaire himself, when asked once for some biographical details, responded, "I have no past, and for that reason I should be happy, like peoples without history. A few travels in Europe, *La Revue blanche, Le Festin d'Ésope*, defending painters I like, literature, poetry—that is all there is on the credit side of my ledger. I am writing a novel and a play and am preparing a collection of my poems. That is my entire personal history. My assets consist of a total lack of money, a knowledge of literature that I believe extensive, a few languages living and dead, and a rather varied experience of life. . . ."

As Picasso once told Gertrude, "One had to break to make one's revolution and start at zero," to leave behind a provincial existence and staid family life, to come to Paris, to be reborn.

These were expatriates but not the exiles they would have been if they had remained at home—onlookers, outsiders, malcontents. "Living abroad," one American poet, Laura Riding, once declared, "I don't do that. America was living abroad to me." They needed a place where everything was accepted and most things understood, "a sort of painted background," as Henry James described, ". . . which is always there, to be looked at when you please, and to be most easily and comfortably ignored when you don't." Gertrude would explain it later in her homage to Paris, "the place where tradition was so firm that they could look modern without being different and where their acceptance of reality is so great that they could let any one have the emotion of unreality." And from the emotion of unreality would come a new reality. It was the place where they could paint pictures ("and naturally," Gertrude said, "they could not do that at home"). It was the place where they could write ("they could not do that at home either, they could be dentists at home"). It was the place they could create, not only their art, but themselves, as they wanted to be.

Without roots, without the encumbrance of familiar faces, they needed only to exorcise ghosts and memories— or hide them deeply away. Each, seeing the other filtered by a new light, confirmed the new image. The living creation —a new identity—was exhibited with as much bravura as the latest painting. The artist was a Personality. His work could not be separated from his life, his loves, his smile, the intensity of his eyes, his odd costumes. The creation of a new image was celebrated in bold strokes and the clamor of hundreds of bells to self-proclaimed genius. The twentieth century was being born, and with it new legends, figments of brilliant imagination.

Nine

"WITH ALICE'S ADVENT," Annette saw, "a new era opened up for Gertrude—Alice was capable of creating a background of competent showmanship that she had never been able to do for herself, and sorely needed this outlet for her thirst for fame. . . . Alice, at last in Paris, had found the brilliant personality worthy of her talents; now she could concentrate her efficiency and cleverness both in furthering Gertrude's literary career, as well as catering to any indulgences that the spoiled child craved to advance her own success."[88]

By December 1908, when Annette sailed back to San Francisco, Alice had begun her own lifelong career as an impresario. From typist, she gradually took on other duties, one as Sunday cook, another as sounding board for Gertrude's progress on *The Making of Americans*. When *Three Lives* was published in the summer of 1909, she assumed greater responsibility, soliciting the help of friends to distribute copies and subscribing to Romeike's clipping bureau, which she remembered from advertisements in the *Argonaut*, so that Gertrude would be kept apprised of the book's reception. She began, too, to figure in Gertrude's writing, most notably in a brief biography, "Ada."

One Sunday evening, when Alice was substituting as cook for Hélène, Gertrude bustled into the kitchen with a manuscript. "Here I want to show you something," she said to Alice, who at first refused, trying to get the dinner on the table. But Gertrude insisted that she look instead at her latest piece. Since Gertrude preferred to eat her food warm, not hot, Alice knew from the start that she was defeated. Resigned, she sat down and began reading from the small notebook. "I began it and I thought she was making fun of me," she recalled, but by the time she had finished it, she was pleased and flattered.

"Ada" traces the life of a young woman, "twice as old as her brother," who "had been a very good daughter to her mother," telling her lovely stories, until the mother became so ill that "the daughter knew that there were some stories she could tell her that would not please her mother." Her mother died, and the daughter "then kept house for her father and took care of her brother. There were many relations who lived with them. The daughter did not like to live with them and she did not like them to die with them." She confessed her unhappiness to her father, but he failed to respond. "She was afraid then, she was one needing charming stories and happy telling of them and not having that thing she was always trembling." Finally, she told her father that she was going away. The father said nothing, but when she had gone, he entreated her with gentle letters to come home. She replied with "tender letters" but never went back. Then she fell in love.

"She came to be happier than anybody else who was living then. It is easy to believe this thing. She was telling someone, who was loving every story that was charming. Some one who was living was almost always listening. Some one who was loving was almost always listening. . . . Ada was then one and all her living then one completely telling stories that were charming, completely listening to stories having a beginning and a middle and an ending. Trembling was all living, living was all loving, some one was then the other one. Certainly this one was loving this Ada then. And certainly Ada all her living then was happier in living than any one else who ever could, who was, who is, who ever will be living."[89]

Alice's happiness, though, was still not complete. With Harriet in Paris, Alice loyally remained at the rue Notre Dame des Champs. Because she was so often abandoned, Harriet invited a San Francisco friend, Caroline Helbing, to spend the winter of 1909-10 in Paris, rooming at a hotel but taking her meals with Alice and Harriet.

Since she understood little French, Caroline was not as easy to entertain as Ada Joseph. But Alice and Harriet thought she would enjoy the company of Fernande and Marie Laurencin. After a lunch together, Marie invited the group to her apartment. It was an unusual honor, Alice recalled, since no one seemed ever to have been to her home.

Marie, called "Coco" by her friends, was a slight, child-like young woman in her early twenties. Her nose reminded some of a snout, her blue eyes protruded, her lips were thick; she seemed, Alice thought, like "some strange mythological animal." She had begun to paint as a child, encouraged by her mother to practice drawing braids. To be a fine painter, she told her daughter, one had to be expert in braids. Marie's subjects, however, tended toward the whimsical and the artificial. An art dealer who handled her work remembered "dolls, phantoms, beings that cannot possibly be brought to life. . . . Clockwork birds enclosed in cages . . . artificial flowers. . . ."

When her six-year liaison with Apollinaire ended in 1912, sorrowful friends sympathized with the poet. But Marie defended herself as best she could: "People talk of how I threw Apollinaire out," she said, "yes, I shut my door on him and have been attacked for it. He adored me, he loved only me; it's true that he suffered frightfully, but what people didn't understand is that I was twenty-five and he was sleeping with all the women, and at twenty-five you don't stand for that even from a poet!"[90]

Picasso, Fernande told Gertrude and Alice, could not abide Marie because she made "low wild cries like small animals." But Caroline was fascinated by her and was delighted by the delicate tea she served them in the apartment she shared with her mother.

The arrival of Caroline was a great relief to Alice, but it was only a temporary solution to her problem. She was ready to move into Gertrude's home if only Harriet would make her own arrangements. But it was not until July that her wish was fulfilled.

Once again, Sarah and Michael Stein were returning to San Francisco. Sarah's father was very ill—dying—from a brain tumor. On July 26, 1910, the Steins boarded a ship back to America. By August 1, they had arrived in "black foggy Frisco." And Harriet was with them.

Whether Caroline had spoken frankly to Harriet, or whether Harriet had finally seen that she would be doomed to solitude if she remained in Paris, Alice never knew. But she was now free. Harriet had written soon after arriving in California that she would not return, and Alice disposed of the apartment and took up residence at 27, rue de Fleurus, in a small but adequate room.

Leo accepted the intrusion with uncharacteristic grace, probably because most of his energy was directed toward his own love affair with Eugénie Auzias, better known as Nina of Montparnasse. Nina, an artists' model, had fallen in love with Leo when she first saw him in the Luxembourg Gardens in May 1905. Several years later she met him, posed for him, and pursued him in the most seductive way she could—by confiding in him her innumerable amorous entanglements. Leo, grasping his new subject with fascination, patiently offered his counsel and kept faithful track of the details of Nina's affairs. In 1921, he finally married her.

Besides, he was resigned to being replaced in Gertrude's affections. Alice had come to stay. In their "domestic discord," as Leo later described it, Gertrude had won. "She had the victory," Gertrude wrote about herself, "which was the coming and the staying and the telling of that which was the needing. . . ."[91]

From then on, each Saturday evening, Alice took her place with the "wives" while Gertrude surrounded herself with the more interesting men. Occasionally, Alice's talk of hats, perfumes, and recipes was changed for a special guest. Gelett Burgess, whom Alice remembered from San Francisco, had come to Paris to write about the art scene. He and Alice reminisced about old times and talked about the "wild men" whom Burgess was discovering. His visit to the Salon des Indépendants, when it opened in March 1910, was a shocking experience. He asked, as Harriet had asked, "What did it all mean? . . . Had a new era of art begun? Was ugliness to supersede beauty, technique give way to naivete and vibrant, discordant color, a very patchwork of horrid hues, take the place of subtle nuances of tonality? Was nothing sacred, not even beauty?"

Trying to find his way in an aesthetic wilderness, he visited some of the aritists in their studios. From Matisse, who Burgess thought was the first pioneer in the land of the ugly, he learned that the artists were in revolt against impressionism, striving for simplicity and directness, painting with such flaming emotion that beauty could not be achieved. Braque, who also wanted to translate emotion onto canvas, said he was trying to create a new interpretation of beauty, subjective and not decorative. André Derain, whose shyness precluded long explanations, looked at Burgess with kind brown eyes and asked, "Why what, after all, is a pretty woman?" Picasso, of course, wouldn't take his visitor seriously.

"Picasso is a devil," Burgess reported. "I use the term in the most complimentary sense, for he's young, fresh, olive-skinned, black eyes and black hair, a Spanish type with an exuberant, superfluous ounce of blood in him. I thought of a Yale sophomore who had been out stealing signs, and was on the point of expulsion. When, to this, I add that he is the only one of the crowd with a sense of humor, you will surely fall in love with him at first sight, as I did." Picasso, he went on, was audacious: "the doubly distilled ultimate." His paintings were outrageous, an affront to decency, "abominable." When Burgess dared to ask if he used models, Picasso turned, grinned, and winked at "his ultramarine ogresses." "Where would I get them?"[92]

Walter Pach, painter and art critic, sharing Alice's interest in music, invited her to a concert. She accepted, though she made it clear that she felt she was playing hooky from her duties at the rue de Fleurus.[93] She, in turn, typed some articles for him. A 1908 piece on Cézanne had been well received, and Pach was now writing about Matisse and others. Shortly after they met, Pach became the European representative for the New York Armory Show, gathering paintings for the exhibit that would introduce post-impressionism to America. But when his article on Matisse was rejected by the paper to which Pach submitted it—on grounds of Matisse's "insanity"—the success of the Armory show seemed questionable. Pach's undaunted perseverance impressed Gertrude and Alice.

To most of Gertrude's visitors, Alice was invisible or, at most, forgettable. Henry McBride, the art critic for the New York *Sun*, was an early advocate of Gertrude's and therefore endeared himself to Alice. They met at a restaurant where McBride was lunching with Roger Fry, and McBride was a frequent guest at the studio. Yet he could never remember more than the first name of Gertrude's "charming young friend."

An exception was Daniel-Henry Kahnweiler, the art

dealer who championed the cubists and, as Gertrude said, made secure their present and their future. He thought Alice was extraordinarily modest, intelligent, and well-bred. But generally she was overlooked, the resident friend of the family—or at least of Gertrude—quietly sitting by as Leo and his sister held court.

Most guests never realized they were being scrutinized and mercilessly evaluated. Alice never did and never would cease in her analysis of Gertrude's friends, sorting in her mind the acceptable from the discardable. She could forget but not forgive, she had admitted. And rarely did she forget.

It was not until the summer of 1911, however, that she wielded her growing power with Gertrude and began the disintegration of a friendship. She and Gertrude visited the Villa Curonia in July and Alice, for the first time, met Mabel Dodge.

The ancient villa, situated in the hills of Florence, had been named by its former owners for their homeland, the province of Kurland, in Russia. Mabel never changed the name, but her husband, and architect, substantially changed the interior to his wife's tastes. The house featured an Italian garden bordered by cypresses, and filled with gardenias, statues, and a few white peacocks. In her ninety-foot parlor, Mabel had gathered old paintings, tapestries, statuettes, gilded boxes, china dogs, renaissance bric-a-brac, Venetian glass candelabra, and innumerable figurines atop heavy refectory tables. The villa, one friend noted, was the perfect reflection of her personality.

Mabel reigned in white, usually in a long silk dress and a white turban. Her room was white—whitewashed walls, white curtains—but the room she gave to Gertrude was hung with gold and crimson silk. Alice was relegated to a small bedroom next door. Besides her numerous guests, her husband Edwin, and her young son, she had a dog, Climax, and a monkey, Emma Bovary.

Mabel was eccentric but astute. She noticed at once that Alice was usurping Leo's position in the ménage, making herself so indispensable that Gertrude would not be able to do without her. She was sure that Alice was pushing Leo out of the house, and Leo obliquely confirmed her suspicions. When she commented on Alice's incessant ministrations, Leo agreed, adding that he had seen trees strangled by vines in the same way. Alice, Mabel thought, was a perfect errand girl and a willing handmaiden. "Pensive, pale and black-haired Alice, 'tender-eyed,' like Leah, she began by being so self-obliterating that no one considered her very much beyond thinking her a silent, picturesque object in the background. . . ."[94] But Mabel knew otherwise.

She disliked Alice immediately, not only for hurting Leo, but because she thought her insidious, somehow dishonest. "She was slight and dark, with beautiful gray eyes hung with black lashes—and she had a drooping, Jewish nose, and her eyelids drooped, and the corners of her red mouth and the lobes of her ears drooped under the black, folded Hebraic hair, weighted down, as they were, with long heavy Oriental earrings." Alice's batik dresses, Mabel went on, made her look like someone out of the Old Testament, and Mabel derided her "half-Oriental get-up—her blues and browns and oyster whites—her black hair—her barbaric chains and jewels—and her melancholy nose."

Alice seemed to have no interests other than manicuring her nails, something of a fetish with her, Mabel noted. Her hands, Mabel thought, looked like a courtesan's with their shaped and polished nails. And moreover, she didn't eat— at least not with Gertrude's gusto. Gertrude's amplitude was sensuous, Mabel thought, and very attractive. She loved to watch her devour five pounds of rare meat at a sitting and admired the "pounds and pounds and pounds piled up on her skeleton." Alice on the other hand, ate a little slice of meat "daintily, like a cat."

Their first meeting was brief, and Alice remembered especially one scene of Mabel's son standing on the terrace threatening to fly. "Fly my dear, fly if you want to," Mabel caroled. Fortunately, the child did not, and Edwin Dodge merely commented. "It is easy to be a Spartan mother."

One pleasant spot in an uncomfortable visit was Alice's meeting Constance Fletcher, whom she liked at once. Mabel sent Alice to the station with instructions to meet "a very large woman who would wear a purple robe and who was deaf." But instead, Alice found a large, laughing, golden-haired woman with big blue eyes. Grotesque to some, Constance seemed delightful to Alice.

The author of *Kismet*, once engaged to the grandson of

Byron, now had grown so obese that rumors had it she sometimes got stuck in her own bathtub. She was nearsighted but refused to wear glasses, and her abiding passion was the worship of her mother's memory. With her stepfather, the painter Eugene Benson, she turned her home into a shrine for her mother, daily strewing rose petals on the stairs. "Mamma's" chair, Mabel noticed, was always kept empty.

Alice was more interested in her fascinating embroidery. A wreath simply took form as she stitched without a pattern to guide her on the linen. And Alice was amused by her affection for ghosts.

The Villa Curonia reportedly had two, one the spirit of a young governess who had killed herself in the house. One morning, when Alice called on Constance because she had not felt well the evening before, she found her lying peacefully on her bed. "I had a delightful night," she told Alice. "The gentle ghost visited me all night, indeed she has just left me. I imagine she is still in the cupboard. . . ." She asked Alice to check, but even when she reported seeing nothing, the enraptured Constance merely sighed, "Ah, yes."

Constance's presence, however, did not diminish the effect of Mabel's. The visit was long enough to establish a fierce mutual hatred between Alice and Mabel, but not long enough for the forces to clash. Besides, Alice could not yet risk a confrontation with someone of whom Gertrude was very fond and with whom Leo was very close. But her position, over the next year, became more secure.

In May, she and Gertrude left on an extended trip through Spain. Alice had never visited Spain but, owing to her California heritage, claimed she was predisposed to anything Spanish.

The two went first to Burgos and visited the Gothic cathedral, where they were annoyed by a miniature "Becky Sharp"—a small green-eyed girl who pestered Alice for "A penny, kind sir?" Then they proceeded to Valladolid. More and more, Alice was enchanted. On one of the altars of the cathedral, she noticed "two beaten and painted ornaments with arabesque designs to imitate artificial flowers." She thought they were so lovely that she inquired of the sexton if she might know who made them—and eventually she found two which she brought home.

Alice liked Spain immediately and immensely. When she and Gertrude arrived at Ávila, she decided to stay forever.

"I am not going to leave here," she said to Gertrude. "I am staying."

"What do you mean?" Gertrude asked.

"I am enraptured with Avila and I propose staying."

Gertrude was mildly upset by the passionate outburst. She, too, thought the ancient walled city was magnificent and was inspired by being at the birthplace of St. Teresa, but, she told Alice, "I could not work here, you know that."[95] She compromised, however, by offering to stay two weeks instead of the planned two days.

Even the food in Ávila seemed to Alice superior to that in other cities. They found a pastry shop where they watched dishes being decorated, salads assembled to look like a cathedral, desserts precariously mounted and topped with meringue.

They visited the Cathedral of San Salvador, the Iglesia San Pedro, the Capilla de la Santa, and strolled beyond the massive towered walls to the stark countryside. On these excursions they were accompanied by two members of the Civil Guard to protect them against annoyance by the populace. The stay was too brief for Alice, whose feelings about Ávila echoed St. Teresa's own words:

> . . . for if a person has to go and settle in another country, it is a great help to him, on undergoing the fatigue of his journey, that he has discovered it to be a country where he may live in the most perfect peace.

The gaiety of Madrid mitigated her disappointment about leaving Ávila. Their hotel on the Carrera de San Jerónimo was near enough to El Prado to enable them to visit often, and was surrounded by antique shops, where they made numerous purchases. In the evenings they found a striking diversion: La Argentina, a vibrant flamenco dancer. Years after, Alice still recalled her stunning appearance.

She wore the classic Spanish dancer's costume of the full fairly long skirt trimmed with chenille balls, sleeves to the elbows, the bodice cut in a modest V, a large tortoise-shell comb in her hair. With her famous smile, she danced the classic dance of Spain in which she did not move more than a few feet from the center of the stage.[96]

They sat through a bland variety show to see her astounding performance. The audience was spellbound, and Alice and Gertrude were so impressed that they returned for the midnight show. Everyone, Alice recalled, was bewitched, clapping in time with her step. "It was more exciting," she thought, "than the Russian ballet." They remained in Madrid for several weeks, returning again and again to watch her dance.

Like many tourists, they attended a bullfight. Though they had excellent seats, Alice's view of the spectacle was limited by Gertrude's admonitions to look away when a horse was being gored.

From Madrid they went further south to Toledo. It was then early June, and they were in time for the Corpus Christi procession. From the balcony of their hotel, they watched the candle bearers and listened to the children singing canticles. They saw the collection of El Grecos, and Alice decided that, though the painter had been born in Crete, he had become thoroughly a Spaniard.

At El Escorial, Alice was overwhelmed by the beauty of El Greco's *Conversion of St. Maurice*, and, at Cuenca, Gertrude was overwhelmed by the height. The village, built on the steep sides of a hill overlooking deep valleys of the Júcar and Huecar, made Gertrude afraid to keep the windows open, and forced Alice to sleep in a stuffy hotel room.

In Cuenca, Alice changed what she called her "Spanish disguise"—black satin coat, black hat, black fan, and black gloves—for her comfortable batik. As they walked in the pine woods around the village, the children came up to touch the strange fabric, remarking that it was not silk. They were curious, too, about the lovely flowers on her hat, which Alice explained were made of silk and velvet. Among their purchases in Spain was a clasp they found in Cuenca for Gertrude: a huge rhinestone turtle.

Córdoba, sultry in the middle of summer, was already uncomfortable. Unable to sleep, Alice spent the night sprinkling cool water over her body. She disliked the town, not only because of the temperature, but more because of its atmosphere, more Moslem than Christian, she thought, dominated as it were by the mosque, La Mesquita.

Seville was no cooler than Córdoba, and Alice and Gertrude tried to keep comfortable by eating ices all day. Gertrude's sensitive stomach was disturbed and after a few days she succumbed to a violent attack of colitis.

They had barely had time to see the cathedral, stroll along the Calle de la Sierpes, and walk down to the Guadalquivir, when Gertrude's illness frightened Alice enough to cause a quick departure to Gibraltar, where Gertrude found sufficient medical help to recover within a short time.

They returned to the mainland, staying for several days in the mountain village of Ronda, whose architecture reminded Alice of an Elizabethan town. On one of their walks, Gertrude blithely crossed a river by stepping from one stone to the next, a feat which Alice was not sure she could copy. "Come on, why do you hesitate?" Gertrude asked her. But Alice, sure that they were not stepping-stones, but "skipping-stones," was fainthearted and had to be coaxed across.[97]

Alice liked Granada nearly as much as she had liked Ávila. She and Gertrude were struck with the color and costumes of the gypsies. But anything in Spain could delight Alice: the sounds, the shadows, the special light.[98]

By August they had returned to Paris, and by mid-September they left once again—this time to Florence, where Mabel Dodge had succeeded in drawing them back to her villa. Gertrude spent much of her time writing. Alice typed what Gertrude relayed to her. Mabel—with her husband in New York—pursued an ardent interest in her son's twenty-two-year-old tutor. "The days," Gertrude wrote, "are wonderful and the nights are wonderful and the life is pleasant." But if they were pleasant for Gertrude, they were less so for Alice. Her animosity toward Mabel was growing. Gertrude's famous creation during her stay at the Villa Curonia was her "Portrait of Mabel Dodge," which she alternately titled "Mabel little Mabel with her face against the pane. . . ." To Alice, the alternate title would seem apt.

Mabel was still puzzled about Alice. She was not an

artist, like Gertrude. She was not a sensuous, struggling soul, as Mabel pictured herself. She seemed to have no interests but her manicure. Finally, Mabel asked outright, "Well, I can't understand you. What makes you contented? What keeps you going?" Alice answered honestly, "Why, I suppose it's my feeling for Gertrude." But Mabel failed to heed her warning.

Despite her preoccupation with her young friend, Mabel sensed that Gertrude herself was attracted to her. Mabel had long flaunted her bisexuality, and when Gertrude looked at her across the lunch table one afternoon, her glance "seemed to cut across the air . . . in a band of electrified steel. . . ." Apparently, Mabel was not alone in sensing the meaning of Gertrude's look. Alice quickly rose and left the room.

When she failed to return, Gertrude went after her but came back to the table a few minutes later alone. "She doesn't want to come to lunch," she told Mabel. "She feels the heat today."[99]

The friendship was ended. Though Mabel promised to publicize Gertrude in Europe and America, though she wrote effusive praise of her work, Alice's "feeling for Gertrude" was put above everything else. Violently jealous of her relationship with Gertrude, Alice—"poco-poco" as Mabel put it—slashed all ties between the two women.

Mabel tried to communicate. She had three hundred copies of Gertrude's portrait of her bound and brought them to New York when she returned a few months later. She wrote glowingly about Gertrude for the *Arts and Decoration* special issue on the Armory Show. "You are just on the eve of *bursting!*" she told her a few days before the show opened in 1913. And indeed, Gertrude had reason to be grateful for Mabel's efforts. The Armory Show—and Mabel's article—did spur her notice in America. But Alice would permit no healing of the breach. As Gertrude had written in the "Portrait," ". . . the union is won and the division is the explicit visit." Mabel could not intrude. "There has not been that kind of abandonment. Nobody is alone."[100]

Ten

THE RELATIONSHIP BETWEEN Gertrude and Leo in the fall of 1912 was raw and difficult. They disagreed constantly. Leo belittled Gertrude's thirst for *la gloire*, ridiculed her writing, chided both her and Alice for their acceptance of cubism. He thought Gertrude's "Portrait of Mabel Dodge" was "damned nonsense. A portrait of a person that I know pretty intimately which conveys absolutely nothing to me," he wrote to a friend, ". . . seems to me to have something the matter with it."[101] Gertrude and Picasso, he thought, were producing "Godalmighty rubbish," and he could no longer abide it.

He claimed to have reached an important point in his life. After years of experimenting with diets, he was feeling physically fit on a self-imposed regime of bread, milk, and fruit and intellectually fit on a diet of mathematics and philosophy. But philosophical books were now a source of amusement rather than the source of a "possible solution." He felt closer to Nina than ever before, happy that she did not make demands on him, lean on him, smother him. "I have come to the end of something and perhaps the beginning of something else," he wrote.[102]

Certainly he had come to the end of his life with Gertrude. "The presence of Alice was a godsend," he wrote to his friend Mabel Weeks, "as it enabled the thing to happen without any explosion."[103] Mabel Weeks, who knew Leo and Gertrude from their undergraduate years, tried to understand the final break. "I think Leo felt," she wrote, "after Alice joined the household, that there was less place for him there, and he began to feel impatient and was glad enough to ease off." Mabel's sympathies were with Leo, though she had once shared an apartment with Gertrude and had corresponded with her frequently when Gertrude settled in Paris. Alice, of course, was aware of Mabel's feelings and helped make sure that the friendship with Gertrude was ended.[104]

Alice would say nothing about the causes of the break except to reiterate Gertrude's statement that Leo's disparagement of her work "destroyed him" for her. She was well aware of the ramifications of the destruction. Until 1911, Alice wrote to a friend, there had been no closer devotion than that between Leo and Gertrude. And when Leo died—exactly a year and two days after his sister— Alice blamed the shock of Gertrude's death as the cause of his own.[105]

Several days before his death, Leo once again returned to the break, and once again tried to explain publicly what had happened.

There is in the reviews of my book on *Appreciation* so much said about the relations between Gertrude and myself that it seems to me something should be said to put the matter straight.

The differences between Gertrude's character and mine were profound. My interest was a critical interest in science and art. Gertrude had no interest whatever in science or philosophy and no critical interest in art or literature 'til the Paris period and, apart from college texts, never, in my time at least, read a book on these subjects. Her critical interest was entirely in character, in people's personalities. She was practically inaccessible to ideas and I was accessible to nothing else. She was much influenced by people and I was not influenced by them at all but only by ideas.

From childhood on our private lives were entirely independent. At a very early time before our teens we had come to an explicit understanding not to interfere with each other, and this developed in many implicit ways.

In Paris her critical interest in art and literature was awakened by her personal problems in writing. The Cézanne, Matisse, Picasso pictures that I bought were of great importance to her in respect to her work and then became an interest independent of that and in time this interest in pictures came to be only second to her writing.

Some reviewers speak of a feud or quarrel between us. We never quarreled except for a momentary spat. We simply differed and went our own ways. Later I would sometimes criticize her work or comment on her character in reference to it as I would do in the case of any other writer, not thinking that the hearers would interpret this as a consequence of personal relations. There is no more quarrel or feud in my relations to Gertrude than in my relations to Picasso. In both cases I have impressions and opinions which are not necessarily in agreement with certain opinions widely prevalent. That is all.[106]

But that was not all that was happening in 1912. The break was not a mere academic shrug. More than once Leo tried to win back his sister's sympathy. He stopped coming to the Saturday evenings at the atelier, but he tried to revive their mutual affection by explaining and analyzing their differences. Even Gertrude admitted, "He had the faculty of expression."[107] But no amount of rhetoric could alter the shift of power. The more Leo said "No" to Gertrude's work, the more strongly Alice countered with "Yes." Finally, Gertrude and Alice could no longer bear the emotional confrontations. They decided not to see him. "Do you remember how we decided that indeed if he came we would have it said that there be no admittance. Do you remember that we decided that we had entertained him as frequently as we would and that now when he came we would have him told that we would not receive him. Do you remember that."[108] By February 1913, Leo decided to move out, to divide the paintings, to settle the accounts. As Gertrude always remembered, "He and the beginning was not the pleasant time. . . ."[109]

Meanwhile, Gertrude's unpublished manuscripts were quickly mounting. She had completed more than two dozen portraits, similar in style to "Ada," and three longer pieces of psychological explorations of her friends and family: *Many Many Women, A Long Gay Book*, and *G.M.P.* Her style had evolved considerably since *The Mak-*

ing of Americans, culminating in *Tender Buttons*, a fragmented rendering of familiar objects re-created in the cubist mode. Some of her writing was languishing in America, being prodded along by one agent or another; Mabel Dodge, in New York, was enthusiastic about publishing possibilities but had no real offers. It was time, Alice thought, for them to act on their own.

On the advice of Mira Edgerly, a miniaturist whom Alice remembered from a Mark Hopkins Mardi Gras in San Francisco, Alice wrote to several English publishing houses, describing Gertrude's work and requesting an interview. In January 1913, the two set off for London.

The visit began with a relaxing stay at Riverhill, in Surrey, the home of Mira's friends Colonel and Mrs. Rogers. Mrs. Rogers, Alice thought, was delicately beautiful. Her children, too, were gentle and lovely, especially one little girl who showed a great deal of affection for Gertrude; even the maids looked angelic. The home itself was gracious and elegant. In Alice's room, there was a piece of Chinese porcelain so fine that she thought it should have been in a museum.

Alice enjoyed English country life: the drives, the gardens, even a meeting of the hunt at which she was introduced to an ex-Viceroy of India. After a few days of leisure and gentility, they left for London. There they saw the editors to whom Alice had written, but received only polite refusals to offers of Gertrude's works. Only John Lane was interested but at the time could offer no contract. With their hope placed solely in Lane's press, the Bodley Head, they went for a day in the country with Roger Fry before going home.

Roger Fry, who once told Lytton Strachey that the Old Masters made him sick, had been a curator at the Metropolitan Museum of Art in New York from about 1905 through 1910 and had acted as adviser for J. P. Morgan's art collection. A dynamic and active "Bloomsberry," he daringly introduced French post-impressionism to England. On November 8, 1910, "Manet and the Post-Impressionists" brought modern painting across the Channel. On October 25, 1912, just months before Gertrude and Alice arrived, his second post-impressionist exhibition opened at the Grafton Galleries. This one caused a greater furor than the first. Even Lytton Strachey, who seemed to exist "in an atmosphere of rarefied thought,"[110] noticed the impact. "It made me feel very cold and cynical. I must say I should be pleased with myself, if I were Matisse or Picasso—to be able, a humble Frenchman, to perform by means of a canvas and a little paint, the extraordinary feat of making some dozen country gentlemen in England, every day for two months, grow purple in the face!"[111]

Strachey's curiosity about the artists was partly satisfied by Alice. At a party given by "the incorrigible old Sapphist" Ethel Sands on February 13, 1913, he found Gertrude and her "Spanish-Jew-American lady-friend." Alice engaged him in a long conversation about Picasso. It was interesting, Strachey thought, but it kept him from listening to another guest, George Moore.

Roger Fry, enthusiastic about Gertrude's work, offered to help publicize her and to spark John Lane's incipient interest. With the hope that English gentlemen might soon grow purple in the face from *Tender Buttons*, Alice and Gertrude went home.

Having a small audience, Gertrude decided in retrospect, was the reason for her outsized publicity. In 1913, her inner circle was increased by one. At the second performance of Stravinsky's *Sacre du printemps*, Gertrude noticed a "tall well built young man" wearing a pleated evening shirt sitting behind them. Though they didn't speak to him, Alice was sure that he was either American or British, and in a whisper warned Gertrude not to comment aloud, for fear of being understood. When Gertrude returned home that evening, she was inspired to write a word portrait of the elegant young man and entitled it, simply, "One."

Her attention may have been focused on the stranger because neither she nor Alice could hear any of the performance above the noise from the audience. "No sooner did the music begin and the dancing than they began to hiss. The defenders began to applaud. We could hear nothing. . . ." They tried to watch the dancers, but even this was distracted by a violent fight in the next box. "It was all incredibly fierce," according to Gertrude.

On the following Saturday, Gertrude and Alice prepared

to receive a dinner guest invited after he had forwarded to them a letter of introduction from Mabel Dodge. The young man, assistant music critic of the New York *Times*, had met Mabel in New York a few months earlier, heard her enthusiastic description of Gertrude's work, and left with a copy of the "Portrait of Mabel Dodge" and a curiosity about its author. A popular, reputable journalist, the young man would, no doubt, be useful. Hopefully, he would be congenial. Happily, and to everyone's surprise, he turned out to be the same one in the box at the ballet.

Carl Van Vechten, blond, with clear blue eyes and buck teeth, appeared, some thought, deceptively innocent. "He should have been a wasp-waisted dandy," one writer decided.[112] He and Gertrude shared a love of gossip, an easy sense of humor, and the strong conviction that Gertrude was a genius.

Coming from the bland complacency of Cedar Rapids, Iowa, Van Vechten was a harbinger of the avant-garde first in music, then in literature. He embraced the new with a fervor that his more conservative colleagues sometimes rated. Edmund Wilson thought Van Vechten belonged to the *Yellow Book* era bracketed by Baudelaire and Arthur Symons. "The decadents," Wilson wrote, "talked much about 'paganism,' but their point of view was not pagan: it was a reaction against Victorian Christianity by people who were still Christians and Victorians."[113] The thrill of shocking the conventional with the unexpected was fun, and Van Vechten, like Gertrude, was fun-loving. He had his doubts about the work of his contemporaries, as expressed in his fictionalized autobiography, *Peter Whiffle*:

> Never did I feel less sure of the meaning of art than I do here, surrounded by it . . . although I have never been more conscious of it, more susceptible to real beauty, more lulled by its magic. Yet I do not understand its meaning. The trails cross. For instance, here is Edith [i.e., Mabel Dodge] leading her own life; here are we all leading our own lives . . . here is Marinetti shooting off fire-crackers. . . . Here is Loeser, always building new houses and never completing them . . . here is Leo Stein, collecting Renoirs and Cézannes for his villa at Settignano. What does it

all mean, unless it means that everything should be scrambled together? I think a great book might be written if everything the hero thought and felt and observed could be put into it.[114]

But the great book would not be Van Vechten's. His own career shifted from journalist to novelist to photographer. In none was he outstanding, and he remains most noted as a popularizer and supporter. In the 1920s, Harlem's renaissance in art, music, and literature was brought downtown by Van Vechten. He was among the first to recognize Faulkner. He established Ronald Firbank's American reputation. And he was, until his death in 1964, unceasingly loyal to Gertrude Stein.

Within a year after they met, Van Vechten found a publisher interested in Gertrude's work. His friend Donald Evans had just begun his own press, named for a certain Claire Marie Burke and destined to appeal to a select few. Claire Marie, its advertising brochure proclaimed,

believes there are in America seven hundred civilized people.
Claire Marie publishes books for civilized people only.
Claire Marie's aim, it follows from the premises, is not even secondarily commercial.

Though Gertrude was warned by Mabel Dodge that Claire Marie was "in bad odor" in New York, she decided to accept Evans' offer and sent him *Tender Buttons*, a book not likely to find a home elsewhere. In June 1914 the volume was brought out, and in the August issue of *Trend*, Van Vechten announced its "majestic rhythm . . . the virtuosity with which Miss Stein intertwines her words. . . ." Adjectives never failed him: the book was sensuous, fresh, irresistible—no less than perfect. And if the style did not immediately enrapture, Van Vechten recommended that the reader think of its sense. "Here," he admitted, "one floats about vaguely for a key to describe how to tell what Miss Stein means. Her vagueness is innate and one of her most positive qualities." Understanding, he suggested, was facilitated by a "certain sleepy consciousness." Though he offered little help in interpreting Gertrude's style, hoping

111

the reader would follow his own bubbling enthusiasm, he painted an intriguing portrait of the writer herself. "She is massive in physique, a Rabelaisian woman with a splendid thoughtful face; mind dominating her matter. Her velvet robes, mostly brown, and her carpet slippers associate themselves with her indoor appearance. To go out she belts herself, adds a walking staff, and a trim unmodish turban. This garb suffices for a shopping tour or a box party at the Opera." He dropped such fascinating tidbits as her favorite food—roast beef; her working habits—words surged through her brain and flowed out of her pen; and a few of her friends—Marsden Hartley, John Reed, Matisse, Picasso. If the writing was not irresistible, certainly the writer was.

The publication of *Tender Buttons* seemed a happy portent. In July, Gertrude and Alice prepared for another visit to England, where John Lane again expressed interest in adding Gertrude's name to his list of authors. But England, he thought, was not ready for her newer pieces. He felt more comfortable with *Three Lives*, the tales Gertrude had published, at her own expense, in 1909. The limited edition of *Three Lives*, praised by her friends and purchased by her faithful small audience, had come to Lane's attention, and he gave it to his wife to read. Camille Lane, who reminded Alice of her former piano teacher, predicted an easy success for the book in England and advised her husband to publish it.

While they waited for the contract to be drawn up, they visited with the family of a "delightful young creature," Hope Mirlees, whom they had met in Paris. Alice enjoyed the English, finding them gracious and civilized. But their breakfasts were barely endurable. She took nothing but coffee in the morning and wanted it as soon as she awakened. But English country breakfasts required her to sit through four courses begun at nine—hours after she woke —and to remain amiable through witty remarks and intelligent talk until coffee was finally served.

She was pleased with Gertrude's success. The English treated her like a lion, Alice wrote to her friend Harriet Levy, and arranged meetings with writers and scholars of lofty stature. One evening at a dinner given by Hope Mirlees, Alice found herself sitting across from her third genius, Alfred North Whitehead, and beside the poet A. E. Housman, interesting, but not quite a bell ringer. Both were interrested in David Starr Jordan, whom Housman knew as an ichthyologist and Whitehead as a pacifist.

After dinner, Alice joined Whitehead for coffee in the garden and was impressed by his "benign sweet smile and a simplicity that comes only in geniuses."[115] She and Gertrude saw Whitehead and his wife Evelyn again in London and accepted an invitation to visit them at their country home in Lockeridge, near the Salisbury Plain.

Though Gertrude was fortunate in her many new contacts and buoyed by intimations of future literary renown, Alice experienced what she claimed was her "unique lost opportunity." She failed, once again, to meet Henry James. On July 27, she and Gertrude had tea with the photographer Alvin Langdon Coburn, whom James had commissioned to do the frontispieces for Scribner's New York edition of his works. They had met Coburn in 1913 after he had written for permission to see Gertrude's "splendid collection of paintings by Matisse." He visited with his bride of a few months, Edith Clement, a prim Bostonian whom Gertrude took to be his "adopted mother." Gertrude was pleased by his photographs of her, and pleased even more by his praise. "Gertrude Stein . . . I think has something to tell us which the world will come to appreciate, which many are now beginning to recognize and which many in the future will value."

Coburn, to Alice's intense excitement, offered to arrange a meeting with James. But James, closeted at Lamb House, would not see them. Coburn graciously proffered the excuse that James was ill, when in fact he had simply declined to receive visitors. Alice embellished the episode even further when she recalled it later. ". . . It had been arranged that we should spend a day with him at Rye, but to my bitter disappointment we received word that he was too indisposed to receive us on the appointed day, would we come some day on the following week? Alas, we had to return to Paris before then."[116] Though they remained in England until mid-October, Alice never was to meet her much-admired author.

By the beginning of August, they were at Lockeridge with the Whiteheads, following with incredulity the events reported in each day's paper. The assassination of Arch-duke Francis Ferdinand and his wife on June 28 had not prevented Gertrude and Alice from traveling to England, nor prepared them for the news which followed. One month later, Austria declared war on Serbia; within days, Germany, in support of Austria, declared war on Russia, then on France. On Tuesday, August 4, with England's entry, the Great War had begun. Both Alice and Gertrude were shocked.[117] The days before England's entry, Alice said, were interminable, and the days afterward, intensely painful. Since it was impossible for them to cross to France, the Whiteheads insisted that they stay with them in the country. What was to have been a weekend visit lasted, instead, for six weeks.

All conversation, naturally, centered on the war. The English maintained that they had entered to aid Belgium against the Germans, and the Whiteheads worried con-stantly over the possible destruction of Belgian libraries. Both Gertrude and Alice failed to understand their ap-parent detachment from their own peril, and Alice finally burst out, ". . . Why do you say that, why do you not say that you are fighting for England, I do not consider it a disgrace to fight for one's country."[118]

Alice helped Evelyn Whitehead in planning relief work while Gertrude and Dr. Whitehead took long walks, talk-ing about philosophy and history and stopping on the way to chat with gamekeepers and mole-catchers. There were occasional visitors, the least pleasant of whom was Ber-trand Russell.

Even the pacifist Bloomsbury group thought Russell's articles in the *Nation* were alienating the populace, and at the Whiteheads' his incessant arguments against the war disturbed everyone. Gertrude, to change the subject, drew him into a discussion of education, about which he had equally strong views. American education, he said, suffered from the neglect of Greek. Gertrude argued for Latin—advocating the language of a continent over the language of an island, and both became eloquent as the talk became more and more abstract. The subject was sufficiently di-verting to occupy everyone until bedtime.

Whitehead's sister-in-law tried to convince Gertrude to use her political influence in France. Though Gertrude explained that her influence was only among painters and writers, the woman would not be dissuaded. "I think it would come very well from a neutral like yourself," she said, "to suggest to the French government that they give us Pondicherry. It would be very useful to us." Gertrude continued to demur politely until after lunch, when she turned to Alice and asked under her breath, "Where the hell is Pondicherry?"[119]

Their nerves became more worn with each day's battle reports, and by the beginning of September, Gertrude was so worried about the fate of Paris that she could no longer bear to be present at breakfast. One morning Alice appeared at the table alone, excused Gertrude by saying that she had a cold, and braced herself for Whitehead's rendering of the news. But before he could begin, a call from London brought the excited word that the Germans had been turned back at the Marne River, north of Paris. Immediately Alice rushed to Gertrude's room and told her that the Battle of the Marne had been won. "I can't believe it," Gertrude said, crying. And Alice, also in tears, could only repeat that it was true.[120]

Though the news of the battle eased their worry about France, Alice suddenly became very worried about Nellie Jacott, who was then living in Boulogne-sur-Seine. She sent her a hasty telegram and received a quick reply: *"Tout va bien nullement de danger t'embrasse Nellie."* Alice thought Nellie's carefree answer was ridiculous, but the Whiteheads considered it a sign of optimism.

Periodically, Gertrude and Alice would go to London, sometimes accompanied by Evelyn Whitehead. They stopped in at Cook's travel offices to try to determine when they might be able to return to Paris, and they retrieved money which had been sent to them by Alice's father and Gertrude's cousin.

When Harriet Levy arrived home alone, it became apparent to Ferdinand Toklas that his daughter meant to stay in Europe permanently. Though Alice wrote to him at least weekly—in Paris often penning her letters at the Closerie des Lilas—he felt an unexpected loneliness at her absence. He frequently visited the families of her friends, dropping by at the Rosenshines' and coming each Sunday to the Moores'. Clare, by then married to William de Gruchy and the mother of Billie-Anne, enjoyed sharing Alice's letters, and Ferdinand's visits became a ritual. He would arrive in the afternoon, read the latest voluminous letter aloud, and then stay for tea. Clare was always amused when he asked Mrs. Moore if her cookies were homemade; she assured him they were, even if they came from the local pastry shop. He would leave at five, returning to the men's club where he lived.[121]

When Sarah returned home, she too called on Ferdinand to give him news of Alice. One afternoon, she succeeded in painting such a glowing picture of his daughter that Ferdinand was "walking on air."[122]

Though Alice never saw her father after 1907, she was able to express more warmth in her letters to him than she could when she lived with him. Sometimes, of course, she wrote when she needed money, and this Ferdinand wired as needed. But her funds were becoming exhausted. Finally, her father warned her that she would have to make some definite plans about her finances. She would have to live on a limited income, she decided, but even living frugally would not augment the inheritance upon which she was drawing, and she knew that soon she and Gertrude would have to sell some paintings or make a strong effort to earn what they needed through Gertrude's writing.

Now, with the war, even John Lane could not go ahead immediately with his projected publication of *Three Lives*. There was no choice but to wire relatives. At each visit, London appeared grimmer, and Alice and Gertrude were increasingly anxious to return to Paris. Finally, on October 15, Cook's advised them to apply for a temporary passport to cross into France. At first the young man who interviewed them at the American Embassy was reluctant to supply the necessary papers. Gertrude, however, reminded him that the procedure had been effected for a friend of hers—Mildred Aldrich—and insisted that the papers be issued for her and Alice. Humbly he replied, "You are right," and asked if they would stand up and take an oath of loyalty to their country. "Oh, I would love to," Alice replied enthusiastically.

In two days they were home. Alice could describe Paris only as "wonderful."[123] She admired the calm bravery of the French and felt secure and tranquil back at the rue de

Fleurus. The house, which had been recently painted and renovated, had never seemed more homelike and welcoming. But their happiness at being back in Paris was marred by their worry about a friend, Mildred Aldrich, who was living in a small cottage on a hilltop near the Marne River. After unpacking their trunks, they packed a suitcase and hurried north to find out how she had survived the battle.

Mildred Aldrich, whose childhood memories included the Civil War, was an American journalist living in Paris. She was one of Gertrude's first friends and always a loyal supporter—even when she did not understand Gertrude's work. Though she had trouble with *The Making of Americans* and *Tender Buttons*, she was sure, she said, that Gertrude knew what she was doing. But her doubts about Picasso and Matisse became so upsetting that she sought Alice's advice. ". . . Tell me is it alright," she asked her, "are they all fumisterie, is it not all false?"[124]

When Alice first met her, she lived on Boulevard Raspail, on the top floor of a building, with a huge cage of canaries always in her window. As Alice learned later, a friend had asked her to mind her canary, and another friend, noticing Mildred's careful attention to the bird, provided a mate. After a few years, her aviary had increased and the first small cage was replaced by a larger one. Only after she gave away all her birds did she finally disclose to Alice that she never could bear canaries.

In the spring of 1914, Mildred decided to leave Paris for a small cottage in Huiry, a village some thirty miles north, where she could live more economically than she could in the city. Always generous with her friends, she was frequently in debt. Once, Alice remembered, she borrowed some money to send a cable to America. When she repaid the loan a few days later, she brought a huge potted azalea worth much more than the cost of the cable. Her extravagances, however, only served to endear her to those who knew her. Gertrude and Alice were worried that she would feel isolated in the village and, when they visited her there shortly after she moved, found her somewhat downcast. "What am I going to do in the evenings?" she asked them. She had completed her chores, done her mending, written her letters. Mustering up their own enthusiasm, they assured her that she would soon be busy tending flowers and vegetables and picking berries. But privately they wondered if she would not succumb to loneliness.

When they visited her in October, however, they found her spirits high. She was healthy and happy, had managed to grow a delightful garden, and with the help of a faithful housekeeper, Amélie, had turned the hundred-fifty-year-old gabled cottage into a lovely home. She was bursting with stories of the battle and writing a book about her unique view of the war.

Hilltop on the Marne was Mildred's day-to-day account of the fighting from September 5 through 12. From her first glimpse of belching black smoke to the final retreat of the Germans, she reported on what one French officer told her was the *"bataille décisive de cette guerre."* Written in Mildred's simple, unaffected style, the book, Alice thought, was charming. Mildred, in fact, was one of the few people they knew who was still cheerful.

Though Paris had not yet suffered zeppelin raids or real scarcity of food, war was in evidence everywhere—wounded soldiers, women in black, dressmakers who advertised quickly filled orders for mourning clothes, cafés filled with nurses and officers but few others. It was not until January that Alice experienced her first real fright. She had gone to bed early, as usual, and left Gertrude working in the studio. Later, she heard Gertrude calling to her softly. "What is it?" she asked. "Oh nothing," Gertrude said calmly, "but perhaps if you don't mind putting on something warm and coming downstairs I think perhaps it would be better . . . there has been an alarm." Alice was about to turn on the light when Gertrude stopped her, took her hand, and helped her make her way down the stairs to the couch. When she finally sat down, she found her knees shaking uncontrollably. Gertrude offered to get a blanket, but Alice was too frightened to be left alone. They heard a few loud booms, and soon there were horns signaling the end of the alarm. They lit the lights, Alice said, and went to bed. But she had discovered something she never thought to be true, "that knees knocked together as described in poetry and prose. . . ."[125]

In the early winter, many believed the war would be short and that the troops might be home for Christmas. after all. Even Picasso quipped that if there weren't a war there would be so many fewer good stories to tell.[126] But as the new year progressed, it became clearer that the war was not about to end. By March, Alice and Gertrude had had enough. They were worried about their friends— Braque, Derain, and Apollinaire had enlisted. They were growing short of funds and the prices of food and fuel had risen steeply. They decided they could exist more economically and more peaceably if they left France, and they started for Palma de Mallorca, via Barcelona, in mid-March. As they were packing to leave, Paris had its first zeppelin raid.

Eleven

THEY STOPPED FIRST at a pension recommended by some English friends, but found it disappointing. Instead, they took rooms at the luxurious Hotel Mediterráneo overlooking the harbor and the town's early Gothic cathedral. Within a short time they located a furnished house at 45 Calle de Dos Mayo, high on a hill, two hundred sixty steps above the sea. There was a garden with almond, fig, and pomegranate trees, a terrace bordered by carnations and tuberoses, and a lovely landscape somewhat like that of Monterey. They would have been content to be alone together—indeed, they preferred their solitude at times—but they found several people on the island whom they had known in Paris. William Cook, an American painter, and his French wife, Jeanne; a Swedish count to whom David Edstrom had once introduced them; the French Consul and his wife. They bought a dog, a deerhound, and fondly named him Polybe Bouton Geborue Reinach, after the nom de plume of military critic Joseph Reinach, a writer for *Le Figaro*. Alice knitted with a supply of wool from Scotland; Gertrude wrote; and though they longed for Paris, they were distracted, as much as they could be, from the war.

During the hot summer months, Alice was uncomfortable and sometimes irritable. She became extremely sensitive to light, and the long walks in midday which Gertrude loved distressed her even more than usual. They went to a local powder factory, Gertrude perspiring profusely and Alice trying in vain to shield the sun from her eyes. On the way, however, they discovered a patch of lovely yellow flowers and sheep grazing in a field, sights which compensated for the discomfort of the hike. At night, Alice slept protected by a mosquito net and cooled by their electric fan. On Sundays, when there was no electricity, or once when the fan broke, she nearly wept from the heat. But autumn brought a respite, and Alice was bothered only by lizards, which she hated, and thunder, which she always feared.

From time to time they took a steamer to Barcelona to shop on Las Ramblas, with its plane trees, or to visit the American dentist they had happily located. With the Cooks, they attended the *juegos florales* and bullfights in Valencia at the end of July, and traveled by train to Inca, where Jeanne saw her first bull killed and Alice failed in an attempt to drink aqua vitae without touching her lips to the bottle.

When Alice was not knitting, gardening, or overseeing the housekeeper, she tried to train Polybe, a task which repeatedly ended in frustration. Polybe, it seemed, thrived on tuberoses and enthusiastically chased the neighbors' goats. Though Alice thought he was "quite a dear," he refused to obey—even when, at Gertrude's suggestion, she gently whispered to him—and eventually he had to be given away.

Both Gertrude and Alice were preoccupied with the war, adamant in their hatred of Germany, and worried about the fate of their friends and their city. They didn't understand the war, Gertrude wrote, and therefore they were nervous about it. A civil war, she thought, would have been comprehensible; but a war between countries was terrifying. "What is the use in worrying?" Michael Stein wrote to them, but still they worried, knowing they could do nothing but wait. Day after day, Alice waking at seven-thirty, Gertrude at nine, they went about their independent tasks, relying on each other almost completely for companionship. Increasingly, Gertrude came to depend on Alice for approval about her work and for the management of their life. The year in Mallorca solidified their roles. Alice became so necessary to Gertrude that the threat of infidelity, the merest intimation of disloyalty, was shattering.

Gertrude's writing had evolved into verbal collage, the assembling of experiences from everyday life. Bits of conversations intermingle with descriptions of the physical settings in which she walked and worked. In the pieces she wrote during 1915 and 1916, Alice was everywhere. Significantly, the pieces are often blatantly erotic. Alice was her sweetheart, her little dove,[127] her gay baby,[128] her dear wife. There are kisses and caresses for "Mrs." and promises from her devoted husband that he will be faithful, true, hard-working, flourishing, successful, rich, and adoring. Alice was persistent in her hopes for Gertrude's success, partly for Gertrude's sake and partly, Gertrude knew, for her own. "Success is what she was supposed to favour. How was she supposed to favour success. She was supposed to favour success by being fond of money."[129]

Where earlier pieces centered on the guests that had passed through their salon each Saturday or the various anecdotes provided by their friends, Gertrude's Mallorcan pieces revolved around her love affair with Alice. She reconstructed their relationship from their first meeting—the quarrel when Alice arrived late, the nervousness Gertrude felt when she first asked Alice about her loves, her break with Leo and the distress it caused. "The first day that Leonard [i.e., Leo] went away it was very considerate of him. I remember all about sleeping. I remember all about waking. I remember thinking do we mean to be serious."[130] Though Gertrude was not afraid of a sexual relationship, she was afraid of being hurt by a casual relationship. She needed Alice's constant reassurance of her love: her questioning went on for a prolonged time in their early years together and "answering was everything."[131]

Throughout the pieces, Gertrude is seen coddling Alice, who cries, balks, and frequently becomes angry because of the physical discomforts of Mallorcan life. Gertrude apologizes for upsetting her, and Alice could be upset easily and often. "I am sorry I spoke as if I were not pleased," Gertrude simpers.[132] "My blessed baby nothing must bother you or be any annoyance to you. Nothing must cause you any irritation. You must be very happy and have no annoyance. You must see to it that you will be pleased and that you will not suffer in any way. You must be sure to express yourself and to have what you want when you want it."[133]

Gertrude repeatedly expresses her love for Alice. Hardly a piece lacks a word about her happiness—happiness that depends solely on her wife. "We have been very happy here," she wrote. "Yes but that has nothing to do with the people. No it hasn't."[134] They had each other, and the days passed quickly. "We do understand our pleasure," Gertrude wrote:

> Our pleasure is to do every day the work of that day, to cut our hair and not want blue eyes and to be reasonable and obedient. To obey and not split hairs. This is our duty and our pleasure.
> Every day we get up and say we are awake today. By this we mean that we [i.e., Alice] are up early and we [i.e., Gertrude] are up late. We eat our breakfast and smoke a cigar. . . . Do not be upset by anything,

she pleads with Alice, who replies, "No I won't be." And Gertrude, relieved, can only murmur, "Dear one."[135]

Gertrude reiterates her promise to fulfill Alice's growing pressure for success. "I am going to conquer," Gertrude assures her. "I am going to be flourishing. I am going to be industrious. Please forgive me everything." Even in Spain, where living was comparatively inexpensive, their funds were quickly diminishing. Alice felt the pressure more than Gertrude, since she was the one concerned with shopping and running the household. Her worries troubled Gertrude and intruded into what would otherwise have been complete contentment.

"If one loves one another," Gertrude felt, "by that means they do not perish."[136] Sure that any difficulties would be worked out, she proclaimed theirs as the most blissful of marriages. "When they were engaged she said we are happy. When they were married she said we are happy. They talked about everything they talked about individual feeling."

". . . I have so much to make me happy," Gertrude announced. "I know all that I am to happiness, it is to be happy and I am happy. I am so completely happy that I mention it."[137] And she mentioned it again and again: Alice was everything.

> Baby mine
> All the time
> Be Light

Nestle tight
Shall giggle
With
Splendour
and
Courage
and beauty
and goodness.[138]

With Alice as her entire audience, Gertrude began to use an idiosyncratic vocabulary that would be perpetuated even after they left Mallorca. There is repeated reference to cows and Caesars, their own terms for various stages in their lovemaking.

Though Gertrude's pieces were written for publication, both she and Alice thought them obscure enough not to invite speculation about their private life. Often, their real meaning was addressed only to Alice, who read them critically and typed them all. Gertrude invariably relied on Alice's opinions and became uneasy if she could not give unqualified praise. "You don't understand me you don't understand the manner of my writing," Gertrude complained, though she conceded "you do see that here and there there is something to admire. You are convinced of that."[139] Without Alice's complete support, she was insecure. She reported a more pleasant conversation:

You agree with me.
Yes I agree with you.
Do you always agree with me.
You know that I always agree with you.
Then that is satisfactory.
To me.
And to me too.[140]

Her reliance on Alice is evident in many pieces: "explain looking," she asks. "Explain looking again. Alice explain looking again."[141] Alice, she thought, "read marvelously," and "was pleased" by what she read.[142] She supplied etymologies of words,[143] references for poets,[144] pronunciation of Spanish. . . .[145] And she kept the house filled with bouquets of acacia, honeysuckle, and roses.[146] Meals were served promptly, piping hot, even if Gertrude liked them lukewarm. Orders for books were sent to Mudie's Lending Library in London, sparing Gertrude the tedium of going through the catalogue. All the chores of running the ménage were taken up by Alice. "Would you have another," Gertrude wrote to her love. "What," Alice asked. "Kiss."[147]

The fighting in Verdun in the spring of 1916 caused Alice and Gertrude deep anxiety. Day after day they waited for news, placing their hopes in Pétain's ability to avert defeat. Their hearts were in Paris, and late in June, when the battle seemed to turn in France's favor, they decided at last to go home.

Though Alice had been knitting feverishly throughout the war—having been taught the skill by Madame Matisse some years before—she and Gertrude now wanted to take a more significant part. About a month after they returned, they were walking down the street when Alice noticed a girl dressed in dark blue driving back and forth alongside the curb. They watched her for a while, determined that her dark blue dress was a uniform, and were curious about who she was. "Wait a minute," Alice told Gertrude, "I am going to inquire about this."[148] Her inquiry led her to Mrs. Isabel Lathrop, who, though she appeared to be a frilly American clubwoman, was actually the competent head of the American Fund for French Wounded. If Alice could procure a vehicle, Mrs. Lathrop told her, she and Gertrude could deliver hospital supplies. Meanwhile, they could do office work at the rue des Pyramides headquarters in Paris.

Their official title was "delegate," but Alice referred to herself as "errand boy" and Gertrude—as soon as she learned to drive—would be a driver. While they waited for Gertrude's cousin to send them a Ford, Gertrude was given driving lessons by William Cook, who also had returned to Paris. Her driving reflected her personality: she objected to night driving, hated going in reverse, and had inordinate difficulty keeping in her lane. Alice never drove at all, preferring, instead, to direct Gertrude. Usually she was very patient with Gertrude's idiosyncrasies, though she admitted that some violent arguments broke out over the touchy subject of backing up.

By mid-January, the Ford had come and was taken to a local garage to be transformed into a truck. Befitting its passengers, it was a motley assemblage of wheels, cubes, and cylinders, much of which was collapsible. The new addition was nicknamed "Auntie," after Gertrude's Aunt Pauline, who, legend had it, was undaunted in an emergency and "behaved fairly well most times if she was properly flattered."[149] One snowy morning, the ebullient driver and her errand boy left on their first long-distance assignment to Perpignan.

". . . You will drive the car," Alice had agreed with Gertrude, "and I will do the rest."[150] Among her duties was procuring gasoline for Auntie. It was necessary to see the major in command of the army's commissary department, a task which Gertrude flatly refused to undertake. She would crank the car, she told Alice; she would even get up early in the morning to drive—as impossible as the notion seemed to her—but she would not interview army officers. The major courteously directed Alice through a maze of official business. Taking Alice to be the driver of the car, he addressed her as Miss Stein, an error which she did not bother to correct until he graciously invited her to dinner, explaining that his wife was anxious to meet her. Timidly, she replied that she was not, in fact, Miss Stein. "Mademoiselle Stein is the driver and I am the delegate and Mademoiselle Stein has no patience she will not go into offices and wait and interview people and explain, so I do it for her while she sits in the automobile," she told the major, who by now had changed into a stern and unsympathetic bureaucrat. Nevertheless, he accepted her confusing statement, followed her downstairs, and met Gertrude. To Alice's relief, they became friends immediately and both were invited to dinner, at which, Alice reported, they had a good time and unexcelled soup.[151]

Since supplies were scarce, Alice tried to think of ways to aid the American Fund. She had a photograph taken of her and Gertrude in Rivesaltes, in front of the birthplace of Marshal Joffre, the hero of the Marne. Reproduced as postcards, they were sold to American friends. She wrote to her father, who had his lodge donate an ambulance and some x-ray equipment. She managed to gather surgical supplies and bandages from a number of friends. But management of the supplies required her ingenuity and a certain deviousness. When she received a bounty of five thousand thermometers, she knew she would have to hide them or the cache would be immediately depleted. She kept everything sealed, arranged so that she knew where the various items were, and piled one upon the other to form a series of steps which she could climb.

She quickly learned how to shuttle what was needed to the right people, ignoring a request for silk pajamas by the director of the military hospital in Perpignan, but making sure that the "pitiable, gentle, sad" young soldiers were helped. The first wounded soldier whom Alice came upon had been the elevator boy for a San Francisco department store. She asked if he felt sorry, seeing how severely he had been wounded. But he replied that he didn't know if he regretted enlisting. Distributing supplies, she thought, was like a perpetual Christmas. With a real compassion for the soldiers, she persevered tirelessly. She proudly called herself "a professional worker," but for many of the young men she was a surrogate mother, a comfortable maiden aunt in whom they could confide and to whom they could write. She and Gertrude had many godsons among the soldiers, and it was Alice who knitted mittens and scarves, promptly answered their rambling letters, and gave them the kind of advice they might have heard at home and missed hearing in France.

The Americans who began appearing in France in July, especially those who joined the ambulance corps, were usually well-educated and highly idealistic. Not content to observe the war from the safety of the States, they rushed to the midst of battle and found themselves isolated, lonely, homesick, and frightened. In America, they had believed fully in the war, and not participating would have seemed close to treason. But in France, they came to doubt their convictions, to wonder why they were there risking their life. As the San Franciscan had told Alice, sometimes they weren't sure whether or not they were sorry they had come. The war, one of them wrote to Alice, seemed like a dream. But she and Gertrude were reality.[152]

From Perpignan they returned to Paris and soon set off again, this time for Nîmes. They settled at the Hôtel Luxembourg, where one evening they noticed an American private having dinner alone. Always interested in meeting

American soldiers, they approached him a few days later in the lobby of the hotel. "I am Miss Toklas," Alice announced, "and this is Miss Stein." They invited him to tea, during which Alice revealed, "Miss Stein writes." They found out from him whatever they wanted to know: he was a New Englander, from Massachusetts, went to Amherst, was in France as a member of the Amherst ambulance unit. He was William Garland Rogers, whom they affectionately called "the Kiddie."

When they learned that he was on a ten-day furlough, they suggested that he accompany them on some jaunts, provided he comply with certain conditions. "Miss Toklas did not invite me," he recalled, "she 'propositioned' me." He would be mechanic-in-residence for Auntie; he must sit on the floor with his feet on the running board, on a pillow, his knees tucked under his chin, so as not to crowd Gertrude when she drove. "Miss Toklas," he soon realized, ". . . devoted practically all her adult life to the prevention of any crowding of Gertrude Stein."[153] They went to Orange and Arles—though Rogers had never heard of Van Gogh. Auntie barely survived the climb to Les Baux, almost running out of water. They stopped at the site of Caesar's defeat by Vercingetorix and visited the walled city from which St. Louis departed on one of his crusades. The trips were narrated by his hostesses, Gertrude offering bits of history, and Alice aesthetic judgments on the passing scene. She preferred the Roman theater at Orange to the one at Arles, and thought Les Baux approached perfection as a town—even in its ruins. Rogers' impression of Alice changed swiftly in ten days.

At first glance, the Miss Toklas whom I first saw in 1917 . . . was and has remained a little stooped, somewhat retiring and self-effacing. She doesn't sit in a chair, she hides in it; she doesn't look at you, but up at you; she is always standing just half a step outside the circle. She gives the appearance, in short, not of a drudge, but of a poor relation, some one invited to the wedding but not to the wedding feast.

But in the first moment after the first glance, the impact of her wit, her tonic acidity and her amazing vitality makes itself felt unmistakably. Though you assumed you would devote all your attention to Miss Stein, you found yourself obliged to direct a generous share of it to Miss Toklas, even against her wishes.[154]

She was, admittedly, odd-looking. She had just cut her hair, and the short, dark ends showed out of her helmet-shaped hat. She wore a long, baggy skirt and a long, baggy coat. She was tiny, wiry, and walked with short quick steps alongside Gertrude's easy strides. Despite her friendliness, she seemed somewhat unapproachable. ". . . I was a little afraid of Miss Toklas," Rogers wrote later, "and still am. I was never afraid of Miss Stein."[155]

He wrote to Alice throughout the war, though, asking for her prayers, thanking her for knitted gloves, advising her and Gertrude about the care of their Ford. He confided a wistful dream—being home, going to an all-night dance —and the despondency he shared with the other soldiers. He told her that she needn't bother to respond to his letters; just knowing that she received them was "an immense relief."[156] But she always did reply, with comfort and support and warmth. She had adopted him as one of her many military godsons. But the most winning, she admitted, was a young man named Abel.

One day Alice lost her purse, an annoying recurrence, made more irksome this time because it contained a good deal of money. The same evening, at dinner in their hotel, the waiter called them from the dining room and Alice saw waiting for her a man holding her purse. She offered him a generous reward, but he asked for a favor instead: Would Alice be his seventeen-year-old son's godmother for the duration of the war? Of course, she agreed, and asked that the young man come to see her the next evening.

She immediately loved Abel Leglayle, "the youngest, the sweetest, the smallest soldier imaginable. . . ." She doted on him, proud of his being decorated with the Legion of Honor, and after the armistice entertained him for a week in Paris. It was the young man's first visit to the capital, and he was awed. "I think all that was worth fighting for," he told Alice. But Paris in the dark seemed to frighten him more than being sent to the front; he would not go out alone. Abel and Alice corresponded for a short while until he and his family moved, and she lost track of her favorite godson.

Alice and Gertrude were still in Nîmes on November 11, 1918, when bells tolling throughout France celebrated the Armistice. Alice wept with happiness, but Gertrude stopped her. "Compose yourself," she said. "You have no right to show a tearful countenance to the French whose sons will no longer be killed."[157] Both women, on their errands, brought the news to many of the small surrounding villages. No longer needed in Nîmes, they were sent to Alsace, where they were to work with the refugees. With newly purchased sweaters and fur-lined aviator jackets, they traveled north on icy roads. Irritation from physical discomforts, which had often set Alice to weeping and complaining, abated during her war work. When the war was over, Alice and Gertrude were both awarded the Reconnaissance Française,[158] and Alice's bore the added honor "*sans relâche*"—without respite.

The trip from Nancy to Mulhouse, though it justified her complaints, was met with humor. On a desolate road, Gertrude suddenly discovered that the fan belt was broken. After an unsuccessful attempt to mend it with a hairpin, Gertrude hailed an approaching military car. "Carefully, my dear," Alice said as she glanced at the car. "He is a general."

"I do not care," Gertrude replied, and in a short time was ready to drive away with a fan belt tightened by the soldiers. Alice thanked them with "a sufficient quantity" of cigarettes.[159]

In Alsace, while they distributed clothing from their stock in a gymnasium, they tried to communicate with the friendly populace. Gertrude, Alice saw, "spoke a fluent incorrect German which the Alsatians understood," but Alice could hardly recall the little German she had once learned. When she tried to speak to a woman one day, the Alsatian turned to a friend and said, "She is a Prussian." The remark pleased Gertrude.

While Alice was fully occupied with her position as "delegate," Gertrude found time to continue writing. Besides soliciting funds from friends, the two had contributed their own money to the American Fund, and their accounts were quickly diminishing. By the end of the war, Alice said, they were "dead broke," and Gertrude's writing would be the only way they could support themselves. Still, Gertrude would not or could not write for commercial success. She continued in the repetitive, elusive, nonsensical style which characterized her work from the time of *The Making of Americans*.

Alice, of course, looms grandly in Gertrude's war work, most notably in a 1917 piece, "Lifting Belly," a long rhapsody of Lesbian love. "Lifting belly is in bed," Gertrude wrote, and its object is "making/A cow/Come out."[160] References in the piece indicate that it was probably begun in Mallorca, where she and Alice had seen a spectacular meteor fall into the Bay of Palma, sizzling the water. "Miracle you don't know about the miracle," she asks. "You mean a meteor," is the prosaic answer.[161]

But most of the piece is a love song to Alice. "I love cherish idolise adore and worship you. You are so sweet so tender so perfect."[162] Gertrude recounts a conversation:

> Frankly what do you say to me,
> I say that I need protection.
> You shall have it.
> After that what do you wish.
> I want you to mean a great deal to me.
> Exactly.
> And then.
> And then blandishment.[163]

And she recalls intimate exchanges:

Kiss my lips. She did.
Kiss my lips again she did.
Kiss my lips over and over and over again she did.[164] . . .
I say lifting belly and then I say lifting belly and Caesars.
I say lifting belly gently and Caesars gently. I say lifting belly
again and Caesars again. I say lifting belly and I say Caesars and
I say lifting belly Caesars and cow come out. I say lifting belly
and Caesars and cow come out.
Can you read my print,[165]

she asks Alice. Alice could.

Alice appears under Gertrude's pet names for her—

pussy and baby—in many pieces, including "Lifting Belly" and another love song, "Accents in Alsace." "Baby winks and holds me tight./In the morning and the day and the evening and always."[166] Alice, the "accent" in the town and in Gertrude's life, is "Sweeter than water or cream or ice. Sweeter than bells of roses. Sweeter than winter or summer or spring. Sweeter than pretty posies. Sweeter than anything. . . ." And Gertrude's only desire is to "express the love which is hers to inspire."[167]

In May the two returned to Paris, stopping for a few days with Mildred Aldrich in Huiry. Mildred, like Gertrude and Alice, had practically no money left after donating a great deal to the local war effort, throwing a Christmas party for the soldiers, and being as generous toward her new neighbors as she always had been toward her old friends.

Paris, Alice remembered, "like us, was sadder than when we left it." There was not enough money for the former Saturday-evening gatherings, and besides, the old crowd had dispersed. Matisse had moved south; Picasso, now married to a dancer from the Russian ballet, was playing the successful, suave husband; Apollinaire was dead, a victim of the 1918 flu epidemic. Many of the writers they had known before the war had gone home, and the new arrivals from America were, Alice thought, very different. These were a "younger generation . . . who came to Paris to write, many of them believing that in the city of boulevard bars (prohibition was at its height in the U.S.) and Baudelaire, writing was a contagious craft."[168]

Prohibition was not limited to alcohol. The Society for the Suppression of Vice and Boston's Watch and Ward Society cast a vigilant eye on publications. Europe, especially France, was just "over there," no more forbidding and much more enticing to the former ambulance drivers and privates than was Greenwich Village. And with the postwar devaluation, they could live cheaply and comparatively well. For less than one hundred dollars, they could book passage and leave home.

The war had inspired restlessness and gnawing disillusionment. War stories in the press, glamorous and glorious battle scenes, were unconfirmed by the returning men. The war which had been perpetrated for such high-sounding reasons had cost 130,000 American and millions of European lives. The world which it involved was left wounded.

Nothing was the same, they said. Yet when the newcomers left for Paris, as Alice had thirteen years before, they came, as she had come, to "fly."

3

New Faces

You shall read that we are commanded to forgive our enemies; but you never read that we
are commanded to forgive our friends.

Attributed to Cosmus,
Duke of Florence

Twelve

THROUGH THE EFFORTS of Mabel Dodge, Carl Van Vechten, and Henry McBride, Gertrude was gaining notice from American writers. Some of her short pieces had appeared in *Life, Vanity Fair,* and several little magazines—*Soil, Rogue, Broom, Camera Work.* McBride had written about her in his column in the New York *Sun*; Van Vechten had reviewed *Three Lives* and *Tender Buttons* in *Trend* and the New York *Times.* And her name was invariably linked with the cubists in the proliferation of articles which followed the Armory Show. Though a dubious measure of success, her works had already begun to be parodied, and the legend of her personality had already begun to radiate with the glow of mystique. There was the general impression, Sherwood Anderson wrote, that Gertrude Stein reigned in Montparnasse, "lying on a couch, smoking cigarettes, sipping absinthes perhaps and looking out upon the world with tired, disdainful eyes."[1]

The new expatriates, however, when they came to pay homage, found instead a gregarious forty-six-year-old writer, with a pile of unpublished works, anxious for recognition and eager for praise. Gertrude would have seen them all, again and again. One after another they came. And one after another—except for a few chosen by Alice —they went. "Alice Toklas always liked a poem that used to go, Give me new faces new faces new faces I have seen the old ones. . . ."[2]

Sylvia Beach, who would make the mistake, Alice thought, of publishing Joyce, was one of the first among their new acquaintances after the war. She had worked with the Red Cross in Serbia, then settled in Paris with her sister Cyprian, an actress. Unable to finance her dream of

137

opening a French bookshop in New York, she managed, with her mother's savings, to open an American bookstore in Paris. Finding Sylvia "the most American after Gertrude Stein," Alice nicknamed her "the flagstaff." She admitted that she was tempted to name her the flag, "but could one do that," she wondered, "would that not be a sacrilege?"

Sylvia's Shakespeare and Company, the only bookshop in Paris with two circulating copies of *Tender Buttons*, attracted Gertrude's and Alice's attention one day when they were out walking. Sylvia was amused by the unmatched pair, thought Alice whimsical and gypsylike, with more finesse and sophistication than Gertrude. It was obvious, she thought, that they agreed on almost everything. The shop was officially opened on November 19, 1919, and the friendship lasted until the publication of Joyce's *Ulysses* on February 2, 1922. During those few years, Sylvia acted as introducer, and both Gertrude and Alice appreciated her for the bright spirit that she was.

Shakespeare and Company was the nexus for literary life as much as 13, rue Ravignan had been the center for artists before the war. A few blocks from the cafés in which writers sought solace or inspiration—the Dome, the Rotonde, the Coupole—it was a meeting place and home away from home for many newcomers. On its walls hung portraits by Man Ray, himself recently arrived from an artists' colony in Ridgefield, New Jersey. Among the many writers he photographed was Gertrude, and when she saw the results, she told him that she liked his photographs better than any other that had ever been taken of her—except, of course, for a snapshot by Alice. Man Ray, unfortunately, did not accept the statement as praise.

Both Gertrude and Alice were familiar figures in their quarter, ambling along the Luxembourg, or riding through the streets in their new Ford, a two-seater in which they sat very high. From her lofty perch in the driver's seat, Gertrude looked down one day and saw the bright blue eyes of the writer Robert McAlmon and next to him a young woman she immediately took to be "an ethical Jewess." Though McAlmon's wife, Winifred Ellerman, who called herself Bryher, came from a long line of English Protestants and German Lutherans, she took Gertrude's remark as a compliment and accepted her invitation to tea. More than her husband, Bryher took an instant liking to the rue de Fleurus and its two hostesses. The studio, she remembered, was "full of paintings, but what I noticed, it must have been some trick of the lighting, was that the atmosphere seemed full of gold." Gertrude's talk, too, was sparkling. Her phrases rose and spun hypnotically. "She offered us the world," Bryher wrote, "took it away again in the following sentence, only to demonstrate in a third that it was something that we could not want because it had never existed."[3] But Gertrude did not try to include the young woman in those ethereal conversations, and Bryher took refuge at Alice's side.

Alice, for Bryher and many of the other "wives," was nothing other than "Miss Toklas." Even when amusing her charges with stories of San Francisco, Alice exuded a dignity that subdued those around her. Sometimes, she would allow a guest to accompany her to the kitchen, where the talk would be of cooking or gardening, but once Bryher remembered being scolded by Gertrude for their absence. "I am afraid that while I had a profound admiration for Gertrude," Bryher admitted, "it was Miss Toklas whom I loved. She was so kind to me."[4] In her company, Bryher felt completely at home.

In Alice, Bryher understood a devotion similar to her own for the poet Hilda Doolittle, whom she met in 1918. To the twenty-four-year-old Bryher, Hilda Doolittle—H.D. —"was the most beautiful figure that I have ever seen in my life, with a face that came directly from a Greek statue and . . . the body of an athlete." H.D., born in Pennsylvania, had come to England in 1911 and gained attention as one of the Imagists, closely associated with Amy Lowell and Ezra Pound. Though she was married to the writer Richard Aldington, whom she later divorced, her friendship with Bryher lasted until her death in 1961, an expression of the kind of love in which she fervently believed. "You must love," she had told Bryher when they first met. "A person, an island, an idea, but it must be completely and with utter dedication."[5]

Bryher's marriage to the moody Robert McAlmon was a practical pact which each felt would work to their mutual advantage. Bryher wanted independence from her family; McAlmon needed money to go to Paris. "I put my problem before him," Bryher wrote later, "and suggested that if we married, my family would leave me alone. I would give him part of my allowance, he would join me for occasional visits to my parents, but otherwise we would live strictly separate lives."[6] Their arrangement lasted until 1927, when they were amicably divorced.

Unexpected liaisons always interested Alice, and she followed them with endless fascination. Especially amusing was Ford Madox Ford's romance with Violet Hunt. Ford had noticed Gertrude and Alice riding in their first car and saw them often then and again in the twenties. Alice confessed a weakness for him and later boasted that she had known him "intimately" through his three marriages. She was especially fond of alluding to his love affair with Violet Hunt.

Violet, whom Alice thought "ever so good looking and very distinguished," was nearly fifty when she met the thirty-six-year-old writer in 1909 at a dinner party given by John Galsworthy. Still Ford Hermann Madox Hueffer—he would change his name after the war—he had been married to Elsie Martindale since 1894 and had two children. But the flamboyant Violet—the woman Henry James called "The Purple Patch" because she wore a purple veil and coat, and carried a purple pillow for her back when traveling—was determined to attract him. He tried to obtain a divorce, but his wife, a Roman Catholic, refused. Violet, undaunted, took his name anyway—a brazen action in the eyes of English society.

Violet, however, had never been reticent. H. G. Wells, conjuring up her horoscope, noted her vitality, strong will, and emotional nature. She was

> just a trifle nervous, and not very ambitious, and would not be very brilliant at necromancy, alchemy or other branches of Occult Science. She has a strong faculty for immediate apprehension, or intuition, and is very sentimental. She has a moderate affection for the opposite sex. . . . If she takes to keeping cows she will be successful. . . .[7]

While Wells apparently found her enjoyable, Henry James thought she could be exceedingly irritating. Once, visiting him at Lamb House, she began breakfast with the mention of someone she had deeply loved. "I actually used the word of awe in his connection," she remembered, and James appeared shocked. He got up, cleared his throat nervously, and pointed out the portrait of his mother which hung near. The author, Violet decided, had "dyspepsia written all over the cover of him."[8]

The eccentric Violet was just the kind of personality that Alice found amusing. Like Gertrude, she usually found the men more interesting than their wives. Among the many new faces brought to the rue de Fleurus, she felt a warm affection for Sherwood Anderson.

It was Sylvia Beach who brought Sherwood Anderson to see Gertrude when he came to Paris in June 1921. Alice was not at home when he visited for the first time, but when she did meet him, she approved immediately. "He had a winning brusquerie, a mordant wit and an all-inclusive heart—the combination was irresistible."[9] He was, besides, very sweet. He had published four well-received books, and at forty-four seemed more sure and settled than many of the younger writers Gertrude was meeting, who all, she said, seemed to be twenty-six.

The author of *Windy McPherson's Son, Marching Men, Winesburg, Ohio,* and *Poor White* was tremendously excited by *Tender Buttons.* "Here was something purely experimental," he wrote, "and dealing in words separated from sense . . . an approach I was sure the poets must often be compelled to make."[10] He vowed to try her method in his own writing; but if he did, he never published the results. Nevertheless, his praise was so sincere that he won Gertrude's trust, and Alice's. "He was very handsome," Alice also noted, "and incredibly charming," and, to Gertrude's delight, an excellent storyteller.

Apparently, Anderson mentioned to Gertrude that he might write an essay or article about her—a suggestion she would not let him forget. A few months after he returned to America he wrote proposing that he provide the introduction to a book she had finally assembled, *Geography and Plays.* "I wonder if you are still interested in doing an essay on me," she asked. ". . . I would like that because as I told you, you are really the only person who really knows what it is all about." He was, also, one of the few established writers she knew who took her seriously.

Geography and Plays would be published at Gertrude's

expense by the Four Seas Press, a Boston firm economically run by Edmund Brown. Harry Phelan Gibb, an English painter, aware of Gertrude's hoarded manuscripts, was adamant about her publishing a new book. But Gertrude was sure no editor would be interested. Frustrated in his attempt to prod Gertrude into action, Gibb finally turned to Alice. "Alice, you do it," he said. And Alice did.

During the typing of the collection, Alice discovered in a piece called "Sacred Emily" the line "Rose is a rose is a rose is a rose" and pounced upon it. ". . . It was I who found it . . . and insisted upon putting it as a device on the letter paper, on the table linen and anywhere that she would permit that I would put it. I am very pleased with myself for having done so."[11] Indeed, she should have been. The "device" became Gertrude's trademark, indelibly impressed on twentieth-century literary consciousness, and a symbol of Gertrude's own blossoming.

To find a publisher, Alice asked the advice of Kate Buss, a friend and writer, who suggested Brown's press since he had printed some of her own work. Alice wrote, and by July 1922 arrangements were made for Gertrude's new book. Brown himself applauded the choice of Anderson for the introduction. Though Gertrude was carefully choosing pieces for the collection, Brown thought she would benefit by a little help. Anderson's acceptance endeared him even more to Alice and Gertrude, and the final product completely delighted them. In retrospect, the only mistake Anderson made was sending them Ernest Hemingway.

Thirteen

IN THE SUMMER of 1913, Max Jacob, poet and painter and friend of Picasso, wrote Alice's horoscope. She was more interested in having her fortune told, but nevertheless found his remarks generally amusing. He placed her near "the greats" and predicted powerful friendships. He saw her strength of character, a sense of daring tempered by good judgment, a certain nobility. Alice was startled by his noting a tendency toward theft—he also mentioned murder, but this she allowed to pass without comment. He recommended prudence: he saw in her passionate nature the threat of adversity.

Gertrude's fear of Alice's infidelity was hidden in her writings, as if the pieces were an ongoing diary, private and cryptic. In the spring after the war, Lilyanna Hansen again came to Paris. The reunion upset Gertrude, and several later pieces attest to the intrusion of another into their relationship. "A Third," written in 1925, vents some of the unhappiness she felt. But she was powerless to stop Alice from seeing anyone she wanted to see. A photograph which Alice took of Lily in the Luxembourg Gardens was kept by her until after Gertrude's death. Gertrude's pain only caused her to be more docile, submissive, and loving. She would do anything to keep Alice, to win her back if she lost her.

Alice, on the other hand, was vengeful when jealous, ruthless when threatened. She would allow Gertrude a friend like Anderson, who was then married and had an easygoing, country-boy admiration of Gertrude. She accepted Picasso, whose taste in women excluded Gertrude Stein. But the young man who came to see them in March 1922, with "dark luminous eyes . . . a flashing smile and the guiches he affected [which] made him look like an Italian" aroused her suspicions.

Ernest Hemingway arrived in Paris late in 1921, checking into the Hôtel Jacob with his wife Hadley. In his wanderings around the Left Bank, he soon came upon Shakespeare and Company, and when Sylvia Beach looked up from her work one day, she saw "a tall, dark young fellow with a small mustache and heard him say, in a deep, deep voice, that he was Ernest Hemingway." Soon he became, by his own calculations, her best customer, borrowing piles of books day after day and stopping at the shop where he knew he would find a sympathetic ear. "He seemed to me," Sylvia wrote, "to have gone a great deal farther and faster than any of the young writers I knew. In spite of a certain boyishness, he was exceptionally wise and self-reliant."

Earning his living as a correspondent for the Toronto *Star*, he had come to Paris to write—not only journalism, but novels and stories. In America, he had already earned the respect of Sherwood Anderson, whom he had known in Chicago in 1920. When he came to Paris he brought with him a letter of introduction from Anderson to his friend Gertrude Stein. Shortly after she met Hemingway, Gertrude gave Anderson her reaction. "He is a delightful fellow," she wrote, "and I like his talk and am teaching him to cut his wife's hair." Hemingway, however, wanted more useful instruction from Gertrude.

From their first meeting, Hemingway was a frequent visitor to the rue de Fleurus. In the beginning, he would sit in front of Gertrude and listen and look, while Alice would serve liqueurs and cakes and listen and look. He brought all his work for Gertrude's appraisal—poetry, stories, sketches. His poem "They All Want Peace—What Is Peace?" was submitted to *The Little Review* only after Gertrude gave her approval. "Her method is invaluable," he thought. "She has a wonderful head."[12] Soon he was coming more and more often, staying later, taking Gertrude on long walks. When he and his wife found an apartment at 74 rue du Cardinal Lemoine, Gertrude and Alice were among his first guests. They sat on the bed while he showed Gertrude everything he had written so far, including stories he would choose for a collection, *Three Stories and Ten Poems*. He asked her opinion on the format of the book, the appearance of the contents page—even the kind of type. He seemed so hungry for her advice, and took her comments so seriously, that she was pleased and flattered. "Gertrude Stein and me are just like brothers, and we see a lot of her," Hemingway wrote to Anderson. And, hastily scribbled at the end of a letter, he added, "We love Gertrude Stein."[13]

Though he was unusually sensitive to criticism, and easily hurt, he welcomed Gertrude's help and opinions. With her, he could drop his pose—what Robert McAlmon called "a boy's need to be a tough guy, a swell boxer, a strong man." Gertrude had no doubt that he was serious about writing—obsessed with the need to learn everything he could. Her estimation of him was in agreement with that of at least one other important figure in the literary circles of Montparnasse: Adrienne Monnier.

Adrienne Monnier was the well-loved proprietor of the bookshop across the street from Shakespeare and Company, La Maison des Amis des Livres. A close friend of Sylvia Beach, she shared her interest in young writers and often sponsored readings and gatherings. Writers kept rendezvous at one or the other of the shops. "There should have been a tunnel under the rue de l'Odéon," Sylvia suggested.

Monnier, as she was always called, was stout, fair, and rosy-cheeked, and her simple, unstylish clothing made her appear older than her thirty years. She usually wore a long gray skirt, velvet vest, and white silk blouse. In her journal *Le Navire d'argent* she published Hemingway's first story to be translated into French—"The Undefeated," as *Invincible*. She was respected throughout the quarter for her instinctive judgment of writers, and her opinion of Ernest Hemingway was not easily forgotten.

"Hemingway will be the best known of you all," she said one day. Her blunt statement surprised her listeners, and Bryher, who was present in the group, asked her why she thought Hemingway better than the others. "He cares," she replied, "for his craft."[14] At the time, Monnier knew what few others did—that after a day's writing Hemingway proceeded to a local printer's each evening to learn how to set type so that he would know exactly how his manuscripts, with all punctuation, would look when completed. It was this dedication which impressed Gertrude. As she had once told Annette Rosenshine, "It is better to be a journeyman than an apprentice."[15] Besides, Gertrude thought he "had a truly sensitive capacity for emotion." She believed in his talent and enjoyed his company. Both she and Alice had a real affection for Hadley, who was friendly, open, and warm.

Alice, however, disliked Hemingway from the start, for no ostensible cause except that Gertrude confessed a "weakness" for him. Though for Alice that was reason enough, she did not actively intervene in their beginning friendship. The intensity of the relationship, in any case, was interrupted by each couple's travels: Gertrude and Alice went south to St. Rémy in the summer and fall of 1922—and sent the Hemingways a luscious casaba melon; Hemingway and his wife went to Spain in the summer of 1923, on Alice's recommendation. Because Hemingway had especially liked Pamplona, the town was forever ruined for Alice—more than forty years later, she still admitted a prejudice against it "on account of Hemingway." Between the trips, Hemingway was away on several assignments as a reporter for his paper. One of his articles, in fact, seemed influenced by his conversations with Gertrude. On a flight from Paris to Strasbourg, he looked out of the window as the plane ascended and "the ground began to flatten out beneath us. It looked cut into brown squares, yellow squares, green squares and big flat blotches of green where there was a forest. I began to understand cubist painting."[16] In twelve years, when Gertrude would take her first flight, her reaction would be strikingly similar:

It was then in a kind of way that I really began to know what the ground looked like. Quarter sections make a picture and going over America . . . made any one know why the post-cubist painting was what it was. The wandering line of Masson was there the mixed line of Picasso coming and coming again and following itself into a beginning was there, the simple solution of Braque was there and I suppose Leger might be there but I did not see it not over there. . . . The earth does look like that and even if none of them had seen it and they had not very likely had not but since every one was going to see it they had to see it like that.[17]

When they were together, Gertrude repeatedly gave him the same strong advice. "If you keep on doing newspaper work," she told him, "you will never see things, you will only see words and that will not do, that is of course if you intend to be a writer."[18] She suggested that if he and Hadley had enough money to live simply, he should give up his job on the *Star* and devote himself to serious writing. He mulled over her words until late in the summer of 1923, when he arrived at the rue de Fleurus one morning at ten, obviously distraught. He stayed for lunch, spent the afternoon, remained for dinner—becoming more gloomy as the day went on. Finally, at about ten that night, he announced that Hadley was pregnant. "And I, I am too young to be a father." He left after Gertrude and Alice did their best to console him, and when he came back, he announced that he and his wife were returning to Canada, where he would work, save his money, and come back to Paris to "make himself a writer." It was a decision Gertrude applauded. In August 1923, he and Hadley left Paris.

Warm letters were exchanged between Paris and Toronto. When John Hadley Nicanor Hemingway—Nicanor, after a renowned bullfighter—was born on October 10, 1923, Gertrude and Alice sent their hearty congratulations. Hadley was boosted by their interest. "You've no idea how we miss you two," Hadley wrote. She and Ernest spoke of them often, referring to Gertrude by a special pet name, and probably calling Alice "Miss Tocraz," a mispronunciation that lasted well into the Hemingways' friendship with the two. Hadley missed their visits, wished they were together to share some chocolate cake and tea—and couldn't wait to get back to Paris. Life in Toronto was dull in comparison; there was no one to talk with, Hadley complained and, more important, "not a one to listen to." Ernest reiterated his promise to Gertrude: he would soon "chuck" journalism. When they came back to Paris, newspaper work would be over forever.

In January 1924, the Hemingways returned and the friendship resumed between Gertrude and Ernest with even more affection than before. Gertrude and Alice were to be John's godmothers, an honor about which Alice had certain misgivings. "Writer or painter god-parents are notoriously unreliable," she thought. "That is, there is certain before long to be a cooling of friendship."[19] Nevertheless, after the Episcopalian baptism—the church was chosen because the two godmothers and Chink Dorman-Smith, Hemingway's wartime friend and the baby's godfather, were all of different religions—Alice began to fulfill her new obligation. "I embroidered a little chair and I knitted a gay colored garment" for "Goddy" as she and Gertrude called him, or "Bumbi," as his parents nicknamed him. Her disapproval was only for Ernest.

Alice's response to Hemingway was not unique. Especially after his return from Spain, and more evidently after his return from Canada, friends reacted against his bravado and veneer of hardness. To Robert McAlmon, he was an enigma:

Hemingway was a type not easy to size up. At times he was deliberately hard-boiled and case-hardened; again he appeared deliberately innocent, sentimental, the hurt, soft, but fairly sensitive boy trying to conceal hurt, wanting to be brave, not bitter or cynical but being somewhat both, and somehow on the defensive, suspicions lurking in his peering analytic glances at a person with whom he was talking. He approached a café with a small-boy, tough-guy swagger, and before strangers of whom he was doubtful a potential snarl of scorn played on his large-lipped, rather loose mouth.[20]

Hemingway, despite his public performances, was sensitive to such responses and realized that he was being judged. "Living in a world of literary politics where one wrong opinion often proves fatal, one writes carefully. I remember how I was made to feel how easily one might be dropped from the party, and the short period of Coventry that followed my remarking when speaking of George Antheil that I preferred my Stravinsky straight. I have been more careful since,"[21] he wrote in 1924. Yet, though he feared being "dropped from the party," he could only live out the "Hemingway hero" that he was creating. Many critics, moved by the toughness and violence he wrote about, saw him as the spokesman for a war-beaten generation. "This Hemingway of the middle twenties," Edmund Wilson wrote, ". . . expressed the romantic disillusion and set the favorite pose for the period. It was the moment of gallantry in heartbreak, grim and nonchalant banter, and heroic dissipation. The great watchword was 'Have a drink'; and in the bars of New York and Paris the young people were getting to talk like Hemingway."[22] It was a rare critic, like Wyndham Lewis, who had the insight to know that the Hemingway hero was not a hunter or fighter, but "a man things were done to." Gertrude, too, realized what lay beneath the bold exterior. Though he claimed that he was trying to learn to write by taking as his themes "one of the simplest things of all and the most fundamental," violent death, she tried to urge him against it. Her review of his *Three Stories and Ten Poems,* published when Hemingway was in Canada, carries her warning. "I should say," she wrote, "that Hemingway should stick to poetry and intelligence and eschew the hotter emotions and the more turgid vision."[23] Sex, too, was frequently a topic of Hemingway's conversations with Gertrude, and she was interested at first, believing that he was, at heart, romantic, vulnerable, and shy. Alice, repulsed by his outspoken manner and refusal to use euphemisms, disagreed. After all, she had been brought up to say "compromise" for seduce; "outspoken" for shameless; "impure" for bisexual; and "inadequate" for dead drunk.[24] Clearly, Hemingway shocked her.

But Gertrude, though she knew his fascination with violence and sex, thought he was uneducated in some matters, and he himself admitted "certain prejudices against homosexuality." Before he went back to Toronto, Hemingway was probably not certain whether or not Gertrude and Alice were friends or lovers, and, given his own feelings about homosexuality, hoped Gertrude was not a Lesbian. Her attempt to defend female homosexuality puzzled him:

"You know nothing about any of this really, Hemingway," she said. "You've met known criminals and sick people and vicious people. The main thing is that the act male homosexuals commit is ugly and repugnant and afterwards they are disgusted with themselves. They drink and take drugs, to palliate this, but they are disgusted with the act and they are always changing partners and cannot really be happy."

"I see."

"In women it is the opposite. They do nothing that they are disgusted by and nothing that is repulsive and afterwards they are happy and they can lead happy lives together."

"I see. . . ."[25]

But he wasn't sure he understood. Homosexuality, he thought, was perverse. He loved Gertrude, not only as a mentor but as a woman. As he openly admitted later, she exerted upon him an undeniable sexual attraction. And he was sure that she was equally attracted to him. Alice was convinced of it.

"You know, I made Gertrude get rid of him," she announced to a friend later.[26] And getting rid of Hemingway, no easy task, would stand as Alice's most notorious triumph. He was, after all, so charming. Whatever Alice would say about him failed to affect Gertrude. "Sure, sure," she would reply, "but I have a weakness for Hemingway." And he was becoming unquestionably useful.

With dauntless enthusiasm, he tried to interest some of his friends involved in the many little magazines in Paris to publish Gertrude's work. Finally, Ford Madox Ford agreed to print *The Making of Americans* as a serial in *Transatlantic*. Hemingway tirelessly helped Gertrude assemble the manuscript, proofread, took upon himself the tasks usually relegated to Alice. Her hatred was growing, fired by her jealousy of her position in Gertrude's life. She tried to convince Gertrude that Hemingway played only a trivial part in obtaining Ford's commitment. "I have never known what the story is," she still maintained years later, "but I have always been certain that there was some other story behind it all. That is the way I feel about it."[27]

She tried to expose Hemingway for what she thought he was: an opportunist, concerned only with creating and nurturing his own legend. *"La légende, toujours la légende*,"[28] she said disparagingly. He was crude, she thought. He wasn't virile.[29] He was a rotten pupil who "never got past the second lesson," she told Gertrude.[30] He was using her. He was insincere. But Gertrude would only reply, "but he is so wonderful."

He quoted her in his epigraph for *The Sun Also Rises*. He provided continuous "praise, praise, praise"—the kind she had had only from Alice. Finally, Alice could endure it no longer. "Don't you come home with Hemingway on your arm," she warned Gertrude,[31] but Gertrude kept seeing him until, suddenly, it was over.

The overheard conversation which Hemingway transcribed in *A Moveable Feast* may or may not have actually occurred, but his first certainty that Gertrude and Alice were sexual partners was shocking. The alleged conversation took place while he was waiting for Gertrude.

> . . . I heard someone speaking to Miss Stein as I had never heard one person speak to another; never, anywhere, ever.
>
> Then Miss Stein's voice came pleading and begging, saying "Don't pussy. Don't. Don't please don't. I'll do anything, pussy, but please don't do it. Please don't. Please don't pussy."[32]

Gertrude, of course, would not let Alice leave her. And Hemingway's reaction is paralleled in his very short story "The Sea Change," in which the male protagonist is personally confronted by Lesbianism when his girl friend discloses that she is leaving him for a woman. He realizes that his friend cannot help herself, and yet his reaction is violent. "I'll kill her," he tells his girl friend. "I swear to God I will."

"Couldn't you just be good to me and let me go?" his friend asks him, but he is incapable of really understanding. Lesbianism, to him, is a vice. He struggles to remember some lines of poetry to explain his feelings, but can remember only the first line, "Vice is a monster of such fearful mien," and even this he misquotes. Yet in the title itself, taken from *The Tempest*, there is a measure of compassion:

> Nothing of him that doth fade
> But doth suffer a sea-change
> Into something rich and strange.

After the break, Alice apparently convinced Gertrude of the truth of her intuition about Hemingway. Gertrude's subsequent evaluation of him reflects completely Alice's enduring beliefs. ". . . He began to develop, as a shield, a big Kansas-City-boy brutality . . . and so he was 'tough' because he was really sensitive and ashamed that he was. Then it happened. I saw it happening and tried to save what was fine there, but it was too late. He went the way so many other Americans have gone before, the way they are still going. He became obsessed by sex and violent death."[33] She criticized his writing; his newspaper training, she said, gave him a false sense of time. And in *The Autobiography of Alice B. Toklas,* in Alice's voice, she struck and struck again. Even Sherwood Anderson, once Hemingway's victim, wrote to Gertrude that he was "a bit sorry and sad on the night after that number [in the *Atlantic*] when you took such big patches of skin off Hemmy with your delicately held knife. . . ."[34] She called him yellow, disparaged his talent, wrote about him as if he were an incorrigible—if precocious—child. And he responded in kind.

"She's just jealous and malicious," he wrote. He thought he never should have helped her. "It's a damned shame, though, with all that talent gone to malice and nonsense and self-praise. . . . You know a funny thing; she never could write dialogue. It was terrible. She learned how to do it from my stuff and used it in that book. She had never written like that before. She never could forgive learning that and she was afraid people would notice it, so she had to attack me. It's a funny racket really. But I swear she was damned nice before she got ambitious."[35]

Shortly after *The Autobiography* was published, he retaliated in an article about Miró's *The Farm*, in which he praised the painter for producing a masterpiece by working at it every day for nine months. ". . . It is good to have something around that has taken as long to make as it takes a woman to make a child (a woman who isn't a woman can usually write her autobiography in a third of that time). . . . If you have painted "The Farm" or if you have written *Ulysses,* and then keep on working very hard afterwards, you do not need an Alice B. Toklas."[36]

He could not resist another gibe when, in 1933, he supplied a blurb for the dust jacket of James Thurber's *My Life and Hard Times:*

> I find it far
> superior to the auto-
> biography of Henry Adams. Even in the
> earliest days when
> Thurber was writing under the name of
> Alice B. Toklas we
> knew he had it in him
> if he could get it out.

But eventually he forgave Gertrude for not being the woman he could have loved. He understood that it was Alice who caused the break: she could not bear a rival. And Pope's lines, which he had used in "The Sea Change," made sense:

> Vice is a monster of so frightful mien,
> As to be hated needs but to be seen;
> Yet seen too oft, familiar with her face,
> We first endure, then pity, then embrace.[37]

Alice, for her part, neither forgot nor forgave. She followed his career with rapt attention, reveling in what she considered amends for the hurt he had caused her. She was "strangely" upset by a rumor, in 1950, of his mortal illness. Though she felt little compassion for him, she knew how much he was suffering. And somehow his suffering seemed to her justified.[38] She watched what she deemed the pitiable disintegration of his legend, and felt she was being rewarded in the biblical sense of an eye for an eye.[39] Her comment on his suicide was, "What an inheritance to pass on to his children!" She never regretted having banished him from Gertrude's life. He had made the mistake of loving her too well, and Alice had to get rid of him. "And when you think of all the wives he had," she said later, "I think I was right."[40]

Fourteen

ALICE, TOO, HAD her weaknesses, and one of her favorite young men—"the most sensitive . . . the most distinguished —the most gifted and intelligent of all his contemporaries," was F. Scott Fitzgerald. His being Hemingway's rival— and, Alice thought, his victim—only made him more attractive. She and Gertrude read *This Side of Paradise* soon after it was published in 1920, and thought it "the definitive portrait" of his generation.

Fitzgerald had recently arrived in Paris in the summer of 1925, when Hemingway met him at the Dingo Bar. He thought Fitzgerald "looked like a boy with a face between handsome and pretty" and he soon brought the writer to see Gertrude. Alice noticed at once the contrast between the two. Fitzgerald, unlike his friend, was modest about his own talent and deferential toward other writers. When Gertrude expressed "her unfailing appreciation of his work and belief in his gift," he would not believe her. He said he was only second-rate, especially when compared with Gertrude, and her praise made him aware of his own insignificance. His achievement was minimal: ". . . I have only hope," he wrote to her.[41]

As Hemingway had come when he learned he was to be a father, Fitzgerald came when he approached a crisis in his own life. "You know I am thirty years old today and it is tragic," he told Gertrude one afternoon. "What is to become of me, what am I to do?" Gertrude calmly told him not to worry, "that he had been writing like a man of thirty for many years," and that he should go home and write the best novel he could. *Tender Is the Night* was sent to her later with the inscription "Is this the book you asked for?" It was, she replied.[42]

For Alice, Fitzgerald was "one of those great tragic

American figures. . . ."[43] Yet as much as she liked him, she found his work repetitive in theme. Gertrude predicted that he would be read long after his contemporaries (i.e., Hemingway) were forgotten, but Alice thought otherwise. His characters, like Fitzgerald himself, were young and troubled—but, Alice saw, "they were not made unhappy by too many different reasons." His narrow conception of suffering was "a slight reproach," she wrote later after a collection of his stories was published, and she added what faint praise she could: ". . . one must gratefully acknowledge the variety of examples chosen from the limited range offered by normal middle-class youth."[44]

Fitzgerald's shortcomings were easier to overlook than Ezra Pound's, whom Alice found disagreeable and pretentious. At the time she knew him, in the early twenties, he was interested in Japanese prints, political economy, and oriental music, but Alice doubted the depth of his knowledge about any of them. "He reminded me of Queen Victoria's remark after someone had most unfortunately selected to sing to the Queen 'The Wearing of the Green,' so sad and so very mistaken."[45]

Fortunately, his visits were short-lived; he failed to return after he fell out of a chair. Gertrude captured their final conversation, tensely conducted in the presence of Scofield Thayer, editor of the *Dial*, whom Pound had brought to meet her.

Conversation.

I have hoped to see you often. I had hoped to have the privilege of making your house my home. I had hoped to remain here permanently. I had meant to make good my footing with you. I had indeed hoped to remain indefinitely in this city.

Indeed had you.

I had hoped to find it permissible to explain to every one everything and further than that to write it. I had indeed hoped not for that alone but for myself. . . . I knew that you were not favorably impressed but after all am I not a person of importance. I am accustomed so to consider myself.

> And we have considered you so but we do not want to
> have you in our home.
>
> So nearly have we explained ourselves,

Gertrude concluded, turning to her other guest. "And now
for Thayer. . . ."[46] When they met Pound sometime later
near the Luxembourg Gardens, they turned away his request to visit with an unarguable excuse. "I am sorry,"
Gertrude told him, "but Miss Toklas has a bad tooth and
besides we are busy picking wild flowers."[47]

Pound, Alice remembered, wanted everyone he knew to
subscribe five dollars for a fund to support the poet T. S.
Eliot so he would be able to give up his job at a London
bank and devote himself completely to writing. But in
Alice's estimation, Eliot was hardly more interesting than
Pound. He was brought to see Gertrude by his friend and
patron Lady Rothermere on the afternoon of November
15, 1924. Alice had been in the midst of sewing a new
evening dress when the guests arrived unexpectedly. She
and Gertrude had planned to meet them that evening at
Lady Rothermere's reception for Eliot, Alice wearing her
first new dress since the war. Eliot, thirty-six, was a somber
man, who for his own reasons refused to relinquish his
umbrella to Alice's care and sat clasping its handle
throughout the visit, "while his eyes burned brightly in a
non-committal face."[48] He was the editor of the *Criterion*
and asked Gertrude two important questions: first, on what
authority did she use the split infinitive?—"Henry James,"
she replied—and second, would she contribute her very
latest piece to his magazine?

Gertrude's portrait of Eliot, which she brightly titled
"The Fifteenth of November," was long in appearing in the
Criterion, though Eliot professed continued interest in her
work.[49] In April 1926, he printed Edith Sitwell's laudatory
review of *The Making of Americans*, in which she called
the book "the product of one of the richest, and at the
same time most subtle, minds of our time. . . . It is the
history of the growth, the flowering, and the decay of all of
us." By the next year, however, Eliot himself had changed
his mind about Gertrude. "As a person," he wrote in one
issue, "Miss Stein equally resents agreement and curiosity,

any attitude in fact except one of devotion and faith. . . . She recalls the sophists rather than Socrates."[50]

Inevitably, Alice preferred Edith Sitwell to T. S. Eliot. She even liked an earlier review by Sitwell of Gertrude's *Geography and Plays*, which appeared in the *Athenaeum*. "The review was long and a little condescending but I liked it," she admitted.[51]

"To sum up the book as far as possible," Edith Sitwell had written, "I find in it an almost insuperable amount of silliness, an irritating ceaseless rattle like that of American sightseers talking in a boarding-house (this being, I imagine, a deliberate effect), great bravery, a certain real originality, and a few flashes of exquisite beauty. . . ." The ceaseless rattle of American tourists was a theme that James had used in *A Bundle of Letters,* a collection which Alice knew, and Sitwell's recognition of the originality and beauty in Gertrude's work no doubt pleased her.

When the editor of the *Athenaeum* brought her to meet Gertrude, their friendship warmed immediately. Gertrude thought Edith had the mind of a man[52] and Edith thought Gertrude was a literary pioneer. Alice, like most who met Edith, was impressed by her unusual appearance. ". . . She looked like nobody under the sun, very tall, rather the height of a grenadier, with marked features and the most beautiful nose any woman had."[53]

At the rue de Fleurus one day, Edith met one of their young painter friends, the erratic Pavel Tchelitchew, and there began, Alice noted, a long and violent affair. Gertrude was rightly concerned about the liaison and warned her new friend, "The fact that you have met Tchelitchew at my house does not mean that I will be responsible for him."[54]

Alice disliked the young Russian at once. "Pavlik was not interested in life as he saw it, as it was. . . . He wanted to use it. . . . Pavlik was a dreadful little arriviste. . . . As I see him beside other men of his generation, his attitude toward life wasn't clear. If you get into Pavlik deeply, you'd find a weakness," she told an interviewer later. Her first objection to him was his haircut, but as she knew him better, she found other faults: he was, for example, malicious.[55] Gertrude, though, was interested in him because, she told him, she didn't understand what he was doing.

And Edith Sitwell thought he was "tragic, haunted and noble . . . one of the most generous human beings" she knew.[56]

Tchelitchew was brought to meet Gertrude in 1925, two years after he arrived in Paris from his native Russia—via Kiev and Berlin—after the Bolshevik Revolution of 1917. He began his career as a scenic designer, quickly moving into whatever mode of art was fashionable at the time. His paintings were often terrifying and grotesque, reflections, some thought, of his multiple inner demons. He seemed most comfortable, both artistically and emotionally, among the surrealists.

To Alice he was a derivative artist and a dangerous personality. Fortunately Gertrude's interest in his work quickly waned, and Tchelitchew's interest in Gertrude was diverted by Edith Sitwell, who took Gertrude's place as publicizer and patron. Tchelitchew was very much aware of Alice's disapproval. Years later, lecturing at an exhibition of Gertrude's paintings, he told his audience that one reason for his talk was to show "Miss Alice B. Toklas, the faithful companion of Gertrude Stein, that painters not only paint but also can think sometimes."[57]

Though he declared an abiding affection for Gertrude, his portrayal of her in his monstrous world-view *Phenomena* caricatures her as an Indian chief surrounded by broken canvases, sitting beside Alice, who is demoniacally knitting. His artistic rendering of his friend is incongruous with his claim that she was good, kind, thoughtful, and feminine and reminded him of his dearly beloved mother.

In addition to his other faults, he had the misfortune of being Russian, one of the nationalities to which Alice was unsympathetic. She was not surprised, then, that he was "absolutely cannibal" in his relationships, counting among his victims even his sister Choura, whom Alice thought lovely, mysterious, and tragic, and who later refused to see her because of Alice's hostile treatment of her brother.

Tchelitchew's one redeeming act was introducing Gertrude and Alice to René Crevel, one of Alice's favorite young men. "I adored him," she wrote, "he was blue-eyed and demi-blond, with irregular features that made him look like a sailor. He spoke very quickly and brilliantly and made sharp gestures. He was, alas, tubercular."[58] Forced to spend the winters in a Davos sanitarium, he sent lonely letters to his friends in Paris, whimsically illustrated with hearts and flowers.[59] His tousled fair hair, his charming way of calling Alice "Miss Touclas" endeared him to her; and his suicide in 1935 seemed, to many who knew him, the inevitable consequence of his too trusting heart.

Far different from the aspiring young men who clustered around Gertrude Stein were the women who met at the rue Jacob mansion of Natalie Clifford Barney. Barney's Académie des Femmes was conceived as a female counterpart to the all-male French Academy, and the readings and presentations which she held in her salon were offered, ostensibly, to bring about a better entente between French and American writers and artists. Her gatherings were notorious for the guests, including ladies in suits and ties, who would retire by couples to private rooms throughout the evening. Her private Isle of Lesbos on the Left Bank was featured in the privately printed roman à clef The Lady's Almanack, Djuna Barnes's account of Barney's circle. Charming, blond, and wealthy, Natalie Barney was born in Dayton, Ohio, in 1877. She came to Paris at the turn of the century after realizing that she could not live among American women, who, she thought, were born with a Bible in their mouth.[60] Paris provided her with attractive company—the poetess Renée Vivien, artist Romaine Brooks, and writer Elizabeth de Gramont, the Duchess of Clermont-Tonnerre. "Upon the disorders of my life I have built my throne," she boasted.[61] And for her epitaph, she suggested, "She was the friend of men and the lover of women, which for people full of ardor and drive is better than the other way around." Alice, who admired her independence, followed with amusement her succession of love affairs, the last beginning when Natalie was eighty. Alice thought it astounding.[62]

"At Natalie Barney's there were many comfortable chairs and a very large round table where tea was served," Alice remembered. The refreshments often featured a velvety chocolate cake from Colombin's, served, in season, in a Grecian temple of friendship in the garden.

Natalie's colorful reputation had come largely through a series of letters which began to appear in the Mercure de

France in 1910. Written by the poet and novelist Rémy de Gourmont, they were directed to an undisclosed woman called only L'Amazone. The object of his adoration was Natalie Barney.

Natalie, who habitually rode in the Bois de Boulogne each morning, had a personality as overpowering as her stature on her horse. The aging poet, who would die only a few years after he met her, was stimulated by her charm, vivacity, and wit, and his adoring letters were an expression of love disassociated from the carnal. One of the great moments in human history, he thought, was Christianity's separation of carnal pleasure from the idea of love. With that shift of consciousness, man rose to a higher level of humanity. "The Egyptians were so far incapable of understanding such a disassociation," he wrote, "that the love of a brother and sister would have seemed nothing to them if it had not led to sexual intercourse."

With Natalie, who was involved in love affairs with various women throughout the time he knew her, he had no fear that his idealized love would fall from its state of grace. Much of the talk at Natalie's gatherings, in fact, was Lesbian gossip; and Gertrude and Alice often discussed Natalie with their own friends. Gertrude, who was always interested in Natalie's latest attachment, listened attentively as one of her friends wondered, "Well, here she is a world-famous Lesbian practitioner, but who does she do it with and where does she get 'em?" Alice replied with her usual wit, "I think from the toilets of the Louvre Department Store," but apparently the answer did not satisfy Gertrude's curiosity. Sometime afterward, on one of her walks around the quarter, Gertrude met a woman who happened to be, coincidentally, Natalie's lover of the moment, and began questioning her about Natalie in front of a café where all could hear. When Gertrude's indiscretion got back to Natalie, she was furious. At her next opportunity, when Lesbians were being identified and Gertrude and Alice were mentioned, Natalie burst out, "Oh, nothing like that there at all. It's entirely innocent." She had taken her revenge.[63]

At Natalie's salon, Alice and Gertrude met the Duchess of Clermont-Tonnerre, who soon began appearing at the rue de Fleurus. The model for Proust's Duchesse de Guermantes, she was statuesque, and one of the few women who, after the First War, still had long hair. One evening, however, she arrived at one of Gertrude's gatherings very late, with her hair cut. "Do you like it?" she asked Gertrude. "I do," Gertrude replied, and that night, decided to follow the fashion. "Cut it off," she said to Alice. Alice did.

One of Alice's worries after the war was Mildred Aldrich. Always in a precarious financial state, Mildred suddenly disclosed that a small annuity she had been receiving had been cut off. Her situation was so serious that she considered leaving her home in Huiry, and her friends were concerned about her future. Having succeeded in obtaining for her the Legion of Honor, they now set to ensuring her income. Alice and Gertrude, especially, scoured their friends to try to secure the needed money. Gertrude wrote to the editor of the *Atlantic Monthly*, who, Alice said, showed "bad taste" in advertising for funds in the magazine. But he did raise money. Mildred, however, felt somewhat humiliated by accepting charity. "You would not let me go elegantly to the poorhouse," she told Gertrude, "and I would have gone elegantly, but you have turned this into a poorhouse and I am the sole inmate." Mildred, whose gentle nature won Alice's affection, always became "rather weak in gratitude" from kindnesses. A few years before she died, she learned that her house was to be occupied by a young family after she was gone. Her happiness was complete. "I should love to think of young people enjoying what I have loved," she wrote to Gertrude.

Alice, Gertrude, and their friend William Cook were with Mildred when she died. Her neighbor and housekeeper had phoned to tell them that Mildred had had a heart attack, and the three drove to Huiry, then back to the American Hospital at Neuilly. She was buried in the small village where she had spent her last years.

The continuing problem of finding a publisher for Gertrude's work persisted throughout the twenties. Of the many small publishing houses begun in Paris and New York, Contact Editions seemed a likely outlet for her writing. "At intervals of two weeks to six months, or six years," its editors decided, "we will bring out books by various writers who seem not likely to be published by other publishers, for commercial or legislative reasons. . . . These books are published simply because they are written, and we like them well enough to get them out."

Contact Editions grew from the journal *contact*, coedited by Robert McAlmon and William Carlos Williams in New York. Transplanted to Paris, the press helped launch Hemingway, Hilda Doolittle, Ezra Pound, Dorothy Richardson, and Edith Sitwell. McAlmon had been in Paris for several years before he was invited to tea at the rue de Fleurus. Expecting to dislike Gertrude, he was surprised to find her "almost shy" and left her studio "thinking that one could become fond of Gertrude Stein if she would quit being the oracle, descend from the throne-chair, and not grow panicky every time someone doubted her statements, or even bluntly disagreed." He had been favorably impressed by *Three Lives*, disclosed that he had "a suspended respect" for her other work, and felt that her critics had not presented her in the best light. ". . . All of the articles I've seen on you insist too much on a quality you undoubtedly have, that of refreshing the language and of sensitizing it, but it strikes me they don't dwell enough on the zip of intelligence, and whoop of personality power, you get in *The Making of Americans* and 'Melanctha,'" one of the stories in *Three Lives*.

As Gertrude and Alice had hoped, the "whoop" of Gertrude's personality was enough to persuade McAlmon to accept for publication *The Making of Americans*. Gertrude promised fifty subscribers to help underwrite the cost of printing, and she and Alice agreed to proofread the entire book themselves. But when the five hundred bound copies were ready, McAlmon found that he was left with an unsalable tome. He claimed that Gertrude never tried to attract subscribers; Alice later declared that McAlmon was "irresponsibly drunk" throughout the entire episode. "Contrary to your verbal statements that you would help rid us of your volume, you have done nothing," he wrote to Gertrude, and he became even more enraged when she ordered the entire shipment sent to New York for distribution by another publisher, without ensuring payment for McAlmon himself. He threatened to pulp the volumes which she had not already given as gifts to friends and reviewers—but never did.

The publication was still another failure to bring Gertrude to a larger readership and, equally important, to make money. Still they had no one to depend on but friends. Shortly after the publication of *The Making of Americans*, Edith Sitwell invited Gertrude to speak at Cambridge and Oxford, and Harold Acton, president of the "Ordinary," Oxford's literary society, seconded the invitation. In May, Gertrude and Alice left for London.

They were honored at a party given by Edith Sitwell and her brother Osbert, whom Alice thought delightful if prosaic. Osbert, Alice remembered, was of great comfort to the nervous Gertrude. "He so thoroughly understood every possible way in which one could be nervous that as he sat beside her in the hotel telling her all the kinds of ways that he and she could suffer from stage fright she was quite soothed."

On June 5, 1926, Gertrude sent a message to friends in Paris: "Here is where I did it," she wrote, "about 100 in audience and it lasted about 2 hours, and I did not get scared and Alice was quite proud of me. . . ."[64] Her lecture at Jesus College, Cambridge, and the one following at Oxford left the audience entranced. "Composition As Explanation," which she claimed to have written in a garage while waiting for her Ford to be repaired, was uncharacteristically intelligible. "The illusion that we were living in a continuous present was certainly there," Acton remarked. "When the reading came to an end life moved considerably faster." She had successfully dispelled the prevailing image the students had of her.

Owing to the critics [Acton wrote] the popular conception of Gertrude Stein was of an eccentric visionary, a literary Madame Blavatsky in fabulous clothes, the triumph of the dream and escape from life personified, with bells on her fingers as well as on her toes, or a mermaid swathed in tinsel, smoking drugged cigarettes through an exaggerated cigarette holder, or a Gioconda who had had her face lifted so often that it was fixed in a smile beyond the nightmares of Leonardo da Vinci. One was aware of the rapid deflation of these conceptions, as Gertrude surpassed them by her appearance, a squat Aztec figure in obsidian, growing more monumental as soon as she sat down. With her tall bodyguard of Sitwells and the gipsy acolyte, she made a memorable entry.[65]

The "Ordinaries" came away thinking her a brilliant exponent of Modernity, a refreshing diversion from normal Oxford fare. Gertrude was able to handle the assault of questions with a calm, motherly assurance of her own artistic beliefs. ". . . We are having a beautiful time," Alice wrote to friends back home: Gertrude was again a lion.

But Alice was becoming more and more concerned that Gertrude's rising reputation was not bringing in any money. Gertrude mentioned Alice's feelings in "A Diary," written the year after the English lectures. "She . . . asked me if I would not like to receive . . . a great deal of money and I agreed, I certainly would find it to be a very great pleasure to be abundantly paid. She and this was in another case told me I should not give anything away for nothing and I would very much like not to do so."[66]

In 1924, Daniel-Henry Kahnweiler suggested the idea of his publishing some of Gertrude's work. He saw in her pieces the same quality that he found in the paintings of the cubists or in the music of Schönberg. "In Gertrude's case," he wrote, "it was a question of language, or more exactly of English vocabulary. The poetry with her comes from an entirely new use of this vocabulary, no longer accepting any law antecedent to the act of creation but freeing this act and leaving it abandoned to its interior logic."[67] *A Book Concluding With As A Wife Has A Cow. A Love Story* seemed suited to his taste and it was published in 1926. But the limited edition, illustrated with Juan Gris's lithographs, again was not meant for a large audience. It was, instead, a sentimental souvenir of a friendship.

Juan Gris, who died the year after the book was published, was among Gertrude's favorites. Alice had a special devotion toward him and credited him with heightened intuition that was a part of his artistic nature. Even beyond his knowledge of his art, he seemed to have a deep understanding of other people, a rare and gentle concern that she always felt.[68] When he died of uremia, at forty, both Alice and Gertrude were deeply grieved. They knew that he felt his work was still incomplete, and they knew, also, that he had suffered greatly.[69]

But the slim volume, though treasured, would not meet their expenses. Nor would the volume published by Leonard and Virginia Woolf's Hogarth Press in 1926, the transcription of Gertrude's English lecture, "Composition As Explanation." Nor would the publication of several pieces in *transition*, the journal founded in 1926 by Eugene and Maria Jolas, and coedited by Elliot Paul. And even when John Brewer, an English publisher, agreed to bring out a volume of Gertrude's work in 1928, the results were disappointing. Payson & Clarke published *Useful Knowledge*, but Brewer did little to advertise the book. When sales did not reach his expectations, "instead of continuing and gradually creating a public for Gertrude Stein's work," he did nothing.[70]

Alice was convinced, finally, that if Gertrude were to be a success it would have to be her own doing. She decided to become publisher, director, and managing editor of her own press, which would be devoted to only one author: Gertrude. Tired of shoving the unshovable,[71] they decided to take it upon themselves to make Gertrude's reputation in the literary world. Alice asked Gertrude to invent a name for the firm, and Gertrude, laughing, said, "call it Plain Edition."[72] Alice did the rest.

"All that I knew about what I would have to do was that I would have to get the book printed and then to get it distributed, that is sold," she said. Clearly, she needed advice, and she began to ask all their friends about publishing. For a short while, she thought of working with someone else on her project, but quickly saw that no one could meet her standards. ". . . I decided to do it all by myself."

To finance the venture, Gertrude sold a painting, Picasso's *Girl with a Fan*, which saddened Alice, but there was little choice. In the postwar art market, Picasso brought the best price. Alice chose for her first book *Lucy Church Amiably*, a novel which Gertrude completed in 1927, and engaged the Union Printery on the rue Méchain for the printing and binding of the volume. Publicity, she knew, was everything. Armed with a list of American booksellers, she began sending advance notices of the first offering of her press. She wrote to Bennett Cerf, asking if Random

House would distribute the edition, but he replied that "at the price she was paying for printing and the price they could ask for it it was not interesting."[73]

Lucy Church Amiably, offered at three dollars—less a thirty-percent discount for book dealers—was described simply as "a novel," with no reference to its stylistic eccentricities. Alice pointed to Edmund Wilson's "detailed article" on Gertrude in his recently published *Axel's Castle*, but must have hoped that booksellers would remember only the positive remarks and not Wilson's more qualified comments. "Most of us balk at her soporific rigmaroles, her echolaliac incantations, her half-witted-sounding catalogues of numbers," Wilson wrote, "most of us read her less and less. Yet remembering especially her early work, we are still always aware of her presence in the background of contemporary literature. . . . And whenever we pick up her writings, however unintelligible we may find them, we are aware of a literary personality of unmistakable originality and distinction." Though he admitted that Gertrude wrote nonsense, he did add that "one should not talk about 'nonsense' until one has decided what 'sense' consists of. . . ."[74]

Optimistically, Alice had one thousand copies of *Lucy Church Amiably* printed. The book was ready by January 1931, and Alice was faced with the larger problem of making it known and selling it. Her letters to American booksellers resulted in a few orders; she found distribution in English bookstores in Paris fairly easy. Gertrude took to wandering about the city, looking for copies of the book in shopwindows, and reporting back to Alice. "This event," Alice said, "gave Gertrude Stein a childish delight amounting almost to ecstasy."[75]

But Alice was still unsatisfied with the venture and, with her next book, decided to confront her problems more professionally. For *How To Write*, a collection of short pieces, she looked for another firm for the printing and binding because she had been displeased by the quality of the Union Printery work. At a party, she met Maurice Darantière, formerly of Dijon, who had begun a press in Paris. Because he was one of France's master printers, Alice told him her troubles only to ask for his opinion, since she thought she could not afford to hire him. But his idea of printing the books "on good but not too expensive paper" and binding them in paper and providing sturdy slipcases seemed practicable. "And I will be able to sell them at a reasonable price," she asked. "Yes, you will see," Darantière assured her.[76]

Alice's press published a limited edition also: one hundred copies of *Before the Flowers of Friendship Faded*, thirty-six pages, autographed and numbered, which sold easily at four dollars each. By 1930, Gertrude—with Alice's help—had accumulated enough broken friendships to make the title appropriate.

The piece was originally supposed to be a translation of *Enfances*, a poem by their friend Georges Hugnet. Even Alice admitted that Hugnet was devoted to Gertrude's work and he had translated—"so he felt," she added— some of Gertrude's portraits. Hugnet, like Hemingway, was handsome and appealing. "Hugnet's big black eyes were like a mechanical toy," she thought, "they wandered about his white face in the manner of the man in the moon."[77] Gertrude's rendering of *Enfances* was more interpretation than translation and included some romantic passages which apparently frightened Alice. Claiming that she "wanted only to protect Gertrude,"[78] Alice manipulated the break with Hugnet by inciting Gertrude to argue over the placement of her name in the final publication. The quarrel went beyond a literary disagreement, however, and marked the end of the friendship. When Gertrude later published her translation, it bore a title suggested by Alice.

In a restaurant one day, Alice overheard two Frenchwomen gossiping, one saying to the other, "Before friendship fades, the flowers of friendship fade. . . ." Realizing how appropriate the idea was to Gertrude's situation, she translated the sentence for Gertrude, and Gertrude took it as her own.

The break with Hugnet was not unusual. Mabel Dodge and Ernest Hemingway had been ousted. Tchelitchew had been rejected. Leo was long gone. The case of Bravig Imbs was typical. He had come to Paris from Dartmouth, worked as a proofreader for two American newspapers, and met Gertrude and Alice late in 1926. Brought to the studio by Tchelitchew's sister Choura, he was given over to Alice at first, who nearly hypnotized him with her constant flow of conversation. Alice, he saw, "acted both as sieve and buckler; she defended Gertrude from the bores and most of the new people were strained through her before Gertrude had any prolonged conversation with them." Alice found out everything she needed to know to make a judgment, a process which took, Imbs recalled, about three minutes. ". . . She would dart questions like arrows . . . would know your place of birth, your environment, your family, your connections, your education, and your immediate intentions. And she never forgot what she acquired. I remember, years later, when conversation would come to a dead center and Gertrude seemed to have nothing to say, I had only to ask some questions about an American family in Paris, and Alice would spend the rest of the evening giving their history with most complete and fascinating detail."

Though he would have preferred to talk with Gertrude, Imbs realized that Alice was important, and he "nodded and yessed and noed while Alice . . . talked on and on. . . ." Finally, Alice released him and, in his brief contact with Gertrude, found her pleasant and accessible. His ultimate assessment of the two, made after five years of friendship, was that Alice, "elegant and detached," had a much surer feeling for painting than did Gertrude, though Gertrude managed to acquire the reputation for her feeling for art. "Her flair was for people," Imbs thought, "and particularly for genius. . . . Her capacity for sizing up a person's character in a relatively brief time was of an uncanny precision. . . . She was always much more interested in the painter than in what he was doing and she measured his artistic worth by the amount of his resistance to her." When Gertrude sold her Matisses to buy more Picassos, Imbs thought it was her feeling for the Spaniard, more than her love of his work, which prompted her devotion. Alice, on the other hand, came to a definite opinion of Matisse as an artist: "He never knew what size canvas to use," she told Imbs.

Alice's cooling toward Imbs began at a party when she ran to tell him some fiery bit of gossip about some people they both knew. But he put her off, saying he didn't want to hear about it and would rather find out for himself.[79] Though he could be amusing and helpful, Alice had no plans for his usefulness. A mistake, it was clear, would not be forgiven, and in 1931 Imbs made his mistake.

Alice and Gertrude were spending some months at Bilignin, their country home in Belley, a small village in Savoy. Imbs had brought his pregnant wife Valeska to a boardinghouse nearby, and it was obvious to Gertrude and Alice that they would be present throughout the final stages of her pregnancy. Gertrude's aversion to childbirth apparently was well known to everyone but Imbs. And Alice's swift termination of the friendship left him stunned.[80]

Annette Rosenshine, on successive visits to Paris in the twenties, noted for herself Alice's power over Gertrude. In 1920, on her way to Zurich, where she was to be analyzed by an associate of Jung, she stopped to see Gertrude. Her brief stay allowed her time for a ride through the city in Gertrude's Ford, and Annette "was surprised to find that Alice seemed to be in the driving seat, directing Gertrude and deciding what streets would hold the most interest for me." In 1928, she again visited Paris and was invited to the rue de Fleurus for tea.

> The day of the tea, as I entered the room with a smart new Paris hat and my best antique earrings, Gertrude rose to greet the stranger. In a split second she recognized her mistake. I was not a stranger, but her past psychological experiment.[81]

But from the moment she sat down, she realized that she was being deftly eliminated from Gertrude's life—by Alice. "It was first-rate team work," she said. "It was most evident that Alice with her fine Italian hand would manipulate and plan my visits, Gertrude would merely recognize my presence. The door was not closed but I realized Gertrude was completely disinterested."[82]

One evening, especially, Alice's feelings were most apparent. With her San Franciscan friend Lawrence Strauss, whom she had known in Paris in 1906, Annette came to the rue de Fleurus with a few samples of her sculpture, hoping to spur Gertrude's interest in her work. As they entered the salon, they noticed that Gertrude was writing;

they were taken by Alice to the opposite side of the room, where Strauss unpacked Annette's sculptures and showed them to Alice. Her response, Annette remembered, "was dead silence." Then, as Gertrude got up from her work, Alice switched off the overhead light, putting the room in semidarkness. Only one small lamp illuminated a far corner of the room. Annette's sculpture was hidden in obscurity.[83]

Annette was hurt and confused by what she thought were Gertrude's feelings against her. "Naively clinging to my Victorian feeling about friendship, I kept trying to imagine what dire unpardonable sin I had committed that made her wipe out all traces of her help to me." Only later did she realize that Alice was carrying out her own feelings, ending with finality Annette's formerly close friendship with Gertrude.[84]

Alice's vigilance was also directed to a benign cause. With Gertrude, she shared in the care of two young boys, nephews of Margaret Anderson, the editor of the *Little Review*. Fritz and Tom Peters were the sons of Margaret's sister, Lois Peters, who was hospitalized in 1923 and could no longer care for her children. With her friend Jane Heap, Margaret undertook the task and brought the children to Paris. But when the two women had to return to New York in 1925, they asked Gertrude and Alice to watch over the boys, who were living at the Gurdjieff Institute for the Harmonious Development of Man, run by the Russian faith healer, Gurdjieff.

Margaret, Alice thought, was so emotional that she frequently became inarticulate. She had fierce hatreds and equally strong loves and she often pursued her beliefs with outsized passion. In 1921, she was tried and convicted for obscenity when she serialized *Ulysses*; for fifteen years she edited the *Little Review*, until one day in 1921, the Paris *Tribune* quoted her reason for discontinuing the magazine. ". . . Even the artist doesn't know what he is talking about," she said. "And I can no longer go on publishing a magazine in which no one really knows what he is talking about. . . ." Alice was more comfortable with Jane Heap, though she did not sympathize with her interest in Gurdjieff.

Fritz Peters, eleven, was surprised when Jane told him that Gertrude was going to be "watcher-over or something." But after he met her, he found her wonderful. He was, however, "a little scared of Alice. She came and went so mysteriously. And although she often came in bearing some wonderful cake or other concoction I gave Gertrude the credit for it. I knew Alice was doing it for her." The two women took the boys all over Paris, and during the winter of 1925–26 they visited the rue de Fleurus every other Thursday. Their visits commenced with Thanksgiving, when Alice traditionally made a stuffed turkey.

Gertrude, however, as much as she liked the children, was not pleased with the way they were being brought up. She argued with Jane about their living at the Institute, and finally felt she could no longer take a role in their lives. She visited them alone and handed Fritz a box of candy which she explained was a farewell gift. She said she wanted to see him, rather than say good-bye in a letter, but that both she and Alice would not be coming again.

Fifteen

SINCE 1923, Gertrude and Alice had revisited Belley, first staying at the Hôtel Pernollet, famous for its cuisine, which figures in Gertrude's works. The waitresses Zénobie, Marie Jeanne, and Hélène; the maids, Thérèse-Joséphine and Louise; and a local horticulturist, Fred Genevrey, who provided the ladies with fresh flowers—all make sporadic appearances. Gertrude and Alice liked the region so well they extended their stays from April through the grape harvest in the fall.

In 1926, driving around the countryside, they glimpsed a house that they wished could be their own. "I will drive you up there and you can go and tell them that we will take their house," Gertrude told Alice, seeing no obstacle to the fulfillment of her wish. When she noticed that curtains were floating from the window, Alice suggested, "I think that proves someone is living there." But Gertrude continued undaunted. Alice managed to keep her from the house that day, but they did ascertain that the occupant was an army officer who rented the house, and that it could be theirs if by some chance the officer were transferred.

By 1929 the officer had, indeed, been transferred, and though Alice admitted that her conscience sometimes troubled her, she revealed that she and Gertrude had been the cause of his moving. "We talked to the owner of the house who plainly showed he considered us quite mad," she explained, "but he told us that his tenant was a captain, and that there were too many majors in the battalion. That was enough to inspire us. We would get two influential friends in Paris to have him promoted, he would be ordered to another garrison and the house would be free for us." Somehow the two friends arranged for the officer to be tested for a promotion, but to Alice's dismay, the officer failed. "Don't worry," she was told. Another test could be arranged in three months. But again he failed. Clearly, another path had to be explored. At this point, a raise in pay was suggested, compensation for transfer to Africa. "The captain accepted, the friends became active again and soon we were ecstatically tenants of a house which we had never seen nearer than two miles away."[85]

Though the house needed some modernization, both Gertrude and Alice thought it lovely. From the first summer they were there, Alice worked untiringly in her garden, experimenting with various vegetables, sifting the advice of her neighbors, and providing their many guests with a young and tender harvest. At first she dismissed the counsel of her neighbors, thinking them superstitious. "They told me never to transplant parsley and not to plant it on Good Friday," she recalled. "We did it in California," she replied weakly, but the farmers' opinions were unshakable. "They said not to plant at the moment of the new or full moon," to which she answered impatiently, "The seed would be as indifferent as I. . . ." But before long, she found that they were often right. "Experience is never at a bargain price," she decided, and she became weather-wise and a firm believer in local lore.

The first year was spent cleaning out the rubbish, weeding, clearing the terrace of snakes' nests, and planning the garden plots. Though she uncovered some snakes as well as their habitats, she found, too, that strawberries and raspberries still grew near the house. With the help of a village boy for the heavy work, she began to turn and fertilize the soil. But the parched topsoil frequently blew away, and new weeds implanted themselves from the airborne seeds from neighbors' gardens. "The weeds remained a tormenting backbreaking experience all the summers we spent at Bilignin," Alice wrote, though she was able to joke about it with Gertrude, who had the easier job of tending the hedges and flowers. "What do you see when you close your eyes," Gertrude would ask Alice. And Alice replied, "Weeds."[86]

Her gardening began soon after her morning coffee, taken at about six. For an hour she would gather strawberries for Gertrude's breakfast; guests, if they wanted fresh berries, were invited to gather them for themselves. Beginning in May, she would harvest salad vegetables and herbs. ". . . Radishes and herbs made me feel like a mother about her baby," she sighed. "How could anything so beautiful be mine." With each successive vegetable, her wonder would increase. "There is nothing that is comparable to it, as satisfactory or as thrilling," she decided, "as gathering the vegetables one has grown."[87] Gertrude's success, of course, was an exception.

By the time they moved into the house at Bilignin, the ménage had increased by one: a white poodle puppy with blue eyes and a pink nose. Alice, who had read *The Princess Casamassima* years before, had always wanted a white poodle; and because he seemed elegant enough to carry a basket of flowers in his mouth, suggested his name. Basket was more manageable than Polybe had been. Though he grew large and leggy, he liked to climb onto Gertrude's lap and rest there for hours.

Not long after Basket joined them, they were given another dog, a Chihuahua, by their friend Francis Picabia. This dog was called Byron because, Gertrude explained, he was to be mated with either his sister or his mother. But Byron died suddenly one night, and Picabia replaced him with another Chihuahua, this time named Pépé. Though Basket had a moment of intense jealousy when Pépé first arrived, they soon lived in peaceful coexistence.

Francis Picabia, Alice thought, had a definite talent, though his paintings were sometimes shocking. His appearance was incongruous with his work: small, plump, he reminded some of a Basque ball player or a Spanish peasant. His skin was rough and dark, owing to his Cuban heritage; his eyes large and round; his hair white. He looked too well-fed to be a revolutionary artist. "I've never seen such a rational sort of man in front of painting that seems so irrational," one gallery owner told him. On his canvases, one might find an eye on a buttock, a dolphin swimming into a woman's mouth, the *American Girl* as a spark plug. "Life," he wrote once, "has nothing to do with what the grammarians call *Beauty*."

Picabia's pleasant friendship with Alice and Gertrude lacked the intensity of their relationship with his friend Francis Rose, whose paintings they had seen in the late twenties at the gallery of Jean Bonjean. Shortly afterward, Gertrude and Alice were invited to tea by Méraude Guevara, a painter friend of Picabia. ". . . There is going to be someone at the house that you will want to meet," she told them. "Francis Rose." Though Gertrude claimed she was not interested in meeting new artists at the time, she and Alice accepted.

When Rose arrived, he heard a great commotion coming from the drawing room, and was greeted by the sight of a large black and white dog chasing a smaller dog, and a very large white poodle chasing the black and white dog. Besides the melee caused by the animals, all the people in the room were standing and shouting, adding to the din— except, Francis noted, "for one woman . . . in the middle of the room quietly eating a cake." When she finished eating, Gertrude turned to Francis and asked calmly, "You are Francis Rose! Do you want to see your pictures?" Surprised, he said yes, and was taken across the threshold of the famed 27, rue de Fleurus.

> We went through a porte-cochere with a shabby concierge's lodge in which sat an old concierge wearing a postman's cap and blue workman's trousers; the small flagged courtyard we crossed was shabbier still, and facing us was a large lock-up studio which might have been a garage or workshop with a small residence attached.
>
> The studio was higher than it was wide; the furniture was heavy and Renaissance; a great sofa and armchairs stuffed with horsehair filled the middle; two tiny Louis XV chairs stood near-by; they were covered with jewel-like petit-point tapestry, one in bright yellow, black, and red, the other in green and white. These were the work of Alice Toklas from the designs Picasso had painted on the canvas. The atmosphere was like that of a cultured Spanish house—but the walls! The walls were covered tier over tier with paintings, one over the other until one could hardly see them near the ceiling. Paintings of the kind that only people who love paint will have. . . .
>
> On entering the studio for the first time, I immediately noticed an ostrich egg made into a lamp with the shade of Negro raffia-work, and next to it, an egg-cup

and spoon cast in lead, painted with dots. It was the first sculpture collage, made by Picasso.

His eye then moved from one painting to the next, Picasso's, Juan Gris's—and then his own.

Next to these pictures hung three rows of paintings which made me feel bewildered and alone; I had forgotten painting most of these pictures, and nothing is more tiresome for an artist than seeing his finished works. The shepherd sleeping in the ruins painted in 1928 on absorbent board, the little chair painted in 1929, Byron meditating, the big blue man, L'Italienne, a fog at sea, a river in Spain (which was painted in Brittany)—in fact I cannot remember all my pictures that were there.[88]

Francis, Alice noticed, "flushed rosy" at the sight of his paintings on the walls next to Picasso's. There was a winning quality about the twenty-year-old painter, and Gertrude consulted Alice about him. "Yes," she said, "Francis must come again."

When they met, Rose was living in Montmartre in one room papered with black tar paper and draped with black oilcloth curtains. He had recently begun smoking opium, which he thought "clears the mind, gives peace, removes nervousness and indecision, and destroys neurotic complexes and pain."[89] Though he traced his career as an artist to his somewhat erratic childhood when he painted "dreams, flowers and lots of moons and suns," he marked the beginning of his life as 1925 when, at sixteen, he visited his mother at her villa in Villefranche and met Cocteau and Christian Bérard. Comfortable in their surreality, he attained a reputation for being "exotic" and even mentally unbalanced. Gertrude agreed that he was sometimes unbalanced, but added that he was "elegant . . . and intelligent." Francis described himself even more kindly: "That I am wildly passionate and do everything with a fervour is true; that I romance I am willing to admit; but that I am unbalanced and weak is false." With his romantic nature, he immediately became attached to Gertrude and Alice. Each

177

in her own way reminded him of his mother, who had recently died.

Gertrude supported his efforts in painting, arranged for him to meet artists she knew, and talked with him about "painting, people and herself." Alice plied him with tea and cookies. "She acted like a shadow behind Gertrude and was really the power behind the throne. It was she who always made the final decisions; whether it was concerning the dismissal of friends . . . or their reinstatement, but her real devotion was for Gertrude Stein's mind and this almost amounted to adoration."[90]

Though Francis's misadventures would one day be Alice's burden, their friendship at the beginning was loving. At Bilignin, they would go for rides in the country—Gertrude speeding on the narrow winding roads, and Alice clutching her hat; and Francis and Alice would endlessly pick berries, Francis bending while Alice walked beside him with her basket.

Evenings at Bilignin, Francis remembered, were quiet and homey, with Alice resting after her busy day, working on a needlepoint tapestry that Picasso had drawn for her. Her first petit-point, which Francis had noticed on the small chairs, had been designed at her timid suggestion. She was reticent about asking Picasso to draw a pattern for her, but Gertrude agreed that the results would be striking. "All right," Gertrude said, "I'll manage." When Picasso came by one day, Gertrude brought up the subject of Alice's needlework. "Alice wants to make a tapestry of that little picture," she said, pointing to one of his paintings, "and I said I would trace it for her." Picasso, of course, would have no one tamper with his work. ". . . If it is done by anybody . . . it will be done by me," he replied. Quickly, Gertrude placed a piece of tapestry in front of him. "Well, go to it."[91]

The piece she was working on the first summer that Francis visited was not her favorite. Picasso had given it to her as a gift and left her to choose the colors by herself. Picasso, she told Francis, had been unhappy about her choice of yellow, a criticism which upset Alice. While Alice worked on her needlepoint, Gertrude rocked slowly beside her, with Basket curled on her lap.

At Bilignin, Alice found, it was easier to surround Gertrude with amiable company than it was in Paris. Guests were invited singly or in twos or threes; there was none of the pressure of a crowded salon.

One of their favorite visitors was Bernard Faÿ. Faÿ, who came from a family of Catholic royalists, met Gertrude and Alice in 1926. Gertrude, he thought, was like a Roman emperor, and he felt immediately the power of her intelligence. Alice, dark, modest, nevertheless revealed a strong discernment and a stronger will.[92] The real nature of their relationship was apparent to him almost at once. "Between the two women," he saw, "one seemingly stronger and the other more frail, one affirming her genius and the other venerating it, one speaking and the other listening, only a blind man could ignore that the most vigorous one was Alice, and that Gertrude, for her behavior as much as for her work and publications, leaned on her, used her and followed her advice."[93]

He praised Gertrude in a 1930 article in *La Revue européenne* as "*le plus puissant écrivain américain d'aujourd'hui*," one who was singlehandedly conducting a great revolution in literary art. And he was in the process of translating *The Making of Americans*, a book he thought so fine that he feared the translation would be unable to convey its force. He had proven himself loyal and devoted to Gertrude, and for his efforts and emotional enthusiasm he was rewarded by Alice's approval.

"Alice," Faÿ saw, "kept house. On her fell the tedium of servants, provisions, upkeep and finances. Alice knew how to entertain, listen to, stimulate Gertrude and to calm her. She knew how to guide her and divert her. In a word, she gave her good advice. Even in her friendships, she played a discreet but influential role, because she drew in or rejected those who came near Gertrude, according to her own judgment."[94] Alice once tried to explain to Faÿ why she remained quiet during conversations. "I am always beaten in discussion," she told him.[95] It was necessary for her to prepare her answers well in advance of the moment she could say them—and she could not compete with Gertrude's quick retorts.

Gertrude and Alice had been brought to meet Faÿ by Virgil Thomson. It was Bernard Faÿ, Alice thought, who had helped Virgil Thomson become a Parisian. Faÿ had urged Thomson to come to Paris to study music after having heard him sing with the Harvard Glee Club. Thomson himself had been brought to the rue de Fleurus by George Antheil, the faun-like composer who interested neither of the two women. "Alice Toklas did not on first view care for me," Thomson recalled.[96] But Gertrude was warm to the young musician and kept seeing him. "Virgil," Alice said, "had a gift of producing an opera with only himself and a piano."[97] Eventually, he wrote the music for several of Gertrude's pieces: *Four Saints in Three Acts*, "Susie Asado," "Preciosilla," "Portrait of F.B.," "Capital Capitals," and *The Mother of Us All*.

Among the young men who brightened the summers was Paul Bowles, whom Alice and Gertrude called Freddy. Bernard Faÿ happened to be at dinner the first night Bowles arrived and was amused at Freddy's direct response to the question, "What does your father do?" "My father is a dentist," the young man replied with no reticence.[98]

Though Alice could not recall why she nicknamed him Freddy, Bowles later said that Gertrude simply could not call him Paul "because it was a romantic name and I didn't have one ounce of romanticism in me."[99] Always dressed in shorts and sneakers, Bowles shocked the villagers when he and Alice went to town.

Aaron Copland met Bowles at Bilignin and along with Gertrude and Alice tried to give the twenty-one-year-old writer and musician some direction. He seemed to be doing little professionally and that worried them. When he mentioned to Alice that he might go to Villefranche to visit Cocteau, she suggested that he travel, instead, to Tangier. Just as she had once sent Hemingway to Spain, her advice to Bowles opened up a new path in his life, and eventually he even bought an island off the coast of Algeria.

In Bilignin, Alice found the temperate climate she so much enjoyed, and a measure of peace and contentment that she could not find in a city. But whatever respite Bilignin provided, Alice had her real work in Paris.

Plain Edition had gone on to publish two more volumes —*Operas and Plays* and *Matisse, Picasso and Gertrude Stein*—but Alice despaired of inspiring serious reviews of Gertrude's work. Parodies were becoming common, and these, in their way, pleased Gertrude: she thought that she had proven unforgettable to her detractors. But they irked Alice. There were few who wrote about Gertrude as if she were an artist—only friends like Sherwood Anderson, Edith Sitwell, Carl Van Vechten, and Bernard Faÿ.

Despite the loyalty of a few who tried to publicize Gertrude's writing, she could boast only her faithful small audience and, at fifty-eight years old, was still far from real fame. Alice was impatient and saw that if Gertrude were to have success it would come only through a popular book. But the last conventional work that Gertrude had published was *Three Lives*, her first book. Of all the manuscripts that she pulled out of her cupboard, there was just one that met the general criteria of intelligibility, and this Alice would never permit to be printed.

Until 1931, Alice did not know of the existence of *Quod Erat Demonstrandum*, or *Things As They Are*, which Gertrude had written in 1903, buried at the bottom of her pile of work and claimed to have forgotten until she accidentally found it one day. The novel was a faithful rendering of Gertrude's first love affair—never consummated—with a fellow student at Johns Hopkins, May Bookstaver.

May was an independent young woman not unlike Viola Startup, the student Alice admired at the University of Washington. May was daring as a horsewoman, impetuous, defiant of her family. She found Gertrude innocent and naïve, spurned her for another woman, and left Gertrude deeply hurt. *Q.E.D.* was probably written to exorcise the pain of rejection and, Alice said, was closely based on May's letters to Gertrude.

The novel's epigraph is taken from *As You Like It* (Act V, Scene ii), Shakespeare's comedy of mistaken identity and women protesting their love for other women disguised as men. Phebe, a shepherdess, is in love with Ganymede, who is actually Rosalind, the banished daughter of a duke, in disguise. Orlando, a well-born young man, also loves Rosalind. Silvius, a shepherd, is in love with Phebe and has the unhappy task of delivering Phebe's love letter to Ganymede (Rosalind). Ganymede, or Rosalind, mocking the young woman's declaration of love, reads the letter to Silvius, who of course is despondent that his beloved loves another.

Phe:	Youth, you have done me much ungentleness,
	To show the letter that I writ to you.
Ros:	I care not if I have: it is my study
	To seem despiteful and ungentle to you.
	You are there follow'd by a faithful shepherd;
	Look upon him, love him; he worships you.
Phe:	Good shepherd, tell this youth what 'tis to love.
Sil:	It is to be all made of sighs and tears;
	And so am I for Phebe.
Phe:	And I for Ganymede.
Orl:	And I for Rosalind.
Ros:	And I for no woman.
Sil:	It is to be all made of faith and service;
	And so am I for Phebe.
Phe:	And I for Ganymede.
Orl:	And I for Rosalind.
Ros:	And I for no woman.
Sil:	It is to be all made of fantasy,
	All made of passion, and all made of wishes;
	All adoration, duty, and observance,
	All humbleness, all patience, and impatience,
	All purity, all trial, all obedience;
	And so am I for Phebe.
Phe:	And so am I for Ganymede.
Orl:	And so am I for Rosalind.
Ros:	And so am I for no woman.

When Alice read the novel and then the letters, she became enraged. She destroyed the correspondence and forbade Gertrude to publish the book. Three friends had already seen it: Bernard Faÿ, the novelist Louis Bromfield, and William Aspinwall Bradley, a literary agent whom Gertrude knew in Paris. Bradley and Bromfield thought the book was well written, but advised Gertrude that it would probably not interest a publisher because of the theme. But their opinions were a minor influence compared with Alice's. All she knew, she admitted later, was that she did not want it read during her lifetime.[100] She took *Q.E.D.* from Gertrude and kept it hidden until after Gertrude's death.

There remained, therefore, the problem of producing a popular book. And the only solution seemed to be for

Gertrude to write one. Many of Gertrude's friends, knowing who had passed through the salon at the rue de Fleurus, suggested that she write a memoir. Slowly it became apparent to Gertrude that such a book would be able to find a publisher and make a good deal of money. She was, after all, known as much for whom she knew as for what she was doing in the way of literary innovation. Her artist friends, especially Picasso and Matisse, had already gained fame. Hemingway, Anderson, and Fitzgerald had established their own reputations and their own legends. A memoir would very likely be a success. But Gertrude did not want to write one.

Completely devoted to her own genre, she felt that writing a popular book would be selling herself short of her real genius. She would be bowing beneath the demands of the publishing world, which did not understand her avant-garde pieces and did not recognize her talent. A memoir would exploit her famous friends, but that would be of less importance than the exploitation of Gertrude Stein herself. She suggested that Alice write the book, and thought of appropriate titles: *Wives of Geniuses I Have Sat With, My Twenty-Five Years With Gertrude Stein, My Life With The Great*. But Alice refused to take Gertrude's jest seriously; Gertrude was the writer. The decision, however, was difficult.

"It does not bother me not to delight them," Gertrude tried to explain to Alice. But Alice had been bothered for long enough. "Shove is a proof of love," Gertrude decided, and, in the summer of 1932, she began to write something very different from anything she had done before.

Above left, Annette Rosenshine, 1897, photo by Arnold Genthe *(Courtesy, The Bancroft Library)*. Above right, Clarence Toklas, 1909 *(Courtesy, The Bancroft Library)*. Bottom, Alice Toklas and Annette Rosenshine, tintype *(Courtesy, The Bancroft Library)*.

Above left, Oil portrait of Sarah
Dix Hamlin, photo by Hal Randall.
Above right, Harriet Levy, c.
1886 *(Courtesy, The Bancroft
Library)*. Emma Marwedel
*(Courtesy, The Hamlin School,
San Francisco)*.

Alice B. Toklas, c. 1906, photo by Arnold Genthe *(Courtesy, The Bancroft Library)*.

Above left, Maria Bonifacio
*(Courtesy, Monterey Public
Library).* Above right, Fernande
Olivier *(Courtesy, The Collection
of American Literature, The
Beinecke Library, Yale University).*

Pablo Picasso, 1904 *(Courtesy,
French Cultural Services).*

Oil portrait of Gertrude Stein, by Pablo Picasso, 1906 *(Courtesy, The Metropolitan Museum of Art, Bequest of Gertrude Stein, 1946).*

Gertrude Stein, 1913, photo by Alvin Langdon Coburn *(Courtesy, International Museum of Photography)*.

Above left, David Edstrom *(Courtesy, Swedish Information Service)*.
Above right, Guillaume Apollinaire *(Courtesy, French Cultural
Services)*. Below, Michael, Leo, and Allan Stein, 1912 *(Courtesy, The
Collection of American Literature, The Beinecke Library, Yale
University)*.

Above left, Sarah Stein
(Courtesy, The Baltimore Museum of Art, Cone Archives). Above right, Sherwood Anderson *(Courtesy, Sherwood Anderson Papers, The Newberry Library, Chicago)*.

Oil portrait of Sylvia Beach, by Paul Emile Bécat, 1923 *(Courtesy, The Princeton University Library)*.

Ernest Hemingway *(Courtesy, The John F. Kennedy Library and Mrs. Mary Hemingway).*

Alice, Gertrude, and Bumbi Hemingway *(Courtesy, The John F. Kennedy Library and Mrs. Mary Hemingway).*

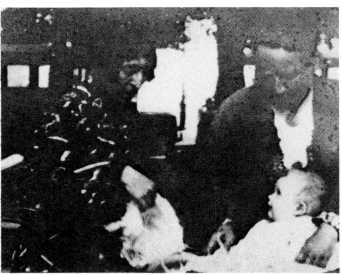

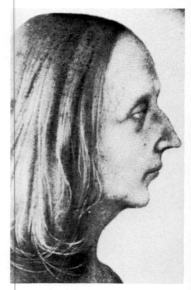

Above left, Pavel Tchelitchew,
Self-portrait *(Courtesy, Hutchinson
Publishing Group)*. Above right,
Portrait of Edith Sitwell, by
Tchelitchew *(Courtesy, Hutchinson
Publishing Group)*.

Henri Matisse *(Courtesy, French
Cultural Services)*.

Portrait of Alice Toklas, by Pavel Tchelitchew, 1927 *(Courtesy, University of California, Los Angeles).*

Bust of Alice B. Toklas, by Annette Rosenshine, 1929 *(Courtesy, Paul Padgette).*

Above left, Thornton Wilder, photo by Gisele Freund *(Courtesy, Magnum Photos)*. Above right, Max White, photo by Consuelo Kanaga *(Courtesy, Max White)*. Below, Petit-point chairs, design by Picasso *(Courtesy, The Collection of American Literature, The Beinecke Library, Yale University)*.

Gertrude, Alice, and Basket, photo by Cecil Beaton *(Courtesy, Sir Cecil Beaton)*.

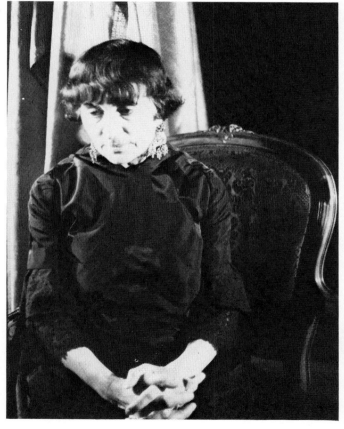

Alice B. Toklas, 1934, photo by Carl Van Vechten *(Courtesy, The Estate of Carl Van Vechten)*.

Alice B. Toklas, photo by Carl Van Vechten *(Courtesy, The Estate of Carl Van Vechten).*

Sixteen

"How I wish I were able to say what I think," Gertrude sighed, as she wrote about everyone she knew—writers, painters, sculptors, dancers, expatriates, and odd characters —in a voice she knew well: Alice's. "She will be me when this you see," Gertrude hinted in a piece she was writing at the same time. Using Alice's comments and viewing their friends through Alice's special lens, Gertrude slightly mitigated her responsibility for the book. Though she once said that she began the book as a joke, a tour de force, even a literary experiment, in reality she wrote it under pressure from Alice. "Who is winning," she asked despondently, "why the answer of course is she is."[101]

Once the decision was made, however, and the literary device found, Gertrude still had trouble getting started. Her first notebook for the manuscript contains abortive starts and convoluted sentences. Gertrude was on her trail of repetition, endless sentences, unintelligible paragraphs. Alice, frustrated, probably would have liked to quote to Gertrude the advice she once gave Hemingway: "Begin over again and concentrate." But she effected the same result without having to invoke her enemy's name.

Alice had always provided the definitive version of any story, and Gertrude, whose memory was undependable, frequently turned to her to find out exactly what had happened, and when. Virgil Thomson recalled many times that Gertrude began a tale, "a recent or a far-away one, and then as she went on with it got first repetitive and then uncertain till Alice would look up over the tapestry frame and say, 'I'm sorry, Lovey; it wasn't like that at all.' 'All right, Pussy,' Gertrude would say. 'You tell it.' Every story that ever came into the house eventually got told in Alice's way. . . ." Later Alice confessed to have prompted Ger-

185

trude on some of the anecdotes in the book, and even revealed that certain remarks were included on her insistence. Gertrude's dismissal of James Joyce, for example, as one of "the incomprehensibles whom anybody can understand," a comment attributed to Picasso, was written, Alice told a friend, because she wanted Gertrude's opinion known. Joyce had for too long been her literary rival.[102] Of course, Gertrude's flaying of Hemingway was inspired by Alice.

The stories were written as though Alice dictated them, with her deadpan humor and acerbic comments. So closely did Gertrude capture Alice's style that friends could almost hear her gritty voice delivering gossip with mischievous pleasure. Some were not completely convinced that Alice did not play an active role in the writing of the book, a suggestion taken by Alice to be an accusation—and vehemently denied. And though Alice denied many things which were subsequently found to be true, there is no evidence that she wrote her own autobiography in 1932. There would have been no need, in any case, for her to have made the effort: Gertrude had been listening to her for a quarter of a century.

The Autobiography of Alice B. Toklas was completed in six weeks, Gertrude claimed, and while she was writing she often asked Alice if she thought it would be popular. Unexpectedly, Alice said no, it was not sentimental enough. Eventually she admitted that she had been wrong. According to Gertrude, Alice demurred at having her name included in the title, especially with her middle initial. But her objection must have been very weak, since she did not get her way. Her life before she met Gertrude is kept closely private. There is a brief glance at her years in San Francisco, but in most of the book she cavorts with the "greats" from a vantage point beside and sometimes slightly to the rear of Gertrude Stein.

Publicity, they both knew well, was everything. The right names were dropped with devilish irreverence. If, as Gertrude supposedly told Hemingway, remarks are not literature, they proved to be grand entertainment. William Bradley, acting as Gertrude's agent, quickly found a publisher: Harcourt, Brace; a magazine which would publish an advance abridgment: the *Atlantic*; and a book club: the Literary Guild. Gertrude, at last, was on her way.

She was overwhelmed by the praise which the book engendered, never having succeeded in exciting anyone "except the publisher of Plain Edition, Alice B. Toklas. . . ." Finally, after thirty years of writing, she was recognized. But her happiness had a troubled undertone. She had achieved success, but not for what she considered her art. She had written a lighthearted, whimsical, popular book, aimed at an audience who would devour gossip with gusto. Long-awaited success was not what she had hoped it would be. "I have always quarreled with a great many young men," she wrote:

> and one of the principal things that I have quarreled with them about was that once they had made a success they became sterile, they could not go on. And I blamed them. I said it was their fault. I said success is all right but if there is anything in you it ought not to cut off the flow not if there is anything in you. Now I know better. It does cut off your flow and then if you are not too young and you are frightened enough you can begin again. . . .
>
> What happened to me is this. When the success began and it was a success I got lost completely lost. You know the nursery rhyme, I am I because my little dog knows me. Well you see I did not know myself, I lost my personality. . . . Here all of a sudden, I was not just I because so many people did know me.[103]

Before, writing for herself, for Alice, or even for her small audience, she was prolific. Now, conscious of thousands of readers, she could not write. Finally, when she did write, her thoughts returned to the changes in her life and personality that came with growing publicity. "Authors need not authorship," she decided.[104] "I have wished for success and I have it and now I will about arrange that I have no thought of change. But changes come," she knew. She questioned the sincerity of her sudden plethora of well-wishers. "Of course they annoy," she said, and tried to accept their praise, "Naturally with joy."[105] Glad of the money from the various publications of her book, she nevertheless rued the interruption of her calm daily life. "Do not disguise what has happened," she warned herself, "or its effect upon what has happened." Of all her adoring public, there was still just one in whom she believed and trusted. "You can remember two things," she wrote. "Make it three things. When as a child you could get your way by being cuddling. When as young you could get your way by being intriguing. And when you are old and you can get your way by being angry if they do or if they don't go away. Three things make them. When this you see say all to me. There is only one loved one."[106]

She wrote "that no one is disillusioned"; but she was disappointed. Faced with the absurdity of having gained success through a popular book while she failed to be recognized for writings which she felt stemmed from genius, she responded with sad resignation. "I simply wish to tell a story," she wrote. "I have said a great many things but the emotion is deeper when I saw them. And soon there was no emotion at all and now I will always do what I do without any emotion which is just as well as there is not at all anything at all that is better."[107] And one thought which was often in her mind recurred again in her despondency. "What is the difference if there is no question and no answer."[108]

The Autobiography shocked many of those who found themselves the subject of Alice's tart evaluation. Georges Braque thought Gertrude misunderstood cubism, seeing art "simply in terms of personalities. . . . Miss Stein," he said, "obviously saw everything from the outside and never the real struggle we were engaged in. For one who poses as an authority on the epoch it is safe to say that she never went beyond the stage of the tourist. . . ." Countering the gossip in Gertrude's book with his own tidbit, he remembered that during the war, when Gertrude and Alice were working for the American Fund, they met him in Avignon "in their boy scout uniforms with their green veils and Colonial helmets" and excited a commotion among the passersby. About the book as a whole, he could only declare for himself and his fellow artists, *"Nous sommes fixés."*

Tristan Tzara, the Dadaist whom Gertrude characterized as a "pleasant but not very exciting cousin," was likewise disturbed. The book was filled with "sordid anecdotes," and he thought the memoirs of Miss Alice Toklas should have been kept "in the family circle between two maiden ladies." But since these two maiden ladies were obviously "greedy for fame and publicity" there resulted the "exploitation of man by man" which Tzara deeply regretted.

"They tell us the infinite pains they took to lure to their house, where their collection of canvases constituted an irresistible bait, people who might be useful to them in publishing an article in this or that review," he wrote, adding that he had no objection to "their revealing the secrets of their literary kitchen" as long as his name was not entwined with the "superficial and burlesque character" of the enterprise. "The memoirs of Miss Toklas," he decided, "furnish us with an opportunity to appreciate how far the limits of decency can be pushed."[109]

Matisse was offended by Gertrude's comparison of his wife to a horse. Madame Matisse, Gertrude had written, "was a very straight dark woman with a long face and a firm large loosely hung mouth like a horse."[110] As Alice later explained, however, Gertrude was speaking of Madame Matisse's beauty, and Alice admonished Matisse's reaction. "Though he didn't read English," she commented, "perhaps he did not consider a horse beautiful."

One offended reader retaliated in an article dedicated specifically to Alice. Thomas Beer, who admitted once, "The whole 'Lost Generation' movement gives me a headache and I strongly suspect a lot of it being as coldly commercial as a burlesque show," took it upon himself to defend his friend John Reed, who had been dead for twelve years by the time Gertrude wrote *The Autobiography*. The son of a wealthy Portland, Oregon, family, Reed had risen to fame after the publication in 1919 of his account of the Russian Revolution, *Ten Days That Shook the World*. The next year he died of typhus in Moscow and was buried beneath the Kremlin wall.

Alice had met Reed in the coterie that traveled to Europe with Mabel Dodge after the Armory Show. Reed made the mistake of talking to her about his trip to Spain, a country about which Alice could not be impartial. "He told me he had seen many strange sights there, that he had seen witches chased through the streets of Salamanca. As I had been spending months in Spain and he only weeks I neither liked his stories nor believed them." She thought, as Picasso remarked, that Reed was "*le genre de Braque mais beaucoup moins rigolo*—Braque's kind but much less diverting."[111]

In "Playboy," an article which appeared in the *American Mercury* in 1934, Beer admitted that Reed could indeed be a bore when talking down the places he had visited in Europe. His monologue about Paris, Beer said, was one of the more "terrible things" he had ever heard, and Beer "determined to duck when I [he] next saw John Reed."

He came abreast of me on Riverside Drive when I was getting some air between doses of Columbia Law School. This happened in winter. I said that the Hudson looked cold as Puget Sound. So John Reed began to talk about the Northwest, and was not a playboy about it. We talked for a long time about Puget Sound and the smell of burning cedarbark in Portland. I told him about a Chinese junk in the bay of Seattle, and he told me about a blind man who grew roses in a back yard in Tacoma. He did all the talking soon, standing with his hands in the pockets of a loose overcoat, staring at the river. He was no more a brilliant talker than he was a brilliant writer, but he talked about Tacoma and the long Sound, mist, Swedes, ramshackle brothels strung up slopes. He said nothing profound, but he made beauty, talking. Men do that when they talk about things they have loved a good deal, and Americans often talk very well when they are not trying to be wise or funny.

"God what a liar she is!" Leo wrote to his friend Mabel Weeks. "If I were not something of a psychopathologist I should be very much mystified. Some of her chronology is too wonderful. . . . Practically everything she says of our activities before 1911 is false both in fact and implication. . . ."[112] Righting the wrongs perpetrated in *The Autobiography* occupied Leo for years after the book's publication. "Nothing of the pre-war period is accurately true," he wrote to another friend, "very little of the whole is accurately true, and very little of it is even approximately true. It's the first time I ever read an autobiography of which I knew the authentic facts and to me it seems sheerly incredible."[113] Besides being a "farrago of rather clever anecdote, stupid brag and general bosh,"[114] the book, Leo thought, was only another example of Gertrude's lack of talent. ". . . I simply cannot take Gertrude seriously as a literary phenomenon," he declared again.[115]

Convinced that Gertrude perverted syntax, was "a barbarian in her use of language," and just couldn't write, Leo sympathized with an article he read in the *Atlantic* in January 1934 whose author, B. F. Skinner, purported that Gertrude Stein had a secret: she practiced automatic writing. Attempting to understand the difference between Gertrude's intelligible work—*Three Lives* and *The Autobiography*, for example—and such pieces as *Tender Buttons*, Skinner turned to Gertrude's own revelation of her undergraduate work in psychology, where she was part of a group conducting experiments in spontaneous automatic writing. *Tender Buttons*, which Skinner described as "the stream of consciousness of a woman without a past," seemingly contained no intellectual content, nor drew upon any literary sources. "If there is any character in the writing whatsoever," he wrote, "it is due to [the] savor of the schoolroom, and the one inference about the author that does seem plausible is that she has been to grammar school." He saw words strung together as sentences but lacking meaning; the book was "intellectually unopinionated" and "emotionally cold. . . ."

Skinner offered proof of his thesis drawn from Gertrude's own description of her working habits: "(1) *Tender Buttons* was written on scraps of paper, and no scrap was ever thrown away; (2) Miss Stein likes to write in the presence of distracting noises; (3) her handwriting is often more legible to Miss Toklas than to herself (that is, her writing is 'cold' as soon as it is produced); (4) and she is 'fond of writing the letter *m*' "—which Gertrude had disclosed was the general trend of her subjects in the Harvard experiment. If his theory were borne out, Skinner felt it necessary to ask the next logical question: "Why, then, did she publish?"

If the work she produced was very likely as unintelligible to herself as to her readers, why did Gertrude place such importance on it? Here Skinner decided that Gertrude had been influenced by Picasso, Matisse, and other artists, who had been repeatedly confronted by viewers asking what their work meant. What should have remained merely "the interesting and rather surprising result of an experiment" was seen, instead, as part of a larger art movement, as serious an endeavor as anything the cubists had created. It was lumped with their art merely because it could not be understood.

Skinner himself attached no importance to Gertrude's unintelligible work, and thought it obscured enjoyment of her more lucid pieces. "I welcome the present theory," he wrote, "because it gives one the freedom to dismiss one part of Gertrude Stein's writing as a probably ill-advised experiment. . . ." Leo considered the article "very good and probably valid," though he admitted that Skinner worked under a limitation: "of course he didn't know that Gertrude couldn't write plain English effectively."[116]

The problems encountered in reading Gertrude's obscure pieces did not trouble a growing audience delighted by *The Autobiography* and wanting more of Gertrude Stein. William Bradley, aware of Gertrude's popularity in America, brought a lecture agent to see her, a somber man whom Gertrude did not like. "I decided that if lecture agents were like that that certainly I would not go over and so I told him not to bother."[117] Bradley advised Gertrude to reconsider, but Gertrude merely repeated her response to her friend Jo Davidson, the sculptor, when he told her that one should always sell one's personality: ". . . only insofar as that personality expressed itself in work." Her new audience was fascinated more by Gertrude Stein than by *Tender Buttons*, and she could not understand it. "It always did bother me that the American public were more interested in me than in my work. And after all there is no sense in it because if it were not for my work they would not be interested in me so why should they not be more interested in my work than in me. That is one of the things one has to worry about in America. . . ."[118]

Despite her refusal, friends continued to urge her to go to America: she would be returning to her native land in triumph, they told her. She would be going home as a lion. Bradley, acting above her protests, began to make plans for her to lecture. "There are some things a girl cannot do," she decided. But she was being pressed to cash in on her fame, to enjoy her publicity, and to cooperate. ". . . Bradley my agent said he had made all the arrangements for me to get rich and now I was upsetting everything."[119]

The trip seemed inevitable, but still Gertrude said no. She and Alice left Paris for Bilignin. They settled down to their simple country life, received guests, lived quietly. Wavering a bit in her decision, Gertrude began to write lectures "as if we were going to America," and suddenly found that she could think of nothing else. Before the summer had ended, "we knew that we were going to America and I was going to lecture."[120]

It was necessary to find someone to make the arrangements, and Bradley, Gertrude thought, would not do. He would not comply with her many conditions for lecturing, and she was afraid that she would be coerced into doing what she did not want to do. They quarreled, and then "there was a complete explosion." Gertrude refused to deal with him.

On the recommendation of W. G. Rogers and Bernard Faÿ, they engaged Marvin Chauncey Ross of the Walters Art Gallery in Baltimore to make arrangements for the tour. Ross was assigned the task of designing an itinerary which would include lectures before an audience of no more than five hundred, not oftener than three times a week, and a schedule which would allow Gertrude to do whatever she wanted to during the days and nights when she was not lecturing. Gertrude and Alice had been told harrowing tales of the trials undergone by friends lecturing in the States, and agreed that nothing of the sort should be allowed to happen to Gertrude.

There were other requirements: Gertrude was not to be introduced at the lectures. She was not to be expected to attend dinners or luncheons in her honor: she did not like to eat in public. Tickets sold for the lectures were not to benefit any fund or cause. She asked a fee of one hundred dollars from schools, two hundred fifty dollars from clubs. And as for clubs, Gertrude preferred, if possible, to lecture before a mixed group rather than a women's club.

Ross was given his instructions. Gertrude returned to her lecture writing. And Alice took care of the remaining details for the trip, including the gathering of Gertrude's wardrobe. "I now commenced to prepare the costumes for Gertrude's voyage," she recalled, "one to lecture in the afternoon, one to lecture in on evenings, one to travel in, an odd dress or two. Gertrude also had her leopard-skin cap from which she refused to be parted."[121]

Alice, like Gertrude, had some uncertainty about the return home. Gertrude had been away for thirty years; Alice twenty-seven. America began to seem almost as romantic as Europe once had been. Yet they could never forget what they had fled. "What was the America that I left," Gertrude wrote. "It was an America where as Mark Twain said in the first diary he ever kept he got up and washed and went to bed."[122] They wondered what they were coming to. Whenever their doubts arose, Alice would assure Gertrude that they could always go home.[123] On October 17, 1934, they sailed away on the *Champlain*.

Seventeen

"HOME WILL NEVER be like this," Alice thought during the voyage, pleased especially by the excellent cuisine and the luxurious stateroom. They preferred to dine alone, but met congenial passengers on board. On deck one afternoon, they found a New Jersey physician and his family who happened to have a copy of *The Autobiography*, which Gertrude happily autographed. Before giving her first lecture, Gertrude had to call on Dr. Wood for his services as a throat specialist. She had caught a cold, she told him, and her throat bothered her. ". . . Hearing his voice was already soothing," she said, "but having him come and feel my pulse was everything. . . ."[124] With Dr. Wood in the audience at her first lecture, she was sure her voice would not fail her.

They also became reacquainted with the Abbé Ernest Dimnet, whom they had met years before at a party given by Alice Woods Ullman and again at the Café Voltaire for a dinner one Friday. Because of the abbé's presence, when the waiter asked for Alice's order, she chose sole and everyone else, following her lead, ordered fish. "Finally," she said, "the maître d'hôtel asked the Abbé what he was going to have and he said, As for me I shall have beef-steak."[125]

On board the *Champlain*, the abbé was a difficult passenger during the usual fire drill. He commenced the charade by donning the safety belt and life preserver, but when he saw that no one actually was to descend into the small boats, he became angry. "They should get into the boat," he told Gertrude. "Tell the captain," she suggested, and he blustered off. When he returned he was furious. "He said you could not get into the boat unless the ship was stopped it would be too dangerous and to stop the ship was too costly and took too much time," he reported. "Yes that is the way it is they prepare they prepare and they never know whether they can do what they are prepared for."[126]

As for Gertrude's and Alice's trip, he agreed that it would be interesting, but "Oh," he sighed, "oh you should have seen them when they were rich."[127]

They arrived in New York on Wednesday, October 24, with their anxieties somewhat diminished. W. G. Rogers was among the interviewers rowed out to the ship before they docked, and when he expressed concern about Gertrude's handling of the reporters' questions, Alice assured him that Gertrude would not be disturbed. Carl Van Vechten stood waving on the dock, and while Gertrude held the attention of the press, he and Alice saw the customs official. "Here are the keys," she told him, "there is nothing dutiable, I have declared the duty, the clothes that are new were made to be worn here by us, I do not think anything is dutiable."[128] Apparently satisfied with her explanation, the official seemed to be finished and Alice mentioned to Van Vechten that she would tip the man. Van Vechten, horrified at her committing a *faux pas*, advised her to do nothing, not even to shake hands and thank him. ". . . You will not be doing that here," he told her.

They all proceeded to the Algonquin Hotel, where Alice had reserved rooms, and again found a coterie of reporters. Their suite was so filled with cameras and equipment that Alice found she could not unpack. It was not until later in the afternoon that she and Gertrude were finally settled and free to go out for a walk. Immediately, they realized that they were indeed special visitors. A salesman in a fruit shop where they had stopped to make a purchase asked Alice how she was enjoying New York. And the lights in Times Square proclaimed, "Gertrude Stein has arrived in New York"—to which Alice could comment only, "As if we did not know it."[129]

They walked around the city, up and down the avenues, until suddenly Gertrude thought Alice looked odd. "What is it?" she asked. ". . . My knees are shaking," Alice told her. She had just seen the side of a skyscraper and the sight stunned her as nothing had since the raids during the war.

Only one thing puzzled her. "Why do they call Paris *la ville lumière*," she asked Gertrude. Even Gertrude admitted there were more lights in New York than in Paris, "and more beautifully strung than anywhere except in Spain," but she explained to Alice, when Paris earned its epithet, ". . . there were more lights there than anywhere, you cannot blame them that they still think so. . . ."[130]

Their escort and protector during their stay in New York was Carl Van Vechten, who lived on West Fifty-fifth Street, where he had set up a photography studio for the new segment of his career. He took hundreds of photographs of Gertrude—and a few less of Alice—under hot lights which Gertrude, especially, found tiring. He also kept their evenings busy with parties where they could meet his many literary and artist friends. His Negro friends, Alice thought, were sometimes shocking in their "outspokenness."

Carl's "indescribable loyalty" to Gertrude was treasured; Gertrude called him "the Patriarch—Carlo Patriarch," and he replied, ". . . it makes me feel like Moses or Abraham, but I guess I did lead you into the Promised Land. . . ." His enthusiasm for Gertrude's work was boundless. *The Autobiography* was so colorful and exciting, he thought, that it would be perfect as a film. "Of course," he added to Gertrude, "you both would have to appear in the picture. Even Greta Garbo and Lillian Gish couldn't be you and Alice." With Carl as the father, they were drawn together as closely as a family: Carl and his wife, Gertrude and Alice became the Woojums family, Carl as "Papa," Alice as "Mama," Gertrude as "Baby," and the actress Fania Marinoff, Carl's wife, reigned as "Empress."

Though it was assumed that Ross would take responsibility for the lectures, it was left to Alice to regulate life for Gertrude as smoothly as she had in France. Her first dealings were with interviewers. These were allotted a definite span of time in which to question Gertrude, and Alice would not refrain from reminding them if they did not depart promptly. While she tried to remain quietly in the background, it was sometimes necessary for her to see reporters herself.

When a writer from *Art News* arrived at their hotel room, Alice thought it best to set the tone for the interview. "Miss Toklas wished to make it clear immediately," the reporter wrote, "that Miss Stein had no desire to speak of art or artists, painting or aesthetics. 'You see,' she said with that gentleness in which she clothes every movement, 'Miss Stein feels that she has been occupied with art most of her life, and in this time a great deal has been said on the subject. She has still something new to say, but for this she will wait until her forthcoming lectures. For the rest, she feels that everything has been said at one time or another.' " With that bit of encouragement, Alice yielded to Gertrude, who explained further that at her lectures she would "talk not upon art but about paintings. . . ."

The interviewer sent from Columbia University's *Spectator* was not as fortunate as the woman from *Art News*. After waiting for twenty minutes in the lobby of the Algonquin, the reporter was at last met by Alice. Gertrude, Alice explained, was working on her lecture and would not fulfill her promise of an interview. Alice, however, agreed to talk on Gertrude's behalf. The interview was conducted in a dark corner of the hotel lobby, where Alice, in one of her many characteristic hats, "talked a little jumpily" and tried to convey Gertrude's views. Though she said Gertrude thought that newspapermen were "very nice, very kind and gentlemanly," Alice could not help but add her gibe at reporters in general. Seeing the Columbia writer's disappointment at not being able to speak with Gertrude, she told him, "You people should have interviewed Miss Stein many years ago when she was not so well known and not so busy."

She was so well-known that her three scheduled lectures at Columbia University had attracted an audience far above the five-hundred-person limit which Gertrude had set. Though Ross was supposed to have enforced her stricture, Gertrude found that more than three times the number had requested tickets for one of her lectures. At this discovery, she became angered and upset, and contacted Dr. Russell Potter, the director of the Institute of Arts and Sciences, which sponsored the lectures. Potter said she was "very pleasant but quite firm . . . and I believe that she is utterly sincere . . . that she cannot conceive of herself interesting more than 500 people at one time." In a special announcement hurriedly sent to the institute's membership, he wrote that "Miss Stein refuses—flatly, adamantly, stead-fastly, definitely, unconditionally, and absolutely—to address more than 500 persons at any one time" and strictly limited the sale of the tickets. Only one ticket per lecture per member was issued and no mail requests were filled. On Friday, November 2, at 8:15, Gertrude addressed "the curious, fortunate five hundred" in Columbia's McMillin Theatre on "The Gradual Making of *The Making of Americans*."

Gertrude, in a long brown tweed skirt and vest, swaying slightly and reading in her usual low-pitched melodic voice, nearly hypnotized her audience. They laughed when she laughed, applauded her wit, and listened deferentially as she "tweaked the ears of some impertinent questioners" at the end of her almost two-hour talk. Institute members who failed to obtain tickets threatened to give up their membership and tried all means including bribery to gain entrance to the lecture. College students employed as ushers were informed that they would be fired instantly if they dared admit even one friend. But the Institute had kept its promise. " 'Thank you for reducing yourselves to 500,' " Gertrude said as she began, "repeating this in one way or another for a few minutes, interrupting her repetitions occasionally by a deep-seated almost involuntary chuckle." She was a success.

Vassar, where Gertrude was to lecture on November 10, would not make Columbia's mistake. Those advanced literature students and faculty who came were as curious about Gertrude Stein as they were about her writing. "The writer," a local paper reported, "heralded as 'eccentric,' appeared . . . as a wholly normal person, free from any oddities of personality. She wore a dark woolen skirt, a silk open at the throat blouse of simple cut, and low heeled red kid sandals. Her only bit of jewelry was a brooch at the neck of her blouse. Her voice, while exceedingly low-pitched, was audible to everyone in the hall, and her manner was enthusiastic and agreeable. . . . In spite of her stocky, middle-aged figure, Miss Stein appears of indeterminate age. Although her close-cropped hair is gray, her face is unlined."[131] At a coffee reception following the lecture, the audience was able to get a closer look at the genius they had feared might not show up at all and at her "secretary," who generally walked a foot and a half behind her with Gertrude's speech in her handbag.

Though Alice was described as "secretary" or "traveling companion," she had taken over as lecture agent and manager after Ross, because of his failure with Columbia, was fired. In her letters to those who requested Gertrude's visit, she was forthright about "talking business" and enumerating the many conditions of the lecturer. As deftly as she had assumed the role of editor of Plain Edition, she now became a professional impresario.

Audiences were delighted. Bustling onto the stage at the Brooklyn Academy of Music on November 13, Gertrude appeared as "a trim German housewife expecting company. Her gray hair is cut mannish and she has a mannish way of reaching round to smooth it back. She wore a purple-striped shirt, clasped with a garnet pin at the neck and green cuff-buttons. Over this was a quilted sleeveless jacket with Chinese embroidery, caught together at the belt with a jeweled bow. Her skirt was full, brown speckled, and her shoes brown, flat-heeled."[132] Her topic was "The Development of Personality, Portraits, Poetry: Middle Period," and some of the audience thought she was well into the lecture as she was announcing the title. Leaning against a podium, she thrust one hand into her skirt pocket and read from her manuscript, interrupting herself at times with, "Do you see what I mean? Do any of you at all see what I mean?" After the reading, she took off her glasses and tried to deal with the many questions. "Do you understand?" she asked one man. "I understand perfectly," he bravely replied, to a roar of applause from the crowd. But whether or not they understood, they enjoyed Gertrude's show. As one listener commented, "She spoke twice as much as she said."[133]

After her lecture at Bryn Mawr on November 14, the campus was plunged into a discussion of Gertrude Stein's theory of writing. ". . . One went to sleep with the tale of how Miss Stein came to write *Tender Buttons* for a bedtime story, and one talked about punctuation and rhythm in prose and poetry at every meal. Almost everyone who heard Miss Stein was interested in the writer's theory and was fascinated by her personal charm."[134] She had lectured on poetry and grammar, digressing on the function of various punctuation marks and the use of capital and lower-case letters. Her comments on poetry struck the Bryn Mawr audience as especially thought-provoking: "Poetry," Gertrude told them, "is really loving the name of anything. One can love a name, and if one does, then saying it over and over only makes one love it more. Early poetry, such as that of Homer and of Chaucer, was drunk with nouns. . . . Being in love makes for poetry."[135]

At Princeton, Gertrude's limitation of five hundred seemed "a great joke" to the head of the English department. For other speakers, he told her, he almost had to bribe students to assemble an audience of two hundred. And for Gertrude, he had difficulty keeping her audience down to five hundred. "I think it is a great joke," he said. Gertrude, however, "was very solemn."[136]

Among the Princeton five hundred was a "young and very good-looking" student who had sent Gertrude some of his manuscripts. Donald Sutherland was very nervous, she thought, when he met her after the lecture at a reception given by one of the professors. Sutherland described himself and the other students as "agitated and awkward." Gertrude watched the group for a while and then, sweeping her hand in front of her, said, "How is one to describe all this?"

. . . There was nothing in front of her but a casual bunch of Princeton boys, who, I thought, were scarcely worth describing, certainly not as we appeared then. Perhaps we would have been worth describing separately, in single portraits, or doing something more significant or dramatic than just milling about, and perhaps our inner adolescent lives might have been worth describing, but all that was plainly not what she meant by "all this." What she meant was the immediate phenomenon before her, the actual group as it moved and composed itself and made noises before her, that for her was adequate subject matter, the phenomenon or thing which, like all other phenomena or things, was, so they say, in God.[137]

Though the publicity about her limited audience usually ensured a rapt five hundred, the Columbia group at the last of Gertrude's three lectures began to feel restless. Within the first half hour of her talk, a stream of listeners slowly left and a few who remained openly giggled, causing the rest of the audience some embarrassment. Gertrude, however, continued, seemingly oblivious to the mishap. Her topic, "What Is English Literature?," was "rather complicated, to say the least," the college paper reported, and the audience perked up at Gertrude's impromptu comments during her reading. But Gertrude was used to her listeners' density. "Slowly you will see what I mean," she told them. "If not, why not?"

Gertrude's descent on her alma mater was heralded weeks ahead in the Boston papers. "Radcliffe's most famous daughter," the Boston *Sunday Post* announced, "will come to Boston this winter to tell the Athenians of America all about the strange conglomeration of words she turns out in prolific fashion at her Parisian home on the Rue de Fleurus." She would be accompanied, the newspaper said, by one "Annie B. Toklas," who for thirty years ran "the domestic affairs" of Gertrude's establishment, and daily risked her life in driving with Gertrude. ". . . Gertrude Stein has been given the reputation of being the worst automobile driver in the world. They say, along the boulevards, that she takes corners at a great rate, never puts out her arms to signal, drives on the wrong side of the street as often as on the right, pays no attention to traffic signals and never honks."[138]

Interviewed before the lecture, Gertrude was warm and accommodating to the reporters. "Her eyes are like those of a jolly teddy bear, brown and shiny. Her outfit, from hat to skirt, is made of some overcoat-tweed material. She looks as if she expects it to rain at any moment and acts as if she hopes it won't." Her hair, which wasn't gray as it appeared in photographs but white against black, produced a startling effect, one reporter thought. Interviewers tried to bait her, but Gertrude would not succumb.

One reporter quoted an anecdote about Robert Browning, in which a reader had thrust a line of poetry at him, saying, "Dear, dear, Mr. Browning, what does that mean?" Browning then replied, "Madame, when I wrote that God and I knew what it meant. Now only God knows what it means." But Gertrude was not amused. "Every line I have ever written," she told him, "means exactly what I meant it

to mean. It means the same thing now as when I wrote it."
She explained herself further at her Radcliffe lecture.

Speaking on one of her favorite topics, repetition, she
baffled the students, who burst into laughter each time
Gertrude paused and asked, "Do you see what I mean?"
For the five hundred young women, many styled in imitation of Katharine Hepburn, the squat writer, dressed in
tweeds with a yellow flowered jacket, horn-rimmed glasses,
and unfashionable haircut, gave a strange appearance. Further laughter was evoked when Gertrude read from her
published works in an attempt to clarify her theory of
writing. Finally, after assuring the audience that they
would come to understand her, she reconsidered and
added, "Maybe you will but I doubt it."

For the Radcliffe community, the return of Gertrude
Stein held a special interest. Members of the class of '98
were sought out for memories of their famous schoolmate.
One woman remembered that Gertrude had tried to hypno-
tize her; another that Gertrude had liked hiking, bicycle
riding, and reading French psychologists; she loved operas
but had no interest in feminism, the suffrage movement, or
politics. And though the other Radcliffe students were preoccupied then with clothes and Harvard men, Gertrude
showed no interest in either. "She wasn't easy to know,"
one woman recalled, "but once you knew her, you found
her to be charming." Asked for their reaction to her
present appearance, at least one classmate decided, "I'd
know her anywhere."

Even those who had not known Gertrude in college
knew the dimensions of her mythical personality from the
New Yorker's "Talk of the Town" column in an October
issue. Gertrude and Alice were depicted as lovable eccen-
trics, one waking at ten and bathing in an outsized bathtub; one rising at six and "dusting and fussing around."
Gertrude, after her bath, wrapped herself in a woolly robe
and wrote, looking at the rocks and cows around her home
in Bilignin. Frequently, they would drive into the country,
where Gertrude would write as she watched Alice prod a
cow around a field. When inspiration flagged, Gertrude
would drive on to seek another cow, while Alice rode in
the back seat "squealing and jumping" at Gertrude's odd
habits of motoring. When not on bucolic outings, Gertrude

was often involved in quarrels with friends—quarrels, the article pointed out, which were long-lasting and passionate. Alice, who went to bed early, was usually awakened by Gertrude to hear the gossip about their friends. Gertrude's clothes—the "odd dress or two" which Alice had chosen— were, of course, a source of amusement: her sandals, wool stockings, fedora, tweeds, and tunics—even her alleged blue-and-white-striped knicker-length underwear.

Added to the revelations of the *New Yorker* article, a recent *Journal of Medical Opinion* had diagnosed Gertrude as having "distortions of the intellect," and one psychiatrist thought she was schizophrenic. Moreover, she had attended a performance of her opera *Four Saints in Three Acts* wearing a bright red evening gown and white woolen stockings.

Four Saints in Three Acts, the opera on which Gertrude had collaborated with Virgil Thomson in 1927, was performed in Chicago at the beginning of November. Gertrude and Alice, who had never seen it produced, attended the opening night and were enchanted. Florence Stettheimer's costumes, a dreamlike combination of cellophane and velvet, and Frederick Ashton's choreography heightened the effect of a text which some critics said was "meaningless but musical" and undeniably unconventional. For some, it was the introduction to Gertrude Stein, and phrases like "Pigeons on the grass, alas" traveled from *Four Saints* to campuses across the country. The opera, which involved episodes in the lives of several real and imagined saints in sixteenth-century Spain, was given a setting appropriately ethereal and, many thought, thoroughly delightful.

In Chicago, they stayed at the home of Bobsie Goodspeed, where, Alice remembered, their supper one night began with a clear turtle soup and ended with a "fantastic pièce montée of nougat and roses, cream and small coloured candles. The dessert," she added, "reminded me of a postcard Virgil Thomson once sent us from the Côte d'Azur, delightfully situated within sight of the sea, pine woods, nightingales, all cooked in butter."[139]

At a tea party, they met Hadley Hemingway, by then remarried to Paul Mowrer. Both Gertrude and Alice were friendlier with Bobsie Goodspeed than with her husband, who seemed not to share her interests in painting, music, and ballet. One evening, Alice recalled, he appeared in his pajamas and announced to the lingering guests that it was time for them to leave.

Fresh from her success at the opera, Gertrude went on to speak at the University of Chicago, where she met a young lecturer of comparative literature who showed immediate understanding of her work. Thornton Wilder, who had already won his first Pulitzer Prize in 1928 for *The Bridge of San Luis Rey*, felt he shared with Gertrude the sense of breaking away from nineteenth-century novelists who created for their audience a milieu which the reader could not doubt existed. Twentieth-century writing imposed a new and different challenge: an incredulous reader and a new sense of time. One of the few writers who sustained a friendship with Gertrude uninterrupted by petty quarrels, Wilder received Alice's full approval and he was among the few rare people to whom she would defer.

Gertrude had less success conveying her ideas to Robert Hutchins, president of the university, and Mortimer Adler, a professor there. One night at a dinner given by Hutchins, they began explaining a series of classes they had initiated on the world's great ideas. Gertrude took issue with their assertion that all the ideas must be sociological or political. "Government is the least interesting thing in human life," she told them, "creation and the expression of that creation is a damn sight more interesting. . . ." Both Hutchins and Adler took the opposite view, and the talk became heated. ". . . we were saying violent things to each other," Gertrude recalled, when suddenly the maid entered and announced, "Madame, the police." Adler reddened; the talk stopped; and then everyone burst out laughing. Gertrude and Alice were being called for by the homicide squad for a tour of nighttime Chicago.

"It was a raining evening," Gertrude said. "They were big men and we were tucked in with them and we went off with them."

We drove around, we had just missed one homicide it was the only one that had happened that evening and it had not been interesting it had been a family affair and everybody could understand everything. The sergeant said he was afraid not much would happen, it was raining and when it rained nobody moved around and if nobody moved around there could not be any homicide unless it was a family affair . . . someday he said when it is a really nice night I will let you know and then you will see something. . . .[140]

After they had been taken to "various parts of doubtful respectability,"[141] the police returned them to the safe and comfortable neighborhood where Bobsie Goodspeed lived.

Among Gertrude's engagements in Chicago was a lecture where she found one of her stipulations ignored. She would appear on a stage only if she were alone, she said, but when she entered the auditorium, she found three occupied chairs on the speaker's platform. "What are they doing there?" she asked the woman in charge of the arrangements. "Oh, they are the president, vice-president, and the treasurer of the club," Gertrude was told. They were reading the minutes. "All right," Gertrude said, "we will wait here until they finish." At this, the woman was upset. They meant to remain on stage, she said. "Oh no," Gertrude insisted. "I will wait until they go away." There was, Gertrude admitted, "rather a dreadful moment," before they left the stage and she entered to speak. "There is a difference between making speeches and lecturing," she explained, "and that difference made all the difference to me. I might have made speeches but I was lecturing and lecturing had to be alone to see and I was."[142]

With plans to return to the university in January, when Gertrude and Alice would live in Wilder's Drexel Avenue apartment while he moved into the Preacher's Suite in a men's dormitory, the two went on to the University of Wisconsin, and then to Minneapolis. There, lecturing before a women's club, "Dizzy Stein" was unable to identify Fannie Hurst. "Fannie Hurst? Fannie Hurst?" she repeated. "Local girl?" Even Alice's prompting—"You know, the writer—Fannie Hurst"—did not spur Gertrude's memory. "No," she replied, and would not discuss the novelist. Saint Paul was less sympathetic to Gertrude's lecture. "I wonder," a reporter mused, "whether, after her lecture on English literature Saturday evening . . . Gertrude Stein didn't take Alice B. Toklas by the arm, wink one eye, and say, as clearly as a tongue in the cheek would let her: 'Well, old dear, we put it over this time, too.'" The sense of her speech eluded much of her audience and her appearance evoked inventive description:

> Her dress—it was a dress—not a gown, nor yet a frock—was of black taffeta short with very dark blue, and cut after a pattern which was neither a cassock nor a man's lounging-robe, but combined the most comfortable features of both. The bit of white neckwear which adorned it suggested the linen bands of the Reformed clergy.

As usual, her digressions were more intelligible to her audience than her prepared speech, and one comment was especially memorable. "Even a slow catastrophe," Gertrude told them, "is quite fast."[143]

From Saint Paul, Alice and Gertrude were to fly to Iowa City via Chicago. Now seasoned air travelers, the two found this flight unexpectedly difficult. When the plane had engine trouble, another one was substituted; but this one suddenly began to descend long before they would have arrived in Chicago. "What are they doing?" Alice asked. "We must get to Chicago to catch the plane for Iowa City." She was so distressed that she called for the copilot, who told her they were landing in Milwaukee. "There if you want you can get the train for Chicago." Indignantly Alice retorted, "Why do you start a plane if it cannot go where it is supposed to go." "The plane can go all right," she was told, "but no plane can go tonight to Chicago." And to her further protests, he added, "But lady . . . wouldn't you rather be even in Milwaukee than in your coffin."[144] When they finally arrived in Chicago and saw the blizzard that had stopped the city, they conceded that the copilot had been right.

In mid-December, Gertrude and Alice were in Detroit prior to a lecture at the University of Michigan. One evening, frightened by a police search for a murderer at large, they both suddenly decided that Detroit was horrible, that they were afraid to stay in their hotel room, and that they wanted to be rescued. Fortunately, help was nearby. Joseph Brewer, who knew them when he had been a

Rhodes Scholar at Oxford and later published Gertrude's *Useful Knowledge*, was president of Olivet College. Alice, who admitted having a *faiblesse* for Brewer, phoned him, and he came to retrieve them.

Though Gertrude gave no formal lecture at Olivet, the college community offered a warm reception to the "strange-looking pair" who wandered about the campus. The school boasted a "new plan of education" which Gertrude saw as a very old plan "known as the humanistic way, based on human contacts. It is the scholastic way, the natural way of education and the way all ancient teachers taught." Endorsing her old friend, she said that Brewer was a competent "and very earnest young man and he will be a good college president."

Several faculty members at Olivet were recruited to transport Gertrude and Alice to Ann Arbor. Her talk at the University of Michigan was being sponsored by the Hopwood Award Committee, a fund which had been established by Avery Hopwood, a graduate of the university and a friend of Gertrude and Alice until his death in 1928. Avery Hopwood had come to them through Carl Van Vechten and, Alice said, "we adored him." Gertrude described him as having "the air of a sheep with the possibility of being a wolf." A playwright and journalist, he once told them that he wanted to write a great novel, but his efforts had resulted in "nothing but confusion."[145]

". . . Gay, irresponsible and brilliant," Hopwood was also emotional and impetuous. Once, at dinner with Gertrude and Alice and writer Beverley Nichols, Nichols contradicted Hopwood with "Hush, young man, you and your opinions mean nothing in my young life." Alice was astounded by Hopwood's reaction: "Avery took out from his pocket a small paper and emptied a white powder into the palm of his hand and swallowed it. Gertrude knew more about this than I did and said, Oh Avery, you must not. But," Alice said, "it was too late." Later Gertrude asked him, "Is that effective, Avery?" And he said, "Well, not always, but I always do it."[146] They had not known before coming to Ann Arbor that he had endowed a fund for the encouragement of young writers, and remembered with sadness his own "great personal ambitions."

On the last night they saw him, he asked to take them to

"his Montmartre." "I know it was your Montmartre long before it was mine," he added, but still he had "a great fancy" to take them to the places he knew. It seemed to Alice that they were always hopping in and out of cabs. "We went to a great many queer places and he was so proud and pleased." He and Gertrude spent much of the evening talking, and Avery seemed never to have been so open and honest. At the end of the evening he told Gertrude that it had been one of the finest times of his life. The next day he left for the Mediterranean, and a few mornings afterward Gertrude received a card from him expressing his happiness once again. Just hours later, they learned that he had drowned.

Gertrude's talk at the University of Michigan sparked a controversy among the professors in the English department. One thought her "a terrible bore. . . . The whole explanation of her work," he decided, "lies in the fact that early she found she could do automatic writing, and she has never ceased doing it. One day she found she could sell it and called it poetry." Another professor countered that Gertrude had been "very intelligible," and a third offered that it was a mistake to apply old criteria to her new mode of writing, just as it would be to modern painting or music. And one warned students against "a quick enthusiasm for her work until they have balanced it with an understanding of what other artists have already accomplished."

After that guarded reception, and an onslaught of snow and slush, Gertrude and Alice headed south for Christmas. Professional obligations were put aside for a week while they visited with some of Gertrude's relatives in Baltimore. At the home of her cousin Julian Stein, his wife and children, Gertrude requested only that she be excused from all social activities so that she could rest before she continued her tour. But she jovially took part in the family's Christmas, hanging stockings, gushing over trinkets, and entertaining Julian's children and their friends. On Christmas Eve, she and Alice visited a friend of their own.

F. Scott Fitzgerald was then living in the city with his daughter Scottie. When Scottie came down to greet Gertrude and Alice, Gertrude apologized for not having a Christmas gift for the little girl. "I did not know I was to see you," she said. But, the child asked hopefully, "Haven't you something in your pocket?" Gertrude had: a pencil. "I shall keep this as a souvenir," Scottie said politely before she went to bed.[147] Fitzgerald's wife Zelda was home for the holidays from the sanatorium where she was being treated for worsening mental illness and was, Alice thought, "thin, eerie and fey." She showed Gertrude some of her recent paintings, one of which Gertrude asked to keep for herself. Fitzgerald, as Alice remembered him then, was "poignant, disturbing and ineffably beautiful."[148] It was the last time they met.

The two were received at the White House by Eleanor Roosevelt, a visit which left both Gertrude and Alice unimpressed. Alice was unable to recall much of the tea, including the name of the official who took the President's place in greeting them. Gertrude had always been more sympathetic to Theodore than to Franklin. At her arrival in New York, when someone quoted the President, Gertrude had retorted that Lincoln Steffens had been correct in his evaluation of Roosevelt. When a reporter reminded her that Theodore Roosevelt was not the current President and had been dead for some time, she responded, "He may not be as dead as you think."

They continued north and by the middle of January were back in New England, first at Choate, then at nearby Wesleyan, where Gertrude held an informal session with some forty students, discussing art, literature, and aesthetics. Though the students sometimes tried to catch her with such questions as "Do you consider yourself a greater genius than Shakespeare?" the discussion for the most part centered on larger issues. She admonished the students not to try to learn too much from any one experience. "The great trouble," she explained, "is that Americans have the idea that to understand something you must be able to immediately restate it." More important, thought Gertrude, was a sure emotional response.

They stopped in New York for Carl Van Vechten before heading south. He had arranged a meeting for them with Ellen Glasgow, about which the novelist had some reservations. Glasgow promised Van Vechten that she would be polite to Gertrude, even if she did not like her, since it usually took her a full day to prepare herself to be rude. But Gertrude's reputation made her wonder about her talent and her alleged influence. "My private opinion is that the writers she has influenced (especially Hemingway) couldn't have been much worse if she had let them alone," she wrote to Van Vechten. But at the dinner she gave for Gertrude and Alice, Glasgow found that she liked both guests very much, was completely won over by Gertrude's personality—though never changing her opinion of her work. At the dinner, seated beside James Branch Cabell, Alice was at first intimidated by the noted writer. But when he asked, "Is Gertrude Stein serious?" she replied forthrightly, "Desperately." "That puts a different light on it," Cabell told her. "For you," Alice declared. "Not for me."[149] After that, they got along perfectly.

The southern part of Gertrude's tour had been arranged by Alice from their suite at the Algonquin. Ross, who had committed Gertrude to several lectures, had delayed in sending the schedule to Alice. But by contacting each university or club, she was able to reconstruct the sequence of engagements. Gertrude lectured at the universities of Virginia, Richmond, and North Carolina, the College of William and Mary, and Sweet Briar. Sweet Briar and Mount Holyoke, she thought, were the only two women's colleges where the girls were not typed. "Vassar, Wellesley and Smith girls will be Vassar, Wellesley and Smith girls all their life," she told an interviewer.

Gertrude's thoughts about the South had been germinating since her youth, when she lived with relatives in Baltimore after her parents died. During a walk around the Sweet Briar campus, she related the special Southern experience to writing and art. Writing, she told her companion, will be true if it is based in reality. "Take that tree for instance. You see it and I see it. You can write about it because it is true. Your writing will be true. But if, because your parents and grandparents have decided it would be better that no tree should appear there, you decide to write as if it weren't there your writing will not be true. It won't convince me or anybody. That's what Virginia is still trying to do and has been ever since the Civil War. They ought to be producing fine writers but they aren't. They are still trying not to see the tree but they know down deep inside that it is there. You can't get away from it."[150]

For Alice, visiting Virginia was the realization of a

dream and the tour through the temperate South a welcome relief after January in New England. New Orleans, with its bountiful market and colorful architecture, she found charming. There she and Gertrude had a reunion with Sherwood Anderson, who drove them into the city in his rattling Ford, with Alice perched on Gertrude's knee.[151]

After Gertrude's lecture at Tulane University on February 18, she and Alice were taken to see the Live Oak Society on the university's campus. The hundred oaks were themselves the society, admitted if it were proven that they had attained an age of one century. Thereafter, some human sponsor ensured their continuing membership by paying annual dues of one hundred acorns, which were then sprouted by the university and distributed for planting.[152]

They returned to Chicago in March and happily settled in Thornton Wilder's apartment, where Alice could keep house. She marveled at the way the milk was delivered each morning by a seemingly invisible milkman, and managed to glimpse him one day slipping his bottles through an opening in the wall. He seemed a bit embarrassed, she reported to Gertrude, who decided that "these things are not supposed to be seen, not like in France where nothing comes out without everything to do with its coming in."[153]

The kitchen in Wilder's apartment, though very small, was efficient and allowed Alice to cook quickly and effortlessly. "Those days are still my ideal of happy housekeeping," she remembered later. From her headquarters at 6020 Drexel Avenue, she worked on arrangements for the rest of the tour. There was so much to see, and so many who wanted to see Gertrude, that Alice once proposed staying in America and not returning to France. But Gertrude replied with a "hmmph" and the suggestion was forgotten. One city Gertrude was especially excited about visiting was Helena, Montana, where a young novelist, Samuel Steward, was waiting to greet her. Gertrude, Alice wrote, wanted to see a gold mine, a ghost town, and, hopefully, a gallows tree.[154] They also wanted to see Steward, who had sent Gertrude his *Angels on the Bough*, which she deemed "a very interesting book. It has something in it that makes literature. I do not know quite what but there it is."[155] Unfortunately, the plan to visit Helena could not be carried out. With several colleges unable to sponsor a lecture, Alice wrote to Steward that the trip to the Northwest—where she had planned to show Gertrude the country in which she had lived as a young woman—would have to be postponed until a future time.

Instead, the two flew to Dallas, where Gertrude spoke at the Hockaday School, a girls' preparatory school and junior college. Alice was impressed by the flowers—"wild and cultivated . . . wondrously beautiful, bright and fragrant"—the students, and the kitchen's copper pots and pans. She took away with her a recipe for what Gertrude considered the only digestible corn bread she had ever eaten.

For the last month of their stay, they went west to California—forever "God's country" to Alice. A party was given for them by a Los Angeles friend of Carl Van Vechten, where they met Charlie Chaplin, Dashiell Hammett, Lillian Hellman, and Anita Loos. "The only films we have seen are yours," Alice told Chaplin, an exaggeration, she admitted, but one which pleased him.

From Los Angeles, Gertrude rented a car for the trip to San Francisco, first taking a driving test which, fortunately for Gertrude, had nothing to do with driving. ". . . It all had to do with your health and your mother's and father's health and with what you would do if anything happened and what the rules of the road are. . . . Alice Toklas who cannot drive at all could have answered all these questions just as well," thought Gertrude. But, she reflected, perhaps "they take it so for granted that everybody can drive they would no more think of asking you about the actual making the car go than they would think of asking you how you make your legs go when you walk."[156]

On the way to San Francisco they stopped in Monterey, which Alice found changed drastically from the placid town she had known. Failing to find Sherman's Rose, she was amazed when a policeman told her that the adobe house had been moved from the site on which it had stood for nearly a century. It had been rebuilt and restored, designated by the Monterey History and Art Association as an historical landmark. "And Sherman's rosebush?" she asked. "Did that go up into the hills with the house?" It had.

They stopped for a few nights at the Del Monte—it, too, rebuilt and restored from the time Alice had dined there. But the food, she thought, was as fine as she had remembered. During the days they rested there Gertrude received a phone call from one of her old friends, but Alice intercepted it. "When am I going to see Gertrude?" Mabel Dodge asked. "I don't think you are going to," Alice replied. Mabel for years had been living in the artists' colony of Taos, New Mexico. But, Mabel said, the poet Robinson Jeffers has asked to meet her. Alice was not moved. "Well, he will have to do without."[157]

Alice was more congenial to a meeting with the novelist Gertrude Atherton, one of the idols of her youth, still exceedingly lovely,[158] who gave a dinner party for Gertrude and one day took them both on a drive to a convent at San Rafael where her granddaughter was a Carmelite nun. Gertrude Atherton, though over seventy, wore what Alice thought was an outrageous shade—a pale blue—and looked very lovely.

"Coming back to my native town," Alice wrote, "was exciting and disturbing. It was all so different, and still quite like it had been." She met many of her former friends. When Gertrude lectured at a women's club, Alice met Nellie Jacott's brother in the hallway. "Not possible!" she exclaimed to Sidney Joseph. "I didn't expect to see you." After Gertrude's lecture, the two women were surrounded by a lively crowd. One of them, trying to get close to Gertrude, told Alice, "You know we were tremendously fond of your father, your mother was an angel, and you are very dear to us." Alice was unimpressed, noting "the descending order."[159] She found time for a brief but warm visit with Harriet Levy. But while she was able to renew a few friendships, her contact with her family had broken almost completely.

Her father had died in a nursing home in 1924. Her brother had been married in 1915 and had one eighteen-year-old son, but Clarence's relationship with his sister was estranged, especially after legal difficulties over land they held. If Alice saw him at all during her stay in San Francisco it was a last visit: he died, a suicide, in 1937.

They both wanted to visit the sites of their childhood homes: 922 O'Farrell Street no longer existed, and when Alice went to 2300 California Street, where she and her family had lived after they returned from Seattle, she could not find the house and thought it had been demolished. Gertrude was more disturbed than Alice by the resurrection of youthful memories. From their fifteenth-floor suite at the Mark Hopkins Hotel on Nob Hill, Alice looked out over the city and found it "natural," but for Gertrude "it was trouble, yes it was, it did make me feel uncomfortable."[160] The only disturbing sight for Alice was the beginning construction of the Golden Gate Bridge. The span, she thought, "would . . . destroy the landscape a good deal."[161]

In San Francisco, Alice allowed herself to share a bit of the limelight with Gertrude. Throughout the trip, she had lurked in corners, saying little and causing reporters to ask Gertrude, "Is there really an Alice B. Toklas?" Gertrude would laugh, "There she is!" as she pointed out her modest "secretary." If an interviewer cornered Alice, she would admit only, "I am just a plain person. I lead a quiet life." When pressed, she would relate Gertrude's views on various questions. First impressions varied little: most people who met Gertrude and Alice at a lecture thought that Gertrude totally eclipsed her friend. Alice was self-effacing, scarcely spoke, would not pose for photographs. Those who met them socially found Alice charming and congenial. Her appearance, they thought, was less unusual than Gertrude's. She was quiet, polite, a lady. Those who entertained them in their homes or on campuses knew that it was Alice who had full charge of all practical affairs, seeing to every detail, making sure that Gertrude's schedule ran smoothly and ensuring her contentment. She was a "firm but gentle manager," one friend observed.[162]

The press focused on Gertrude, audiences cast but a fleeting glance at the dark woman in the corner, and students could hardly recall Alice's presence. Only Thornton Wilder retained a vivid picture of Alice as he first knew her. She had a protuberance between her eyebrows, he recalled—something Picasso had once noticed and likened to the horn of a unicorn—and with her bangs and mustache she looked strange indeed. Her appearance elicited some giggles in America, but in France, he saw later, she and Gertrude were admired rather than mocked. Wilder never knew whether or not Alice understood all of Gertrude's work, but he could see at once that she believed firmly in Gertrude's genius. She knew she was living with a great brilliance, and for Gertrude that was enough.[163]

A week before they returned to France, Alice wrote to tell Harriet Levy that the trip had been so successful they were planning to come back in the winter. Everything had been "marvellous" and Gertrude was very happy. Any doubts Gertrude had were completely dispelled. Before she came, she had worried that Americans might not pay any attention to her. ". . . There is something that I can not remember not really remember did they listen in that America that I remember did they listen to the answer after they had asked the question."[164] She was afraid that she would come to agree with Sherwood Anderson's description of Americans as a "spongy mass of general unintelligence."[165] Instead, her audiences had been excited and interested, her hosts warm and friendly. Throughout the six-month tour, she had been well cared for, and that, of course, was Alice's doing. Except for a few moments of panic when Alice had lost Gertrude's engagement book and lecture schedule, she had steered Gertrude from city to campus, from plane to hotel, from party to podium with no bother at all to Gertrude.

Gertrude gave one photographer an intimation of Alice's duties when he suggested some activities for her poses. "All right," she agreed, "what do you want me to do?" He mentioned first that she might unpack her airplane bag. "Oh I said Miss Toklas always does that oh no I could not do that, well he said there is the telephone suppose you telephone well I said yes but I never do Miss Toklas always does that, well he said what can you do, well I said I can put my hat on and take my hat off and I can put my coat on and I can take it off and I like water I can drink a glass of water all right he said do that and he photographed while I did that and the next morning there was the layout and I had done it."[166]

Before they left, a worried Alice had asked Carl Van Vechten, ". . . Will there be any one over there who will say there goes Gertrude Stein I have heard of their doing that and I would love it to happen." Carl assured her that Gertrude would be noticed and appreciated. "You mean," said Alice skeptically, "you will hire some small boys to do it so as to give me the pleasure of it."[167]

But by the end of the tour, she was convinced that the Gertrude Stein of myth and celebrity was firmly established. Alice was no longer needed as a publisher: Bennett Cerf had assured Gertrude that Random House would publish a book of hers each year. She was no longer needed as publicity agent: admirers promised to flock to the rue de Fleurus and Bilignin. She would be, once again, gardener, hostess, and wife.

Eighteen

THEY SUMMERED, AS BEFORE, in Bilignin. Alice customarily rose at five-thirty or six each morning, gathered *fraises des bois* for Gertrude's breakfast, picked tea roses for their rooms and table, and, when a guest showed special promise, left a bouquet of mauve roses and laurel in his room. While Alice weeded, hoed, clipped, and planted, Gertrude looked on approvingly, meditating on money, the subject of a forthcoming series of essays. Only once did she interfere with Alice's sudden passion for growing vegetables. Alice apparently would not let herself be undone by the Baroness Pierlot, a neighbor whose garden boasted a grand variety of carrots, beets, peas—and especially beans. Climbing on a box to pick some French string beans, Alice fell. Gertrude admonished her and suggested that fewer vegetables would be sufficient for their table. Alice conceded: the more she grew, the more she cooked, and after a day of cooking, she said, "I wasn't fit for much else."[168]

Her devotion to gastronomy entailed unusual outings. One friend recalled a late night ride to gather acacia blossoms still heavy with dew so that Alice could make acacia fritters for lunch the next day. When she was not attending to the household, she retired to her office, a small room overlooking a terrace garden. But Alice, who once or twice declared that she liked a view but preferred to sit with her back toward it, worked with the shutters tightly closed. A single bare bulb hung above the old black typewriter perched on a kitchen table. The room, papered in dark brown, offered no distractions from her task of deciphering, typing, copy-reading, and sorting Gertrude's ever-growing number of manuscripts. In the peaceful years following Gertrude's peak of fame, Alice did what she liked best: devoted herself completely to the loving care of Gertrude Stein.

At sixty, she could have the air of a grande dame. Francis Rose observed her as hostess during many visits. She would sit

> all black, tidy and tiny, on a vast horsehair sofa, with an equally large tray sparkling with more silver urns and teapots in front of her. Some of the teapots were in frail Chinese terra-cotta coloured pottery. The small tables around were covered with beautiful china, heaped with all kinds of homemade cakes, *marrons glacés*, crystallized cherries and violets, and piles of an Oriental fruit like tiny, yellow Japanese paper lanterns.

> Alice Toklas, in her black lace dress, was like an ambassadress entertaining the women guests who generally did not interest Gertrude. She served the tea and cookies, but was always watching the guests like a cat to see that everything was going well and that the good manners, according to the Victorian standards of the house, were being observed.[169]

Her scrutiny often left guests uncomfortable. A few years later, Picasso's mistress, Françoise Gilot, meeting Gertrude and Alice for the first time, was distinctly ill at ease because of the dark figure at the other end of the sofa peering at her with hostility. Alice's clothing, she thought, was somber enough for a funeral, and she was distracted from conversation by her huge black hat. When Alice was not perched at the edge of the cushion, eyeing her new guest, she trotted back and forth from the dining room, replenishing the supply of iced *petits fours*, which Françoise thought were too sticky and sweet. When she spoke, occasionally supplying Gertrude with a detail of a story, her voice was a shock: low, raspy, grating, it reminded Françoise of "the sharpening of a scythe."[170] Though Françoise ultimately decided that it was easier not to see Gertrude than to suffer Alice's company, many others braved Miss Toklas for the pleasure of Miss Stein.

Their only trips aside from the familiar shuttle from Paris to Bilignin were two stays in England. Early in 1936, they went again to Oxford and Cambridge, where Gertrude lectured and was, Alice reported, "a marvellous success." Again, in the spring of 1937, they went for the premiere of Gertrude's *A Wedding Bouquet*, a ballet based on *They Must. Be Wedded. To Their Wife.* Constant Lambert conducted the score written by their friend Lord Gerald Berners, and the Sadler's Wells dancers included Margot Fonteyn, Ninette de Valois, and Robert Helpmann.

They stayed with Gerald Berners at his home in Berkshire, the only house in England, a friend told them, that was well heated. Lord Berners, a short, bald, dark man, pleased Alice and Gertrude with a wit that impressed even Edith Sitwell. "He had a superb power of retort," she noted, "which his adversary would, in self-defence, ascribe to eccentricity."

One of his acquaintances was in the impertinent habit of saying to him, "I have been sticking up for you." He repeated this once too often, and Lord Berners replied, "Yes and I have been sticking up for you. Someone said you aren't fit to live with pigs, and I said that you are."

A pompous woman of his acquaintance, complaining that the head-waiter of a restaurant had not shown her and her husband immediately to a table said, "We had to tell him who we were." Gerald, interested, enquired, "And who were you?"[171]

Among the friends that Gertrude and Alice saw were the Abdys, Lady Diana and Sir Robert—"Bertie"—whom they had known earlier in France. Bertie was a gourmet who held hour-long sessions with his cook each night reviewing the days's repasts and planning for the next day. One afternoon at lunch, Alice asked innocently, "Of what is this sauce made?" He answered unexpectedly, "The dairy and the barnyard, I suppose."

In the summer of 1937, W. G. Rogers, "the Kiddie" who had been adopted by the two women during World War I, brought his wife to Bilignin for a sentimental journey through the same countryside he had traveled with Alice and Gertrude on his autumn furlough some twenty years before. Now a writer, Rogers, with his wife, the poet Mildred Weston, had warmly entertained the two when they

visited New England in 1934, and their visit was anticipated as a happy reunion. In the spring, Gertrude wrote
that she and Alice were very much looking forward to
August. "Mildred will write a little poem about Bilignin,"
she told him, "and I will write a portrait of the Kiddies and
Pépé and Basket will bark and Alice will do all the rest.
. . ."172

Throughout the visit, Rogers noticed that, although
Alice was long used to doing "all the rest," she had to
contend with many domestic difficulties. Organized and
efficient, Alice struggled with a personality unlike hers in
every way. While she rose early and was ready to leave by
eight, Gertrude, under extreme pressure, could be moved
to start by ten-thirty. While Alice preferred to travel
marked roads, Gertrude enjoyed bumpy, narrow, steep
paths, especially when they were posted: "Vehicles not
allowed beyond this point." While Alice endorsed the prac-
ticality of maps and encouraged their use, Gertrude preferred to travel by whimsey and caprice, detouring to a
town whose name sounded pleasant and driving miles off a
planned course to find a picnic spot.

Alice's tactics sometimes consisted of undirected comments—she once remarked that maps were necessary, in
fact absolutely indispensable. "Yet what . . . was the use of
having them if a person didn't follow them?"173 But sometimes she resorted to blatant threat. ". . . I'll walk!" she
told Gertrude when she turned down a forbidden path, and
proceeded to make her way out of the moving car.174
"She was manager and captain of the team," Rogers saw,
"called the plays, ran interference, decided when the
grounds were too wet for a game, even acted as cheer
leader. . . . To find out what happens when an irresistible
force meets an immovable object, it was necessary merely
to watch these two."175

A few months after the Rogerses had left, the irresistible
force again had to move the immovable Gertrude, this time
to a new apartment. Alice and Gertrude had occasionally
thought of leaving 27, rue de Fleurus: the apartment was
dark, the kitchen was inadequate, the rooms were not airy;
but an unexpected visit from their landlord late in 1937
made the move inevitable. The landlord wanted the pa-
vilion for his son, who was soon to marry, and the atelier

would be turned into a garage. ". . . We were less shocked than we expected to have been," Gertrude wrote to Rogers, and they promptly set forth to find a new home.

Méraude Guevara, their friend who lived on the rue Dauphine, knew of an apartment on the nearby rue Christine, one block from the Seine. Located on a dark, narrow street in a shabby old building, the apartment itself was a delightful surprise. Gertrude was mad about it; Alice was thrilled. "Have you enough money to tip the concierge liberally?" Gertrude asked Alice when they first saw the rooms. Of course, Alice had come prepared; but the concierge declined. The landlord, he told them, must first decide if they were suitable tenants.[176]

They set a moving date for January 15, 1938, allowing for a short time to pack their effects, which included some one hundred thirty canvases. Gertrude's contribution to the effort was characteristically minimal. When the move was over she disclosed to Rogers that "Alice did not know any longer that she could sit she lost the habit and just went on being on her feet. . . ."[177]

Natalie Barney, now a closer neighbor than before, worried over Alice's exertions. "Alice T. is withering away under the stress of moving into a new flat," she wrote to Romaine Brooks. ". . . I am afraid 'the bigger one,' who gets fatter and fatter and fatter, will sooner or later devour her. She looks so thin. . . ."[178]

Along with their packages and pictures, they took with them the inspired anecdotes of life at the rue de Fleurus, indisputable versions to be told and retold, pieces of the legend which would outlive them both. The real memories were left behind, and in their new home, they began "a new life so completely new" that the past faded. Now in their sixties, they were happiest in the company of their closest friends, or alone together. In quiet moments, they would go up to the top of the building at 5, rue Christine and look out over their city. ". . . We stand by the window as we are and look at the sky with no one to see . . . ," Gertrude wrote.

But what might have been a life of peace and pleasure was shattered by rumors of war. ". . . If they would only leave us alone in our little lost places . . . ,"[179] Gertrude sighed plaintively, they could be content. Though Gertrude denied the possibility of war, declaring that war was unwanted and illogical, Alice—"forethoughtful as always," Gertrude said—conceded its likelihood and set to work copying Gertrude's manuscripts to be sent to America. On the advice of Carl Van Vechten and Thornton Wilder, Gertrude's pieces would be deposited at Yale University, Wilder's alma mater, for safekeeping. It was their one concession. Though friends pleaded for their return to the States, they decided to remain in France—at home.

They customarily stayed in Bilignin through the grape harvest, returning to Paris for the winter. But when battle broke out in September 1939, they changed their plans and canceled their trip to the city. ". . . Stay, stay please stay in Bilignin!" Rogers had written them. "If war does come, it'll be a thousand bombs over Paris before any Paris newspaper can get out an extra. . . ."[180]

Still, it was necessary to make a quick journey to Paris to find their passports and papers and to look after their paintings. A pass was finally secured, permitting them thirty-six hours to travel to Paris, set their apartment in order, and return to Bilignin. In the little time that they had, Alice could uncover only their dog's pedigree—their own papers were so well hidden that she could find them nowhere.

She and Gertrude had planned to take down all the paintings to protect them from falling during bombing raids, but it was soon evident that their large collection could not be laid out on the floor. There was nothing to do but to take with them two of the most valuable—Picasso's portrait of Gertrude and Cézanne's portrait of his wife—and hope the rest would survive.

When they returned to Bilignin, they momentarily wavered in their decision to stay in France. The American Consul in Lyon urged them to leave. Letters from America begged for their return. Once they went so far as to drive to the consulate to have their passports renewed—only to turn back at the crowded government office. They preferred to stay among their friends than flee; they wanted to be in France, where they had lived their lives. Where was there to go? Gertrude asked Alice. She could not think of becoming a refugee.[181]

In the States, their friends were worried. "Alice's handwriting," Rogers wrote, "so fine, so little, so clear, and such a long time between anybody ever seeing any of it!" Thornton Wilder, after what seemed an interminable time without a letter, called Rogers for news. When Rogers said he knew nothing, Wilder took what for him was a drastic measure and wrote to Carl Van Vechten for information. Wilder and Van Vechten, many thought, were rivals for Gertrude's friendship and had a cool relationship with one another.

But Gertrude and Alice tried to face the war with calm resignation. In 1940, Alice filled two glass jars with four pounds of citron, candied orange and lemon peel, pineapple, and cherries, and two pounds of raisins. When the war ended, she decided, there would be a Liberation Fruit Cake. The anticipation of baking it cheered her immensely. Even through the Occupation, the two refused to be downed by the "black cloud over and about one" of the very real danger they faced daily. A neighbor of theirs, an aging spinster, became very frightened each time a German soldier passed down her road, yet she always went out to watch. "Well why," Alice asked her, "if you are so scared do you go out to look." "I go out to look," the woman replied, "because I am so scared."[182] It made better sense, thought Alice, simply to turn from the window and keep busy. Gertrude found some solace in cutting box hedges, convinced that when the hedges were completely cut the war would be over. Alice made raspberry jam in season, and otherwise indulged in the passionate reading of recipes.

In the days of rationing, of a "protracted, indeed a perpetual Lent," when their hunger was assuaged by a monotonous menu, Alice read cookbooks with almost salacious joy. "Through the long winter evenings close to the inadequate fire, the recipes for food that there was no possibility of realising held me fascinated—forgetful of restrictions, even occasionally of the Occupation. . . . The great French *chefs* and their creations were very real. . . . Though there was not one ingredient obtainable it was abundantly satisfying to pore over its pages, imagination being as lively as it is."[183]

Even in the leanest years, Gertrude presented Alice with a sumptuous cookbook each Christmas, from which Alice vicariously devoured such delicacies as lobster, breast of chicken, and black truffle salad. "She is just deep in descriptions of cake she will never make," Gertrude observed, admitting, "I myself do not really like cooking. . . ."[184]

For their own fare, they were pleased when they could barter for an egg, or when one of Gertrude's foraging expeditions resulted in a pound of flour or a bit of butter. The Rhône and the Lac de Bourget kept them supplied with salmon, trout, carp, lavaret, and perch; but Alice dreamed of thick slices of ham floating on a silver dish. "That was all," she wrote. "It haunted me for the six months that were to pass before the blessed black market was organised."[185]

Successful marketing depended, it seemed, on one's personality, and Gertrude accepted the responsibility of procuring supplies. "Has she or has she not the right personality?" a neighbor wondered. Gertrude returned time after time with ingredients that no one else could get. The cost of black market food was astoundingly high and their bank accounts were low. As they were unable to get funds from America, there was no recourse but to sell some valuables —and Cézanne's *Portrait of Madame Cézanne* and Picasso's portrait of Gertrude were their most important possessions. In 1943 the decision had to be made: the Cézanne painting was packed in their car, and the two women crossed the border to Switzerland, sold it, and made the dangerous journey back. "We ate the Cézanne," Alice sadly told friends later. Their friends were shocked, but not by the sale of the painting; few could understand why Alice and Gertrude, having safely crossed into Switzerland, did not seek refuge there for the duration of the war.

Months before, they had been warned by an official in Belley that they were in danger of being sent to a concentration camp. He advised them to flee to Switzerland. But the two women were apparently convinced that their safety was assured by the efforts of their friend Bernard Faÿ. Faÿ, who had accepted the position of head of the Bibliothèque Nationale under the Vichy Government, confided to Pétain his worries about the fate of Gertrude and Alice during the Occupation. Moved by Faÿ's request for their protection, Pétain dictated a letter to the *sous-préfet* at Belley, placing in his hands full responsibility for seeing that the two Jewesses were left undisturbed. Faÿ himself regularly telephoned the man to remind him of his special mission.[186]

Although they felt comparatively secure, they relied heavily on their neighbors for advice and commiseration. They were understandably upset, then, when their home at Bilignin was suddenly reclaimed by their landlord for his own family. Not only would they have to find another place to live, but they would now have to live among strangers. Fortunately, the house they found was not far from Bilignin, in Culoz, located between rocky cliffs and a railroad track, on a large plot, but having as yet no vegetable garden. "It would be starting over from scratch," Alice knew. But there were terraced flower beds running down to the valley, and the house itself was pretentious enough to be called a castle. "When is a castle not a castle," Gertrude wondered. It would seem more like a home with a few goats, and these gave their residence a special ambience. ". . . The goats come out and you go in./That is what is real cordiality," Gertrude decided. "There are so many castles, really castles, some are just called castles, some built like castles and some really castles. And those that are really castles, always have something or some are coming in and going out. Always."[187]

Few guests were among those "coming in and going out," but several times soldiers were billeted. The first group was two German officers and their aides. Rooms were quickly made up, and all provisions hidden. Alice did not have time to gather up their books, but apparently these did not interest the soldiers. The men's dining habits, however, very much interested Alice.

When the orderlies came into the kitchen to prepare their officers' meals the cook went white with rage. How the Germans cooked has no place in a cookbook, but their menu eaten three times a day is offered as a curiosity. Per man: 1 large slice of ham $1\frac{1}{2}$ inches thick heated in deep fat, the gelatinous-glutinous contents of a pint tin (replacing bread and potatoes?), the muddy liquid contents of a large tin (replacing coffee?). Three times a day the orderlies would carry these meals into an empty room adjoining their bedrooms. Apparently the officers sat at table and ate with their orderlies. One day an orderly gave the cook a tin of the substitute for bread and potatoes. She in turn gave it to our most treasured possessions, four hens. They ran eagerly toward it, pecked at it and walked away. The cook, delighting in the *geste* of her French hens, threw the mess into the mountain torrent that ran around two sides of the house.[188]

When the officers left after two weeks, everyone in the house "heaved a deep sigh of relief."

They received next thirty-two members of the Italian Army—two officers who lived in the house and thirty soldiers who crowded into the garages and chauffeur's quarters. Alice, worried that the soldiers might raid her vegetable garden, was assured that they would not, and found they didn't. She thought them friendly, and some of them even sold her some black market cigarettes, "A most welcome relief," she said, "from my tobaccoless state." But the Italians suffered at the hands of the Germans. When they learned of their country's defeat, they destroyed their papers. "You should not have allowed them to do this," Gertrude told the officers. "They were a kind of protection and you are without any now. You are at the mercy of the Germans."[189] With the frontier some 125 kilometers away, Alice and Gertrude hoped that the men would escape unharmed. But they later learned that all had been killed.

Shortly after the Americans landed, the third troops came to Culoz, this time one hundred Germans. Twelve were to stay in the house; the rest, outside on the terraces and in the gardens. Gertrude was put out of sight "with her manuscript and the poodle," and Alice and the servants set out beds for the men. With the soldiers' dogs roaming around the house and their horses and donkeys in the gardens, the scene was "a hideous confusion."

The morning after they arrived, Alice found that a calf had been slaughtered on the terrace, and the soldiers were roasting it. After their midday feast, they pillaged Alice's own provisions—not finding, of course, the jars of candied fruit that she had carefully hidden. Fortunately, their stay was brief.

One of the servants who "came with the house" was a cook, but Alice soon discovered that Clothilde couldn't manage without fresh cream, six egg yolks, and a fine white wine. Though Alice, too, preferred the unctuous to the lean, she could make edible whatever was available. She found some wine and instructed the cook to proceed. Meat loaf for six, using one hundred grams of meat, was among Alice's gastronomic economies.[190] While Clothilde sat by, "old, tired and pessimistic," Alice took over the kitchen—until one afternoon in August 1944.

Like their neighbors, Gertrude and Alice were "wild with excitement" when they heard the news that Paris had been liberated. "The end was near," they knew. Soon, they learned that some members of the Resistance had come out of hiding in the mountains and overcame the hundreds of Germans in Culoz. "It was glorious, classic, almost Biblical," Alice said. She and Gertrude joyfully rode into Belley, where American and French flags were flying from the windows.

Alice, thinking she saw a jeep parked at a curb, rushed over to inspect it and saw what were "undeniably two American soldiers in it." Immediately, she invited them home for dinner and to spend the night. Clothilde and another servant, Olympe, were wild with excitement, crying and hailing the soldiers as *"nos libérateurs."* At last Clothilde agreed to prepare a meal. "Do not worry, madame," she told Alice, "now I can cook even if there is no cream and not enough butter and eggs." From then on Clothilde was a constant amazement, ending one luncheon with a puff-paste tart decorated with French and American flags, laboriously drawn until midnight the night before.

Clothilde's excitement only increased when she soon answered the door to two American journalists, Frank Gervasi and Eric Sevareid, who came to personally liberate Gertrude and Alice. They arrived for a lunch of omelettes and chocolate soufflé, accompanied by an incessant stream of talk from Gertrude. Alice, Gervasi remembered, said little, but followed each word with dark intensity, as vigilant as ever. She was frail, he thought, and "magnificently ugly—her hair was stringy and as untidy as an unkempt wig, and her upper lip was faintly fuzzy. . . ."

Sevareid gave Gertrude news of Thornton Wilder, told her of the death of Alexander Woollcott, whom they had met in New York, and of the marriage of Hemingway. "That makes his third wife. Tch, tch, tch," Alice said disapprovingly.[191] When Sevareid offered them some army rations, Alice was definite about her needs. "Just give me one American cigarette and I will be happy," she told him. Throughout the Occupation, she had been smoking anything that could be rolled in cigarette paper, except fig leaves, which allegedly had poisoned a friend. A few tobacco plants were rationed to men, but none to women, forcing Alice to barter for cigarettes on the black market.

Two days after his visit, Sevareid took them both to Voiron, where Gertrude made a radio broadcast for the United States. For the women who had chopped up and burned an artist's portrait of Hitler, the broadcast was a final victory and Gertrude extolled the greatness of the French, the Americans, and the United Nations. Liberty, she exclaimed, was more important than "food and clothes more important than anything on this mortal earth, I who spent four years with the French under the German yoke tell you so."[192]

For Alice, one task still remained. Her Liberation Fruit Cake, iced with one inch of almond paste, with hazelnuts substituted for almonds, was joyfully baked and sent to one General Alexander Patch, whose troops had liberated the Bugey region.

The war was over.

Nineteen

IN THE MONTHS after the Liberation, Alice and Gertrude tried to go back to Paris, but the enormous job of packing their possessions, the confusion of events, prevented their start. Finally, on a rainy December night, Alice piled their belongings into a hired van, and she and Gertrude and Basket—Pépé had died during the war—set off in a rented car. "It was good-bye forever to Culoz."

Just before daylight, they were stopped on the road by two men and a woman with a gun. "What do you want?" Gertrude asked. They told her that they were members of the Resistance and asked who they were, where they were going, and why they were on the road. As they talked, they leaned into the car and onto the Picasso painting. "Take care," Alice said, "that is a painting by Picasso, don't disturb it." The three were duly impressed. "We congratulate you, madame," they said, "you may go on."[193]

They arrived at daylight, exhausted but happy; and the rue Christine apartment, it seemed to Alice, was intact. But the next morning she was shocked to find that their belongings had been pillaged. A petit-point footstool that she had embroidered after Picasso's design was among the precious items taken. Pictures were tied together, ready to be removed. She was stunned that even her kitchen drawers had been rifled. Gertrude, however, wanted to hear nothing about it. "You don't know what has been taken," Alice told her, but she was firm. "Don't talk to me about it." And later, when Picasso arrived to welcome them back, the three celebrated because "the treasures of our youth, the pictures, the drawings, were safe."[194]

For Alice at sixty-seven, postwar life brought a new excitement. There were trips to Germany and Belgium, where Gertrude spoke to American troops. There were visits from young GIs, for whom Gertrude was as sought after as Coco Chanel's perfume. One of the first, and the closest, was Joseph Barry, whom Carl Van Vechten nicknamed "Mercury" for his dependable delivery of packages to Gertrude and Alice.

In the winter of 1944, still in the Army, Barry came to ask Gertrude to speak to some troops—and stayed on to figure in her new opera, *The Mother of Us All*. When she asked what part he wanted, Barry told her he would like to wander onstage talking to himself while the other characters declaimed their lines. But "Joe the Wanderer" became "Jo the Loiterer" when he told Gertrude that he had once been arrested for picketing—the charge became loitering—while a student in Ann Arbor.

Barry; the "genuine poet" George John; Richard Wright; Donald Gallup of the Yale Library; writer James Lord; and Donald Sutherland, whom they had known at Princeton: "Our home," Alice wrote, "again became a salon." And guests recorded their visits with the same liveliness as they always had. Barnett Shaw, a young actor and composer, was greeted warmly at the door by Alice and immediately served some brandy, which, Alice assured him, "was not ordinary brandy but a very old Spanish liqueur which a friend had given them." He noticed at once that Alice seemed always to speak of herself in the plural, automatically including Gertrude in whatever she had to say. Gertrude, of course, spoke for herself. When Shaw told her that he "wasn't smart enough" to understand her books, she quickly replied, "You're not supposed to understand them. You're only supposed to buy them."

Shaw and Sutherland, like Hemingway before them, had strong responses to Gertrude's magnetism, despite her strange clothing and her age. But Constantine FitzGibbon, a U.S. army captain sent to the two by Francis Rose, found Alice "a charming woman" and Gertrude an offensive egomaniac—perhaps because she told him, as soon as he introduced himself, that "an American army officer is a contradiction in terms." Alice's contribution to the inane conversation which followed Gertrude's remark was, "have another cake."

Ellen Bloom, Gertrude's Baltimore cousin, visited the pair in the fall of 1945 and described the aging Alice as "a hideous witchlike little figure with a large nose and moustached face who was wearing a grey suit which reached to her ankles and a hat which was jammed down over her black bangs." Gertrude, Ellen thought, was as much a forceful presence as she had seemed ten years before in America.

Ellen invited them to lunch with her at the Hôtel Edward VII, her headquarters with the Red Cross. When she called for them, she was dismayed to see that Basket was coming too. "They don't allow dogs in the hotel," she told Gertrude. "There's a big sign in the dining room." But Gertrude dismissed her objections. "He *always* goes with us everywhere," she insisted. "The French love dogs. You'll see." The waitress at the entrance to the dining room did not have the attitude that Gertrude expected, but she strode past her, took a table, and slipped Basket scraps as they enjoyed their meal. In the lounge after lunch, Ellen saw that Gertrude attracted a curious and admiring crowd.

Gertrude had her own theory about why GIs came to see her. As she told Cecil Beaton, "It's quite ex-tra-ordinary the way these boys come to see us. They come to see Pablo, and they come to see me. They don't go to anybody else, and I don't believe they come to see us because we're celebrities, but because we're rebels. They know Pablo and I have had to put up a fight in our time, and we've won, and that gives them a fellow feeling, and a link. They know we can understand their problems, and so, of all people in Paris, they come to Pablo and to me. . . ." If they came wanting help in becoming independent and dealing with their own loneliness, she was happy to help them, provided they "haven't got preconceived ideas that are too strong. . . . But I tell some of them to go away. They've become set in their ideas, and I can't put up with anybody who has set ideas, with anyone who is *parti pris*."[195]

She wanted to see her new visitors, but entertaining what seemed at times like the entire American Army was becoming debilitating. She was becoming increasingly tired, and after her Christmas speaking tour in Belgium she returned to Paris feeling greatly fatigued and weak. They would not go out so much, she told Alice; they would not receive so many visitors. Friends found that she was sometimes uncharacteristically irritable, but no one knew what was wrong, except Alice.

Gertrude was ill. In the spring, a severe intestinal attack

sent her to a physician, who advised that she try to build herself up and then undergo an operation. She refused the operation, began to lose weight, and continued feeling fatigued.

By June, the illness was serious enough to mention in a letter to Rogers, and he scolded the two for keeping from him news of Gertrude's health. "In letter after letter I ask how you are and you never say a single solitary word and all of a sudden it's a bowel infection and it's been going on for nobody-here knows how long and nobody knows how bad."[196] Hoping that Gertrude would be able to get a complete rest, the two planned a trip south, heading for Bernard Faÿ's country home. Joe Barry, as chauffeur and companion, took them as far as Azay le Rideau, when Gertrude again felt ill. A local physician urged them to see a specialist at once, and Gertrude and Alice immediately boarded a train back to Paris, where Gertrude's nephew Allan arranged for an ambulance to take his aunt to the American Hospital in Neuilly.

At first the doctors recommended an operation, but the gravity of Gertrude's condition caused them to change their view quickly. Gertrude, by then even more irritable and impatient, told Alice that she never wanted to see them again. Finally, two specialists agreed to operate; and Gertrude, despite pain, was calm and brave.[197]

For Alice, the unthinkable was becoming reality. Somehow, she had hoped, they would die together. Living on—living alone—would be unbearable.[198] Now she was told it was years too late for Gertrude's operation. The "bowel infection" was cancer. On the evening of July 27, 1946, at six-thirty, Gertrude died.

4

The Altar of the Dead

Sorrow comes in great waves . . . but it rolls over us, and though it may almost smother us it leaves us on the spot, and we know that if it is strong we are stronger, inasmuch as it passes and we remain. It wears us, uses us, but we wear it and use it in return; and it is blind, whereas we after a manner see. . . . Everything will pass, and serenity and *accepted* mysteries and disillusionments, and the tenderness of a few good people, and new opportunities and ever so much of life, in a word, will remain.

Henry James,
Letter to Grace Norton

Twenty

SHE LEFT the American Hospital a widow, grieving deeply over Gertrude's death[1] and frightened that she would be forsaken and forgotten by Gertrude's many friends. But from Sarah Stein—who sent her "loving and heartbroken thoughts" from San Francisco—to Hadley Hemingway Mowrer, friends responded with sympathy for Alice. Like most who had known Gertrude, Hadley was shocked at the news of her death, not having heard "the faintest rumour of her being ill. . . . It is you I keep thinking of," she wrote to Alice, "for such a change as this must bring about after a lifetime of complete understanding can hardly be understood by anyone from outside, no matter how great their affection & loyalty. I do hope . . . that my friendliest good wishes, sympathy & affection that I have always felt for both of you will mean a little something in the way of comfort."[2]

"Everything was alive in her," wrote Bernard Faÿ, "her soul, her mind, her heart, her senses. All that life that was in her was at the same time so spontaneous and so voluntary. It is a most shocking thing to think of her as deprived of life. I trust that God in some way, somehow has given her His Life as a reward for all the life she spread around her, for the lives she welcomed, stimulated, cared for and glorified through her genius of understanding and of describing. . . . Dear Alice I can still hear her voice—I shall hear it as long as I live."[3]

Francis Rose, who would design Gertrude's tombstone, was so shattered over Gertrude's death that it was his wife Frederica who wrote to Alice first. "Francis talks continuously of you and longs to be with you," she told Alice. "Miss Stein was the foundation of his life: mother protectoress and inspiration. He is still able to paint but little else and I think it will be some time before he can go on with life again. He looks to you as his dearest friend and wants to do everything in his power to help you."[4]

When Francis himself was able to write, he more than confirmed his wife's sentiments. "You know I love you," he assured Alice, "and will always come when you need me. Dear Alice you will have a lot of work to do now, because you must carry on for Gertrude. She could only leave us in person, which is just hard for us, but she is more than ever alive in her work. It is now up to you to see that all this is made perfect and in order for the world to love."[5]

In the days and weeks after Gertrude's death, Alice was hungry for reassurance that those who had been close to Gertrude would maintain their friendship with her. She asked Carl Van Vechten's forgiveness, when there was nothing to forgive, and begged for his love.[6] More than once, in despondent moments, she grieved over the loss of her one source of joy.[7]

But as Francis Rose had written, Gertrude was gone only physically from Alice's life. She was still the reason for Alice to live. Francis's admonition for Alice to "carry on for Gertrude" was taken up immediately. As tirelessly as she had worked when Gertrude was alive, Alice plunged into work again. Four days after Gertrude's death, she instructed Van Vechten that according to Gertrude's wishes he was to become her literary executor.[8] Though Gertrude had once considered naming Thornton Wilder to that responsibility, the pressure of his own work probably caused her to change her mind and appoint Van Vechten. Alice, however, took upon herself the responsibility of prodding, urging, reminding, and exhorting him to keep Gertrude's spirit alive. Her barrage of letters speak of little else. He must try to publish all of Gertrude's work, she wrote in September, adding that both she and Gertrude were sure he could.[9]

In her will, made on July 23, 1946, Gertrude had provided for payment to be made to Van Vechten for his expenses in facilitating the publication of all her work. Alice and Gertrude's nephew, Allan Daniel Stein, the only child of Sarah and Michael, were named joint executors, with Allan and his children to receive whatever remained of Gertrude's estate after Alice's death. Of her immediate family, only Michael would have been expected to receive a bequest, and he had died in 1938.

Her manuscripts, letters, photographs were all to be sent to Yale, where many were already being kept. Gertrude's art collection was to be left with Alice, with provision for the sale of paintings for Alice's support and for the publication of Gertrude's writing. Only Picasso's portrait of Gertrude was given to a museum, the Metropolitan Museum of Art, in New York.

Alice persevered to carry out Gertrude's every wish, but Van Vechten, when he learned of the terms of the will, was momentarily taken aback.

> Nobody was more surprised than I . . . that she had made me, in some of her last conscious moments, her literary executor, with instructions to publish what material of hers still remained unpublished, for which purpose she instructed her attorney to provide me with the essential sums of money. My initial feeling was that Gertrude had bitten off more than I could easily chew, a feeling greatly intensified after I had inquired of certain publishing friends of mine how much it would cost to print and bind the vast pile of manuscript still unpublished. The sums mentioned were so enormous that my heart sank at the thought of the project ahead of me.[10]

But his loyalty, as always, was unswerving, and his efforts proportionate.

Alice's immediate task was seeing about Gertrude's burial. Arrangements were made for a plot at Père Lachaise; Francis Rose began designs for a headstone with "a little garden . . . for Gertrude's garden must be there."[11] It was not until October 22, however, that the actual burial took place, and for Alice, it was another parting, almost as painful as the first. Prayers were read by Dean Beekman in the American Cathedral. Then Alice, Allan, and his wife continued to Père Lachaise.[12]

But Alice's sorrow was somewhat alleviated by the publication in November of Carl Van Vechten's anthology of some of Gertrude's published work. The book was exceedingly lovely and most impressive, she wrote to Van

Vechten. She praised his taste in editing the book, thought his notes "admirable," and pronounced *Selected Writings* true evidence of his love and friendship for Gertrude.[13]

But the collection had been conceived, compiled, and sent to the printer before Gertrude's death, and the republication of Gertrude's writing, however happy it made Alice, was not bringing her nearer to fulfilling Gertrude's will. Not until the end of November did she see some progress in those efforts: Yale University Press expressed interest in publishing Gertrude's *Four in America*, provided Thornton Wilder, who was much impressed by the book, would write an introduction. Describing herself as most excited over the possibility, Alice set about writing to Van Vechten and to Donald Gallup at Yale to try to determine if Wilder would do the work; by spring she had definite word that *Four in America* would be published in the fall—an event she celebrated in her letters to friends.

Her love for Gertrude still sustained her,[14] she admitted, and for those who would help her keep the memory alive, she offered enthusiastic help and boundless praise. In November, Henry Rago sent Alice an article about Gertrude which he had written for *Poetry*, the journal he edited. More memoir than critique, the article painted an affectionate portrait of an exuberant and generous writer. Of the artistic problems Gertrude considered, Rago was struck, especially, by her questioning of time:

She was interested . . . in the nature of the twentieth century: its beginnings in the American civil war, its need to concentrate on "existence" rather than events, because events were too common an occurrence in our time. . . . She said one day that because the French have a great sense of realism, they know that the elegant is à la mode; and because the English have a sentimental view of life, the elegant for them is the démodé. Time was the reality which she could not forgive the English for sentimentalizing. . . .

Time was her subject,—just as it is the subject of perhaps the greatest philosopher of our century, the inseparable factor in the universe charted by our physics, and the preoccupation of what will probably endure in our literature. . . . It was the timeless which she was seeking in her quarrel with tenses; it was basically not continuous motion she wanted in her narrative, it was the avoidance of discontinuities and perhaps it was even the neutralization of motion. Whether she laid nouns side by side in verses which were almost tactile, or made verbs almost liquid in their fluency in her prose, she wanted a pattern which would keep the beginning from being isolated from the end. She was aware somehow that the nemesis in the modern consciousness is time, the floor of particulars overwhelming the permanently significant.[15]

Alice thought Rago's explanation lucid and precise.[16]

She was equally enthusiastic about Donald Gallup's idea for a collection of letters written to Gertrude by her friends. And her unreserved excitement was for W. G. Rogers' proposed memoir of his long friendship with Gertrude, which he began early in 1947. Reminding him how "very sweet and winning" he was, she recounted their first meeting in the Hôtel Luxembourg in Nîmes and their jaunts through the South of France. Throughout the winter and spring she asked about the book's progress and expressed her eagerness to finally see it. In June, she cautioned Rogers to omit any comments that were not "literature,"[17] but her support was not diminished—not even after reading a first draft.

Trusting Rogers to be as loyal to Gertrude in print as he had been in his friendship, she turned to her own duties, primarily with the dispensing of Picasso's portrait. At first she thought she would not mind its being taken, but as time went on, she realized how much the painting was a part of her life. Whenever she looked at the picture over the fireplace, she could not help but imagine Gertrude sitting contentedly across from it.[18]

When arrangements were finally made to remove it, Alice wondered at the endless formalities. She and Gertrude had thought nothing of bringing it to Bilignin during the war and traveling with it back to Paris. Now, she was even asked to have Picasso attest to the authenticity of the portrait, but refused. It would be an insult, she replied. When the lawyers surmised that the signature could be authenticated by any expert, she kept her silence: the portrait wasn't signed. How could they doubt that the artist was Picasso? she thought.[19]

Early in March, a few days before the painting was to be taken down and shipped to New York, Picasso came to say a final farewell. Neither of them would see the painting again, he told Alice. The last remnant of their youth was gone and for Alice it was another difficult parting. She was deeply upset to see the painting go and replaced it with another, which, she said, filled the wall but left the room empty. More devastating, though, was the news which came to her in the fall that the Metropolitan Museum had lent the painting to the Museum of Modern Art.

Misunderstanding the terms of the loan, Alice was sure the painting would now be able to be sold to a wealthy industrialist or some other collector; or worse; it would find its way into the museum's own collections, something Gertrude would have adamantly opposed. She quickly protested to the Metropolitan, reminding them that Gertrude had never approved of the Museum of Modern Art and had specifically donated her portrait to the only museum whose aims she supported. When she was assured that the loan was only temporary, her fears were quieted; and she accepted with "deep appreciation" a certificate naming Gertrude a benefactor of the museum. Still, she added, she hoped the painting would soon be returned.[20]

Fortunately, she could turn to the success of Gertrude's work. *The Mother of Us All*, Gertrude's last opera, was performed at Columbia University in May 1947, and Alice read with pleasure the clippings Rogers sent. The opera presents a resigned and suffering Susan B. Anthony, who expresses some cynical views on men, marriage, and politics. A letter from the suffragette's grandniece praised Gertrude's characterization, and the young Susan B. Anthony wrote Alice that Gertrude had "caught the essence of the struggle Aunt Susan led—and its pathos" and brought to light her mistreatment by politicians who used her for their own purposes.[21]

Alice was "passionately" interested in a book begun by Donald Sutherland, then a professor of classics. She was impressed by his insights into Gertrude's work and judged him to be one of the few writers she knew who could present Gertrude as she should be understood. When she read the first chapter of his book, she was sure that he would provide the definitive work about Gertrude.[22] In warm, frequent, lengthy letters to Sutherland she repeated her appreciation for his sound interpretation of Gertrude's work. "Her art," he wrote, "like that of Henry James or that of Mozart was a thoroughly intellectual and secular art, essentially, and in the great sense, comic."[23] To Gertrude, as to James, "the consciousness was very much alive, more brilliantly alive than human nature with all its biographies."[24]

For Sutherland, Gertrude's work was "as immediate and exciting as anything America has produced in this century."[25] In her determination to destroy nineteenth-century syntax and word order, he thought her

comparable to what Gerard Manley Hopkins was doing with syntax in his poetry, but there is a very great difference between them. Hopkins had as a Jesuit casuist training in very fine distinctions of idea, a training corresponding considerably to the medical and philosophical training of Gertrude Stein. But, as I believe this is important, Hopkins was a straight baroque poet. . . . The baroque means, as a conquest, to bring everything under a closed system and within reach of the authorities. . . . All in all it leads to a closed and finished art, the stuffing of something inside something else, even if it wrenches the container considerably. Joyce, in the twentieth century, went on with this, cramming everything into the scheme of the *Odyssey* or cyclic time, so that one may say that he was the last hypertrophy of the nineteenth century and destroyed it by overdoing it.[26]

Calling his study a biography of Gertrude's work, Sutherland was more concerned with tracing the evolution of her writing than in uncovering personal details of her life. Alice, always protective of her privacy and Gertrude's, strongly endorsed this view, and equally as strongly opposed the efforts of another writer, Julian Sawyer, who attempted to explain sexual references in Gertrude's work. Gertrude, Alice wrote to Sawyer, would have certainly objected to his speculations. His approach, she thought, was uninformed and boorish.[27]

After nearly forty years of creating and publicizing the legend of Gertrude Stein, Alice would not permit a negative word or a prying eye. Her reaction was always swift and hard, and she mustered whatever forces she could from among those few she trusted. For Sawyer, whose lectures on Stein would have only a limited audience, a word was enough. But for Katherine Anne Porter, whose less than enthusiastic article on Gertrude appeared in the *Atlantic*, Alice called for help.

Porter's piece depicted a childish Gertrude, egotistical, "tepid, sluggish," and monotonous. "It was not that she was opposed to ideas," Miss Porter wrote, "but that she was not interested in anybody's ideas but her own, except as material to put down on her endless flood of pages." Her political views were at best naïve, and her judgments in general were "neither moral nor intellectual, and least of all aesthetic," but "limited, personal in the extreme, prejudiced without qualification, based on assumptions founded in the void of pure unreason."

About Katherine Anne Porter's article, Alice wrote to Rogers that she thought it hostile and offensive.[28] She enlisted the help of both Joe Barry and Donald Sutherland to answer Porter's view and explained to friends that the real reason for Porter's hatred of Gertrude was an unkind remark made about Porter when the writer's nephew once visited Gertrude after the war. Unable to recall whether or not she had ever read Porter, Gertrude asked Alice. Not realizing that the young GI talking to Gertrude was a relative of the writer, Alice replied with a definite "no" and left the scene. This, she considered, was the basis of the article.[29]

But the episode with Porter was a minor frustration compared with what seemed the endless procrastination of the Baltimore lawyers for funds which would make possible Van Vechten's fulfillment of his duties. Finally, in the fall of 1947 the funds were sent, the "nightmare" was over, and the works would begin to appear—except, Alice hoped, for one. In 1933, after deciding not to publish *Q.E.D.*, or *Things As They Are*, Gertrude gave the manuscript to Alice. If Donald Gallup had not asked about it in the spring of 1947, Alice would have kept it hidden, at least, she said, until all the other writings were published. But Gallup's query could not be denied. She acknowledged the manuscript's existence. But she added that she did not want the book published while she was alive, and knew Gertrude would have agreed, she told him. Even after Gertrude's death, the disclosure of her early love affair would be too painful. Alice sent it to Yale reluctantly, but, once admitting its existence, there was little she could do. In any case, she thought, it would be better to have the manuscript at Yale than in her apartment where Allan Stein might someday find it.[30]

Her energy was devoted almost exclusively to Gertrude, diverted by only one other task—and this, too, was carrying on for Gertrude. In whatever way she could, she worked for the release of her friend Bernard Faÿ, who had been arrested on August 19, 1944, and accused of collaboration with the Germans. Faÿ's imprisonment had saddened and worried them both. He had taken the position as the head of the Bibliothèque Nationale, he said, in order to save the books from destruction by the Germans and to keep the library intact. Now, along with many others who worked with Pétain, he was accused of disloyalty to France, of anti-Semitism, of persecution of the Freemasons. Neither Alice nor Gertrude doubted his innocence, and they were concerned that prison would deteriorate his already poor health. It was, for her, a grave responsibility, Alice wrote to a friend for whose help she asked.

After an eight-day trial late in 1946, Faÿ was sentenced to hard labor for life. For two years Alice was tormented by her friend's fate, trying as best she could to find influential people who might act to free him. Finally, in the summer of 1948, his sentence was reduced to twenty years, and she hoped that under De Gaulle an amnesty might be declared which would ensure his release. Though Alice's efforts seemed to have had little to do with Faÿ's commuted sentence, he had no doubt of her complete loyalty, nor she of his. She was sure that it was because of him that she and Gertrude had been spared harm during the war; he named her in his defense as one who would confirm his claim of loyalty to France and protector of two Jewesses.[31]

Alice's enduring affection for Faÿ was almost unique in

her own history of faded friendships. Devotion to Gertrude's memory was, for Alice, the truest proof of friendship. Any deviation from Alice's view of reality was suspect, and those who failed to sustain her own level of adoration were scolded or simply dismissed. Any who dared to write about Gertrude risked Alice's wrath with every word. Her requirements were so exacting that few could hope to come through her critical reading unscathed. In 1948, when Rogers published his warm and loving memoir of Gertrude, *When This You See Remember Me*, he was met with fury.

The draft she saw, Alice claimed, bore little relationship to the finished book. In what she described as a scathing letter, she pointed out to him his many errors—describing Gertrude as aloof, for example; including too many references to herself; giving inaccurate information about Gertrude's death, about *The Making of Americans*, about her desire for success, and her need for "confirmation of her gift." Though her letter to Rogers was less than abominable, her mention of his book to friends showed her distress. It was truly horrifying, she wrote to Samuel Steward,[32] and she doubted Rogers' genuine good will toward Gertrude. Moreover, in his introduction he implied that she endorsed the book, a statement she considered unforgivable.

In his foreword, thanking Alice for her help, he had written that she had read his manuscript, "charitably refrained from objecting to opinions of mine with which she disagreed; and severely charged me with devoting too much space to her." Now, to her loud objections, he offered some defense:

When I turned that foreword in, I had written that you had seen an early draft of the book, and refrained from objecting to opinions of mine, etc. etc. It was suggested that an author doesn't talk of several drafts, that the public is supposed to think words run off his pen just like that, or like this, fluently, without labor, and so early draft was changed to manuscript. That seemed to me all right because I made it perfectly plain that there were some things with which you disagreed. I wouldn't for all the world have anyone

read into that foreword the suggestion that this was a
book of which you approved; not that I wouldn't want
dearly to have you approve. . . .

Because of her unhappiness at his calling Gertrude aloof,
he again tried to explain:

When I said that Gertrude was aloof, I didn't mean to
exclude the fact that she was approachable; she was
on a height that inevitably made her aloof; she could
be approached as one billiard ball approaches another,
touches it and then bounces away at once. And if you
reply to that, as you well might, that if she was aloof
how could she have been so kind to me, I don't know
what the answer is. The Lord knows I didn't think,
and don't think, I had anything to offer her, except
that I was so very fond of her . . . and people who are
fond of you can be the worst nuisances in the world,
so that's another count against me. But it still seemed
to me that there were areas in her living when she was
not merely aloof but impossibly distant; you have to
be very near people, but also a godawful long way off,
too, to write "Three Lives," for instance.

After patiently explaining his sources for the stories she
doubted, he finally arrived at her severe charge of appearing too often in the book:

There were so many things about you that you wanted
taken out, that was the one thing that we disagreed on
most commonly, and I think I should be thanked for
what I did omit, instead of being found fault with for
giving you credit for knowing everything.[33]

He hoped, he added, that though she claimed to be able to
forget, but not forgive, that in this case, she would forgive
him. She did not. Declaring that the book had that acidity
that taints New England cooking, she pointed out to Donald Sutherland the existence of fabrications and several
errors. Even a year after its publication, she could still
write of the "pang" it had given her only just fading away.
It seemed at times that only Basket, Gertrude's dog, could

offer unquestioned loyalty. And his age and illnesses often worried Alice.[34] The Basket she was then coddling was actually Basket II, the replacement of the first poodle, who had died in 1938, and as lovable in spirit. He was her one constant companion.

Twenty-one

EVER PRESENT, like a background farce, was Alice's trouble with her servants. "Unfortunately there have been too many of them in my service," she wrote later. "Unfortunately there have been too many unsatisfactory ones, and too many satisfactory ones did not stay long." The first, whom she and Harriet hired, was Célestine, the niece of Gertrude's concierge. According to Gertrude, one could judge a servant's competence by one question: did she make a good omelette, and Célestine assured Alice that she could.

Experience proved otherwise. Not only was Célestine unable to make an omelette, but she had never marketed, and failed to produce an edible morsel. Though she was shy and sweet, she was fired; her uncle reconsidered and proposed that she might become, instead, a lady's maid.

The Basque woman hired next, Maria Lasgourges, was one of Alice's jewels who stayed too briefly. She was followed by Maria Enz, Swiss, who had "all the Swiss virtues and limitations." Though she was an excellent housekeeper, her cooking, Alice thought, was indifferent. But Alice and Harriet were content with her services until she, too, left—to be married. "A white orange blossom wreath and a lace-bordered veil," Alice remembered, were gifts from her and Harriet.

Once Alice moved into the rue de Fleurus with Gertrude, she was faced with the formidable Hélène. Hélène was one of the few servants who won Alice's respect. "It was Hélène," she saw, "who made all the practical decisions. A friend noticing this observed that it was to be hoped that her servant left a free choice of the Picassos to Gertrude Stein." Calmly efficient, Hélène was not only an excellent housekeeper, but—more rare—"an invariably perfect cook." Moreover, her observations on life and art —delivered humorlessly, as befitting her personality—were of lasting amusement to Gertrude and Alice. She had concluded that there must be no artists in America; they were, she told Alice, all in Paris. When Alice asked what she thought Americans did, she replied matter-of-factly that they must be dentists. She had strong opinions about Gertrude's guests. She did not, for example, like Matisse's way of asking what was to be served for dinner before he invited himself to stay. She did, on the other hand, like Picasso and usually cooked him her best meals.

Unfortunately for Alice, Hélène would teach her nothing about cooking. "A lady did not cook," in Hélène's view. Nevertheless, Hélène's presence was strongly missed when, in 1914, she retired to care for her husband. Léonie, who joined the household after the First War, while not comparable with Hélène, was still more than adequate. An aging woman, she worked, Alice thought, with "boundless energy and reckless courage. . . . With her long arms and frail body she would climb a step-ladder with the agility and the unnatural smile of a professional acrobat." Her ability at cooking, though, was questionable and when she one day offered to make some cakes, Alice accepted, "more curious than hopeful."

Her cakes turned out to be excellent and gradually Léonie came to do more of the cooking and Alice more of the housework. Alice gave her some of her own recipes, but soon discovered that Léonie did not measure any of the ingredients, preferring, she revealed, to pray. "To tease her," Alice said, "I told her she did not always pray to the right saint." After three years of devoted service, Léonie left, for a reason Alice could not remember. But she made way for the mysterious and seductive Jeanne.

Like her cooking, Jeanne was "unknown, delicate and . . . exotic." She exerted a strange charm over both Alice and Gertrude, who wondered what it was about her that seemed unfathomable and alluring. Then, after working for them for some eight months, she failed to come one morning. A series of messages was received by Alice which said that Jeanne was very ill, but explained nothing further. When they visited her concierge, she said nothing but that Jeanne was ill and messages would continue to be sent. In the midst of their short visit, to Alice's and Gertrude's surprise, Jeanne entered, her arms filled with packages from a gay shopping expedition. The quick-thinking concierge shooed her from the room and explained the seemingly unexplainable to her employers. Jeanne, it seemed, had strange working habits: she would work for several months, then suddenly stop, indulge in shopping sprees, and as suddenly begin to work again. Because they were so enamored of her, Alice and Gertrude requested that she return, despite her apparent unreliability; the next morning, she appeared at work and nothing, Alice said, was mentioned.

A few more blissful months with Jeanne followed, until once again she failed to appear. This time, Alice set about to find a replacement. But amazingly, after just one day, Jeanne was back. "Then," Alice said, "the inevitable occurred." Jeanne's absence from her morning duties caused Alice to bring a breakfast tray up to Gertrude. "Never one without twice and thrice," they said in unison, and they quickly sent word to Jeanne's concierge firing her.

But the memory of Jeanne was not easily forgotten. Alice would often detour in her walks to pass her apartment with the hope of seeing her, but never did. And the young women who came and went after her were no match for her cooking or her gentle, enticing manner.

A series of amiable housekeepers tossed crepes and arranged flowers for Alice and Gertrude in the twenties and thirties. But it was becoming increasingly difficult to find servants. Once, Alice resorted to an employment office, an experience she found humiliating, "not certain whether it was more so for me or for the applicants." Finally she placed her own ad in a newspaper and interviewed several applicants, from whom she chose Trac. The young man, Indo-Chinese, could speak only some dozen words of French and was a deft and delicate chef. Though he, like Léonie, eschewed measurements, he cooked with secrets that did not depend on the saints, but on instinct and skill. When he left, he warned Alice that if she hired any other Indo-Chinese, she wouldn't like them; none, he told her, was as nice as he. A train of cooks which followed taught her that he was correct, and when he returned from a trip home, she happily rehired him. But again his employment was brief: this time he married and opened his own restaurant.

Margit, from Finland, was a perfect cook in Alice's estimation, but her melancholy personality caused her to be nicknamed "Miss Hamlet" by one of Alice's friends. Nevertheless, her work was impeccable, her recipes varied, her interest in Gertrude's writing genuine and enthusiastic. Though she was not inventive, she was, Alice wrote, "forethoughtful, rose to emergencies and met all unexpected situations with calm." Unfortunately, her even temperament did not extend to her personal life; in the late thirties, when war threatened, she fled home, convinced she was being persecuted by the police and was in constant peril.

Clothilde, the dour old woman who came with the castle in Culoz, forced Alice to take over the kitchen until the Liberation; and when she and Gertrude returned to Paris, the servant problem began again.

Alice, of course, was not an easy mistress. She was a perfectionist in her demands of a housekeeper and equally hard in her requirements of a cook. When she prepared a meal for guests, she would rise at five and begin chopping, grating, simmering, and braising; but only if she had not already begun the day before. Her expectations were severe, and her means of dealing with her subordinates could be unkind. Friends were sometimes appalled at her impatience with servants; but she merely wafted away their objections by assuring them that replacements could be easily found. At the time of Gertrude's death, she was left with the colorful Gabrielle.

Gabrielle, Alice ultimately decided was unbalanced; but in her stable moments, she was devoted to Alice and kind to Basket. She was clean but not overly neat. Yet her presence was not odious, despite recurring quarrels. One argument was reported to Rogers. Gabrielle, it seemed, would habitually come down in the morning with an ever-lengthening string of complaints, ranging from the weather to the current government and including such trifles as a record player played too loud. Gracefully accepting the blame for all that Gabrielle found unbearable, Alice told her that she would try to correct her ways if only Gabrielle would not ever again mention one more complaint until she found a single positive quality which Alice possessed.

After having delivered her ultimatum, she prepared to withdraw haughtily from her tiny kitchen—an undramatic exit—when Gabrielle, in a quiet voice, admitted that she always had thought well of American integrity and sense of justice.[35] The quarrel, Alice determined, was ended.

Some of Gabrielle's adventures were amusing, especially when they fed Alice's own love of gossip. In the spring of 1949, she became involved in the efforts of some art students to claim squatter's rights in an empty building next door. "With more regularity than she bastes a roast," Alice reported, Gabrielle would check on the students' progress, sympathizing with them against the owner of the building. Then she decided to intervene actively. Slipping two of the students into the courtyard of Alice's residence, she instructed them to use the roof to gain entrance to the next building by way of a trapdoor. Unfortunately, the students, once on the roof, failed to find the trapdoor, their comrades below were arrested, and Gabrielle's heroism was foiled. Gabrielle's mood then became very unpleasant, Alice disclosed, and she and Basket tried to keep out of her way.

But in the fall of 1951, Gabrielle went too far. Bernard Faÿ had successfully escaped from prison the preceding spring, and it was speculated that a heavily veiled lady had been seen waiting for him in a car nearby. Apparently, Gabrielle surmised the identity of the lady and threatened Alice with blackmail. Frightened by Gabrielle's imaginings, Alice was relieved when, finally, Gabrielle quit. It was, Alice announced to her friends, like another war's end.

Besides the attention Alice enjoyed from her old friends, she renewed her friendships with women she had known from her youth: Annette Rosenshine, Harriet Levy, Louise Hayden, and Lilyanna Hansen. Even combined, they hardly filled the void left by Gertrude, but it was a comfort to reminisce, to share a common past. Each realized how much Alice needed her, including Annette, who could not forget Alice's cold last treatment.

When Gertrude died, her friend Clare Moore de Gruchy contacted Alice at once, telephoning her several times from California. Alice was shocked at the expense to her friend but pleased by her concern, and the two, who had seen each other only briefly during Gertrude's American tour, agreed to meet. But by the time arrangements could be made, and Alice wrote saying, "Dearest Clare, I am ready at last," Clare had been dead for two days. She was left with only the memory of seeing Clare in San Francisco, and nothing more, Alice wrote to Fania Marinoff Van Vechten.

Annette had returned to Berkeley, where she continued sculpting and had her own following of students and young artists. At The Forum, a café on Telegraph Avenue, she was a popular figure, talking about her Parisian experiences, her psychotherapy in Zurich, her study with Gurdjieff, and her own art work. She never ceased in her search for psychological understanding and in 1964 found a psychiatrist who allowed her to try LSD.

Louise Hayden had married an American colonel, Emmet Addis, in 1922. After he died, she married a British colonel, Redvers Taylor, some twenty years younger than she. Colonels were her weakness, her second husband remarked. Louise, living in England, was a welcome visitor. In 1950, when she was about seventy, she dropped by with her husband on her way to Palma de Mallorca. To Alice's amazement, they were carrying their luggage in backpacks.

Lilyanna had become a teacher, first at the Catlan School in Portland and then at the University of Oregon, where she and her close friend, librarian Ethel Sawyer, pursued an active interest in the theater. After Ethel Sawyer's death, which came at about the same time as Gertrude's, Lilyanna lived in devotion to her friend's memory as much as Alice did to Gertrude's. She made valuable contributions to the Ethel Sawyer Library at the university, including many of Gertrude's books and many editions obtained through Alice's help.

Harriet, back in San Francisco, was still writing. In 1947, she published two books: *920 O'Farrell Street*, a memoir of her early years in San Francisco, and *I Love to Talk About Myself & Other Verses Concerning God & Man & Me*. Alice thought that Harriet should have held back from the outpouring of her memories. But in Harriet's lighthearted account of her youth, Alice's family became "the Levinsons," a comic and colorful group, and Alice herself was well treated as the oppressed granddaughter. In 1948, Harriet decided to write about her early years in Paris and asked Alice for names, dates, and anecdotes. Alice offered some memories in one letter to Harriet, in which she included the episode of Edstrom's quaking in anticipation of his wife's visit. She outlined the episode as it actually happened—to Harriet. Years later, after Harriet was dead and Alice was writing her own memoirs, she took the anecdote as her own and made herself its heroine.

In her eighties, Harriet took to dressing very ostentatiously, Alice was told, in bold colors and fantastic styles, her eccentricities reminding some of Dickens's Miss Havisham. And she was still active, going to parties, leading a bright social life, until she died in 1950.

In her seventies, Alice began to suffer real physical distress from arthritis. She wrote to Lilyanna, who was also afflicted, for advice on diets and methods of finding relief. It was a considerable effort to go marketing or to take Basket on the walks he loved. Her friends brought her gossip, she told Annette, which she found completely satisfactory.[36] Letter-writing to friends—old and new— became a major occupation. So, too, was the entertainment of those who visited her on their trips through Europe— Donald Gallup, Carl Van Vechten, Thornton Wilder and his sister Isabel.

Wilder's visits always boosted her; he and Isabel were cheerful and encouraging, and her respect for him was undiminished through the years. She confessed to a friend that in Wilder's presence she always felt as if she were walking on eggs—he was so fine.[37] And to Sutherland, she asked if he didn't agree that Wilder was unique in not having to run after culture because he had always had it.[38] Sure that he was more sensitive than most people realized, she was reluctant to burden him with shows of emotion.[39]

She was convinced of his devotion to Gertrude's work, which he admitted, though he added that he did not always understand her writing. Gertrude, he thought, wrote on eight levels, only the first three of which he understood. Though that satisfied him, it sometimes frustrated Gertrude. At Bilignin when she was writing *Ida*, she decided that he must collaborate with her on the book, since she could not write narrative. He dutifully read her manuscript but could understand little of it and told her so. "Well just

read it. It's in plain English, why can't you understand it,"
she admonished him. Believing that a guest should always
try to please his hostess, he tried once more but again
failed. Finally, he gave up. But, he said, his own *Ides of
March* was one book where he felt Gertrude's influence.
Because he was writing about Caesar, he had to confront
the audience's incredulity; the story could not be told in
the confident manner of nineteenth-century fiction.
Thomas Hardy's readers, he thought, had no doubt that
Tess of the D'Urbervilles was a true story; his readers—
and Gertrude's—presented a greater problem to a novelist. His solution was including letters and diary entries as if
they were historical documents. Gertrude's manner of dealing with the problem, he knew, was far different.[40]

Her extreme simplicity, her real love of people were
evident in all his conversations with her. "The important
thing," she once told Alice, "is that you must have deep
down as the deepest thing in you a sense of equality."[41]
When she compared herself to Jesus and Aristotle in her
revolutionary perception, she "cracked the sky open" for
Wilder. But her disclosure was offered with no expression
of egotism, he said, just as if it were a straight fact. Because Alice realized Wilder's sincere love for Gertrude, she
esteemed his friendship as she did that of few others. ". . .
The only confidence I ever gave," she remembered, was
given to Wilder: she would write a book.

Though her effort was to be merely a cookbook, Wilder
was surprised. "But Alice, have you ever tried to write?" he
asked. She was slightly crushed by his doubt. "As if a cookbook had anything to do with writing," she thought. But
his question continued to worry her for years.

The idea for a cookbook had come to her and to Gertrude years before Gertrude's death, and there had even
been a sketchy plan for a combined cookbook and memoir.
In the late forties, Rogers tried to interest his own publisher in Alice's venture, and Alice frequently wrote to
friends asking for their opinion of the project. It was one
which excited her, though she admitted that she had never
tried to write since she was eleven years old and had made
an abortive attempt at writing a play. It was to be a tragedy
in the manner of Shakespeare, and in the first scene, which
took place at court, she announced: "The courtiers speak

among themselves in a spiritual fashion." Unfortunately, she could think of no spiritual phrases to continue the dialogue, and the effort came to an abrupt end.[42] But a cookbook, she thought, must be different. Was experience really necessary, she asked writer friends. Couldn't one build upon one's own "prejudice and passion" for cooking? She was sure the task was not beyond her "inadequate equipment," and the idea for the book was kept alive for many years.

Cooking for friends was, she said, a pleasure, but some of her friends saw it as an exercise in masochism. After a trip at dawn to Les Halles for fresh ingredients, she would spend the entire morning dicing and peeling, painstaking and fastidious in every detail that went into the preparation of one of her multicourse meals. Whole poached apples in a puff pastry was her version of apple pie; a drop of Drambuie set her whipped cream apart from anyone else's. Eggs and butter were the only thickeners she allowed—cornstarch and flour, she said scornfully, were cheap substitutes.

Despite the cuisine, luncheon with Alice could be an uncomfortable experience. Otto Friedrich, then a young writer whom Alice deemed one of the most interesting of his generation, remembered sitting alone with his wife for ten minutes while Alice disappeared into the kitchen to see about their meal. Finally she emerged, followed by Gabrielle—still a member of the household—with the first course of shrimp.

We began to eat, and Miss Toklas asked a few questions, but before she had finished her own shrimp, she was off to the kitchen again, leaving us to contemplate the works of Sir Francis Rose. Then she returned with a chicken, with Gabrielle lurking behind with a plate of zucchini. Miss Toklas jabbed at the chicken with a large fork and then began sawing away at one of its legs. Gabrielle stood watching for a while, concerned, and then set down the plate of zucchini and retreated to the kitchen. Miss Toklas carved with skill, but she was so tiny that she could barely reach across the high table to get at the animal, like a bullfighter lunging forward for the kill. Once she had served three helpings, she vanished again, and we sat in silence for several minutes until she returned with the orange sauce. Once again, desultory questions, compliments on the sauce, gossip about a new novel, and then Miss Toklas slipped out of her high chair again and was off to supervise the dessert, a complicated custard. The dessert was delicious, but it was a relief to have the struggle ended, the meal over with. . . .[43]

After the ordeal of lunch, Alice would sink into an armchair. Well-dressed in a formal suit and wearing some of her baroque, weighty jewelry, she seemed, in repose, to blend with the special feeling of her home.

The apartment, paneled in white, was furnished with the heavy antiques that had come from the rue de Fleurus. Carefully arranged bouquets were set on the Florentine tables, along with china figurines and silver miniatures, faïence jars and ashtrays. The sofa and armchairs were upholstered in brown satin. A corridor and bedroom were papered in blue, with an ethereal pattern of large white pigeons. The kitchen was small, ill-equipped, and hardly an inspiration for her culinary marvels, though eventually she acquired from indulgent friends "American gadgets" which her mother would have envied.

Those who had visited the rue Christine when Gertrude was alive remembered a different woman from the one who greeted them in the late forties. Alice, in her widowhood, had taken on a regal air, stooped though she was and weighing less than one hundred pounds. Enthroned in her armchair, smoking her inevitable cigarettes, she had a presence and an authority that only intimates had known before. She who had sat quietly by listening to Gertrude's endless expositions now delighted in the entertainment of all her visitors. "To talk with Miss Toklas was a pleasure," wrote James Lord, a comparative newcomer, "and she herself seemed to accept with candid satisfaction that this should be so, as if from the beginning it had never been otherwise."[44]

Lord, a young writer who had visited Gertrude and Alice after the war, had pitied Alice for being neglected and ignored while Gertrude shone for her guests. Invited to see Alice after he sent her a letter of condolence, he was surprised at her strength and composure in the face of her evident loneliness. When he mentioned that the large, high-ceilinged living room did not seem the same without Gertrude's portrait, she conceded that there was indeed an irreplaceable emptiness. "You're right," she told him. "Without the portrait it's not the same here at all. But nothing at all is the same, anyway."

Yet with her guests she could, in the only way possible, relive the past. Life for Alice, one friend remarked, had no meaning, but a great many good stories. And those who came to see Alice were not disappointed. "She knew perfectly well," Lord said, "that some of them saw in her only the Alice B. Toklas who had lived with Gertrude Stein, but that, of course, was what she had been all her life, and to find herself assigned the auxiliary role even after Gertrude's death can hardly have been a surprise. . . ."[45] If many of them came to meet Gertrude's alter ego, they left with the impression of a forceful, independent woman.

"The lives of most people," James Lord commented, "are shaped by mindless and uncontrollable chance. I never felt this to be true of Alice Toklas. As she talked and talked of the past and of her life with Gertrude Stein, I became convinced that it had been as it had been because she had had the wit and the self-possession to sense from the beginning what might be, and had purposefully and deliberately chosen to live the life which she and Gertrude lived together for forty years."[46]

Soon, as Gertrude had done before her, Alice took up the role of godmother and protector of young writers, reading their manuscripts, recommending them to publishers, putting them in contact with her now-influential old friends. Her judgments were no less stringent than they had always been, but her loyalties were no less fierce.

Of the young American writers in Paris today there are the GIs with their Bill of Rights and their second novel on the way who are taking a course at the Sorbonne called French Civilization, for which at the end of the year they will be given a certificate for attendance. And there are the more serious Fullbright scholars who are writing tomes for their doctorate. There is a young, very young man named Otto Friedrich who is now working on his fourth novel and who may easily become the important young man of the future. And young George John, whose early poetic achievement so greatly impressed Gertrude Stein and whose present development she foresaw.

It would be well if one could end on this encouraging note but one can not completely ignore the highly colorful group in and about the cafés of Place Saint-Germain des Prés. They publish and contribute their writings to at least one little review. They may be gently dismissed with an "unpredictable future."[47]

The very young Otto Friedrich had sought out Alice Toklas in the winter of 1948, arriving unknown to her, and therefore uninvited, with a friend who knew enough to bring a bouquet of Alice's favorite flower, lilacs. "Miss Toklas," Friedrich remembered, "was incredibly ugly, uglier than almost anyone I had ever met. A thin, withered creature, she sat hunched in her chair, in her heavy tweed suit and her thick lisle stockings. . . . She had a huge nose, a dark moustache, and her dark-dyed hair was combed into absurd bangs over her forehead."[48] But somehow, for Friedrich, her appearance did not detract from her presence, and he noticed "qualities that never appear in photographs—the shrewdness of the large, dark eyes, the cultivated and slightly grainy quality of her voice, the warmth of her malicious laughter. . . . She knew what she admired and what she despised, and she saw the two in perpetual combat, and she was quite fierce about which side she was on."[49] For her own reasons, she found Friedrich's friend dull, but Friedrich himself worthy of interrogation. He left promising to bring her some of his still unpublished novels.

Gradually, he was introduced to the practices of the rue Christine: drinking Armagnac from a cut-glass decanter, ignoring the interruptions of Basket, watching Alice endlessly approach the lighting of her cigarette with one of the long kitchen matches that stood in a box beside her. His visits were not in vain. Not only did Alice offer him sincere praise—a high achievement for a hopeful twenty-year-old writer—but she offered to help him find a publisher. She invited him to tea, once with Carl Van Vechten and once with Thornton Wilder; she introduced him to David Higham, a London literary agent; she arranged for him to meet the Paris correspondent of the New York *Times*. But there was no change in Friedrich's unpublished state and, planning to be married, he left Paris for Munich to take a job as copy editor on the sports desk of the Army's *Stars and Stripes*. In that less than inspiring position, he received encouraging notes from Alice keeping him apprised of her efforts. When she wrote of him in her own article in the New York *Times*, several publishers perked up. Coincidentally, however, through his own tenuous connections, he was able to get a novel published, and this was met by Alice's unqualified approval. Comparing him to Juan Gris, she praised his "flawlessness" and predicted a sparkling future. Though other critics were tepid, Alice never lost her fire. She was still an ardent supporter when, six years later, he left Paris for New York; and nine years after that, when he returned to visit, she greeted him with the inevitable question, "So, tell me your news. You're still writing."

But what Friedrich saw in the eighty-five-year-old Alice was a clearer exposure of what had existed when he first came—a loneliness that required her to bring as close as she could anyone who might need her, who might depend on her—anyone whom she could serve as she had for so long served Gertrude. ". . . She could not resist peering out through the mist," Friedrich wrote, "and reaching out a hand for someone to hold onto."

Twenty-two

SHE DESPERATELY WANTED the dead not to be dead, she wrote to Lilyanna; and she lived alone with Gertrude's memory. When young people came to talk about Gertrude, she would patiently try to explain whatever they wanted to know.[50] She was intent on setting the record straight, on making certain that her version of Gertrude's life was recognized as reality. Predictably, she was suspicious of biographers.

A letter from the poet John Malcolm Brinnin in the summer of 1950 was worriedly reported to Gallup. Brinnin wanted to see her, she said, for his proposed book on Gertrude. But Alice advised him that he had best do his research at Yale. If he required anecdotes, she added in a hastily written second letter, she would have to refuse him. Remembering her mistake with Rogers, she would now help no one. Nevertheless, she did not flatly bar him from Gertrude's home, recalling, perhaps, a poem he had written about Gertrude which Carl Van Vechten had sent her a few years before. "A Little Elegy for Gertrude Stein," Alice had written to Brinnin then, had touched her deeply and she found herself rereading it several times a day. She sent him, in gratitude, a small wood carving—a horse ridden by an octopus—which had belonged to Gertrude.[51] But apparently she had her emotions under control when at last he did come in September 1950. She was annoyed, however, that he seemed in awe about being in Gertrude's apartment, and reported her reaction to Carl Van Vechten. At their tea, which Brinnin remembered as somewhat formal, Alice was not as hostile as her letters had led him to expect. He had, in fact, come "with enormous trepidation" and was surprised by her generosity.[52] At least she allowed him to return with whatever questions he might have of her.

She invited him back many times, Brinnin said, sent him flowers and rare editions of Gertrude's works, gave a party for him at the rue Christine. Though he could see that she was trying to evaluate him at their first meeting, he noticed a perceptible change midway through the second session. And suddenly she threw up her hands and exclaimed, "Why didn't someone *tell* me you were like this!" From that moment on, she relaxed.[53]

Her own reports, however, show a tense and protective sentinel of Gertrude's memory. She complained to Van Vechten that Brinnin's questions were superficial and showed doubtful understanding of Gertrude's work. She was afraid that he would try to portray Leo sympathetically and prided herself in having convinced him that anything he wrote about Leo would hurt Gertrude's reputation. Finally, he agreed that the subject of Leo would be avoided. And most important to her, he agreed to minimize her own appearance in the book. After all, she told him, the countryside at Bilignin had been a stronger influence than she had ever been.[54]

She had a respite from these worries, however, when Brinnin, only half finished with the work, put it aside while he devoted himself to Dylan Thomas, whose American visit would be his subject for another book, long years away from his biography of Gertrude. It was not until 1959 that *The Third Rose* was published—to Alice's dismay and horror. Even her friends, though, thought her feelings were unfounded.

As much as she protested that Brinnin troubled her, she was distracted in October by wonderful news—news which made all else seem trivial. Yale University Press would publish all of Gertrude's works, bringing out one book a year, with the first volume to be ready in the spring. Donald Gallup, Thornton Wilder, Donald Sutherland, and Carl Van Vechten would be editors and compilers. Alice's dreams were more than realized.[55]

It was one wish fulfilled, but Alice did not rest with that success. She still had plans in carrying on for Gertrude. She wanted to keep all of Gertrude's paintings together and sell them as a collection to a museum. Though she knew she could sell a painting if she needed money for her own welfare, she staunchly refused to do so. The thought that the precious collection might someday be separated by buyers haunted her. But her hope of offering the works to Yale as the Gertrude Stein Collection was blocked by Allan Stein, who suddenly, she said, began to show force.

Having known Allan since his childhood, Alice thought him to be the unfortunate product of an unnatural and erratic upbringing; his mother, Sarah, coddled him whenever she noticed him, and his father, Michael, failed to provide the atmosphere for a proper childhood. As a young man, he was appealing if irresponsible, with ever-changing business interests and, Alice thought, little inner strength.

He was divorced from his first wife, Yvonne, a British dancer from the Paris Opera Ballet, and with his second wife, Roubina, and their two children, Gabrielle ("Mimi") and Michael, lived just outside of Paris. At the time of Gertrude's death, he was involved in a perfume business which Roubina was forced to run almost completely alone, since Allan was often ill.

Alice seemed to have a qualified admiration for Roubina, and alternately felt pity and impatience toward Allan. Allan, who was a Christian Scientist—though not as ardent a believer as his mother—nevertheless gave in to a plethora of various illnesses, some of which Alice found unbelievable. When she visited him in the spring of 1949, she found him deeply enmeshed in worry over his health, and he vented a long monologue describing his illnesses. When he finally permitted her to speak, she brazenly suggested that his illnesses might well be psychosomatic.[56]

But as much as she pitied Allan, she was afraid that his health costs, his lack of business sense, and the debts of his son Daniel, the product of his first marriage, would cause him to vandalize his aunt's art collection. Daniel, in California with Sarah, had lost a good deal of money gambling and dabbling in horses. Sarah had sold some of her Matisses to pay his debts, but Alice thought that Sarah's pictures might soon be exhausted and Gertrude's would be the only resource. Not knowing what else to do, she stamped on the back of all the paintings, "This picture belongs to the estate of Gertrude Stein," hoping that the precaution would prevent Allan from taking any by force.

As Allan's health deteriorated further, she consulted a lawyer to see what possible measures could be taken to ensure that the collection was not broken up. After the meeting, though, she commented that perhaps all her efforts might not be necessary, since she intended to outlive him.[57]

She did. In mid-January 1951, Allan suddenly worsened and died. Alice was now left to deal with the future heirs, Roubina and her children. But Roubina, she decided, was honest and trustworthy. Briefly, her fears were abated.

Living at the side of the gregarious Gertrude, Alice believed there was little in her own personality that acquaintances would find interesting. But in the decades that followed Gertrude's death, she formed many close friendships of her own.

Harold and Virginia Knapik met Alice soon after their arrival in France in the summer of 1948. He was a musician, planning to devote a year to the study of counterpoint, and she worked at the American Embassy, a fortuitous position for Alice, since it provided her with many more cigarettes than she might otherwise have been able to procure.

They met when the Knapiks were staying in Chantilly with friends who had invited Alice to lunch. Harold and Virginia were to do the cooking, and the results pleased Alice—especially the dessert, a rich mélange of spongecake, raspberries, cream, and liqueur. She asked Harold if he had actually made it himself, and when he replied affirmatively, she could only murmur, "the courage of youth."

Shortly after, when the Knapiks were invited to the rue Christine for lunch, Harold immediately realized that the compliments meant more than he thought they had: Alice was an excellent cook.

Nearly neighbors, the Knapiks and Alice saw a good deal of each other. Virginia, claiming Alice was her "aunt," was able to share her privileges of rationed goods. Both, Alice said, were "angelic." In the summer of 1950, when Alice decided to take her first vacation alone, they offered to drive her to Bourges, where she had arranged to stay at a pension, while they continued on a trip.

La Régie, which Alice found through the recommendation of a friend, was a large estate, partially farmed for tobacco, on which a large, rambling house had been turned into an elegant inn. Madame Debar, the gracious and efficient proprietress, assigned to Alice a large room with six windows and an entrance to the garden, which Alice thought was enchanting. Since the estate was walled, Basket would run free. Unfortunately, the only other guest for a time was a dull Swedish girl, who had witnessed eighteen aurora borealises unmoved, but who had, Alice thought, the body of an angel.

For five weeks, Alice spent most of her time in the garden of La Régie writing letters to friends. Glad to have escaped Parisian August, and claiming that the inn offered her the peace and rest she badly needed, she was, nevertheless, lonely; and when the Knapiks called for her after their trip to Salzburg and Vienna, they realized that Alice would have much preferred their company to her solitary stay in a bucolic setting.

The next summer, the three rented a furnished house in the South of France. At first, Alice and Harold were to share the cooking chores, but the arrangement failed. ". . . In a household of three," Harold decided, "two cooks were too many—especially two temperamental cooks." Alice deferred to Harold.

Observing Alice's technique firsthand, though, made Harold reconsider his admiration for her talents. She scorned the use of herbs and spices, which she thought had gained popularity only during the postwar meat rationing. Harold thought she had too heavy a hand with both and didn't understand their qualities. He remembered with musement her first try at making *rouille*, a Provençal sauce made with the Spanish equivalent of paprika.

Alice had tasted *rouille* for the first time when Picasso took us to lunch at Juan-les-Pins. The lunch was excellent, and Picasso demonstrated his enthusiasm for the *rouille* (which, although intended to accompany the broiled lobsters we had ordered, had been placed on the table the moment we were seated) by dipping pieces of bread into it and then into freshly grated Gruyère cheese that was also on the table. He devoured the morsels of his improvised hors d'oeuvre with great relish. In any case, when we were back in

Paris after vacation, Alice dropped in one evening and announced that she had served *rouille* to an American guest for lunch that day. I don't recall the name of the guest, but I think of him from time to time, because Alice had made her *rouille* with cayenne pepper.[58]

Also among her cooking prejudices was a dismissal of such things as calories and vitamins. "It was calories in World War I and vitamins in World War II," she said disparagingly, pronouncing the first syllable of vitamins to rhyme with sit, Harold said, "which made a preoccupation with them inane." And as for calories, while she admitted a predilection to egg yolks and cream in her recipes, she told guests that she would usually have only fruit and broth for dinner after one of her own elaborate lunches.

But Harold, himself a fastidious chef, acknowledged that Alice was a good cook. She was, most friends agreed, more than qualified to write a cookbook; and in the spring of 1952, Jennie Bradley, the wife of Gertrude's former agent, presented Alice with just such an offer. Harper's would advance a thousand dollars when Alice completed thirty thousand words and give her until the following spring to finish her book.

To friends, she modestly said that the book was undertaken for "the pennies" only: that it was by no means a serious effort at writing. But to her editor, Simon Michael Bessie, a "delighted" Alice declared that she was eager to begin immediately. Comparing herself with the sensational Mary MacLane, she wrote that she intended to pour everything into the book. At seventy-five, she was finally going to reveal herself to the world.

At Harper's the feeling seemed cooler toward the recipes than toward the prospect of getting Alice to intersperse her stories among them. It was, they thought, perhaps the only way she would ever be coerced into writing her memoirs. While they had heard that "the old girl is supposed to be quite a cook," it was for her cache of anecdotes that they were most enthusiastic.

In March, a few months before the book was due, the pressure of producing forty thousand additional words sent Alice writing to her friends. One chapter would be borrowed recipes—undoubtedly the only interesting part,

Alice sighed, in the whole book. The eclectic dishes included a doctored mayonnaise—"garlic ice cream"—from Carl Van Vechten; lamb curry from his wife Fania; designer Pierre Balmain's chicken; Francis Rose's Chinese-style zucchini; Cecil Beaton's Greek apple pudding; laurel-leaf soup from the painter Dora Maar; two Hungarian dishes from Harold Knapik; and a small problem from one of Alice's acquaintances, painter Brion Gysin:

Haschich Fudge [sic]
(which anyone could whip up on a rainy day)

This is the food of Paradise—of Baudelaire's Artificial Paradises: it might provide an entertaining refreshment for a Ladies' Bridge Club or a chapter meeting of the DAR. In Morocco it is thought to be good for warding off the common cold in damp winter weather and is, indeed, more effective if taken with large quantities of hot mint tea. Euphoria and brilliant storms of laughter; ecstatic reveries and extensions of one's personality on several simultaneous planes are to be complacently expected. Almost anything Saint Theresa did, you can do better if you can bear to be ravished by *"un évanouissement reveillé."*

Take 1 teaspoon black peppercorns, 1 whole nutmeg, 4 average sticks of cinnamon, 1 teaspoon coriander. These should all be pulverised in a mortar. About a handful each of stoned dates, dried figs, shelled almonds and peanuts: chop these and mix them together. A bunch of *canibus sativa* [sic] can be pulverised. This along with the spices should be dusted over the mixed fruit and nuts, kneaded together. About a cup of sugar dissolved in a big pat of butter. Rolled into a cake and cut into pieces or made into balls about the size of a walnut, it should be eaten with care. Two pieces are quite sufficient.

Obtaining the *canibus* may present certain difficulties, but the variety known as *canibus sativa* grows as a common weed, often unrecognised, everywhere in Europe, Asia and parts of Africa; besides being cultivated as a crop for the manufacture of rope. In the Americas, while often discouraged, its cousin, called *canibus indica*, has been observed even in city window boxes. It should be picked and dried as soon as it has gone to seed and while the plant is still green.[59]

Having already decided not to go to the expense and bother of testing recipes, Alice naïvely slipped Gysin's entry into her manuscript when she sent it to Harper's in May. The editors, however, noting that the recipe featured marijuana, cautiously advised that it be dropped.

Her British publishers, Michael Joseph, Ltd., were less prudent. To Alice's horror, she found that readers soon believed they had a new key to the understanding of Gertrude Stein. Protests to friends were filled with dismay. She had been ignorant of the meaning of the botanical terms, she assured them. Gertrude had met Gysin only once, said little to him, and even Alice did not know him well. To think that she and Gertrude had been indulging in hashish all these years and to think that the resulting state of mind might account for Gertrude's writing infuriated her. Only after the book was published, she wrote to Donald Gallup, did she notice the recipe.[60] Thornton Wilder told her it might well be the publicity stunt of the year, but Alice was not amused.

While the British version received the expected attention, even the expurgated American version was a success, after it was honed into a book by Harper's. Though the style and stories pleased the publisher, the manuscript Alice submitted was not like the neat, carefully typed versions she had made of Gertrude's books. Misspelled and badly typed, it set a record, one of the staff thought, in sloppiness. And the recipes seemed too rich and extravagant to be useful to most readers. Eight eggs—set, not scrambled—required no less than one-half pound of butter; a four-egg omelette, appropriately *"sans nom,"* was enriched with three-quarters of a cup of heavy cream. Truffles appeared frequently and liqueurs were added freely. Neglecting even to proofread her recipes, Alice nearly ruined one dinner party given by a friend of Lilyanna.

With a menu made up exclusively of dishes from Alice's cookbook, the young woman was combining the ingredients for croissants when she found the batter undeniably soupy. Filling every container she had with extra flour and butter, she produced a large—but edible—quantity of croissants. But, she wrote to Alice, wasn't the amount of milk she recommended too large?

Alice, "ashamed and confused," confessed that the total quantity should have been two cups—not the five that appeared in the British version of the book—and blamed the mistake on her own trust in the publisher's proofreaders. The pressure of writing so much in so little time, she explained, precluded her revision.[61]

Critics, however, were kind. The *New Yorker*'s Janet Flanner, who had known Gertrude and Alice for many years, called it "a book of character, fine food, and tasty human observation." *Time* thought "its special charm is the stream of Alice's prattle, in which the recipes appear like floating islands. . . ." Joe Barry, in the *New Republic*, wrote a self-described "bread-and-butter review" of his friend's effort. Amid the recipes, he wrote, was the essence of Alice's character. "The Cook Book just published is, of course, a cook book and *Moby Dick* is the story of a whale hunt. But in it are the Comments of a richly provisioned life, of a cool temperament found only at high altitudes."

In her spare, distilled style, which Gertrude had imitated so precisely in *The Autobiography*, Alice offered unexpected glimpses into her life in the kitchen, explaining at length her experiences with murder. Enticingly called "Murder in the Kitchen"—the title she had suggested to Harper's for the entire book—one chapter is devoted to her various techniques of killing, beginning with the murder of a lively carp. "The fish man who sold me the carp," Alice told her readers, "said he had no time to kill, scale or clean it, nor would he tell me with which of these horrible necessities one began." Deducing the sequence, she considered pummeling the fish with a mallet, but feared the wriggling animal would escape her blows. A knife seemed a better choice, and, protecting her left hand with a dishcloth, she grasped her weapon in her right and plunged it into the base of the spinal column. "Horror of horrors," she said. "The carp was dead, killed, assassinated, murdered in the first, second and third degree. Limp, I fell into a chair, with my hands still unwashed reached for a cigarette, lighted it, and waited for the police to come and take me into custody." But after a second cigarette she calmed, emptied the fish "of what I did not care to look at," and stuffed it with chestnuts.

Her second experience as a murderess occurred when, one day, a crate of six white pigeons was delivered to her apartment with an accompanying note from a friend suggesting that Alice's cleverness would inspire her to cook something delicious with them. "It is certainly a mistake to allow a reputation for cleverness to be born and spread by loving friends," Alice decided. "It is so cheaply acquired and so dearly paid for." Fortunately, Gertrude was out when the gift arrived: she could not bear the sight of such work. And though Alice knew she had plenty of time to kill and clean the birds, she lacked courage to do so. "A large cup of strong black coffee would help," she thought. "This was before a lovely Brazilian told me that in her country a large cup of black coffee was always served before going to bed to ensure a good night's rest. Not yet having acquired this knowledge the black coffee made me lively and courageous." After downing her tonic, she picked up one "poor innocent Dove" and pressed its throat. Suddenly, the unpleasant realization came to her "that one saw with one's fingertips as well as one's eyes." But as she saw the six dead birds before her, she reflected that "one could become accustomed to murdering." With more fortitude than she had felt after killing the carp, she proceeded to braise the birds in butter.

Her next murder could not be avoided. A duck, near death from fright of a dog, was brought to Alice in the arms of her cook. "Her heart was beating so furiously I saw there was but one thing to do." Giving the bird three tablespoons of brandy to ensure "a good flavour," Alice deftly killed her. "How does Madame wish her to be cooked?" the pale but placid cook asked. Weakly, Alice replied, "With orange sauce."

Though she admitted having thought at times of killing "a stupid or obstinate cook," she apparently held her passions under control, and her victims were sautéed and sauced, braised not buried.

Alice's selection of recipes did not include one which she shared with friends: her sure cure for insomnia. One clove of garlic, she recommended, should be cooked for ten minutes in one portion of vegetables; three hours after ingesting this, she guaranteed, sleep would come.

Twenty-three

ALICE'S COOKBOOK WAS not her sole foray into writing. She had, as her book blurb advertised, touched the greats, and her opinions on literature and art were weighted with a special authority. In August 1950, "They Who Came to Paris to Write" was featured on the cover of the New York *Times Book Review*. In a telescoped view of literary life since 1907, Alice slid in and out of her many friendships, beginning with the first writer she met: Gertrude Stein. Of that relationship, she said little. Gertrude "so often wrote of her work, her friends and herself with intimacy and precision that one hesitates to add to the choice she considered appropriate to tell." Slipping past the post-World War I writers, Alice noted that after 1918, "American lady novelists, poetesses and fashion writers had gone home and after the peace were replaced by a younger generation of Americans," among them Sherwood Anderson, F. Scott Fitzgerald, John Dos Passos "with his Latin charm," Glenway Wescott, and even Ernest Hemingway. Hemingway, she remembered, once speaking about a rich American and his wife who had come to Paris to become writers, "said that he had known them before they could read or write. And in a kind of way," Alice said, "I feel that about Hemingway, that is that neither reading nor writing is a natural inevitable necessity for him."

The right names were dropped throughout the article— Ezra Pound, Thornton Wilder, T. S. Eliot—until Alice concluded with the present group. But there were few contemporary writers in whom she took an interest. Most new publications she read were the works of friends, who sent her a copy hoping for her praise. When she did choose for herself, she returned to Henry James, the "witty and amusing" Ivy Compton-Burnett, Lillian de la Torre's mysteries, the inevitable cookbooks, or a book which linked her to her past.

Leo Stein's death in July 1947 drew hardly a comment from Alice; but when his journal and letters were published in 1950, she wanted to read his *Journey Into the Self* to rid herself for all time of his memory—and, she wrote to Van Vechten, of the suffering he had caused.[62] When she did read it, she found many blatant errors and misjudgments, but she expected no better from Leo. She was annoyed, but admitted that Leo was finished for her.[63]

She dabbled in young writers but was often offended by what she found. The sex life of Truman Capote's characters bored her; James Purdy, she thought, lacked taste; Françoise Sagan's first novel, *Bonjour Tristesse*, was vulgar. One novel based on the life of Scott Fitzgerald was too offensive even to read. Her maternal protectiveness of Fitzgerald extended to her review of his short stories, which appeared in the New York *Times* on March 4, 1951.

Remembering that *This Side of Paradise* had seemed to her "the definitive portrait of his generation," she admitted that reading his stories was "a melancholy pleasure, for Fitzgerald had become a legend and the epoch he created is history." She related Gertrude's commiseration with the writer on his thirtieth birthday, and her subsequent praise of *Tender Is the Night*. But even with generous feelings, she could offer only qualified praise of the collection and confided to Fernanda Pivano, Fitzgerald's Italian translator, that she thought the stories actually "very very poor."

Hemingway's career, of course, was followed carefully, and any chink in the legend was reported to friends with delight. Lillian Ross's 1950 interview for the *New Yorker*, "How Do You Like It Now, Gentlemen?," seemed to Alice to have odd revelations and disclosures by himself and his wife, which might, she speculated, be explained by the rumor that he was extremely ill. She felt almost vindicated by Alfred Kazin's "The Indignant Flesh," a review of Hemingway's *Across the River and into the Trees*. Nothing, Alice thought, could ever be as destructive to Hemingway's myth as Kazin's review.[64]

The novel, Kazin wrote, "can only distress anyone who admires Hemingway," and he wondered whether readers would feel pity or embarrassment "that so fine and honest a writer can make such a travesty of himself, or amazement that a man can render so marvellously the beauty of the natural world and yet be so vulgar." The Colonel, the archetypal Hemingway hero, was nothing more than "an American big shot who has been in all the countries and seen all the twentieth century wars and has charmed a whole generation into believing that toughness is the same as valor." The Colonel, Kazin went on, represented "the flesh—the flesh in its most automatic impulses, with the sensory machine dying down, the heart threatening to burst at any moment, and the brain throbbing weakly on old obscenities." And though Kazin was thankful that Hemingway's illness was not at all fatal, and that the book was "not his last words," Alice was sure that the myth was crumbling. Friends, she reported incredulously, seemed to think the article would please her, but she said she felt pity about his comedown. Of course she could not refrain from adding that she thought herself justly rewarded.

While not reticent about expressing her literary opinions to friends, she was forced into an uncomfortable position in the fall of 1950, when Yale University Press asked her to write the foreword to the first volume of Gertrude's work. Extremely upset, she wrote to Thornton Wilder, pleading for him to use his influence so that the travesty would not occur. Gertrude, she told him, would never have agreed to such a plan; she accepted only because Van Vechten had implied that her refusal might impede the publication of the book.

Wilder's help came quickly, relieving Alice of her terrible burden. Her replacement was Janet Flanner. Though Alice thought Flanner was not familiar enough with Gertrude's work to write an introduction to *Two: Gertrude Stein and Her Brother,* she acquiesced to Van Vechten's decision. But she was completely unsympathetic to Flanner's probing questions about the pieces, considering them an invasion of Gertrude's private life. She must only read the portraits, Alice told her, to understand them. Frustrated in her attempt to analyze the difficult pieces, Flanner presented an introduction that was based more on her friendship with the two women than on the pieces themselves. And Alice, still unsatisfied, doubted that Flanner had read them at all. She was soothed, however, by Donald

Sutherland, who suggested that Flanner's introduction would convey to readers that having a key to Gertrude's work "is not the point,"[65] and he recommended that Alice not concern herself with prefaces that were closer to reminiscences than dissections.

Her request of Wilder had been couched in apologies. Not only did she hesitate to impose on his time and efforts, but she knew that she was pitting him against a man he did not like: Carl Van Vechten. Each was jealous of his special relationship with Gertrude, and each sought to exert his strength in the publication of Gertrude's works. Van Vechten was more sympathetic toward those who wanted to read Gertrude with *une clef* than were Alice and Wilder. In her own relationships with them, Alice was tender and careful. They were, after all, among her closest friends and they were both working for Gertrude. Her aversion to writing the introduction was so strong, however, that she risked Van Vechten's thinking her a traitor—which, she said, he did—by going to Wilder.

Whatever her reservations, her loyalty to the four men involved in publishing Gertrude was unwavering. Donald Gallup, she knew, besides editing, suffered endless day-to-day drudgery in the production of the books; Van Vechten and Donald Sutherland tried to assemble the volumes with as much taste, delicacy, and logic as they could; and Wilder, she thought, was the project's strength. She flooded them with expressions of endless gratitude—constant thanks—continual love.

As difficult and volatile as Alice was in her later years, she was not without compassionate and devoted friends. In July 1952 she traveled to Spain with Joe Barry and his wife, a trip which resurrected memories.[66] They traveled along the Mediterranean coast and then inland to Córdoba, Seville, Toledo, and Madrid, Segovia, Ávila, Burgos, and Valladolid. Coming back to France, they stopped in Bayonne and Lascaux, where Alice found the cave paintings surprisingly modern. She promised herself that the following year she would definitely return to Castile.

But the following September, though she did go to Spain, she did not go to Castile. This time with Harold and Virginia Knapik, she traveled to the Costa Brava, where they rented a house in San Feliu de Guixols, a fishing village where the only other tourists were English and Spanish—save for one American. The house the Knapiks found was, Alice thought, typically Spanish, a sprawling house with many bedrooms, a poor bathroom, and a multitude of chairs. There was a fountain in the garden, and fragrant trees. Alice was pleased.[67] The Knapiks had rented the house sight unseen, knowing only that it was large and faced the Paseo del Generalíssimo, a promenade along the sea.

The air and sun and Spanish cooking provided a welcome respite, and Alice reported that she felt well doing nothing but indulging herself in sampling luxurious food and enjoying an occasional trip to Barcelona and Madrid. The trip to Barcelona, Harold found, was somewhat treacherous. "There were said to be 365 turns, one for each day of the year, on the road to Barcelona from our town, which meant that the rear of the bus, where we customarily sat, was at least half the time over a cliff. The road, although a good one, was narrow, and it was surprising to note just how well the mules and donkeys had grasped the situation. If in negotiating a turn the bus came on an approaching mule or donkey cart, there was no business of horn-blowing or extra careful driving; the mule or donkey simply headed for the ditch and got out of the way. Virginia, who had begun to suspect that this was not the safest of roads, once questioned the Barcelona agent of the bus company about the possibility of going by another route. I remember his answer: 'Senora, every day and nothing. . . .' "

Though he decided that there was no cause for alarm, one return trip "gave us what is known as an insight." From their places in the back of the bus, they noticed a good many passengers making the sign of the cross, and soon the bus slowed to a crawl. Wondering what was happening, Harold went over to the window and looked out. "What I saw was the sea, about 250 feet below."[68]

For the last two weeks of their vacation, Virginia had to go to Rome, and Alice and Harold were left alone. Often, Harold remembered, when Alice wanted to talk, he would hear her calling "from what seemed a block away." The house suddenly felt as if it had grown to "ghastly dimensions." To lessen the effect of Virginia's absence, the two dined out for those weeks, enjoying local specialties which were prepared excellently. The fruits and pastry, she wrote to Van Vechten, were incomparable.[69]

Besides the comfort of her friends, she had finally acquired a competent housekeeper, Madeleine Charrière, whom Joe Barry had known since 1946. Madame Charrière, "a handsome seamstress . . . with comfortable hips, haunches, and carriage . . . is the Frenchwoman," Barry wrote, "we used to meet in the villages during the war, when the men were away fighting or in the camps—towers of strength, imperturbably running everything. . . ."[70] Alice had finally met her match in servants, and Madeleine, far from being Alice's underling, became her majordomo. As Alice's health declined, as she grew more and more crippled by arthritis and blinded by a cataract, she came to depend on Madeleine for her existence. It was an uncomfortable position for a woman who nurtured the dependence of others. On November 24, 1952, Alice was astonished to discover how very much she needed to be needed.

Basket died that morning, she wrote sadly to Van Vechten. Nearly blind and suffering from various frequent illnesses, he had an attack so severe that he collapsed. Alice was shocked. Now, she wrote to friends, there was no one and nothing that needed her. She felt completely alone.[71]

Still, she had Francis Rose. During the war, Francis had married Frederica, the writer Dorothy Carrington. He seemed totally changed from the eccentricities of his youth, and the change, Alice thought, was undoubtedly caused by his marriage. Frederica was strong, stable, respectable, and made Francis truly happy. But after a few years of marriage, Francis's life had become as "fantastic" as it had been when he was twenty and cavorting with the surrealists. His misadventures often demanded Alice's attention.

Once, Francis claimed that Luis, his valet and paramour, was really his illegitimate son. And Sir Francis wanted to officially declare his paternity so the youth could inherit his title. The disclosure, Alice found, was not made to any of his English friends who would know better about bastards inheriting titles. But she, among his other American friends, was allowed the confidence. Eventually, Francis got his wife's permission to recognize the young man. He hoped to obtain Spanish nationality for him, he told Alice, so that when he came of age, he could benefit from Francis's heritage of Spanish aristocracy.[72]

Alice's involvement was really on Frederica's behalf. Convalescing from an operation, Frederica asked Alice to keep Francis on her side of the channel until she recovered. Alice considered the task formidable, since all she knew of Francis's whereabouts was that he was roaming through the South of France. She could intimidate him more easily, she said, if he were nearby.

That "Francis story," as Alice called it, had a comparatively peaceful ending; but a few years later Alice was once again involved in an escapade. A late-night telephone call brought news that Francis had been beaten up in a drunken brawl by another of his boyfriends, who then brought him to a hospital claiming that Francis had had a heart attack. But the doctors could find nothing wrong with him, Alice reported with a sigh.[73]

Francis's stories, she knew, could not be believed without verification. In his autobiography, *Saying Life*, which is dedicated to Gertrude, he wrote of visits to Goering, Hitler, and Mussolini—at a time, Alice said, when he was staying with her and Gertrude at Bilignin. He also described Gertrude as Episcopalian and, in an article, once disclosed that Alice had in her youth been engaged to a sailor. Some of her friends wondered at Alice's patience with Francis; but Alice had no question of his love for Gertrude.

When her time was not spent in ministering to others, her days were busy with work she had just begun with a young doctoral student—kind, intelligent and perceptive— who was annotating Gertrude's early notebooks. The notebooks, which Alice had never read, were voluminous and intimate. Assured by Yale that they would not be published "for a considerable period," she agreed to be interviewed intensively about their contents. With her love of gossip and her curiosity about what Gertrude had written, she seems to have relished the sessions with Leon Katz.

Gertrude, she soon found, went beyond honesty in her characterizations of those she knew.[74] The notebooks contained her early character analyses and her diarylike revelations about friends and acquaintances. Katz, she saw, read the notes with the eye of a detective.[75] He had already obtained information from several interviews, including those with Annette Rosenshine and Mabel Weeks, and he knew the letters and papers at Yale. Sometimes Alice refused to answer his questions; sometimes she tried to lie. But he posed knowledgeable opposition.

Since the notebooks included the years of Alice's arrival in Paris, her character is given as thorough an analysis as that of anyone else Gertrude observed. When Gertrude's original estimation of her was finally revealed, Alice was understandably upset. Alice, Gertrude thought at first, was a vicious liar, venomous, cruel, unfeeling, base, and lacking high ideals.[76] Shocked, Alice could not explain Gertrude's description of her. Other people, she told Katz, must have influenced Gertrude's perception. The adjectives, she thought, could not possibly have reflected the way Gertrude really felt.

But nothing, she admitted to friends, could have prevented her from continuing the work with Katz, and though she felt the information she provided for him was innocuous, she knew he knew enough about Gertrude to be a danger to her own privacy. At the suggestion that he write a preface to one of the Yale volumes, she felt as if "a bomb" had been dropped. At once, she wrote to Donald Sutherland telling him that she understood that he, and no one else, was to write the preface and that she firmly vetoed Van Vechten's suggestion of Katz.[77] Only because she thought Katz's own work would be sealed and deposited at Yale did she continue until March 1953, when, ill with pernicious jaundice, she finished the sessions with him.

Describing herself as a lovely shade of Oriental yellow, she attributed her recovery to Madeleine's competent and faithful care. Rest and a diet which excluded fats were her physician's prescription, and rest she did, though she was completing her cookbook to send to Harper's by May.

The summer offered more leisure, and in July came the added boost of Donald Gallup's collection of letters written to Gertrude, *Flowers of Friendship*. Privately, Alice had wondered once if the collection were really necessary, but she encouraged Gallup with the idea because of his devotion to Gertrude. And she knew that the collection, carefully annotated and chosen with taste and integrity, would be a boon to Gertrude's admirers. More interesting, however, seemed Van Vechten's idea for publishing Gertrude's own letters to her many famous friends. It was a project he never pursued.

Her strength was sufficiently recovered during the weeks spent in Spain with the Knapiks, and she returned to spend the Parisian winter huddled beside her radiator. On Christmas Eve, she fell down some stone steps and wounded her leg, enough to require half an hour of bandaging each day. Though it slowed her pace, it did not stop her, and in April, a few weeks before her seventy-seventh birthday, she was again traveling, this time to Italy. Elizabeth Gordon, the editor of *House Beautiful,* had invited Alice south to talk with her about American architecture and household furniture of 1900. She wondered to Van Vechten if there weren't anyone else who could remember the last century.[78] But the ten days in Venice, Padua, and Florence—especially Florence—were lovely. She was thrilled at the gardens, the cuisine, the faces of the people.[79] But Fiesole, about which she harbored deeply personal memories, disappointed her. The town had changed from a quiet, charming village to a bustling tourist mecca. The plaza was filled with scores of sightseeing buses from all over Europe, and the hills were crowded with the noise and fumes from automobiles. It was awful, she thought. Though the town hardly resembled the place she knew, she somehow found the Casa Ricci, only to discover that its façade had been ruined with stucco and innumerable balconies. Instead of the beautiful fifteenth-century well she remembered, there was a goldfish pond. Heartbroken, she quickly left.

On her birthday, she reflected that she was only hanging on, not needed and easily forgotten; but an underlying depression did not keep her from feeling real delight at occasions that returned her to her vivid past. A startling retrospective of Picasso's paintings from 1900 to 1914 brought her much pleasure. No matter what Picasso did in his art, for Alice he could do no wrong.

In October 1948 some of his recent paintings and drawings were exhibited at the Galerie Leiris in Paris, and as usual Alice attended the opening. She thought his line was more adept than ever, and ever as beautiful, and was surprised at the magnificence of his landscapes. Though she considered him indisputably a great painter, she was overwhelmed by a 1950 exhibit of his sculpture, pieces she had seen in his studio and wrongly surmised were merely a diversion from painting. The exhibit, she wrote to Donald Gallup, showed how wrong she had been. Picasso, she was now sure, was as important a sculptor as a painter.[80]

Her devotion to Picasso as a friend and artist was unshakable, and she was convinced of his deep loyalty to her. Though she rarely saw him—he spent little time in Paris—he was her strongest and most vibrant link to her first years with Gertrude. Of his painting, she offered continuous and unqualified praise. His work in the mid-fifties, she thought, was as fine as anything he had ever done, the color more sensuous and the composition more relaxed and better integrated.[81] It was to be the source, she decided, for future painters.[82] Picasso was, as always, young.[83]

When he turned to designing pottery—pottery more beautiful than anyone else's, she said—she admitted her preference for his drawings but did not lessen her enthusiasm. Like Gertrude, Alice was firm in her response to personalities, and her love for Picasso inspired her ever-flourishing praise.

Far different had been her response to Matisse, and when she was invited to furnish an article about him for the *Yale Literary Magazine*, she responded that though she rarely saw him after his anger about *The Autobiography*, she would do her best to write about him.[84] The article, which appeared in the Fall, 1955 issue, was tepid in comparison with her bouquets to Picasso.

"The first picture of Henri Matisse that I saw," she began, "was in 1906, brought by Michael Stein to San Francisco. It was a small head of Madame Matisse with a vivid green shadow down the nose. It was of course like nothing one had ever seen before. The strength of the drawing and the force of the color were obvious." When she finally met Matisse and his family at Gertrude's home, she found his daughter Margot "a sweet winsome child— though she greatly resembled her father. . . ." Until 1914, Alice said, she and Gertrude saw Matisse fairly frequently and enjoyed his lively stories. His description of his wife's modeling for him particularly amused them. "Exhausted from household work she would doze," he told them, "her head bent lower and lower over the guitar, her fingers would pass over its strings—twang—she would awaken, straighten herself and resume the pose. Later this was repeated and Matisse would say 'Look here, this interrupts my work,' well knowing this would be effective."

But their friendship ended when Gertrude allied herself more and more with Picasso and the cubists, whose work first irritated Matisse and then, Alice wrote, exasperated him. "He had frankly placed himself in the opposition—with the commonplace majority." Among that majority, of course, was Leo Stein. Alice wrote more sympathetically of Madame Matisse, pointing out her "unconscious, almost tragic beauty," and the awesome way she inserted hatpins on either side of her hat. "Gertrude Stein once said: 'You are certain of what you are doing but to us it does look as if those pins traversed your brain.'" Immortalizing the comment, Matisse made an India ink drawing of his wife's gesture and gave it to Gertrude.

Of the final falling-out, Alice admitted that Gertrude had compared Madame Matisse's beauty to that of a horse, but she was surprised, she concluded, that Matisse did not think a horse beautiful.

The article, for which Alice found it difficult to draw together memories, was part of an issue devoted to Matisse, who had died in November 1954. The idea of a "Homage to Henri Matisse" seemed, despite her less than ardent appreciation of the artist, entirely appropriate. It was an effort she endorsed for Gertrude, and one she hoped would result from a biography which had been undertaken by Elizabeth Sprigge.

On November 16, 1953, Alice wrote to her editor at Harper's expressing her pleasure that Miss Sprigge had begun a work on Gertrude's life, and she recommended that Harper's publish the book, which they eventually did. It was a recommendation that Alice came to regret.

Sprigge, a translator and biographer of Strindberg, seemed to Alice to be eminently qualified to write about Gertrude. In her study of the dramatist, she was, Alice thought, faithful to his books; she wished no less for Gertrude. But she soon was disappointed to find that Sprigge, like John Malcolm Brinnin, wanted to include personal details in her biography—a practice Alice would not allow. Elizabeth Sprigge, she decided by 1955, was pretentious, ignorant of Gertrude's work, and wanted only to shock her readers with intimate disclosures. With a sharper venom than she had written about Brinnin, Alice duly warned Gertrude's friends against Sprigge's questions. And when Elizabeth Sprigge tried to interview Alice in 1956, a vigorous quarrel ensued. As she had told Brinnin, Alice informed Sprigge that she had no place in the book except, perhaps, as the editor of the Plain Edition. But Sprigge disagreed. The resulting manuscript, Alice was sure, would be vulgar and mistaken.[85]

Sprigge's research continued to irritate her, and she complained to friends each time she heard of the writer's visits to various people she and Gertrude knew. Sylvia Beach, she said, told her that Sprigge believed Alice had written Gertrude's book, to which Beach supposedly replied that many who never read Joyce similarly pointed to her as the ghostwriter.

When the book was finally published, in 1957, Alice felt herself partially avenged by two reviewers: her friends Donald Sutherland and Gilbert Harrison, then editor in chief of the *New Republic*.

Harrison thought Sprigge's account of Gertrude's life might interest readers who knew little about Gertrude. "But," he asked, "I wonder why she wrote it. She never met Gertrude Stein. She does not appear to feel strongly about her subject—either way. . . . She does not lead us to any greater appreciation of the more difficult Stein texts." While admitting that the writing was "pleasant" and the reporting "not unintelligent," he could find "nothing more worth saying about her book." The rest of his review was devoted to Gertrude, particularly about her influence on such writers as Hemingway, Sherwood Anderson, F. Scott Fitzgerald, Thornton Wilder, and Marianne Moore. To Alice's happiness, he burnished Gertrude's image:

. . . There was a ruthless rightness about her judgments concerning creativity. She was exceptionally alert, she did not talk or write to please others, what she knew she *knew*. She enjoyed praise, she saw the joke, but she never stooped to conquer. She talked to younger writers as if she were the Lord Himself, and they listened because she was demanding uncompromising disregard of the demands of the audience. She asked them to see "things as they are." She did not tell them what or how to write. . . .

Her simplicity, he continued.

was the result of intense concentration. She meditated about how we know whatever we know, and thought about time and how all that changed from generation to generation and from place to place is the externals and our way of looking at them. She used words as if they were alive, exploring them singly and in relation to each other, regarding them as if they had been born this instant. She had no use for hand-me-downs: the present was her preoccupation. The force of her vision knocked pretensions flat.[86]

"Excellent!" Alice exclaimed when she read the review, and if Gilbert Harrison had not earned her lasting love some twenty years before, he did for his article on Sprigge's book.

In 1937, Harrison remembered, he was a guest at their home in Bilignin, and one day took a walk with Gertrude past a pond where a water lily was floating. "Oh reach for it and bring it to Alice," Gertrude told him, "and she will love you the rest of your life." The prospect, Harrison wrote, was irresistible.[87]

Though she admitted that the publication of *Gertrude Stein: Her Life and Work* had been a disheartening experience, she told friends that the pain—eased by Harrison's review—was quickly passing.

The biography itself was hardly an intimate portrait of Alice. References to her were usually in connection with Gertrude's work, such as her typing of *The Making of Americans*, when she found that the sentences produced a particular rhythm and "made a music of its own. I don't mean the script I mean the typewriter. In those complicated sentences." Alice told Sprigge, "I rarely left anything out. And I got up a tremendous speed. Of course my love of Henry James was a good preparation for the long sentences. I remember being given Balzac when I was quite young and so much preferring Henry James."[88]

Occasionally, Alice's opinions were included, none of which harmed Gertrude's memory. She agreed that Gertrude could well be compared to Bach. "She introduces her theme contrapuntally and turns to the minor key and has the same exactitude."[89] She disagreed with Sprigge's assertion that Gertrude had wit, a quality Alice thought was peculiar to the English, and should not be confused with Gertrude's special kind of humor.[90] Commenting on Leo's liberal political views, she offered the suggestion that had he been English, "he would have been on the Manchester Guardian." And once, she disclosed about herself: "I am a person acted upon not a person who acts. . . ."[91]

The book had no allusions to Lesbianism, nor to Gertrude's repeated sexual themes in her work. Nevertheless, the book was a nightmare, she said, and she was often troubled by it as it was being written from 1953 to 1956. Fortunately, she was not obsessed by Sprigge's project, and what she called her old woman's maliciousness was easily directed to other victims.

In the summer of 1955, Janet Flanner brought Dorothy Miller and two others from the Museum of Modern Art in New York to see Alice's paintings. Given Alice's opinion of the museum, her conduct—she served them sherry and her best cakes—was admirable. And when one of the men mistook a Picasso for a Braque, she managed to hold her tongue. The story, of course, too good to keep to herself, was repeated in her letters.

The contretemps was, in the private metaphor she had shared with Gertrude, "A Henry McBride's Braque." Henry McBride, it seemed, had once praised a Picasso as the finest Braque he had ever seen, which both Alice and Gertrude admitted it would have been if it had not, of course, been painted by Picasso. But Gertrude did nothing to point out her friend's error, and forever after similar cases of mistaken identity were called a McBride's Braque.[92]

One of Alice's criteria of aesthetic sophistication was the ability to discern a Braque from a Picasso. An Associated

Press reporter, interviewing her in 1950 about Picasso and Hemingway, incited her ire when he not only spoke of Picasso and Hemingway in the same sentence, but thought a Picasso was a Braque. Alice became so enraged that in the argument which developed she found herself defending Hemingway, which she was certain she would never do again.[93]

Twenty-four

THE PUBLICATION OF her cookbook seemed to spur Alice's social life. New names were dropped in her letters and new faces appeared at the rue Christine. After attending a rehearsal of Thornton Wilder's *The Skin of Our Teeth* with his sister Isabel, Alice gave a tea for the stars, Mary Martin and Helen Hayes.[94]

She was invited to give a talk in Iceland and responded, "I'd go like a shot if they will pay my air passage." Wondering about her topic for the gathering, she asked, "Should I give a *causerie* in drawing rooms on Picasso or onion soup or both? Oh my dear what a lark—off to Iceland! which will be Gulf-stream comfortable all new new new. To slip out some spring morning in a place one doesn't know has always been my idea of pleasurable excitement."[95]

Her idea was realized—but instead of Iceland, she found herself planning a trip to Belgium. She was invited, in January 1956, to give a talk in Brussels. She accepted gladly; she enjoyed traveling, especially when her expenses were paid. She discussed the subject of her talk with friends, one of whom advised her to make a list of possible indiscretions so that she might avoid saying them. But Alice was afraid that, once they were brought to mind, they might too easily slip out. Entitled "Memories of the rue Fleurus," her talk in March at the American Women's Club was a happy experience. Cocktails preceded dinner at the Poets Club—with Alice honored by the first toast. She met the Queen Mother—sprightly and vivacious at eighty-two—who wanted Alice to send her a copy of her cookbook; Stephen Spender, also a guest at the Poets Club; and Anne Bodart, a seventeen-year-old Belgian writer whose first book Alice had translated.

The Blue Dog and Other Fables for the French had been written when Anne was fourteen and published when she was sixteen. "Anne," Alice discovered, "is completely absorbed by her desire to express the truth—her fear is the false." The fables, which include "The Diary of a Dog," "The Poet," "Mister Poodle," and "The Cat Who Wore Spectacles," are sweet, wistful, and innocent. Anne's gentle Poet, on a quest for beauty and the "souls of things," picks a marguerite, unknowingly observed by two rabbits.

"Who is it?" asked the younger one, worried.
"I do not know," said the other rabbit.
"He plucked a marguerite," said the first one, his throat dry.
"He is certainly one of the worst creatures alive," said the second.
The first rabbit who had never seen a man said:
"He is an assassin of souls."

"Each story of this book," Alice wrote in her preface, "shows sensitive observation, delicate choice in its recording, distinction in the relationship of its characters (for the insects and animals are full-length portraits and only once is a moral value noted). First books with these qualities are indeed rare. The reader will be surprised, pleased and moved by the considerable gift of Anne Bodart."

Translating Bodart's book was a pleasant diversion, but more interesting writing projects seemed imminent. Shortly after she returned from Belgium she began to think seriously about writing her memoirs. John Schaffner, a friend and literary agent, had suggested that she write her book for Holt, Rinehart and Winston. The idea, she wrote him, was definitely exciting—but to sign a contract with Holt, she would have to first fulfill her contract with Harper's, which had an option on her next book.

A new cookbook, it was decided, would be the best solution to her problem, and *Aromas and Flavors of Past and Present* was begun shortly after the contract for it was signed on May 22, 1956. For this book, Alice was required to supply only recipes—fifty thousand words pulled out of her recipe box, she said—and another writer, Poppy Cannon, would assemble them and provide introductions and comments.

Poppy Cannon, the author of *The Can-Opener Cook Book* and an advocate of short-cut cooking, differed sharply from Alice's approach to cuisine. As food editor of *House Beautiful*, she had met Alice in Venice in 1953 and admitted that she had been totally unprepared for the "small, regal figure" with whom she dined at the Hotel Royal Danieli. Alice, she thought, was no less than an "Edwardian lady," and everything about her seemed to burn with an inner strength.

> The first feeling was about her eyes. It is not only that they are so large but that they are so bright, giving out sparks. When she is about to say something especially wise or critical or amusing, she telegraphs it first with her eyes.[96]

Miss Cannon admired what others often mocked. Her bangs, she wrote, and the "dark down over her lips" made "other faces seem nude by comparison." Dressed in heavy, luxurious fabrics, wearing her ornate jewelry, scented with Balmain's *Jolie Madame*, Alice appeared to Cannon elegant and feminine.

> . . . Despite her tiny figure she can dominate a room, a group, a conversation. In the most fashionable places, like Maxim's or Le Moutier at Saint Germain or at dinner parties among the greats of the Cognac or the Champagne country where we have been together, all heads turn toward her. No matter how softly or how slowly she speaks, everyone listens. A whole party knots around her.
>
> Nothing escapes her analytical attention—nothing about the relationships of people. Never a single nuance is disregarded concerning food and wine. Her memory of fragrance and taste is so well developed that years afterward she can recall and often re-create a dish that she has tasted only once.[97]

Despite Cannon's professed admiration, she and Alice disagreed about short-cut cooking. Alice was firm in her disdain of such innovations as cake mixes and blenders. When Cannon dropped the phrase "creative cooking," Alice reacted with raised eyebrows and an audible snort.

"What would that be?" she asked. And to Cannon's recitation of the "riches of the American larder," Alice had only skepticism. "With our traditions and in our menus," Cannon said, "we can now *cream* the world for our tables. We can have Russian soup, a Chinese vegetable with our American steak, and follow it with a French dessert." "How incongruous," Alice retorted.[98]

Work on the book did not bring them together very often. They met twice for marathon sessions of ten hours each, in Cannon's suite at the Plaza-Athénée in Paris. Several times they worked in Alice's apartment, where, Cannon said, Alice "bustles, sparkles, crackles, lashes out. . . ." Apparently her lashing out did not halt the progress of the book, and on the day the manuscript was completed, Alice and Poppy Cannon celebrated with lobster soufflé. *Aromas and Flavors of Past and Present* was published in November 1958. Alice had received an advance of $1,250 for her work, and, most important, she was now free to proceed with a more exciting project: a book she wanted to call *Things I Have Seen*.

But before Alice set to work compiling her life's stories, she effected a major change in her present existence. After Gertrude's death, Alice often expressed envy for those who found comfort and solace in religion. When Clare Moore de Gruchy died in 1948, she told Fania Van Vechten that only a belief in God could provide meaning for life. Otherwise there remained only emptiness.[99]

Beginning in the mid-fifties, friends noticed a growing reference to saints' days, holy days, and blessings in Alice's letters, and Thornton Wilder saw that she was reading a good deal of devotional literature. Among her friends, many were Catholic, three recent converts.

The attractions of Catholicism had been drawing Alice for many years, culminating at Easter in 1956, when she attended a service at the Benedictine monastery at Solesmes, which she found so indescribably beautiful and moving that it brought her a peacefulness she had not before felt. Following the service, she suffered disturbed days— actually months—but by the end of the year she had made her decision.

She explained to friends that she had been baptized as a

child when a friend of her mother was alarmed that she was growing up with no sense of religion. But there is little likelihood of that early baptism. Relatives remembered Alice and her father at synagogue for several Yom Kippur services, and it appears that the Toklases and the Levinskys practiced at least a token Judaism. Certainly a break with their religion would have been a radical step for the times. The destruction of church records in the earthquake precludes verifying Alice's allegation.

Alice's claim of returning to the religion of her childhood was made, most likely, for expediency. Having been baptized at eight saved the effort and time involved in having to be baptized at eighty. Her embrace of Catholicism, in any case, was not a return to the security of her childhood beliefs, but the fulfillment of her need for an all-consuming passion, an ordered pattern of life, and, most of all, for the conception of a populated heaven where she would find Gertrude.

In the summer of 1957, one of those troubled months when she was coming to her decision, she accompanied Donald Sutherland and his wife on a trip to Albi, which took them also to Lascaux, Vézelay, Souillac, and Saint-Benoît-sur-Loire. From Saint-Benoît, they detoured north to Germigny-des-Prés, where the Sutherlands wanted to see the pre-Romanesque church.

Throughout the trip, Alice had not shown much interest in the Romanesque churches that Sutherland and his wife stopped to see. In Vézelay she stayed in the car while they went to the church; she did not visit the cathedral at Albi, nor did she seem interested in the abbey at Saint-Benoît-sur-Loire. Her reaction at Germigny-des-Prés, however, was far different. She seemed to be immediately entranced. "The apse and the interior of the square fenestrated tower, with pale golden light—some say topaze—coming in over the nearly white and finely cut masonry, had a simple and tranquil finality about them," Sutherland wrote, "which I suppose appealed to her more than the militant and forbidding forms of the Romanesque." As they left the church, Alice noticed some blue enamel plaques which she pointed out to Sutherland. They reminded her of a blue brooch that Gertrude had worn, the same shade and shape as those of the plaques.

Though she said little more about the church then, Sutherland noticed that she seemed especially happy as she walked around in it. Years later, she confessed that "her conversion had come over her, almost completed itself" there.[100]

She had the time and leisure to work out her decision after her return from the trip. In September, she was with the Knapiks near Grasse, where she rested in a garden of olive and willow trees scented by jasmine. And in October she went to Italy, to Acqui, on the recommendation of Anita Loos, who had been successfully treated for a serious affliction of arthritis by the mud baths at a spa there.

Anita Loos, when she visited Alice at the rue Christine, found her badly crippled, barely able to walk aided by two canes. When they talked of Alice's arthritis, Loos recommended the treatment she had undergone the previous year at Acqui Terme, which had helped her after cortisone treatments had failed. Thinking that Alice was too weak to endure the trip to northern Italy, Loos mentioned the spa merely in passing. But in the fall, Alice traveled south and left Acqui Terme walking without a cane.

The relief from physical pain, however, was not as miraculous to her as her entry into the Church. On December 9, 1957, she confessed and was given Holy Communion, a catechism, a missal, and a rosary.[101] Now, she wrote, peace would be hers. She shared her happiness with Van Vechten and expressed her gratitude to Virginia Knapik for her acceptance of her conversion.[102]

If Virginia Knapik was understanding in her acceptance of Alice's new-found religion, other friends were dubious, and some less than kind. But Alice took great comfort in her certainty that Gertrude was waiting for her, that she could pray for her and to her, and that someday they would be reunited. She was convinced that though Gertrude was in limbo—she had, after all, never been baptized —she would eventually be released for the reunion in purgatory and the subsequent rise to heaven.

She discussed the possibility of an afterlife with Bernard Faÿ, who unfailingly supported her conversion, and he affirmed her conception of a place where she would find God and Jesus together with angels and saints—and Gertrude, no doubt at work. After eleven years of loneliness, fearing that Gertrude's presence was becoming more and more elusive, she had revived an even more radiant memory of Gertrude through her conversion.

Her practice of religion, however, was more a form of everlasting-life insurance than a turning inward or a preoccupation with the spiritual life. With renewed vigor, she continued her voluminous correspondence, kept up a diverting social life, and continued writing. In 1958, she published two articles.

"Fifty Years of French Fashions" offered a personal survey of Paris *haute couture* to readers of the *Atlantic*, the magazine in which both Henry James and Gertrude had appeared. Though Alice was modest about appearing in a magazine that had published such eminent writers, she managed to provide a gossipy view of fashion from Monsieur Worth—remembered from her childhood visit—to Pierre Balmain. She admitted a weakness for Balenciaga, because of his Spanish sense of color and design, and described a treasured Balenciaga scarf woven in delicate grays. Balmain, she thought, praising her friend, celebrated freedom of movement for women and instilled the spirit of Renoir and Manet into his clothes. Though Balmain had designed several suits and dresses for Gertrude and Alice, the public often did not realize that the two were so fashionably dressed. "Be sure you don't tell anybody that we are wearing clothes made by Pierre Balmain," Gertrude once told Alice. "We look like gypsies."

Alice discussed fashion as seriously as Gertrude had discussed art. Balmain's use of decoration, she wrote:

> threw the emphasis on the line, which became simplified or complicated according to the inspiration of the moment, never interfering, however, with the free movement of the body, though the length of the steps might be reduced to a matter of inches. To emphasize the line he used stitched bands on wool, flowing scarves on silk, and finally artificial flowers and even ostrich feathers on evening dresses. None of these inventions was shocking, because, good Frenchman that he is, he remained ever in the tradition of the *haute couture*—even in this period of Chaos. Sputniks are not his concern: the survival of the fittest in

French *haute couture* is. . . . He told me that his greatest pleasure had been to find recently in Rome a client wearing a coat which he had made for her two years previously and which had not become old-fashioned. It was beyond fashion.

Balmain had grown up near Aix-les-Bains, where he "spent hours making paper mannequins and dressing them in fabulous gowns fashioned out of scraps of cloth." Later, he developed an interest in theater design, after finding a chestful of old costumes. He went on to study architecture in Paris but returned frequently to help his mother run her boutique in the affluent resort town. She counted among her customers Gertrude and Alice, who were living nearby in Bilignin.

Balmain so much enjoyed the company of the two women that he would bicycle to Bilignin for visits, bringing them darning cotton from Paris; and when architecture was finally abandoned for designing, he made them coats and

voluminous tweed skirts which came down to the ankle, with matching jackets, but the buttons were of embossed silver, and the linings in dove-coloured taffeta. Gertrude always ordered deep pockets in which she plunged her arms up to the elbow to withdraw the paraphernalia of her everyday life. Both of them wore with distinction clothes that would have seemed ridiculous on anybody else.[103]

Gertrude, Alice, and Basket attended Balmain's first press showing in 1945 at his special invitation. "I am counting absolutely on you," he wrote to them. "All the French and American press and several Parisian personalities will be there—there will be photographers and it would flatter me very much if the American magazines published you at the opening of a new maison de couture."[104]

They not only attended, but Gertrude's review of the showing, "From Dark to Day," appeared in *Vogue*. "I suppose there at the opening, we were the only ones who had been clothed in all those long years in Pierre Balmain's clothes," she boasted, adding, "we were proud of it."

Gertrude's death so saddened Balmain that Alice gave

him a memento of her—a black and yellow silk scarf—which he looked upon as a talisman, keeping it with him throughout preparations for his future showings, most of which Alice attended.

One of Balmain's most treasured memories of the two was at Culoz when he visited them there during the war:

> My English was not very strong, and I remember that after one of these outings I told an American friend that I had arrived to find Gertrude Stein walking a ghost in the garden. I meant "goat," of course, but perhaps the mistake did not seem so out of place when it related to Gertrude.[105]

Alice was especially amused by his description of his designs, his mime to show style, and his imitation of his models.[106] Until her death, Balmain considered Alice "almost my godmother."

For her second article, Alice turned to a graver issue: French politics and the volatile situation in France over the Algerian war. The war, Alice wrote to Annette Rosenshine, was a problem that seemed to be getting worse. During the month of May 1958, when De Gaulle was being pressed to return to the government after having been cloistered at Colombey-les-Deux-Églises since 1946, there was an uneasy atmosphere in Paris which Alice described in "The Rue Dauphine Refuses the Revolution."

Alice, like the populace of the street, preferred the status quo to upheaval, and her political views were usually conservative. Strikes inconvenienced and depressed her. National policies, she thought, should be strong and consistent; governments should not meddle in the lives of the people. And the people themselves should not be submissive. ". . . It is a confused world," she admitted. But no matter what the conditions were, to Alice they were never as shattering as the newspapers described them. She could manage with inflation, austerity, rationing, and, as she blithely revealed, rumors of revolution.

In World War I when only a few doughboys had gotten to the front and the Germans were advancing on Paris, a wounded poilu said to Gertrude Stein:

"This is leading to revolution." "Be sensible," she assured him, "you French invented a perfectly good revolution more than a hundred years ago. You won't repeat yourself." This recurred to me the other day when Paris was politically disturbed, very disturbed indeed. Even in the busy working-man's district in which I live, revolution was not spoken of, but people were more excited than usual. One morning when I went marketing there was a long line of women standing before the grocer's. As I passed on the narrow sidewalk a woman came out of the store and announced: "It's a deception. They have a ton of sugar all piled up to the ceiling. They have deceived us." It took no more than this to discourage hoarding.

The city was disturbed, it seemed, because President Coty was failing to find a candidate who could obtain a majority, and De Gaulle, to whom Coty had made overtures at the beginning of May, had not yet clarified his position. The concierges, "all of whom know the worst and are supposed to believe it," Alice wrote, "commenced to spread rumors." With her political sophistication and California sense of humor, Alice decided that if a mob broke into her apartment she should be prepared "Marie Antoinette fashion" to deal with them. Unable to find a taxi, she went out on foot to the Saint-Germain quarter, where, in the finest bakeshop she knew, she found "the best fruitcake now baked in Paris."

There were very few women on the streets—just groups of men of strangely assorted ages and classes. They looked like conspirators from a scene of grand opera. When finally, exhausted, I got to the bakers, I bought the largest fruitcake they had and . . . a large box of small palely frosted cakes. With these I commenced the homeward trek. The odd groups were piling into cars—small cars to hold so many. "What are they up to?" I asked a policeman at the corner, his back turned toward the automobiles. For answer he shrugged his shoulders. "At least we are quiet here," he said. I trudged all the way home again.

Sunday was quiet, but on Monday an unexploded bomb was found in a garbage can on her street. Though a noisy crowd had assembled to see a policeman remove the bomb, Alice commented only, "This was as near violence as it got." Other Americans, she was surprised to note, were not as calm as she. The Place de la Concorde, near the United States Embassy, would be, they were sure, the center of the revolution. An American visitor even feared she heard shouting from that very spot while sitting in Alice's apartment. "Not through the closed windows," Alice replied impatiently, "and from almost a mile away."

With a sigh, Alice ended her article by predicting that De Gaulle would soon come to power—he soon did—with the support of the middle class, and that even the word "revolution" would not soon be repeated—at least not by Parisian concierges.

Twenty-five

THE BOOK WHICH was eventually published as *What Is Remembered* was begun in May 1958. Alice, at eighty-one was unable to work on so imposing a project alone, and a collaborator was enlisted from among her friends. Max White, a writer she had known since 1934, was someone, she thought, who knew Gertrude well and admired and understood her writing.[107] They had met in New York during the lecture tour, after White had sent Gertrude an issue of *Ploughshare*, a journal which published some of his stories set in Spain. The stories, Gertrude told him, had captured "the special brand of realism that is Spain's own." White, she decided after she had read his first novel, *Anna Becker*, "does something that his newer crowd do do he makes a very clear line coming out of his writing, not heavy as the last generation were doing, but clear as if everything was there not in the air but in being clearly there."[108]

White's admiration for Gertrude no doubt touched Alice. He had written to Gertrude in 1937 that she, more than any other writer, had given him a new idea of "the sentence as a unit of composition," and, more important, he recognized in her writing "a stream of reader's consciousness" rather than "of writer's consciousness" that characterized Joyce. ". . . I have felt very strongly about you and Joyce . . . that whereas he takes the direction of death yours has always been that of life. . . ."[109]

They corresponded warmly until Gertrude's death, and then White continued his friendship with Alice. After he visited her in 1952, Alice wrote to a friend that he was very dear to her and with real pleasure she reported his own conversion to Catholicism in 1955. Because he came to Gertrude's work with an intelligence and sensitivity that she respected, he would be, she thought, invaluable for the book her publisher wanted.[101]

Though Alice told friends that she was writing the story of her life with Gertrude, Holt apparently expected a book which related situations and anecdotes to those passages in Gertrude's work which reflected them. But Alice could be depended upon only for the anecdotes; her collaborator— who should, ideally, know Gertrude's work extensively— would bear a great deal of responsibility. But the nature of the book was never revealed to White. This was to have been discussed when he and Alice were in the country, several months after the actual writing of the book had been started. By then, White thought, Alice doubtless hoped that the momentum already picked up would prevent him from refusing to continue the collaboration, even without a proper contract. His agent had failed to get from Holt any contract outlining his responsibilities. Had he known from the beginning what Holt expected he would have had to take some six to eight months to read those works of Gertrude which he did not know. He said later that whereas he knew Gertrude's work in depth—"like Bach she gives herself totally on every page"—he did not know it "*in extenso.*" The thousand-dollar advance he was given by Holt was insufficient to make him sure they were ready to back the book properly when it was done. Nevertheless, even without a standard agreement from the publisher, he kept his commitment to his friend.

Working with Alice on her stories presented another problem entirely. "Nietzsche," White wrote, "has said that everything thought is surely fiction. And indeed, a story has its own rightness that may not coincide exactly with the facts that give rise to it. Gertrude," he thought, "who excelled in the obvious that no one else could see and could speak and write directly and unforgettably, knew more of the truth than Alice could imagine." Alice's version of her life, he came to realize, was nothing but a store of well-wrought anecdotes. White recounted:

As the note-taking got underway, I began to notice that Alice kept staring into the corner of the room beyond Picasso's tawny nude on pink. She was watching a silent film of her own years before she met

Gertrude. It was too good in spots: the truth would never have needed all that plausibility. This could only harm the book and somehow a way must be found to bring her up short, possibly by going her one better.

At hand was a useful reflector that would show her to herself: an old story of which Alice would be bound to know the truth. It concerned Rémy de Gourmont's *Lettres à une Amazone* written shortly before he died in 1915. Apropos of what we were saying one afternoon, I gave Alice Natalie Barney's version of the story as she had told it to me. (Natalie is famous, among other things, for the excessive symmetry of her stories.)

She listened with growing astonishment and when the anecdote was ended exclaimed, "Natalie told you that?" Here was my cue. "It did seem a little pat. I've been writing fiction for a number of years now and believe I know the sound of it." Her eyes went dark with dismay and she glanced into the corner from which so much fiction of her own had come. During the long silence I studied my notes. Then she resumed smoothly. I had got a probative answer and she would go on pretending there had never been a question. Unable or unwilling to recognize the danger or to be the good friend to Gertrude's work she meant to be she returned to her manipulation of what was already tainted material turning comic.

At first, however, the sessions—six days a week for four or five hours each day—seemed to go smoothly. Though White was increasingly sure that Alice could not or would not provide enough information on which to base her autobiography, Alice was content that the work was going quite nicely. She thought White agreed with her that the book would be centered on Gertrude, and that references to her would be discarded—except those that had to do directly with Gertrude's work. While Alice was boasting that the work was advancing rapidly, White was growing more and more frustrated in trying to get Alice to give him real material. "All she can do is lie and deny it and contradict herself. If this were amusing stuff, I'd have been able to make something of it." But as it was, after weeks of work, while he had filled three-quarters of a thick school-child's notebook, he knew the material he could actually use would be minimal. The relationship, which clearly had been deteriorating, reached a climax on the afternoon when Alice was to end her life story with Gertrude's death.

White had worried that this last afternoon would be difficult for Alice, but when she related the scene at Gertrude's death, "it was washed of all emotion and had turned into legend." The two questions which Gertrude was said to have asked before she died: "What is the answer?" and then, after a pause, "What is the question?" were given by Alice in reverse order. The tone of that afternoon, as of her story over the weeks, was hollow.

Alice, knowing by then how White felt, and embarrassed over her own mistake, reacted in anger and made another. As White was leaving, she began to enumerate the faults of someone she referred to only as "a young friend." "A well-trained player," White said, "she made it clear I was the subject of the portrait and vented her feelings with deep animosity." Without a word, White left, knowing that he could no longer work on the book.

> I went the three short blocks from the rue Christine to my hotel in Gît-le-Coeur where I tore my notes into tangled strips and stuffed them into a linen mail sack and took them the few steps that brought me to a public trash receptacle on the Boulevard des Grands Augustins. I made sure no last piece of paper clung to the inside of my mail sack. The dustmen would empty the S.V.P. before dawn.

Four days later he left for Madrid.

On June 14, 1958, Alice received a letter from White breaking off their collaboration. To John Schaffner, she expressed proper shock and wrote that she could not imagine the cause of White's decision.[111] To most friends, she pretended to be the injured party, innocent of fault, and said that White vanished, absconding with notes on which she had worked so long and hard. But to some she revealed what she knew was the truth: White took the book seriously as biography;[112] she saw it, from the very first, as her final opportunity to gild the legend which she had created. She knew White wasn't pleased with her, that he did not see the book as a novel—as she did—and that his persistent efforts to get her to tell the truth led to the parting.

". . . One can't just tell an old woman she's too feeble-minded to work on the book she's proposed," White wrote to his lawyer. Not wanting to hurt her, he chose to keep silent about the causes of the break, instructing his lawyer to tell Holt only that there was not enough material for a book. ". . . I'm surely not going to talk about it to anyone else except to explain that Miss Toklas couldn't remember her memories. I've given her an opportunity to blame me and save her face (a life-long preoccupation of hers) but everything is anecdote beside the real fact that there was no basis for a book. Hoping against hope, I discovered this slowly. . . . I'm the only one capable of judging just how incapable Alice is of any sort of collaboration," he added. "She's completely incapable."

What White found out too late Alice had expressed to Carl Van Vechten when the book was begun. How could it be otherwise, she had asked after telling him that the book was to be, of course, about Gertrude. She herself was unimportant.[113] Yet, in her stories, Alice was not able to evoke the memory of Gertrude, but only the legend and the myth. Her years of providing the precise detail for every one of Gertrude's anecdotes, of remembering the faults, deeds, and merits of all their friends, had ended with Gertrude's death. She once remembered everything with precision, she later told an interviewer, but after Gertrude died, her memory was lost, and images from the past seemed confused and muddled.[114]

When she had first discussed the book with White, she had suggested as its title *Gertrude's Manner*; by the time it had been commissioned by Holt, she proposed, instead, that it be called *Things I Have Seen*. But without consulting Alice—an action she considered ill-mannered at the least—the title was changed to one more fitting. *What Is Remembered* was published in the spring of 1963.

After devoting seventeen pages to her first thirty years, Alice allowed Gertrude to dominate the rest of the book. The dramatis personae were, of course, irresistible, and Alice's laconic style, her wit, her irreverence, and her gossip made the book delightful. If the stories were familiar, they were no less "artlessly droll," as one reviewer commented. But the terse retelling of *The Autobiography* left unanswered questions. ". . . Although we are keenly interested in the pictures in Miss Toklas's album," Laurent LeSage wrote in the *Saturday Review*, "in all the celebrated friends and Gertrude Stein in many poses, it is the delightful lady herself who fascinates us." Who, after all, was Alice B. Toklas? "Did she never wish for a life of her own," he wondered, "for anything of her own?"

Time's reviewer, too, deemed *What Is Remembered* "the sad, slight book of a woman who all her life has looked in a mirror and seen somebody else." Alice, in fact, seemed "to have disappeared without a trace into Gertrude Stein's life." But Joe Barry, writing in the *New Republic*, tried to rescue Alice's image. Ever since the publication of *The Autobiography*, he wrote, "Alice Babette Toklas has been assumed to be the alter-ego or 'at most' the companion of the more illustrious Miss Gertrude Stein. . . . It was, I admit, in search of a stronger word than companion to describe this Platonic pair that I struck on the original Greek meaning of *hetaera*. It is nothing more—or rather nothing less—than companion, thus closing a circle some might call vicious. But what a conception of companion it contains!: the fullness of a relationship that makes wife a feeble household word." Delighting in Alice's memories, Barry thought the book captured the lightness and dryness of Alice's conversations, especially toward the end, when material was actually transcribed from her talk because her eyesight had become so poor.

If *What Is Remembered* was not autobiography it was, nevertheless, what Alice set out to write. "Predictably but a little pathetically," *Time*'s reviewer wrote, "it reads like Gertrude Stein."

The book, besides being an opportunity for remembering —like long visits with Bernard Faÿ or Thornton Wilder— brought Alice some much-needed income. Gertrude had tried to assure Alice's financial comfort by one clause of her will. Except for her papers, which went to Yale, and the Picasso portrait, which went to the Metropolitan Museum of Art in New York—

All the rest and residue of my Estate, of whatsoever kind and wheresoever situated, I give and bequeath to my friend Alice B. Toklas, of 5 rue Christine, Paris, 6e, to her use for life and in so far as it may become necessary for her proper maintenance and support, I authorize my executors to make payments to her from the principal of my Estate, and, for that purpose, to reduce to cash any paintings or other personal property belonging to my Estate.

When Alice died, the estate would go to Allan; but now, with Allan dead, the heirs were his widow, Roubina, and his children. Though Alice received a monthly stipend from the estate, the sum of four hundred dollars was not sufficient for her "proper maintenance." Friends often despaired at her extravagances: expensive perfume, designers' scarves, made-to-order hats. She entertained at luxurious restaurants and, after her conversion, tended to make generous donations to the Church. Yet at home, her horsehair chairs were threadbare, her rugs worn to holes, and the walls of the apartment long in need of painting. In 1959, she reviewed Sylvia Beach's *Shakespeare and Company*, a memoir of her famous bookshop, for the *New Republic*. The thirty-five dollars she received would, she hoped, repair a chair. She assured some worried friends that she always had the right to sell a painting if she were in serious need of money, but she was reluctant to do so. Though she twice made a sale through her old friend Daniel-Henry Kahnweiler, she wanted to keep the collection together and she wanted to keep the paintings on her walls. They were, after all, her memories. She had shared them with Gertrude and it was by their light that she lived.

There was apparently little communication between Alice and Mrs. Stein after Allan's death. Alice's needs were handled directly by the Baltimore lawyers who acted on behalf of Gertrude's estate. But in 1960, Mrs. Stein began to worry about the pictures that lined Alice's walls. They were insured—but for far less than their market value—and Alice was hardly a threat to determined thieves. Concerned about her children's inheritance, she asked for a new inventory to be made, as a prelude to rethinking the insurance requirements. Alice, while irritated by the problem, relegated it to her lawyer. After a hard winter—she had been ill with pneumonia and suffered constantly from arthritis—she was leaving Paris to go to Acqui and then to Rome for the following fall and winter.

She had hoped to live at the Convent of the Blue Nuns, where Santayana had spent his last years, but their rooms were all required for the coming Olympics. Instead, she found comfortable accommodations at the Sisters of the Precious Blood, a Canadian order. For 2,100 lire a day, she had a room with running water but no bath and with good, if monotonous, board. Her room had a view of the sky, and she enjoyed watching the passing clouds; and if the food were somewhat institutional, she had visitors now and then who took her to nearby restaurants. She attended mass each morning at six-thirty, then had her coffee, and later her bath. Her days were passed in reading, writing to friends, and resting. Donald Sutherland, who visited her there, was amused that her choice of books was sometimes incongruous with her surroundings.

> She had arrived at the convent with a variety of large and small luggage, including a zipper bag of the sort used for air travel. All this was heaped into the elevator beside her, and as the old machinery lurched upward the zipper bag fell off the heap. Overpacked and inadequately zipped, it now came unzipped enough to release onto the floor of the elevator a copy of *Lolita*, with its title up. It was a bad moment, because she did not know how severe or how secular this roughly Carmelite order of nuns might be. The nun who was running the elevator glanced down at the book, turned to Alice with a sweet smile, and said, "Oh, my dear—you read *detective* stories?"

Alice soon found out that her embarrassment was unfounded, "since the book turned out to be neither so amusing nor dirty as she had been told." Sutherland promised to send her his own verse translation of *Lysistrata*, assuring her that his version was bound to be "much funnier and dirtier than *Lolita*." "I did, and she wrote back saying, 'We are enjoying it immensely.' Did 'we' mean only herself and some nuns of the pension," he wondered, "or all of them and those of the contemplative wing as well?"[115]

The nuns' life, it seemed to Alice, was enviably peaceful, and she confided to a friend that if she were again young she might well decide to join them in their simple existence. Still, she admitted, there were times when she missed having her delicacies sent from Fauchon's.

She was well cared for by the "good sisters," her room was warm, and she welcomed the relief from the damp Parisian winter. And there were wild flowers—like those she remembered from California—and her favored temperate climate. In November 1960, she attended a papal audience.

The gold and vermilion of the room were dazzling, the Pope—though a small man—was enormously impressive. The chant of the prayers and blessings was hypnotic. Alice was deeply moved.[116]

Her friends visited: Bernard Faÿ, Thornton and Isabel Wilder, Sutherland, Virgil Thomson, Samuel Steward. And in January 1961 she spent a day with Judith Anderson, whom she had met in Paris. The actress brought Alice a passion fruit—but unfortunately forgot to leave it with her at the convent after an emotional good-by. Though Alice did little sightseeing, she was taken occasionally to art exhibits, and passed churches and piazzas that she remembered from a brief trip to Rome with Gertrude. She had affection, she wrote to a friend, for the splendor of Rome.

Her arthritis was slightly less disabling than it had been in Paris, but her feet were so deformed that she could wear only sandals. And a cataract was worsening her vision; she could hardly write and with increasing difficulty she read—often with the aid of a magnifying glass. In June, she returned to the rue Christine. But when she entered her apartment, a shocking sight faced her: the walls were bare. Her paintings were gone.

The inventory made for Roubina Stein showed a number of Picassos missing. Alice explained that she had sold them some years before, for about six thousand dollars, the price suggested by Picasso himself. Though she did this without the consent of the estate, she was acting, she thought, in accordance with Gertrude's will. But the sale of those works for a price far below what they might have brought otherwise came as a disconcerting surprise to Mrs. Stein. The collection, worth more than a million dollars, was unprotected in Alice's apartment—especially with Alice away for months. While Alice had arranged for her concierge or *femme de ménage* to look in on her apartment in her absence, Mrs. Stein believed this precaution was far less than the needed security. She sued for removal of the paintings and won. By the time Alice returned from Rome, the collection was in a vault of the Chase Manhattan Bank.

The walls were not only bare but ghostly. James Lord, visiting the apartment soon after the paintings had been removed, described the barren rooms:

> The apartment had not been repainted for more than fifteen years with the result that where each picture had hung a discolored area of its exact size now remained. Like drab and disconsolate ghosts, these shapes were far more insistent and inexorable presences than the paintings themselves had been, because they never for a moment allow one to forget that what had been was now no more.

Alice took the event with unexpected calm. It was tedious, she wrote to her friend Fernanda Pivano. To visitors she was stoic. "It's sad," Lord told her once, "it's sad to see all those blank spots where the pictures were." "Oh, not to me, dear," said Alice. "I can't see them. But I can see the pictures in my memory. I remember each one and where it was. I don't need to see them now."[117]

With her health and eyesight deteriorating—by 1962 she could no longer read and had a secretary or friend take letters from her dictation—her pleasure was remembering. More and more, she lived in a private world of the past—a past which encompassed the unfulfilled dreams of her youth. Once, at dinner with Thornton Wilder, Alice drew out a conversation while nodding and falling asleep at the table.

"Last night I had a dream," she began.

"What did you dream, Alice?" Wilder asked, before she lapsed into a nod.

"I dreamed I played at the Salle Pleyel," she replied when she popped awake.

"And what did you play, Alice?"

"Schumann's *Fantasy*," she answered definitively.

"But Alice," he said gently, "Schumann's *Fantasy* is one of the most difficult pieces for a pianist. How did you do?"

At this Alice managed a sly smile. "Splendidly," she assured him, and fell asleep again at once.[118]

Shortly after she returned from Rome, she slipped and broke her kneecap. Elderly people fall, she informed her friends. But, unable to walk, hardly able to see, she was taken to a nursing home to convalesce. The Ville d'Avray, she wrote, had a strange atmosphere. The rest home itself was located in the middle of a large, ill-tended garden. The staff seemed always to be squabbling, and unexpectedly came in and out of Alice's room looking for one another. The aides were young and generally inefficient. Nevertheless, she found that the massage and exercise were beneficial; and friends brought her candy and flowers, gossip and news. When her knee healed, she returned to the rue Christine for a few months before going back to the convent in Rome. The following year she fell again, broke a bone again, and found herself unwillingly under the care of a grouchy nurse, with only devoted Madeleine for comfort. Madeleine had found a succession of cooks for her, but though they provided amusing stories to relate to friends, they were as much trouble as servants had always been for Alice.

One disclosed to Alice that she was the child of Jesus and Brigitte Bardot. When Alice accepted the revelation without comment, the woman thanked her for her understanding and then promptly reversed herself and left in a fury. Another fell drunk at Alice's feet, was gathered up by Madeleine and put to bed, and was fired by Alice the next morning. Finally, a Spanish maid was found, Jacinta, who managed to serve her often irritable mistress without incident.

Her stay in Rome, besides causing the removal of her pictures, threatened to cause her eviction from the rue Christine. Shortly before she had left, she was informed that the apartments were to be sold by the owner, and she was given the option of buying the flat she had shared with

Gertrude. But she could not afford it, and assumed that her age would allow her to keep the apartment until her death. Her absence, however, enabled the new purchaser to sue for possession.

On May 15, 1963, official action was taken. Alice was in bed when, at seven-thirty in the morning a *huissier* read her an expulsion order requiring her to leave the apartment within twenty-four hours. "I was born in 1877," Alice replied sedately. "If I leave this apartment it will be to go to Père Lachaise."[119] But if she managed to keep her composure in the presence of the official, she shared her fear with friends. At eighty-six, feeble and ill, she was not prepared to find a new home.

Joe Barry, Janet Flanner, the singer Doda Conrad, Virgil Thomson, and other friends she considered "influential" tried in every way they could to help her stay where she was. Even André Malraux, she wrote to Louise Taylor, tried to help.[120] But the law was firm. An apartment could not be vacant for more than four months of the year. If Alice needed to go to Rome for her health, officials suggested, perhaps she should move there permanently. After a frustrating year, she was finally evicted.

Alice, unable to take charge of the move, was sent to the Ville d'Avray for several weeks. Friends found her a home on the rue de la Convention. Madeleine arranged for the contents of the rue Christine to be transported to the new, modern apartment. She immediately disliked it.[121] The building seemed thin and unstable. She could hear her neighbors sneeze through the walls. She was forbidden to drive a nail into the walls: no pictures could be hung. The only one she did have—her portrait by Dora Maar—had to be leaned against a wall. Stark and cold, the apartment was devoid of memories.

But until the spring of 1965, she could hardly see it. The removal of her cataract diminished the pessimism to which, she wrote friends, she felt entitled. When her eye was fully healed, she was cheerful and hopeful. At her doctor's last visit, he asked her to look at him. For the first time, she said, she was able to see him. And for the first time in months she felt joyful.

When Donald Sutherland visited her in 1966, he found her lively and in good spirits. But their light conversation soon became serious. "We both knew it was most likely our last [visit], as indeed it was. . . . I tried to evade the solemnity," he wrote; "Alice took it on. 'Why are you so good to me?' she asked.

> I was certainly not going to say it was because I loved her, which would have been true but embarrassing and ridiculous, without a long description of the kind of love. And I did not like this kind of emotional showdown. . . . So I answered, "Because you have always been good to me."
> "Have I?" It was quite as if she had not realized it, or had not particularly intended to be good to me.[122]

Alice, he thought, never expected goodness or kindness. But she inspired loyalty from her friends and returned their devotion. As her friend Clare Moore had said half a century before, she was the most intensely loyal person she had ever known. For all her fierce and seemingly irrational hatreds, her prejudices, her adamant refusal to forgive, she had retained friends who gave her a love which went beyond compassion and endured what one called "the Calvary of those last difficult years."[123]

"It was not especially I who was being good to her," Sutherland knew. "She might have put that question better to Joe Barry, or Doda Conrad, or Thornton Wilder, or Janet Flanner, or Virgil Thomson, or Picasso . . . or Madeleine. . . ." She might have asked the same of Bernard Faÿ, the Knapiks, Louise Taylor, Francis Rose, Donald Gallup. . . .

To those friends who supported her in her last years, she bequeathed small tokens of her appreciation in her will. A Renaissance Tuscan inkwell was left to Donald Gallup, a mahogany shaving mirror to Harold Knapik, some small silver objects to Francis Rose; some objects which stood on tables and chests in her apartment she left to Virginia Knapik, Joe Barry, Bernard Faÿ. To her "dear friend, dearest Virgil Thomson," she gave an English piecrust table. Royalties went to Madeleine and others. And the rest of her estate was left to her oldest friend, Louise Taylor.

For twenty-one years she lived with only their friendship to ease the pain of loneliness. It was the duty of all her friends, Bernard Faÿ once wrote to her, to do everything they could to show her love and affection.[124] And even when her own sorrow was intense, she tried to face them with the courage she had shown in her youth and the strength that had never failed her. Only when she was completely bedridden and almost blind did she admit to feeling "blue." And though she wished that the world were a gladder place, she refused to be daunted.

She was willful to the last. In a stupor from the sleeping pills she was taking, she could only nod to her maid's questions. "Do you want anything to eat?" Jacinta asked her. Alice shook her head no. "To drink?" Again, Alice shook her head. Impatiently, Jacinta asked her then if she wanted to die. Alice nodded. Yes.[125]

Belatedly, in 1907, her own "new full life began," when, as Gertrude wrote of her, "trembling was all living, living was all loving. . . . And certainly all her [Alice] living then was happier in living than any one else who ever could, who was, who is, who ever will be living." But abruptly, on July 27, 1946, the happiness she knew was ended, followed by a mercilessly protracted darkness as she waited for the end of her widowhood.

She died at one-thirty, on the morning of March 7, 1967. Four days later, her friends watched her small coffin lowered into a vault beneath a large granite block. She had arranged for her name to be chiseled into the stone. Long before, she had planned for the Catholic service. For twenty-one years, she wanted only reunion. She lies beside Gertrude.

Appendix

AN ANNOTATED GERTRUDE STEIN

Many of Gertrude Stein's works are verbal collages of found objects and ephemeral everyday experiences. Like the *papiers collés* of Gris, Braque, and Picasso, they are "applied" reality, and they are punctuated by the appearances and comments of Alice B. Toklas. Though some object to reading Gertrude Stein with a treasure map or even a concordance, others are delighted to have a key. This guide is for them. It may be, after all, that Alice is hidden in the petals of the Rose.

[The following is meant to supplement Richard Bridgman's dissection of Gertrude Stein into pieces, and references to his book are made throughout.]

A WORD ABOUT CAESARS AND COWS

In Gertrude Stein's lyrical, affectionate, or erotic works the terms "Caesar" and "cow" recur with maddening frequency. Bridgman thinks they are erotic symbols (152), but their meaning is elusive. One or the other of these terms appears in many pieces, predominantly in fifteen written between 1913 and 1931, the period of Gertrude's greatest dependence on Alice, when she produced her rhapsodic love songs.

Once, she defines "Caesar": "What are Caesars. Caesars are round a little longer than wide but not oval. They are picturesque and useful." ("Today We Have A Vacation," Haas, Vol. I, 82; 1921). They seem to be tangible, since Gertrude remarks that she is "always willing to wear Caesars. Not down or away but stay." ("A Circular Play," 146)

Occasionally, Gertrude puns with the term: "seize her" or "sees her."

"Big Caesars.
Two Caesars.
Little seize her." ("Lifting Belly," 83)

"Caesar," she tells us, "is plural" ("Lifting Belly," 87), and obedience and docility are among the Caesar's characteristics ("Lifting Belly," 104, 107)

While the etymology of Caesar might include reference to Julius Caesar's reputation as every woman's husband and every man's wife, its meaning for Gertrude and Alice was idiosyncratic to them. Evidence that Caesars are linked to sexual delight is most apparent in "Lifting Belly":

I say lifting belly and then I say lifting belly and Caesars.
I say lifting belly gently and Caesars gently. . . . I say
lifting belly and Caesars and cow come out. (91)

Knowing she has by now thoroughly confused the reader, Gertrude sweetly asks, "Can you read my print."

If Caesars are picturesque, cows are more so. Bridgman notes that cows are "associated with food, with wetness, and with emergence. . . ." (151) In one piece, they seem to have some relationship to defecation:

Little fool little stool little fool for me. . . . And what
is a stool. That was the elegant name for a cow. ("Vacation in Britany")

A cow may be made of "A fig an apple and some grapes. . . . How. The Caesars know how." ("A Sonatina," 20) Alice herself is "so full of a cow factory," able to "manufacture cows by vows." ("A Sonatina," 24) Gertrude pleads with Alice to "have a cow come out . . . a cow come out of baby mine baby mine have a cow come out with time. . . ." ("Old & Old," O&P, 230; 1913) When Alice fails, Gertrude is "overcome with remorse," thinking that it is her fault. She admits her shame, then adds, "This sentence they cannot use." ("Sentences and Paragraphs," 25)

Cows come out after Alice is "covered with kisses" ("The King or Something," 125), and the cow itself is a "blessed blessed blessed planner and dispenser and joy./My joy./The Cow." ("The King or Something," 127)

The cow makes sense best as the end product of their lovemaking. The process is described in rhyming, rhythmic prose:

Love a baby which is thin will he go in will he go in. She
is not so very thin not like a pin not like a pin she is lively

and caressed she is sticky and addressed she is lovely and so large how can I charge how can I charge. I do charge her for a cow ten spots here ten spots now no the lovely wont be teased she will be doing as she pleased as she pleases as she says which is the way of marriedness. Think what I say my tender sweet and little cow will come out complete, my treat." ("Coal and Wood," 9)

The emergence of a cow is followed by mutual satisfaction. "A cow has come he is pleased and she is content as a cow came and went. . . . And now a little scene with a queen contented by the cow which has come and been sent and been seen. A dear dearest queen."
A sleepy Gertrude praises Alice:

> My sweet dear does hear her dear here saying little and big coming and true discern and firmly coming out softly shoving out singly coming out all of the cow that has been registered as a round now. . . .
> Navigation sub-marine of the cow come out of queen my queen. That is what the cow does it sinks and a little it sinks so sweetly, my own cow out of my own queen is now seen. ("A Lyrical Opera," 51)

Cows seem to be synonomous with orgasms. As Gertrude reveals, "Cows are very nice. They are between legs." ("All Sunday," 102)

A

1. "Accents in Alsace" (G&P, 409–15; 1919)
After Leo is dismissed: "Brother brother go away and stay" (409), Alice is celebrated:

> You are my love and I tell you so
> In the daylight
> And in the night
> Baby winks and holds me tight.

The love song is supplemented by "An Interlude," which reminds us of their respective birthdays:

> Thirty days in April have a chance to sing at a wedding
> Three days in February gave reality to life. (414)

Though the piece is subtitled "A Reasonable Tragedy," it is the expression of "but one desire"—the devotion of Gertrude to Alice. "In the midst of our happiness," Gertrude tells us, "we were very pleased" (415).

2. *An Acquaintance with Description* (1926)

"Mary Lake is a pretty name," writes Gertrude. It is also the name of Alice's teacher from 1888 to 1891. Mary Lake's school was "a gay happy one" where Alice met Clare Moore, a lifelong friend.

3. "Ada" (G&P, 14–16; 1909)

In her manuscript, Gertrude began the piece by using the real name of her subject—Alice—and switched midway to "Ada," which was used in publication.

4. "Advertisements" (G&P, 341–46; 1916)

There is an undercurrent of irritability in this Mallorcan piece. The nights were hot; the electric fan broke and was repaired by either Gertrude or Alice (344); but on Sundays there was no electricity to use it. "We sleep easily," Gertrude admitted, but sometimes they were awakened by the same noise (345). Ill humor could be provoked by trivial causes: "I can. I can be irritated. I hate lizards when you call them crocodile. She screamed. She screamed. I do not know why I am irritated." And finally, Gertrude offers blanket encouragement: "I am going to conquer. I am going to be flourishing. I am going to be industrious. Please forgive me everything" (346).

5. "All Sunday" (A&B, 89–128; 1915)

In Mallorca in the summer of 1915 we find Alice making bouquets of honeysuckle, acacia, and roses (105) and removing grease from her face at night (97). The war was a constant worry. "This war teaches us to be certain of our hates," Gertrude declares (113). They are disturbed by censored letters from their friend Emily Chadbourne, and decide to write to Nellie Jacott for wool and flannel for the coming months (111–12). And they remain firm in their decision to stay in Spain. "It is inexpensive, money is easily gotten and there are no victims. They all speak the language" (126).

There are personal disclosures: the two wish they were alone together (89). Alice is allowed a small soliloquy: "I am going to tell all my feelings. I love and obey. I am very sensible. I am sensitive to distraction. I like little handkerchiefs. I like to have mosquito netting over my bed. . . . I like to do my nails" (105). To these characteristics, Gertrude adds, "My baby has suddenly become very sensitive to light. She explains it by saying that it is hot and she cannot cover herself over so as to exclude the light from her eyes" (111).

Alice's brother, Clarence, makes a brief appearance:

Please be rich.
Clarence.
Clearance.
Puget Sound.
Seattle.
Bay.
No mosquitoes at all. (121)

Clarence, having returned to San Francisco from New York, where he was going to try to start a business, was soon to be married.

6. "As Fine As Melanctha" (AFAM, 255–69; 1922)

As Natalie Barney notes in her introduction to this volume, "Our approach remains that of the eavesdropper on situations to which we have not been initiated." We overhear a conversation (258) with someone who "had hoped to find it permissible to explain to everyone everything and further than that to write it." and who, furthermore, "had meant to make good [his] . . . footing. . . ." Once this nameless speaker's feelings are expressed, Gertrude turns to another visitor: "And now for Thayer, and now there." The explainer could very well be Ezra Pound, who visited Gertrude with Scofield Thayer, then editor of the *Dial*; the visit ended when Pound fell out of Gertrude's favorite armchair, to everyone's displeasure.

Alice appears as "pussy," "And so sweetly she purrs" (261). "How sweetly Americans love Chinamen Spaniards and watches. How sweetly they press themselves together. . . . How can you be wedded to me. Oh so very easily" (261).

7. "At Present A Play. Nothing but Contemporaries Allowed" (O&P, 315–24; 1930)

The contemporaries allowed parts in this play include Georges Hugnet, Virgil Thomson, Bébé Bérard, Maurice Grosser, Eugène Berman, Picasso, Alice Toklas, Henry Levinsky, Bernard Faÿ, Kristians Tonny, André Masson, Avery Hopwood, Bravig Imbs, and Ralph Church. "I love my love with an l because she is little," Gertrude reveals. "I love her with a p because she is pretty" (318). No doubt she loved her, too, because "Alice B. tenderly she asks is and are guessing and grading" (317). In less vigilant moments, Alice is overheard talking to a dog (321).

B

8. "A Ballad" (SIM, 256–67; 1931)

"She may be the cause of a ballad," writes Gertrude in another love song to Alice. "And he comes and he sings for her" (265). The two unexpectedly see an eclipse of the moon (264), which Gertrude finds "very exciting," but Alice "May be. Said to be. Not very. Interested" (265). Her pleasure comes from "sitting. There. And working./Pleasantly. As is her wish. . . ." (258). Still, there is cause for singing:

> He did win her. He held her. He did win her.
> And when it is. On the day. When they.
> Said. Very well. On that day. Win her.
> Anyway she was own. And won by him. (262)

Alice is happy being "of two and here" (266).

9. *Before the Flowers of Friendship Faded Friendship Faded* (Meyerowitz, 274–87; 1930)

Intending to translate a poem by Georges Hugnet, Gertrude soon dismisses the French version and writes a love song. "It is easy to put heads together really. Head to head it is easily done and easily said head to head in bed" (282).

> I love my love with a v
> Because it is like that. . . .
>
> I love my love with an a
> Because she is my queen. . . .
>
> I love my love with a y because she is my bride
> I love her with a d because she is my love beside
> Thank you for being there
> Nobody has to care
> Thank you for being here
> Because you are not there. (286)

10. "Birth and Marriage" (A&B, 175–98; 1924)

As Bridgman notes (153), the "she" of this history is Alice, "born on the thirtieth of April" (184), "fond of being the only daughter" (186), and "one of two" children (187). The "he" is Gertrude.

11. "A Birthday Book" (A&B, 128–54; 1924)

In his introduction to this volume, Donald Gallup notes that Gertrude was fond of birthday books, "quite common at the end of the last century," where each day bore an appropriate quotation and a space to note births (xv). The excitement begins to grow on April 28 (138), continuing through the twenty-ninth—the day on which Alice was expected—and culminating on the thirtieth.

The thirtieth of April selects the thirtieth of April. . . . May and might hold me tight, might and may night and day, night and day and anyway, anyway anyway as so gay, gayly, gayly misses. (138)

Other noted days include May 11 "as is necessary all the time" (139), which is Leo's birthday; May 20, "melodrama" (135), which is Ibsen's birthday; and a question appears on "April the twenty-third and was it"—the day attributed for Shakespeare's birth (137). The piece was written for the birth of Picasso's son on February 4.

12. "Bonne Annee" (G&P, 302–3; 1916)

"Bonne Annee" is an affirmation of domestic happiness in Mallorca. Everyday tasks are completed in quiet resignation.

Alice asks, "What are the letters in my name," and Gertrude responds, "O and c and be and tea." When Gertrude decides to delete a portion of a piece from the transcription, Alice dutifully replies, "Yes sir." Tranquillity is evident. "It isn't necessary for me to mention what a good baby," Gertrude writes; only, "Happy New Year."

13. *A Book Concluding With As A Wife Has A Cow. A Love Story* (1923)

The last chapter of this book, "As A Wife Has A Cow," celebrates the event. According to Virgil Thomson, Gertrude called this piece her *Tristan and Isolde.*

14. "A Bouquet. Their Wills" (O&P, 195–218; 1928)

See Bridgman, 199–201. A "chorus of Baltimoreans" who "are distinguished by their management" (197) apparently suggested that Gertrude and Alice make their wills. Gertrude finds wills a curious subject (212) but concedes that they are necessary if each is to leave her money to the other (200). The Baltimore relatives are depicted throughout as prosaic and bourgeois. Gertrude is intrigued to learn that if a husband and wife are killed at the same instant, for legal purposes the man is taken to have lived longer and his heirs inherit his wife's portion. We find out, incidentally, that "My baby loves blue. . . ." (202).

C

15. "Can You Climb In Little Things" (BTV, 201; 1918)

There is discord here: "In the midst of brushes there is war" may be word play: in the middle of the word is "us."

APPENDIX

16. "Capital Capitals" (O&P, 61–70; 1923)
    Concerned in general with the four capitals of Provence, there is a brief allusion to life with Alice:

Hearty kisses.
In a minute.
Shut the door. (65)

17. "Castles they live in. Castles on the wall" (Yale Collection of American Literature, #542; 1943)
    Wartime in Culoz, where the house they lived in seemed like a castle. "If they walked along and met a policeman, were they afraid, no they were not." The piece centers on Claude, a neighbor, and her daughters, but Alice makes a sporadic appearance. "I had to buy a pot of jam," she explains.

18. "A Circular Play" (LO&P, 139; Brinnin, 143–56; 1920)
    Alice's voice filters through as Gertrude writes. "I can hear Alice./So can a great many people" (155). Their happiness is declared: "A miss and bliss./We came together." But intruders were not always welcome. "Then suddenly there was an army./In my room./We asked them to go away" (143).
    The circles which are implied by the title give Gertrude a chance to play with variations on the theme: "The Inner Circle is one in which we hope to engage places" (145), she admits, although there is always the pleasure now of encircling Alice (151) and of bestowing upon her "A circlet of kisses" (155).
    Alice's approval is satisfying: "She can admire me always. She can always admire me," Gertrude repeats (147). And "Whimsies consist in pleasing a wife in instantaneous reference, in pleasure, in fatigue and in resolution" (153). But one question occurs to her. "Do I sound like Alice," she wonders, and then decides, "Any voice is resembling./By this I mean when I am accustomed to them their voices sound in my ears" (155). Also, see Bridgman, 161.

19. "Coal and Wood" (PL, 3–11; 1920)
    "Let me show you exactly how we feel," Gertrude writes. And she does. "I marvel at my baby. I marvel at her beauty I marvel at her perfection, I marvel at her purity I marvel at her tenderness I marvel at her charm I marvel at her vanity I marvel at her industry I marvel at her humour I marvel at her intelligence I marvel at her rapidity I marvel at her brilliance I marvel at her sweetness I marvel at her delicacy. I marvel at her generosity. I marvel at her cow" (4). Later, the wonderment at Alice's qualities becomes more erotic (9).

20. *Cook Book*

The inside cover of Gertrude's copy of James Fenimore Cooper's *The Pilot* contains a plan for a cookbook which has similarity to Alice's later work. The seven chapters included, "My life with cook books, My life with cooks, My life with recipes, The history of cooking," and a final chapter entitled "Eating and not eating, an occupation." The recipes, Gertrude noted, would be interspersed with each one's recollections. Alice's Chapter 11, "Food in the Bugey During the Occupation," may clarify Gertrude's intention.

D

21. "A Diary" (A&B, 201–18; 1927)

Besides learning what Hélène, the cook, is buying or cooking, we find out that she is partial to Bravig Imbs and wonders why the others seem to prefer Virgil Thomson (202). As Brinnin notes, Alice's preferences sometimes differed from Gertrude's: "Several times other people have been here. There is a difference of opinion as to the desirability of their being here" (204). Furthermore, Alice has definite opinions of Gertrude's career:

> She asked me not to introduce surprises nor leavings nor annoyances and I did not but it seems so. She also asked me if I would not like to receive for them [her writings] a great deal of money and I agreed, I certainly would find it to be a very great pleasure to be abundantly paid. She and this was another case told me I should not give anything away for nothing and I would very much like not to do so. She again . . . also said that it would be better to get back what I had loaned. I find that I do not really mind very much if I do not. (203)

But Alice's demands did not interfere with their relationship, as Harriet Levy knew. "Why is Harriet not pleased with two. Because two are one and some" (214).

22. "Didn't Nelly and Lilly Love You" (AFAM, 221–52; 1922)

"Didn't Nelly and Lilly Love You" chronicles the start of Gertrude's relationship with Alice, and begins with Gertrude's birth in Allegheny, Pennsylvania, and Alice's in California. The question itself is repeated throughout. On a walk one afternoon, Gertrude began to wonder "about arms and tears" (225) and was moved to ask Alice the crucial question. Nelly (Jacott) and Lily (Hansen) were girlhood friends of Alice. Gertrude learned of Alice's attachment to them from her letters to Annette Rosenshine. "How can I tell you that she wrote, that I did not write, that we quote . . ." (224).

Much of the lengthy piece is filled with Gertrude's devotion to Alice. "I love her with an a because I say that she is not afraid" (224). "She is an aid to all whom she aids. She aids me and I am sure that she had aided Lilly and Nelly" (230).

> If fishes were wishes the ocean would be all of our desire. But they are not. We wish for land and sea and for a birthday and for cows and flowers. Our wishes have been expressed. We may say that the history of Didn't Nelly and Lilly love you is the history of wishes guessed expressed and gratified. Didn't Nelly and Lilly love you. (230)

"Do you please me. Oh so much" (230). Their union is celebrated. They admit to each other, when they are alone "that we had intended to stay away" (228). And furthermore, they need no one else (234).

The two take on their roles as husband and wife, with characteristics clearly defined. "I am a husband who is very very good and I have a character that covers me like a hood and must be understood which it is by my wife whom I love with all my life . . ." (245). But as a loving wife, Alice was not subservient. "He considers he considers you to be perfect, and what do you consider me," Gertrude asks. "I consider you to be aware of that," is Alice's reply (251).

As in other erotic works, Caesars and cows make frequent appearance:

> Caesars do not turn away but stay. I put the Caesars to bed and this is what I said, I want you to do instead, instead of what, said the Caesars, instead of not doing it and this is what I said. (229)

> I wish that the fish are fishes. And that a cow is a cow. (238)

> . . .

> I wish to mention the practicability of housing a cow. In this way cities prosper and Caesars render that which Caesars owe. I do not say this to intimidate Caesars nor do I implore sweetly caress and impress. Caesars do not reflect they do so well show by the daily activity how useful how tender and how strong and how a Caesar will do not wrong. (239)

"You might just as well announce what you feel," Gertrude advises, "which is faith in Caesars" (249).

E

23. "Every Afternoon" (G&P, 254–59; 1916)

Subtitled "A Dialogue," the piece is a staccato rendering of a conversation between Gertrude and Alice. Though they repeatedly express their happiness ["We are pleased with each other" (254). "We are very happy./Very happy./And content./And content" (257)], there seems to be an underlying disturbance:

When will we speak of another.
Not today I assure you. (254)

Each time the disturbance is brought up, the subject is quickly changed. "Very well then explain" is met with a reply about daisies.

Finally, it is suggested that it all be forgotten: "If you remember you will remember other things that frighten you." Or if not forgotten, at least put aside:

Not now.
You mean not now. (259)

24. "Evidence" (Haas, Vol. I, 153–54; 1930)

The scene pictures "a lady sitting and working at tapestry which although it is of to-day in design and color looks ancient." This is Alice, working at needlepoint with Picasso's design.

25. "An Exercise in Analysis" (LO&P, 119–38; 1917)

"We have suffered" (130), Gertrude writes, referring to her own unconventional marriage. "Please be mannish," she asks first. Then, "Please be womanish" (131), and finally, just—

Please me.
Do please me.
Please me pleasantly. (135–36)

Alice replies, "Yes I will."

"What is the name of the bedding," Gertrude asks later. "It is different," she admits. "Then don't explain," Alice says (137).

F

26. "Farragut or A Husband's Recompense" (UK, 5–18; 1915)

The piece predates "Didn't Nelly and Lilly Love You" and deals with the same theme in a less obvious manner. The actual question is disguised as "Didn't Henry and Herbert love you" (11), but the circumstances are the same.

> I said go home if you like.
> I said I was an authority.
> I said I could be angry.
> I said nothing.
> We went on terrorising.
> Then we came to a hill.
> We settled on the hill.
> I said is it likely that I am stubborn.
> An answer.
> Not such as would be given.
> There came to be then a time when answering was every-
> thing. (15)

When they first met, Gertrude was struck by Alice's appearance not having been able to "picture her physical presence" (10). She did know something of her personality: Alice wanted success and security. "Whatever she said," Gertrude thought, "was earnest and thoughtful and showed rare decision" (11). And Gertrude quickly made her own decision. "Y is for you and u is for me and we are as happy as happy can be" (12).

27. "First Page" (SIM, 282–89; 1933)

A somber tone of resignation characterizes this piece, although Gertrude tells us "that no one is disillusioned. Every day is the same as next year" (283). She has at last attained the success she wanted and now must arrange her changed life. She appreciates her well-wishers, but there are others who annoy (284). "There is," she knows, "only one loved one" (285). "Fortunately we are not alone because of her . . ." (288).

She tried to explain her own work: "I simply wish to tell a story. I have said a great many things but the emotion is deeper when I saw them. And soon there was no emotion at all and now I will always do what I do without any emotion which is just as well as there is not at all anything at all that is better" (289).

"What is the difference," she asks, "if there is no question and no answer" (283).

28. "Forensics" (HTW, 383–95; 1931)

Though she wrote *The Autobiography of Alice B. Toklas* for financial success, Gertrude's doubts about yielding to Alice's pressure creep into many pieces. "At last I am writing a popular novel," Gertrude writes, but quickly wonders, "popular with whom" (391).

APPENDIX

29. *Four Saints in Three Acts* (O&P, 11; Brinnin, 41–86; 1927)

The role of Saint Therese—St. Teresa of Ávila—is seen by both Bridgman and Katz as a tribute to Alice Toklas (see Bridgman, 177ff., and Katz, 277).

Virgil Thomson, who wrote the score for this opera, sees St. Theresa reaching "high sexual delight" in having "had it with a spoon" in the following passage:

Saint Therese. Having happily married.
Saint Therese. Having happily beside.
Saint Therese. Having happily had it with a spoon.
Saint Therese. Having happily relied upon noon. (61)

Perhaps he is correct, since Gertrude admits, "It is very easy to love alone" (75).

There are more lyrics to Alice:

Ring around a rosey.
How many acts are there in it.
Wedded and weeded.
Please be coming to see me.
When this you see you are all to me.
Me which is you you who are true true to be you. (83)

As Bridgman notes, "Saint Theresa is the presiding and efficient force" (186) in this piece.

30. "A French Rooster. A History" (SIM, 213–22; 1930)

Praise for Alice, whose aptitudes include knowing "the difference between lily and lily white and tube roses," and rise to greater needs:

And who has held whom
When they are all well. . . . (217)
. . . after all it was she
Who found the link that was lost and by me. (218)

G

31. "A Grammarian" (HTW, 103–11; 1930)

Gertrude interrupts her treatise on grammar to let us know, "I love my love with a b because she is precious. I love her with a c because she is all mine" (105).

H

32. "Harriet Fear" (TWO, 343–46; 1908–12)

Harriet Levy's fears, indecision, and worries are contrasted with someone's strengths—"not needing being at all afraid in being living" (345). Alice was "certainly satisfying some one" (346) and succeedng in the life she chose for herself.

33. "Here. Actualities" (PL, 11–13; 1932)

In celebration of Alice's birthday, Gertrude gives her a "spring bouquet of wild primroses wild violets and little rosy a little rosy paquerette . . ." (13).

34. "He Said It" (G&P, 267–74; 1915)

"We have been so happy here," Gertrude writes of their stay in Mallorca. "Yes," Alice agrees, "but that has nothing to do with the people" (274). They picnic on eggs, salad, vegetables, and brown bread (274), and Gertrude finds that at last she is able to stop worrying about the war (268), rise leisurely at nine (Alice, of course, gets up at seven-thirty) (271), and enjoy her life with a "Mrs." who "kisses most" (271).

35. "A History of Having A Great Many Times Not Continued to Be Friends" (AFAM, 287–327; 1924)

By 1924, the title of the piece had already proven true. "Selections have been nicely planned by those who feel best and most" (292), Gertrude admits. Vague reasons are offered for the various partings, but one is clear: "Particularly as to part two." Though Gertrude warns, "No names mentioned," we find Clara and Bell (229) [Claribel Cone] and Mable (308) [Mabel Dodge] among the severed friendships.

A reference is made to the establishment of Plain Edition, for which friends' advice was depended upon. "Begin to ask every one if they are able to be of assistance" (314).

There are no regrets admitted; separations are inevitable to be "able to safely say so and as much. As much as ever. Together" (318).

36. "History or Messages from History" (A&B, 221–38; 1930)

Love messages to Alice appear throughout:

She is always right.
And beautiful. (224)

"She cherishes me so tenderly," Gertrude tells us. And although some of her admirers will gain wider recognition, although some "will be thought best and most . . .," for Gertrude "she is all" (231).

37. "How Could They Marry Her?" (Haas, Vol. I, 16–30; 1915)

"By good luck I married her," Gertrude tells us at the outset (16). She becomes involved in a discussion about whether or not someone will be going to Serbia as a nurse, and the woman's vacillation disturbs Gertrude. "I said if you are going to Serbia why don't you go. Why do you say you are going if you are not going. Why are you living a life of suffering. Why do you mislead not only yourself but many more, why don't you say earnest I am not going" (21).

The problem seems to fit the situation of Emily Chadbourne and Ellen La Motte. Ellen La Motte, a nurse, wanted to work near the front but was gun-shy. Emily Chadbourne, aristocratic and remote, apparently was not enthusiastic about the prospect, and it was only after meeting Mary Borden-Turner, who ran a hospital at the front, that Ellen La Motte was able to nurse there for a few months. "She was apt to be frightened by those hospitable friends who would not be pacified. She was certainly apt to be nervous. This is not a description of Emily" (22). But it could be a description of Ellen.

Gertrude's involvement in their problem was disagreeable: "Long calling, hours of annoyance, pleasant phrases, bitten curls, really actual places and more than that, sombre fortunes, those together make anyone uneasy" (27). Fortunately she still had Alice. "Caesar kisses. This makes a radiator. All the heat glows" (19).

I

38. "If You Had Three Husbands" (G&P, 377–91; 1915)

Again Gertrude writes of their relationship. "It happened very simply that they were married. They were naturally married and really the place to see it was in the reflection every one had of not frightening not the least bit frightening enthusiasm" (381). Perhaps less than enthusiastic was an unidentified "he" who finally yielded. "He said I would have known by this time. I don't like to think about it," and he found that there were other things to make him happy (382).

Alice's history is given succinctly: "She was brought up by her mother. She had meaning and she was careful in reading. She read marvelously. She was pleased. She was aged thirty-nine. [Actually, she would be thirty-nine in 1916.] She was flavored by reason of much memory and recollection" (377).

She and Gertrude "had likeness. Likeness to what. Likeness to loving" (380). They were able to discuss everything, including "individual feeling" (382). And Gertrude came to know that "If one loves one another by that means they do not perish" (385).

39. "Independent Embroidery" (PL, 81–84; 1915)

Alice merited solicitous treatment, and Gertrude admonishes her to speak up whenever she needs something. She promises to protect Alice from all discomforts, irritations, and annoyances and would see to it that Alice could indulge in "independent embroidery."

40. "I have No Title To Be Successful" (PL, 23–26; 1915)

Success in daily living was possible even through distant disturbances of war. "We are angry at the German flag and we are delighted that they have Italian selections in music," Gertrude writes (26). A calm day-to-day existence was all that was hoped for: "I ask for nothing I use whatever is necessary and I say good-night do not disturb me. I will write in the day-time" (25). They were away from the turmoil of war, but still, "Everybody says something. Mike [Stein] says that it is terrible the way the war does not finish. We know" (25). But their resignation and inner peacefulness are evident:

Deep earnestness shows that there is hope. Denial finds perfect joy. Reasons there things which show. For instance our loving. (25)

41. "I Often Think About Another" (PL, 32–34; 1916)

An undercurrent of infidelity, but Gertrude wants to hear nothing about it. "If you do you need not mention it. If you do and I do not believe you do you need not mention it. I do not think about another" (33). More pleasant thoughts are about teeth: "Dear Sir We found a very good American dentist who made me a very pleasant platinum cap and didn't hurt me and seems to be very good" (32). The dentist was in Barcelona; the two were then in Mallorca.

J

42. "Johnny Grey" (G&P, 167–75; 1915)

Alice:
My gay.
Baby.
Little.

Lobster.
Chatter.
Sweet.
Joy.
My.
Baby. (168–69)

K

43. "The King or Something (The Public Is Invited To Dance)"
(G&P, 122–33; 1917)
Gertrude is learning to drive:

I am learning to say a break.
I am learning to say a clutch.

But this is secondary to the pleasures of life with Alice.

There was a little apple eat.
By a little baby that is wet.
Wet from kisses.
There was a good big cow come out.
Out of a little baby which is called stout.
Stout with kisses.
There will be a good cow come out.
Out of a little baby I don't doubt.
Neither does she covered with kisses.
She is misses.
That's it. (125–26)

Caesars and cows evoke praise (127), and Gertrude's source
of inspiration is clearly Alice (131).

L

44. "Left to Right" (Haas, Vol. I, 155–58; 1931)
Perhaps a pun—Gertrude was left to write after this event—
this piece is Gertrude's version of a quarrel over her translation
of Hugnet's *Enfances*. Gertrude wanted to do a "reflection,"
not a translation, and her eventual rendering of Hugnet's poem
was aptly titled *Before the Flowers of Friendship Faded Friendship Faded*. Here, Arthur William is Hugnet; General Erving
is Virgil Thomson; Frederick Harvard is Bravig Imbs (who
came from Dartmouth).

45. "Lend a Hand or Four Religions" (UK, 170–207; 1922)
References to Alice are preceded by "First religion." Bridg-

APPENDIX

man uses the piece as evidence that Gertrude thought of herself "as one with Alice" (163). Perhaps Alice was, indeed, the first religion and primary devotion: "She is here and perfection" (182). "I need tell you that I see the moon and the moon sees me God bless the moon and God bless me which is you" (206). Alice's abilities were many: "Can you refuse me can you confuse me can you amuse me can you use me. She said can you. Sweet neat complete tender mender defend her joy allow and then say that" (186).

46. "Lifting Belly" (BTV, 65–115; 1915–17)

Of all Gertrude's erotic pieces, "Lifting Belly" emerges as the most graphic recording of Lesbian love. It is a long, raucous celebration of sex. "Lifting Belly is so strong. I love cherish idolise adore and worship you. You are so sweet so tender so perfect . . ." (80). Naturally, Caesars recur:

There are two Caesars and there are four Caesars.
Caesars do their duty.
I never make a mistake.
We will be very happy and boastful and we will celebrate Sunday. (104)

Lifting belly is a miracle.
And the Caesars.
The Caesars are docile.
Not more docile than is right. (107)

Lifting belly, we are told, "is in bed./And the bed has been made comfortable./Lifting belly knows this" (113).

> Lifting belly.
> So high.
> And aiming.
> Exactly.
> And making
> A cow
> Come out. (114)

47. "A Little Love of Life" (SIM, 277–82; 1932)

"If any one is angry with me now I am not angry with them" (277), Gertrude begins, and concedes that Alice was right all along about a painter whom Gertrude mistakenly thought to be a genius (282). Alice is, of course, "A little love of life . . . my own delight . . . ," who likes to have a little dog sit on her lap, but "better than anything" she likes "love . . ." (282).

48. *A Long Gay Book* (*Matisse, Picasso and Gertrude Stein*, 11–116; 1909–12)

Bridgman notes the possibility that "gay" used here and in "Miss Furr and Miss Skeene" means homosexual (96n.). Until after World War II, the term was used as a kind of password with homosexual overtones. First applied to prostitutes in England as early as 1825, "gay" became synonomous with immorality. California writer Jack London used the term to describe hoboes—outsiders to society—in the early 1900s.

Notes in the manuscript of the book reveal Gertrude's intent in exploring the "bottom nature" of women, including Sarah Stein and several of Gertrude's female relatives. Their relationship to men particularly interested Gertrude, and she planned to analyze such diverse personalities as Picasso and her brother Simon. Alice was to be presented as an exception to the other women.

Throughout the work there are enumerations of names, of which two are consistently outstanding in the manuscript: Larr and Ollie. These are the only two names written in a heavily pressed pencil, obscuring whatever name was written originally underneath. The name written beneath Larr seems to begin with an L, is short, and suggests Leo; the name written beneath Ollie seems to be Alice, and one passage might verify the guess. "This is a general leading up to a description of [name in question] who is an xception [sic] in being one being living." The phrasing parallels that in Gertrude's notes, but the name this time seems to be Olive or Ollie.

Two women's names which Gertrude mentions as subjects are Jane Sands and Eugenia. Jane Sands, as Bridgman notes, is a nom de plume which Gertrude used for herself in early works. Alice may have brought to Gertrude's attention the evolution of Aurore Dupin's nom de plume, which at first was J. Sand, a tribute to her lover, Jules Sandeau. Eugenia may have been Eugenia Auzias, later Mrs. Leo Stein.

49. "Look At Us" (PL, 259–68; 1916)

"Bow to the prettiest and kiss the one you love the best," Gertrude tells us (265). The prettiest, we know, is Alice.

Look at us we are so pretty.
Lovely.
Beautiful.
Silky.
Oh yes we are silky. (267)

50. "Louis XI and Madame Giraud" (O&P, 345–53; 1930)

Michael, Sarah, Gabrielle, Allan, and Danny appear in this play, along with ". . . a lady of May from Baltimore," possibly

May Bookstaver. The refrain "Misses misses kisses./Misses misses most" (345) occurs again; and Alice's presence is gratefully noted:

> When I finish a sketch I pass it to some one.
> Who receives it.
> Thank you for flattery. (353)

51. *Lucy Church Amiably* (1927)

Changing identity throughout the book, Lucy Church sometimes exhibits characteristics associated with Alice:

> Lucy Church prefers the sun to the rain but finds both monotonous she prefers a temperate climate where the snow does not stay upon the ground where the mountains are poetical the rivers wide and rapidly flowing the meadows green and the poplars very tall and the newly planted ones very thin and pretty and delicate. She also likes the people to be nearly as well to do as they are and to live in the enjoyment of butter cake nut oil and fowl and also to find many of the natural growth to be pale yellow mauve blue and purple and rose and very miniature also the sun flowers to be planted if they are useful. (111)
>
> Lucy Church rented a valuable house for what it was worth. She was prepared to indulge herself in this pleasure and did so. She was not able to take possession at once as it was at the time occupied by a lieutenant in the french navy who was not able to make other arrangements. . . . (130)

Once, Gertrude informs us, "Alice Babette was sleeping . . ." (150). Among the many names mentioned in the novel, a few are Alice's friends: Carrie Helbing (228), Lilyanna Hansen (56, 181, 195), her sister Agnes (181). Lilies, which may be Lily in transformation, occur frequently as a threat: "Lilies lily they have avoided partially why. Supposing two met at once which one was the one that it was decided might love . . ." (56). A cryptic message is given:

> It is as roses that cows commit suicide.
> It is as lilies that it is as lilies and lilies and as lilies that cows that cows commit suicide.

Lilies lurk in a generally bucolic landscape, the countryside around Belley, in which Lucey Church was nestled.

52. "A Lyrical Opera Made By Two To Be Sung" (O&P, 49–60; 1928)

The sentiment of this opera is caroled in the line, "My wife is my life is my life is my wife is my wife is my life is my life is my life" (49). As Bridgman notes (154n.), the theme is similar to her earlier Mallorcan pieces. Cows and Caesars are abundant. "A cow will be a large and loose Caramel. . . . A cow it will be how a large a loose a cow let it let it pet it get it set it" (50).

"A cow has come he is pleased and she is content as a cow came and went. . . . And now a little scene with a queen contented by the cow which has come and bent sent and been seen. A dear dearest queen" (51).

Alice is compared to flowers: ". . . My babe baby is sweeter than even John Quillies [i.e., jonquils] are" (50).

Rose is a rose and a pansy he chose.
Rose is a rose and he chose a pansy.
Pansy is short for Pussie. (58)

Amid the torrid description of their love (51), there is a small rhyme of appreciation:

Dear April
Which made she
To be
All
To be
April fool
To his sweetie
Which is she
Tenderly
Excessively
Sweetily
My April fool baby.
May June and Jew lie [i.e., July] we love to be by little love . . . her little hair so nicely greasy which is to please he who has to squeeze she in a particular and careful way as you may see on every day as well as to obey . . . (52–53)

We are allowed a glimpse of everyday life—Gertrude writing and Alice embroidering (57)—but for the most part, we are treated to a reiteration of Gertrude's love for Alice. "Of all the flowers of our love which is you and me. When this you see you are all to me and I am all to thee completely and continually" (54).

"She is very necessary to me" (55), says Gertrude, as if we could doubt it; "My sweetie/She is all to me . . ." (52).

APPENDIX

M

53. "A Man" (TWO, 235–52; 1908–12)

The man in question here seems similar to David Edstrom, the Swedish sculptor whose conversion to Christian Science impressed Sarah Stein. "Any one might be one giving to him a religion" (241), Gertrude noted. His physical appearance varies from fat to thin; and a turning point in his existence came when he found " some one" to whom he began talking and reminiscing—thereafter he became "enormously fat. . . . He was exciting" (252). According to Harriet Levy, Gertrude wrote many portraits of Edstrom, which Harriet failed to understand.

54. *Many Many Women* (*Matisse, Picasso and Gertrude Stein*, 119–98; 1910)

As Bridgman notes, the piece "presents a series of females who marry, study, suffer. It is an accomplishment of some magnitude to be able to say even that much. The book's prose is a desert. . . ." (104). The women, described in droning repetition, may seem indistinguishable, yet Gertrude had definite models in mind, listed on the inside cover of her manuscript. Among them are Alice Toklas, Nellie Jacott, Harriet Levy, Fernande Olivier, Sarah Stein, and several of Gertrude's aunts.

55. "Mary Nettie" (PL, 42–48; 1917)

Dressed in espadrilles, the two go shopping for little bowls, an electric fan, and a sugar bowl with the U.S. seal on one side and the emblem of liberty on the other (43). They say a brief prayer for the soldiers: "May the gods of Moses and of Mars help the allies" (46)—and report without comment on a newspaper article: "A spanish newspaper says that the king went to a place and addressed the artillery officer who was there and told him, artillery is very important in war" (44).

Then they return to the personal life:

> You Like This Best
> Lock me in nearly.
> Unlock me sweetly.
> I love my baby with a rush rushingly. (47)

The title is apparently a pun on the name of the futurist artist Filippo Tommaso Marinetti, whose "New Futurist Manifesto," subtitled "Wireless Imagination and Words at Liberty," proclaimed the end of syntax, sentence construction, adjectives, punctuation, and "mannerism or preciosity of style, and will seek to stir you by hurling a confused medley of sensations and impressions at your head." The pun has added humor when one considers that Marinetti advocated the banishment of the female nude from art and the substitution of the male; he wanted his male disciples to bear their own children, and his battle cry was "*Méprisez la femme!*"

56. "Meditations" (Yale Collection of American Literature, #570; 1946)

"Old people write meditations not because they meditate better than when they are younger or young, not at all, but because to write down meditations you do no have to write so long at a time. That is it" (#9). In the last year of her life, Gertrude sat down to write thirty-one brief meditations which often return to the subject of war. "It is funny to think that peace can come out of war," she decides. "Only war can come out of war" (#2). "No use in moon and stars no use in thunder and hail, no use in sun and rain, that is what is after a war" (#29). The despondency is not without hope. "No use in wind and birds, no use in food and water, no use in change of scene and clothes, no use. And yet. Are they ready yet. They might be" (#31).

While the meditations are going on, Alice is at work planning a cookbook and reading recipes. "She is just deep in descriptions of cake she will never make. It is just time to write a cook book about restrictions, it is never too late to do that. Not" (#5). But cooking is not one of Gertrude's passions. "It is very easy to remember how old cooking is when cooking interests some one. I myself do not really like cooking, it is so old that it does fuss me, like eating, cooking and eating bothers me, always has, always" (#10). But then, she notes, ". . . no one can really like anything if things have not settled down . . ." (23).

57. "Mexico" (G&P, 304–30; 1916)

Alice, Gertrude's "little sweetheart," sometimes suffers from bad dreams (304), but Gertrude urges her, "Do dream of me" (305).

A warning is given:

Do I have to choose.
You had better be careful whom you choose.
I will be very careful. (313)

And Gertrude makes a claim for respect:

If you want to be respectable address me as sir.
I am very fond of yes sir.

APPENDIX

58. "Monsieur Vollard et Cezanne" (P&P, 37–39; 1912)

Bridgman notes the edginess of a lover's quarrel (139), but reconciliation is imminent.

> Please me.
> By staying.
> It's pretty nice.
> I asked a question.
> No I'll never think of it again.

"Please, please," Gertrude writes. "Please be good./That's the end of that." The piece seems to have nothing to do with art dealer Ambroise Vollard or the painter he championed.

59. *The Mother of Us All* (Brinnin, 159–202; 1945–46)

Gertrude's views on marriage and men are aired throughout the opera. "Naughty men," she writes, quarrel about everything:

> About how late the moon can rise.
> About how soon the earth can turn.
> About how naked are the stars.
> About how black are blacker men.
> About how pink are pinks in spring.
> About what corn is best to pop. (172)

Arguing is not their only weakness. "Men can not count, they do not know that two and two make four if women do not tell them so. There is a devil creeps into men when their hands are strengthened. Men want to be half slave half free. Women want to be all slave or all free therefore men govern and women know . . ." (183).

Gertrude's views on marriage are sometimes tenuous: "What is marriage, is marriage protection or religion, is marriage renunciation or abundance, is marriage a stepping-stone or an end. What is marriage" (185). Indiana Elliot, effusive in her admiration of Susan B. Anthony for never having married, elicits the response that marriage is a puzzle, for "if there are men and women, it is rather horrible, and if it is rather horrible, then there are children . . ." (198). Susan B. remained single because she had to lead her life independently, "to do what I have had to do," she tells us (186). When her companion Anne protests, "I have been married to what you have been . . . ," Susan B. replies that that is impossible. "No, no, no, you may be married to the past one, the one that is not the present one, no one can be married to the present one . . ." (186).

Bridgman (340–45) has more to say on the piece.

APPENDIX

N

60. "Names of Flowers" (BTV, 217; 1914–15)

A brief appearance by Leo, when the break was fresh: "By being unkind I please brothers./Brother brother go away and stay."

61. "Natural Phenomena" (PL, 167–233; 1925)

Among the natural phenomena in the piece are roses: "There is a great difference between to be and to be rose. There is a great difference between to be rose and to be rose" (195). Though roses appear often since the 1913 piece which expounds that "a rose is a rose is a rose . . . ," Gertrude tells us that natural phenomena "makes it easy to ask about roses whose were they and when are they to be liked and very likely who makes a mistake" (219).

Natural phenomena seem related to a quarrel:

Was I deceived.
All ate too.
All hate to. (199)

"A phenomena of nature," Gertrude continues, "is warm in February and warm in April . . ." (228). Finally, we are assured that all is well: "I choose you. I choose you too" (223).

62. "Nest of Dishes" (PL, 97–107; 1921)

Myra (or Mira) Edgerly is the subject of this piece. Myra, a tall, beautiful woman whom Alice had once noticed at a Mardi Gras ball in San Francisco, had been photographed often by Arnold Genthe, sometimes with a cat. Gertrude recounted her youth (98) and followed her to England, where she attained a certain reputation as a miniaturist. It was Mildred Aldrich who introduced Myra to Gertrude, describing her as "the altruistic enthusiast in search of a great mission." Gertrude noted that she was "very anxious to get three houses in four different blocks in the same part of the city" (104). Perhaps she attained both aspirations by marrying Count Alfred Korzybski, a semanticist, whose works she tried to make known.

We find, once again, cows and Caesars:

Cows are the same as goats.
Not to us.
Cows are the same as cows.
Break of day, break of day, what do the big Caesars say.
They say One Two Three Cow. (107).

63. "A New Happiness" (PL, 151–59; 1914)

Gertrude's happiness centers on her "Little sweet blessing" (155), Alice:

"Oh cherished joy. That's what you are. . . . Oh you cherub. Not cherub thin. Cherubim. Oh lovely cake. I incline to call you awake. That's not teasing, that's love." (155)

64. "No" (AFAM, 35–70; 1915)

"This is a nice story with a happy ending" (49), Gertrude tells us, as she writes love notes to Alice:

> Baby mine
> All the time
> Be light
> Nestle tight
> Shall giggle
> With
> Splendour
> and
> Courage
> and beauty
> and
> goodness.
> Daisy dine
> You are mine
> For
> Thee
> To
> See
> Mastery . . . (59)

Gertrude expresses some fears, but apparently Alice can help her overcome them.

"Please do it," she asks Alice. "Gertrude doesn't like to be frightened" (51). She explains her fear of height, coming from a sense of "no motion." Gertrude promises "to be good and happy and cheerful and not blameworthy or peevish . . . to be good and industrious and patient and loving and earnest devoted equable goodnatured and pious" (60), and asks of Alice only one thing:

> Do be anxious.
> To please.
> Do be anxious to please me.
> Do be anxious.
> To please. (68)

65. "Not Slightly" (G&P, 290–301; 1915)

As in the other Mallorcan pieces, Gertrude seeks Alice's

opinion (290) and listens devotedly (294). They are not completely isolated from former friends: "The Bruces [Patrick Henry and Helen] have left," Gertrude reports (301).

66. *A Novel of Thank You* (NOTY, 3-240; 1925–26)

Carl Van Vechten calls this one of Gertrude's most hermetic books, "and one about which very little has been written, even by Gertrude, or remembered, even by Alice Toklas" (ix). If Alice failed to recall the theme, Bridgman may be correct in thinking that the main movement indicates domestic breakup and reconciliation (173), but it is less likely that Alice had an actual hand in the work, as he speculates (211n.). Though passages in the manuscript are written by Alice, this is not unique in the Stein oeuvre. The passages in *A Novel of Thank You* in Alice's handwriting do not differ stylistically from Gertrude's. Gertrude's statement that the piece is "A novel of thank you and not about it" (185) may mean that the piece itself was a thank-you gift, in the same way some were birthday gifts or love songs. Bridgman thinks, however, that "Gertrude's gratitude was directly manifested, not merely described, by permitting Alice Toklas to share in the composition" (211).

There is evidence of an arranged liaison:

Thank you for having arranged it for me. . . . (179)
How many more than two are there. (3)
I arranged that she had a friend and that that friend would
   show to advantage. (17)
Union.
A conversation between them.
They came every day. . . . (18)

The arrangement causes distress and tears (23), and the straying partner is invited to return. "Come and kiss me when you want to . . ." (106). A "third" is

new especially delivered and attracted and fairly well announced also something that in exchange is received more than usually. Introductions to them to them and introductions. Furtively. (5)

The narrator, having arranged the "attachment," must sit by and wait for its completion. "What else did I do for her," Gertrude writes. "I planted roses in such a way that if she took ordinary precautions and showed determination there would be presently an additional enjoyment confidence and please and this might be at a distance and intelligence."

"Please say it soon," she adds (17).

O

67. "Objects Lie on a Table. A Play" (O&P, 105–12; 1922)

The pupil who appears in this piece may be, as Bridgman suggests, Hemingway (165). ". . . He says I am very willing but I have had to invent something to fill in and I say to him you had better really have it . . ." (108). Various suggestions about writing are cryptically stated, and once the teacher fears that her pupil might think her less expert than she really is. "Do we suppose that a rose is a rose. Do we suppose that all she knows is that a rose is a rose is a rose. He knows and she knows that a rose is a rose and when she can make a song as to which can belong as to what can belong to a song" (110).

68. "One Sentence" (AFAM, 73–107; 1914)

Alice, in the guise of Fanny, shuns dancing partners, though she "was asked by a great many to dance./Fanny does not dance any more" (106). She and Gertrude lead a quiet life in Spain. "Fanny and I are alone the weather is fine and hot./We read aloud to each other in the evening" (105).

69. "Or More (Or War)" (UK, 115–43; 1925)

Part Two of this piece contains personal references to Caroline Helbing (134), to Alice and her hats (136), to Lily Hansen and Louise Taylor (137), and to the course of love:

> You will never be angry with Ida.
> At once more.
> So soothingly.
> This is the way it has to be. It has to be this is the way and
>   not to do it again.
> She has absolutely promised never to mention birds. (139)

P

70. "Patriarchal Poetry" (BTV, 254–94; 1927)

Concerned in general with emotion, Gertrude focuses on Alice in an eighteen-line poem which Gertrude tells us is a sonnet (272).

> To the wife of my bosom
> All happiness from everything
> And her husband.
> May he be good and considerate
> Gay and cheerful and restful.

And make her the best wife
In the world
The happiest and the most content
With reason.
To the wife of my bosom
Whose transcendent virtues
Are those to be most admired
Loved and adored and indeed
Her virtues are all inclusive
Her virtues her beauty and her beauties
Her charms her qualities her joyous nature
All of it makes of her husband
A proud and happy man.

71. "Pay Me" (PL, 137–39; 1930)

"She is everything to me because I see that she eats well and is very happy. My attentions make her happy," Gertrude tells us. Alice is more than a companion; she is necessary for Gertrude's success. Though others "make hopes" of Gertrude's talent, Alice provides the necessities without which Gertrude could not work. "She is my wife. That is what a paragraph is. Always at home. A paragraph hopes for houses. We have a house two houses. My wife and I are at home" (138–39).

72. "Pink Melon Joy" (G&P, 347–76; 1915)

There is repeated mention of eyes and sight, and joy at being "all well. That baby is baby. That baby is all well. That there is a piano. That baby is all well" (349). Recovery is complete and Gertrude is filled with ardor. "Little dove little love I am loving you with much more love." The illness is unexplained:

> I cannot mention what I have.
> I have.
> Guess it.
> I have a real sight. This is so critical.
> Alice. (363)

And the piece ends, expectedly, with a kiss (376).

73. "Portrait of Mabel Dodge at the Villa Curonia" (P&P, 98–102; 1911)

Alice's jealousy of Gertrude strained the visit to Mabel's villa and, as Gertrude saw, "An argument is clear" (98). The uncomfortable triangle persisted, but Mabel did not succeed in coming between Alice and Gertrude. She remained the outsider, with "her face against the pane . . . ," as Gertrude noted in her alternate title to the piece.

74. "Possessive Case" (AFAM, 111–59; 1915)

Alice's subscribing to the Romeike clipping bureau made Gertrude happy. "I am quite touched with Romeike" (112), she wrote. Alice's gesture was one of many kindnesses:

> To marry for love and to be very handsome and very clever and to be deterred by no difficulties and to give her attention to dogs suffering with wounded soldiers is not discovered until some years after it is mentioned. In some things she is a leaf in the wind.

Though Alice provided happiness in the present, future success was always on Gertrude's mind, and she recalls Patrick Henry:

> It is natural to indulge in the illusions of hope. We are apt to shut our eyes to that siren until she allures us to our death. Is it that we are among the number of those who see not and who hear not the best that leads us to salvation shall we be among the number of those who having ears hear not and having eyes see not the things that lead us to salvation. (138)

> It is natural for men to indulge in the illusions of hope. We are apt to shut our eyes against a painful truth, and listen to the song of that siren till she transforms us into beasts. Is this the part of wise men, engaged in a great and arduous struggle for liberty? Are we disposed to be the number of those who, having eyes, see not, and having ears, hear not, the things which so nearly concern their temporal salvation? (Patrick Henry, Speech in the Virginia Convention, March 23, 1775)

75. "The Present" (BTV, 212; 1918)

Alice:

> Tiny dish of delicious which
> Is my wife and all
> And a perfect ball.

R

76. "Readings" (Haas, Vol. I, 81; 1921)

Alice and Gertrude:

Kisses can kiss us.
A duck a hen and fishes, followed by wishes.
Happy little pair.

77. "Reread Another. A Play. To be played indoors or out. I wish to be a school." (O&P, 123–30; 1921)

"My memory does not tell me how and what to remember and so what do I do. I remember everything," Gertrude tells us. But very often, she relied on Alice for answers and judgments. "I can be as stupid as I like because my wife is always right" (125). As Bridgman notes (213), "Gertrude realized that she was not equipped to exercise the selectivity that a history required."

In this piece she does recall Louise [Hayden] and Georgiana [King] (125), but her thoughts turn most often to Alice. "To be wed, I was wed. I said I am led. Twenty-eight, I wait to be led. By she who is all to me" (123).

"I am very happy here," she tells us. "I am so much happier than to-day. Than yesterday. Than everyday" (129).

The reason is evident: "I love my love with a z because she is exact" (129).

78. "Rich in the City" (Yale Collection of American Literature, #186; 1918)

Gertrude's criteria for financial success are simply expressed:

What do you mean by riches.
I mean enough wealth to run around.
Do you enjoy running around.
Very much.

A conversation between her and Alice includes discussion of the health of the French populace (they agree that they are healthy) and their appreciation of parks and forests. The brief piece ends with a familiar note:

That is a question I meant to ask.
It is answered.

S

79. "Sacred Emily" (G&P, 178–88; 1913)

"Sacred Emily" has the distinction of being the first piece (but hardly the last) in which Gertrude made her famous assertion, "Rose is a rose is a rose is a rose" (187). The title is said to derive from a remark made by André Derain about the long-suffering Amélie Matisse: "*Sainte Amélie, la plus grande martyre de notre siècle.*" The piece, however, has little —if anything—to do with Matisse's infidelities or Amélie's plight. Puns and wordplay abound. "Pussy" is celebrated as

"Push sea push sea push sea. . . ." There is a brief recollection of Seattle and Alice's friend Louise:

> Settle stretches.
> Sea at till.
> Louise.
> Sunny.
> Sail or.
> Sail or rustle.
> Mourn in morning. (188)

Gertrude alludes to her collaboration with Alice:

> Put something down some day in.
> Put something down some day in my.
> In my hand.
> In my hand right.
> In my hand writing.
> Put something down some day in my hand writing. (185)

Gertrude reveals that the meaning of the piece is "Not in description" (188). And the rose emerges as "Loveliness extreme" (187).

80. "Saints and Singing. A Play" (G&P, 71–87; 1922)

Bridgman notes references to recovery from an illness or operation (164) and to saints, possibly inspired by a stay in a Catholic hospital.

Gertrude praises Alice's hair (75) and declares boldly, ". . . Treasure treasure I love you without measure" (86).

81. "Sentences and Paragraphs" (HTW, 23–35; 1930)

Supposedly a treatise on grammar, the piece offers an inventory of some friends and acquaintances: Georges Maratier, Genia Berman, Georges Hugnet, Bernard Faÿ, René Crevel, and of course Alice (25).

"I was overcome with remorse," Gertrude laments. "It was my fault that my wife did not have a cow." But cautiously she adds, "This sentence they cannot use" (25).

Alice is the listening ear, always understanding Gertrude's meaning. "Dear do I," she asks once. ". . . Well I guess I do" (34). She proves Gertrude's dictum. "It is to be certain that love is lord of all" (28).

The piece includes two restatements of the word attributed to Gertrude on her deathbed: "What is the difference between a question and an answer. There is no question and no answer" (33); and "Now the whole question of questions and no answer is very interesting" (35).

346

82. "A Singular Addition. A Sequel to an Instant Answer or One Hundred Prominent Men" (PL, 277–86; 1922)

The theme is weddings. "Let us attach ourselves to marriage to proposals of interesting plans. . . . The first wedding. He asked and she was asked and she was asked and she did not ask it for him. She did not ask for it for him. She did not ask for it" (278). Subsequent weddings are enumerated, the eighth dealing with Lilyanna Hansen: ". . . Easter lilies and Nellie's lilies and St. John's lilies and Kitty's lilies and the market lilies all have the same colour and endurance. They are not separated by lilies there. Lily is Scandinavian" (279).

83. "Sitwell Edith Sitwell" (P&P, 92–95; 1925)

Mabel Weeks appears in this portrait of Edith Sitwell: "This is for her and not for Mabel Weeks," and "Weeks and weeks able and weeks." If no one understood the relationship between the English poet and Gertrude's Radcliffe friend, the incongruity most likely did not bother Gertrude. She pairs another two, but this time the relationship is more comprehensible: "No one sees the connection between Lily [Hansen] and Louise [Hayden] but I do." The same line appears in another piece written in the same year, "Or More (Or War)."

84. "A Sonatina Followed by Another" (BTV, 4–32; 1921)

No other piece better deserves to be called "The song of Alice B." (12). "Little Alice B. is the wife for me," Gertrude sings. "Little Alice B. so tenderly is born so long so she can be born along by a husband strong who has not his hair shorn. . . .

"One two one two I come to you. To-day there is nothing but the humble expression of a husband's love. Take it" (12).

Written for Alice's birthday, the love song enumerates her many praiseworthy qualities in tender detail. Gertrude's "little Jew" (4, 31) apparently slept through the creation of the piece, and Gertrude wonders whether to awaken her. The problem is left unsolved, and Gertrude goes on to a riddle.

"Why is pussy like the great American Army," Gertrude asks. "Because she buds so many buddies" (6).

Nature serves the cause of true love:

You are my honey honey suckle.
   I am your bee. (8)

. . .

A red poppy is for decoration a daisy is a humble expression of a husband's love. Together they make a bouquet. Joined to nasturtiums and pansies they show unexpected tenderness. (9)

APPENDIX

"I address my cares, my caresses to the one who blesses who blesses me," Gertrude writes. She finds kindnesses in simple acts. "How can I thank you enough for holding me on the ladder for allowing me to pick roses, for enjoying my fireside and for recollecting stars. How can I thank you enough for all your kindness to me" (10).

Predictably, there are many references to Caesars and cows. "All of us worship a cow," Gertrude admits. "How. By introducing and producing and extension" (31).

Digressing for a moment, Gertrude turns to her own limitations. "This is a list of my experiences. I cannot describe beauty. I cannot describe a square, I cannot describe strangeness. I cannot describe rivers, I cannot describe lands. I can describe milk, and women and resemblances and elaboration and cider. I can also describe weather and counters and water. I can also describe bursts of melody" (21).

She can, of course, also describe Alice.

1. Always sweet.
2. Always right.
3. Always welcome.
4. Always wife.
5. Always blessed.
6. Always a successful druggist of the second class and we know what that means. Who credits her with all this is a husband with a kiss and what is he to be always more lovingly his missus' help and hero. And when is he heroic, well we know when. (32)

85. "Stanzas In Meditation" (SIM, 3–151; 1932)
See Bridgman, 213–17. The piece was written concurrently with *The Autobiography of Alice B. Toklas*, in the evenings, as an apologia for producing a popular book, and references to *The Autobiography* are made throughout:

This is her autobiography one of two
But which it is no one which it is can know. (77)

This is the most obvious. "She will be me when this you see," Gertrude writes of Alice's fictional memoirs. She wants to write pieces in her own style. "How I wish I were able to say what I think," she sighs (79).

I wish to remind everybody nobody hears me
That it makes no difference how they do
    What they do. (108)

Bowing to what the public expects saddens Gertrude: "I have been thought not to respect myself/To have been sold as wishes"

(134). "I could never believe that I could not happily deceive," she writes. But pressure from Alice forces her to continue. "Shove is a proof of love" (146).

Gertrude might have remained content with her small audience and private prose (87). Alice, however, wanted success (90). Gertrude took her "delight in moonlight," writing the five-part stanzas and meditating on her daily work.

"I wish once more to say that I know the difference between two," she assures us (150). But there is a wistfulness in one question to Alice:

> Tell me darling tell me true
> Am I all the world to you
> And the world of what does it consist. (50)

86. "Storyette H.M." (P&P, 40; 1911)

Matisse's infidelity to Madame Matisse—which Gertrude scorned—is the subject of this piece. "The one that was married to that one did not like it very well that the one to whom that one was married then was going off alone to have a good time and was leaving that one to stay at home then."

87. "Susie Asado" (G&P, 13; 1913)

"Susie Asado" is usually coupled with "Preciosilla," two portraits inspired by Gertrude's and Alice's trip to Spain. "Asado" means roasted; in "Preciosilla" we find "Toasted susie is my ice cream." According to Maurice Grosser, "leche helado" (ice cream) rhymes with a flamenco dancer's name. "Incy is short for incubus," Gertrude intrudes in "Susie Asado," referring to the nocturnal evil spirit who has intercourse with women as they sleep.

T

88. "They Must. Be Wedded. To Their Wife. A Play" (LO&P, 204; Brinnin, 87–125; 1931)

Among the players in this piece is Ernest. There is a certain familiarity in his character. Though he "Is obedient. And. Developing" (90), he "May be a victim. Of himself. He may be delightful. Or not. As it happens" (89). The theme or themes of the play are obscure, but there are allusions to possible future success:

> She may be clouded. Or cowed.
> And they will trace. And. They will shape.
> Their destiny. (111)

And there is worry about impermanent friendships, unfaithful friends, especially in light of growing fame. The solution seems to be a selectivity of recollection:

> . . . They have weeded
> Weeds thickly. As a memory. (123)

89. "This One Is Serious" (PL, 20–23; 1915)

Alice is allowed a brief monologue: "Sometimes I cry. Not from anger. I only cry from heat and other things. I love to be right. It is so necessary. No one can deny the necessity. It is pleasing" (20).

90. "Three Sitting Here" (P&P, 124–42; 1927)

"Why do they love me so very well" (124), Gertrude asks repeatedly in this lengthy piece. She wonders why her admirers are "twinkling with love for me" (128) and determines after some consideration that there is "every reason" for their devotion. Sometimes she focuses on Alice's love:

> The reason that I am contenting those who have been and are devoting themselves to be obliging to care very much for me is this, when it is not difficult to look about and see where they are they are here. (127)

Still, there is a hint that Alice might think of "rejoining lilies of the valley . . ." (124)—a prospect which makes Gertrude despondent.

91. "Turkey and Bones and Eating and We Liked It" (G&P, 239–53; 1916)

The play includes dialogues between Gertrude and Alice:

> I do not care to look at any one.
> I do.
> Then please yourself.
> I do not understand electricity.
> I do.
> I do not understand hail.
> I can explain it.
> I do not care for history.
> I can read it.
> I do not care about individual wishes.
> I understand it.
> Plenty of people do love another.
> She. (245–46)

Any hint of a dispute is resolved:

You agree with me.
Yes I agree with you.
Do you always agree with me.
You know I always agree with you.
Then that is satisfactory.
To me.
And to me too. (253)

92. "Two: Gertrude Stein and Her Brother" (TWO, 1–142; 1910–12)

The inside cover of the manuscript, Volume 1, helps explain Gertrude's intent in writing this piece: "Complete sound and then a list of what they did and how. Then do Alice and me what we did and how. Use the introduction for Alice about babies. . . . Sally takes it up and makes it the same. He takes it up and makes it difficult and particular. Noises. . . . This is to be told in diagrams and introductions and diagrams. . . ."

Though Gertrude wrote "Leo and Sally" in large script in the first volume, the piece evidently concerns Leo and Gertrude. Two are a man and a woman, "Different the one from the other one" (2), yet alike in that each seems to be searching for personal identity. Leo is described as "compelling" and "deciding," Gertrude as "accepting" and "asking" (42–43). Leo was becoming increasingly repetitive: "He was needing sound coming out of him in being one needing telling again and again what he was telling" (38). But more important for Gertrude, ". . . he was expressing that he was not loving" (47). She, on the other hand, was looking for understanding and sympathy. The entrance of Alice is obliquely noted. "Each of them was the one that was not one of the two of them" (99). Leo and Gertrude were no longer a pair; Alice and Gertrude were not yet a pair.

Gradually, Gertrude was able to assert herself against Leo. ". . . She was the one who spoke the thing that staying away from home meant everything. She did not escape excusing that she was liberating enough to be returning to every custom" (108).

Moreover, she had support from Alice. ". . . She said what she said and she was agreeing" (109). Communication between Gertrude and her brother deteriorated. "When there was an arbitrary way to see a clear sight that was not particularly there, he explained the origin of something and he meant the rest. . . . He was particular." Gertude conceded that he did have "meaning. . . . He was not doddering. He had the faculty of expression" (123). But Gertrude needed the solid approval and support Alice provided. "She did not deny anything. She agreed and the feeling was perfection" (123).

"Two" is the most detailed, if obscure, version of the breakup between brother and sister that Gertrude was to offer. Alice, in later years, gave no further information—only adding, when Leo died a year after Gertrude, that there were no closer two than they had been before 1914.

V

93. "Vacation in Britany King or Kangaroo King or Yellow King or Marie Claire Suggests a Meadow. And The Use of Thought" (Haas, Vol. I, 77–78; 1920)

Gertrude gives some thoughts on devotion and faithfulness. Men are not to be trusted. "Men say. Leave me and be gay. Men say tenderness today. Men say go away./And leave me."

Devotion is related to Caesars and cows:

Devotion. What is devotion. . . . An opening is covered by Caesars. Sharp wire. Do sharpen wire. Devotion. Devotion is determined by design.

When this you see remember me.

Another definition for cow is invented: a stool. "That was the elegant name for a cow."

94. "A Valentine to Sherwood Anderson" (P&P, 151–56; 1922)

Oddly, the valentine seems to be to Alice:

If you hear her snore
It is not before you love her
You love her so that to be her beau is very lovely
She is sweetly there and her curly hair is very lovely
She is sweetly here and I am very near and that is very
    lovely.
She is my tender sweet and her little feet are stretched out
    well which is a treat and very lovely
Her little tender nose is between her little eyes which close
    and are very lovely.
She is very lovely and mine which is very lovely. (155)

W

95. "Water Pipe" (Haas, Vol. I, 31–33; 1916)

Another Mallorcan piece, it is evidence of Gertrude's dependence on Alice.

I ask you to speak. I ask you to give directions every five minutes. I ask you if you think that it is splendid that photographs are copied in embroidery. I know what your answer will be. I do not mean to say that I can anticipate it. Believe me that I sign myself yours obediently.

Alice's wishes are Gertrude's commands:

You will give me orders will you not. You will tell me what you prefer. You will ask for what you want. You do need the door closed. Please do not mind if I refuse at first. I don't like to find out exactly where the draft comes from. But I see what you wish, you need to have instant obedience and you shall have it. I will never question. Your lightest wish shall be my law.

I have no objection to a signature. I sign with your pen.
I say frequently I have asked that you write it for me.
To you I'll be true.

96. "We Have Eaten Heartily and We Were Alarmed" (PL, 39–41; 1916)

The war was always on their minds. "We Are Nervous Because We Did Not Expect That There Ever Would Be This War," Gertrude exclaims (10). Their dog, Polybe, chased goats and finally had to be given away, but even the dog's antics were no distraction against worry of war (41). They remained in Mallorca "because we are not determined to have our character. We like very much to discuss ice-cream" (39) and not witness the real reprivations of war.

97. "What Does She See When She Shuts Her Eyes" (MR, 375–78; 1936)

Bridgman thinks the "she" in this piece is Gertrude, using gardening as a diversion against "mental suffering" and disquieting thoughts. But it is more likely that "she" (and "Theresa") is Alice, growing flowers and vegetables in Bilignin (377), while another character, Henry Maximilian Arthur, was busy contemplating money. So was Gertrude, resulting in her "Money" essays written in the same year. When they were not at their respective occupations, they found mutual enjoyment. "Once in a while Henry Maximilian Arthur was caressed by Theresa."

"Henry Maximilian Arthur could be tickled by grasses as they grow and he could not caress but he could be caressed by Theresa as well as be tickled by grasses as they grow . . ." (377).

98. "Winning His Way. A Narrative Poem of Poetry" (SIM, 155–209; 1931)

Hope of fame and success gave Gertrude the theme for this

piece. "Fame. Is a pleasure. To the. Beholder," she admits
(192), but "Fame came. Gradually . . ." (199). Gertrude
wonders if she writes for Alice or for herself:

> Does a poem. Continue. Because of. A kiss.
> Or because. Of future greatness.
> Or because. There is no cause. . . . (164)

While Gertrude ponders fame, Alice pursues her tasks,
making tapestries (178), tending the garden (196), overseeing
Gertrude's friendships (157). Gertrude tells Alice:

> It is a very pretty garden you have made me.
> It is full of things. That give me pleasure. (196)

And, in a more personal tribute:

> It is by seize us. That they christen. Baby. With by. Caesar.
> Seize us. That they Christen. A Baby. (160)

Louise Hayden's marriage to an army officer is announced
briefly (193).

99. "Woodrow Wilson" (UK, 104–14; 1920)

"Reading everything again is one of many pleasures," Gertrude tells us. But love affords greater pleasure. "To accom-
plish wishes one needs one's lover . . ." (111), she knows. She
pleads with Alice, "Beseech me, beseech me to love you" (110),
knowing that ". . . love is not protected by charms" (111).

Y

100. "Yet Dish" (BTV, 53–60; 1913)

A note to the piece indicates that A.R. is "a woman Miss
Stein once knew." From Gertrude's description, she may have
been Annette Rosenshine.

> A.R. nuisance
> Not a regular plate.
> Are, not a regular plate.
>
> . . .
>
> A R not new since
> New since.
> Are new since bows less. (58)

If palate and plate are synonomous, the reference here is to
Annette's deformity and subsequent operation and to her annoying dependence on the Steins.

Notes

Most works cited in the Notes are referred to by initials or abbreviations; all sources are cited fully in the Bibliography.

PART 1

1 Will Irwin, "The City That Was," New York *Sun*, April 21, 1906
2 Lena Levinsky Bruml, Oral History, American Jewish Archives, Cincinnati
3 Sharfman, 55
4 *Ibid.*, 83
5 Duncan, 32
6 SOA, 151
7 Duncan, 20
8 "Fifty Years of French Fashions"
9 Duncan, 91
10 EA, 149
11 SOA, 227
12 *Ibid.*, 42
13 *Ibid.*, 227
14 WIR, 9
15 *Southwestern Washington*, 1890, 80
16 WIR, 9
17 Duncan, 65
18 *Ibid.*, 77
19 *Ibid.*
20 *Ibid.*
21 WIR, 9
22 *The Northwestern Real Estate & Bldg. Review*, c. 1896
23 Duncan, 75

24 Rosenshine, 172
25 *Ibid.*, 38
26 SOA, 123
27 Rosenshine, 30
28 Duncan, 5
29 Jordan, *The Call of The Twentieth Century*, 15–16
30 Rosenshine, 30
31 James, *The American* (New York: New American Library, 1963), 73
32 John Cowper Powys, in the *Little Review*
33 Duncan, 74
34 SOA, 115
35 Rosenshine, 44
36 *Ibid.*, 34
37 Duncan, 62
38 *Ibid.*, 63
39 *Ibid.*, 73
40 Rosenshine, 44
41 Cf. Leon Katz dissertation
42 Duncan, 95
43 *Ibid.*, 53
44 Levy, *920 O'Farrell Street*, 25
45 *Ibid.*, 26
46 Duncan, 49
47 Rosenshine, 35
48 *Ibid.*, 33
49 Duncan, 50
50 December 23, 1902
51 Duncan, 64–65
52 *Ibid.*, 57
53 *Ibid.*, 10–11
54 WIR, 17
55 Duncan, 63
56 *Ibid.*, 65
57 ABT, 5
58 SOA, 104
59 Rosenshine, 176
60 In 1893, Sarah Stein wrote to her sister-in-law Gertrude explaining Dr. Mayer's feelings about "self-abuse." Mayer, Sarah's gynecologist, apparently had met Gertrude when she was last in San Francisco, but she did not speak to him then about his treatment or about the problem. Whether Gertrude was interested in his counsel for her own reasons or because of her interest in female psychopathology is not clear from Sarah's letter; but Sarah indicated that she felt Dr. Mayer's talk would have helped Gertrude. Letter at Beinecke Library, Yale University.

61 Duncan, 68
62 Levy, "Recollections"
63 Duncan, 87
64 *Ibid.*
65 Rosenshine, 55
66 WIR, 14
67 Levy, "Recollections"
68 ABTC, 31
69 WIR, 14
70 Thomas & Witts, 151
71 William James, "On Some Mental Effects of the Earthquake," 220
72 Bonner, "The Passing of the Argonauts' City"
73 Genthe, 99
74 WIR, 17
75 Duncan, 68
76 *Ibid.*
77 *Ibid.*, 14
78 H. Kirk to LS, October 7, 1974
79 Sarah Stein to GS, November 1899. Beinecke Library, Yale University
80 Gimpel, 76
81 Pach, 120
82 Gimpel, 76
83 Sarah Stein to GS, September 28, 1896. Beinecke Library, Yale University
84 ABT, 79
85 Miller, Theme written by GS, December 20, 1894.
86 Gallup, *The Flowers of Friendship*, 8
87 QED, 152
88 *Ibid.*, 153
89 Brassai, 162
90 Gilot, 60
91 ABT, 11
92 *Picasso*, 12
93 *Ibid.*, 8
94 Sarah Stein to GS, October–December 1899. Beinecke Library, Yale University
95 Levy, "Recollections," 10
96 Rosenshine, 66
97 *Ibid.*, 64
98 Sarah Stein to GS, October 1906. Beinecke Library, Yale University
99 Rosenshine, 72–73
100 *Ibid.*, 86
101 Duncan, 69
102 AT to W. G. Rogers, November 24, 1960

PART 2

1 The date of Alice's arrival in France is deduced from Duncan (97), where she says that she and Harriet arrived on a fête day. Her description of the costumes worn in Caen matches those worn on the celebration of the Virgin Mary's birth, which was September 8. She must have left San Francisco at the end of August, arriving in New York after August 31, when Lillian Russell came to the city. Also, a letter from Mrs. Milton Eisner to Annette Rosenshine, dated September 16, 1907, mentions that Mrs. Eisner, in San Francisco, knew that Harriet was already staying at the Hôtel Magellan. Letter at Beinecke Library, Yale University.

2 WIR, 20
3 *Ibid.*, 22
4 Duncan, 69–70
5 WIR, 23
6 Duncan, 16
7 Levy, "Recollections"
8 Rosenshine, 82
9 *Ibid.*, 74
10 *Ibid.*, 69
11 *Ibid.*
12 *Ibid.*, 74
13 *Ibid.*, 84
14 Weininger, 26
15 *Ibid.*, 118
16 *Ibid.*, 65
17 *Ibid.*, 112
18 *Ibid.*, 138
19 *Ibid.*, 139
20 *Ibid.*, 189
21 Rosenshine, 78
22 Gallup, *The Flowers of Friendship*, 45
23 Weininger, 66
24 "Value of College Education for Women," n.p.
25 MOA, 175
26 EA, 121, 243
27 Weininger, 188–89
28 Rosenshine, 76
29 *Ibid.*, 74
30 *Ibid.*, 78
31 *Ibid.*, 79
32 *Ibid.*, 107
33 "Didn't Nelly and Lilly Love You," AFAM, 226

34 WIR, 24–25
35 Levy, "Recollections," 9
36 *Ibid.*, 8
37 *Ibid.*, 6
38 SOA, 182
39 ABT, 10
40 *Ibid.*, 9
41 *Ibid.*, 10
42 *Ibid.*, 17
43 *Ibid.*
44 *Ibid.*
45 WIR, 33
46 Rosenshine, 107
47 ABT, 21
48 Parmelin, 114
49 ABT, 21
50 Levy "Recollections," 7
51 *Ibid.*, 6
52 WIR, 35
53 *Picasso*, 9
54 Levy, "Recollections," Chapter V
55 WIR, 37
56 Edstrom, 239
57 *Ibid.*, 240
58 Hapgood, 217
59 Edstrom, 218
60 *Ibid.*, 337
61 Hapgood, 219
62 *Ibid.*, 120
63 *Ibid.*, 131
64 *Ibid.*, 245
65 Edstrom, 242
66 Sterne, 194–95
67 Edstrom, 258
68 Levy, "Recollections," Chapter IV
69 AT to Harriet Levy, October 18, 1948 (in WIR, 47, Alice
   attributed this anecdote to herself)
70 Levy, "Recollections," 38–39
71 Rosenshine, 235
72 Leo Stein, *The New Republic*, April 23, 1924
73 SOA, 319
74 WIR, 64
75 TWO, 42–43
76 Leo Stein, ABC, 206
77 EA, 75–76
78 At the time Alice was reading George Sand's autobiography,
   Gertrude was trying to choose a nom de plume for *Three*

Lives. Three of her possible choices are variations on the name "Sand." Aurore Dupin herself first used the nom de plume J. Sand, a tribute to her lover, Jules Sandeau. Cf. Bridgman, 46; Katz, 73.

79 WIR, 41–42
80 *Ibid.*, 44
81 *Ibid.*, 45
82 *Ibid.*, 48
83 Cf. "Didn't Nelly and Lilly Love You," AFAM
84 Duncan, 101
85 Hapgood, 247
86 WIR, 55
87 Levy, "Recollections"
88 Rosenshine, 83
89 "Ada," G&P, 200
90 Gimpel, 372
91 TWO, 101
92 Burgess, "The Wild Men of Paris," 408
93 Walter Pach to AT, February 4, 1911. Beinecke Library, Yale University
94 Luhan, *European Experiences*, 326
95 WIR, 68
96 *Ibid.*, 70
97 *Ibid.*, 75
98 Duncan, 72
99 Luhan, *European Experiences*, 332–33
100 P&P, 98–102
101 JIS, 53
102 *Ibid.*, 51
103 *Ibid.*, 52
104 SOA, 223
105 AT to W. G. Rogers, August 10, 1947. Beinecke Library Yale University
106 JIS, 298
107 TWO, 133
108 "Didn't Nelly and Lilly Love You," AFAM, 247–48
109 TWO, 133
110 Morrell, 150
111 Holroyd, 69
112 Acton, *Memoirs of an Aesthete*, 257
113 Wilson, *The Shores of Light*, 70
114 Van Vechten, *Peter Whiffle*, 176. Filippo Tommaso Marinetti (1876–1944) announced the birth of futurism in *Le Figaro*, February 20, 1909. His firecrackers would more likely have been bombs, since part of his aesthetic formula incited his followers to bomb palaces, libraries, and museums and set up factories in their place. He exalted the

machine, "aggressive movement, feverish insomnia, the double quick-step, the somersault. . . ." Mussolini was one of his pupils.

Charles Loeser (c. 1866–1928) came to Italy soon after leaving Harvard in 1886. He bought a villa in order to restore it and filled it with paintings chosen on instinct, he maintained, or on the advice of the best critic he knew—his cook, Maria.

115 WIR, 83; see also Duncan, 5
116 "They Who Came . . ."
117 Duncan, 79
118 ABT, 144
119 *Ibid.*
120 Duncan, 84
121 Anne de Gruchy Low-Beer to LS, January 19, 1976. Material on the friendship between AT and Clare Moore de Gruchy was generously supplied by Mrs. Low-Beer.
122 Michael Stein to GS
123 WIR, 85
124 ABT, 114
125 *Ibid.*, 148–49
126 AT to Harriet Levy, Autumn 1915. The Bancroft Library, University of California, Berkeley
127 "Pink Melon Joy," G&P, 366
128 "Johnny Grey," G&P, 168–69
129 "Farragut," UK, 11
130 *Ibid.*, 14
131 *Ibid.*, 15
132 "How Could They Marry Her," Haas, Vol. I, 16
133 "Independent Embroidery," PL, 83
134 "He Said It," G&P, 274
135 "Bonne Annee," G&P, 302–03
136 "If You Had Three Husbands," G&P, 385
137 *Ibid.*, 382
138 "No," AFAM, 59
139 "All Sunday," A&B, 106
140 "Turkey and Bones," G&P, 253
141 "Not Slightly," G&P, 290
142 "If You Had Three Husbands," G&P, 377
143 "Mexico," G&P, 304
144 "He Said It," G&P, 273
145 "Mexico," G&P, 306
146 "All Sunday," A&B, 105
147 "Pink Melon Joy," G&P, 376
148 WIR, 93
149 Rogers, *When This You See . . .* , 17
150 ABT, 159

151 *Ibid.*, 168
152 W. G. Rogers to AT, April 30, 1919. Beinecke Library, Yale University
153 Rogers, *When This You See . . .* , 17
154 *Ibid.*, 30
155 *Ibid.*, 38
156 W. G. Rogers to GS and AT, January 27, 1918. Beinecke Library, Yale University
157 WIR, 101
158 Awarded October 6, 1922
159 WIR, 102–03
160 "Lifting Belly," BTV, 113–14
161 *Ibid.*, 72
162 *Ibid.*, 80
163 *Ibid.*, 96
164 *Ibid.*, 80
165 *Ibid.*, 91
166 "Accents in Alsace," G&P, 410
167 *Ibid.*, 415
168 "They Who Came . . ."

PART 3

1 Sherwood Anderson, G&P, 6
2 EA, 119
3 Bryher, 210–11
4 *Ibid.*
5 *Ibid.*
6 *Ibid.*
7 Hunt, 266
8 *Ibid.*, 39
9 "They Who Came . . ."
10 Sherwood Anderson, *A Story-Teller's Story*, 359
11 ABT, 130
12 Fenton, *The Apprenticeship . . .* , 191
13 *Ibid.*, 146. The letter is dated March 9, 1922
14 Bryher, 212–13
15 Rosenshine, 124
16 Hemingway, *By-Line*, 42–43
17 EA, 191
18 ABT, 201
19 *Ibid.*, 202
20 McAlmon, in Knoll, 226
21 Hemingway, *By-Line*, 132
22 Wilson, *The Wound and the Bow*, 221
23 GS, Paris *Tribune*, November 27, 1923

24 Sutherland, "Alice and Gertrude and Others," 297
25 Hemingway, *A Moveable Feast*, 20; cf. letter of EH to W. G. Rogers, July 29, 1948, at Beinecke Library, Yale University
26 Sutherland, *op. cit.*, 297
27 ABT, 203
28 Conversation with Max White, April 30, 1975
29 SOA, 38
30 ABT, 204
31 *Ibid.*, 207
32 Hemingway, *A Moveable Feast*, 118
33 Preston, 163
34 White, 76
35 Hemingway, *The Green Hills of Africa*, 65
36 Hemingway, "The Farm," 28–29
37 Alexander Pope, "Essay on Man"
38 SOA, 194
39 *Ibid.*, 210
40 Sutherland, *op. cit.*, 297
41 Fitzgerald, *Letters*, 174
42 WIR, 117
43 SOA, 169–70
44 *The New York Times*, March 4, 1951
45 "They Who Came . . ."
46 AFAM, 258
47 ABT, 190
48 "They Who Came . . ."
49 As in a letter to GS, April 21, 1925
50 *The Criterion*, January 1927
51 ABT, 218
52 Salter, 113
53 WIR, 118
54 Salter, 106
55 Tyler, 318
56 Sitwell, *Taken Care Of*, 161
57 Pavel Tchelitchew, Ryerson lecture, 19-page typescript from lecture delivered on February 20, 1951, in connection with a Gertrude Stein exhibition. Beinecke Library, Yale University
58 WIR, 127
59 Crosby, 303
60 Rogers, *Ladies Bountiful*, 44
61 Crosby, 224
62 SOA, 347
63 Wickes, "A Natalie Barney Garland," 115–16
64 GS to Allen Tanner and Pavel Tchelitchew. Beinecke Library, Yale University. Reprinted in *On Our Way* (New

York, 1959), a limited edition of letters by AT and GS from Oxford and Cambridge.

65 Acton, *Memoirs of an Aesthete*, 161
66 A&B, 203
67 Kahnweiler, intro. to PL, xii
68 Duncan, 16
69 SOA, 154
70 ABT, 228
71 GS to Carl Van Vechten, quoted in Ford, *Published in Paris*, 236
72 ABT, 228
73 EA, 99
74 Wilson, *Axel's Castle*, 244
75 ABT, 229
76 *Ibid.*, 231
77 WIR, 132
78 Thomson, "A Very Difficult Author"
79 AT to W. G. Rogers, March 14, 1947. Beinecke Library, Yale University
80 Thomson, *Virgil Thomson*, 183–84
81 Rosenshine, 224
82 *Ibid.*, 225
83 *Ibid.*, 227
84 *Ibid.*, 233
85 ABTC, 102
86 *Ibid.*, 283
87 *Ibid.*
88 Rose, *Saying Life*, 280
89 *Ibid.*, 63
90 Rose, "Gertrude Stein," 135
91 ABT, 175
92 Faÿ, *Les Précieux*, 137
93 *Ibid.*, 145–46 (trans. LS)
94 *Ibid.*, 146
95 *Ibid.*
96 Thomson, *op. cit.*, 89
97 WIR, 128
98 *Ibid.*, 137
99 Bowles, 5
100 SOA, 63
101 "Stanzas in Meditation," SIM, 90
102 SOA, 91
103 "And Now," Haas, Vol. II, 63
104 "First Page," SIM, 283
105 *Ibid.*, 284
106 *Ibid.*, 285
107 *Ibid.*, 289

108 *Ibid.*, 283
109 Braque, "Testimony Against Gertrude Stein"
110 ABT, 33
111 *Ibid.*, 126–27
112 JIS, 134
113 *Ibid.*, 142
114 *Ibid.*
115 *Ibid.*, 141
116 *Ibid.*, 136
117 EA, 50
118 *Ibid.*
119 *Ibid.*, 129
120 *Ibid.*, 163
121 WIR, 139
122 PL, 255
123 SOA, 246
124 EA, 169
125 WIR, 143
126 EA, 181
127 EA, 199
128 WIR, 143
129 *Ibid.*, 144
130 EA, 174
131 Poughkeepsie *Courier*, November 11, 1934
132 Brooklyn *Daily Eagle*, November 24, 1934
133 Brooklyn *Daily Eagle*, November 22, 1934
134 *Byrn Mawr Alumnae Bulletin*, January, 1935
135 *Bryn Mawr College News*, November 21, 1934
136 EA, 181
137 Sutherland, "Gertrude Stein and the Twentieth Century," in Haas, *A Primer for the Gradual Understanding of Gertrude Stein*, 140–41
138 Boston *Sunday Post*, October 21, 1934
139 ABTC, 134
140 EA, 207
141 WIR, 149
142 EA, 210
143 St. Paul *Pioneer Press*, December 9, 1934
144 EA, 223
145 *Ibid.*, 226
146 WIR, 126
147 *Ibid.*, 149
148 *The New York Times*, March 4, 1951
149 WIR, 150
150 *Sweet Briar News*, February 14, 1935
151 Tess Crager to LS, March 26, 1975
152 Frederick Hard to LS, March 29, 1975

153 EA, 270–71
154 AT to Samuel Steward, March 5, 1935. Beinecke Library, Yale University
155 EA, 227
156 *Ibid.*, 248
157 WIR, 153
158 Duncan, 11
159 WIR, 154
160 EA, 288
161 WIR, 155
162 Frederick Hard to LS, March 29, 1975
163 Conversation with Thornton Wilder, April 6, 1975
164 PL, 255
165 Paris *Tribune*, December 18, 1926
166 EA, 218–19
167 EA, 181
168 WIR, 158
169 Rose, "Gertrude Stein," 133
170 Gilot, 69
171 Sitwell, *Taken Care Of*, 146–47
172 GS to W. G. Rogers, March 1937. Beinecke Library, Yale University
173 Rogers, *When This You See . . .*, 137
174 WIR, 135
175 Rogers, *op. cit.*, 134
176 WIR, 161
177 GS to W. G. Rogers, n.d. Beinecke Library, Yale University
178 Secrest, 327–28
179 GS to W. G. Rogers, n.d. [1938]. Beinecke Library, Yale University
180 W. G. Rogers to GS, Spring 1939. Beinecke Library, Yale University
181 Duncan, 106
182 WIHS, 146–47
183 ABTC, 227
184 "Meditations." Beinecke Library, Yale University
185 ABTC, 218
186 Faÿ, *Les Précieux*, 162
187 "Castles they live in." Beinecke Library, Yale University
188 ABTC, 225
189 WIR, 164–65
190 Duncan, 48
191 Sevareid, 458
192 *Ibid.*, 462
193 WIR, 167
194 *Ibid.*, 168
195 Beaton, *Photobiography*, 179

196 W. G. Rogers to GS and AT, July 1, 1946
197 SOA, 4
198 *Ibid.*, 88

PART 4

1 SOA, 12
2 Hadley Hemingway Mowrer to AT, August 28, 1946. Beinecke Library, Yale University
3 Gallup, *The Flowers of Friendship*, 402
4 Frederica Rose to AT, August 8, 1946. Beinecke Library, Yale University
5 Francis Rose to AT, August 8, 1946. Beinecke Library, Yale University
6 SOA, 5
7 *Ibid.*, 15
8 *Ibid.*, 4
9 *Ibid.*, 13
10 Intro. to NOTY
11 Francis Rose to AT, April 1, 1947. Beinecke Library, Yale University
12 SOA, 74
13 *Ibid.*, 31
14 *Ibid.*, 54
15 Rago, "Gertrude Stein"
16 SOA, 57
17 *Ibid.*, 71
18 *Ibid.*, 49–50
19 *Ibid.*, 52
20 *Ibid.*, 107
21 Susan B. Anthony to AT, May 11, 1947. Beinecke Library, Yale University
22 SOA, 86
23 Sutherland, *Gertrude Stein . . .* , 14
24 *Ibid.*, 20
25 *Ibid.*, 21
26 *Ibid.*, 42–43
27 SOA, 83
28 *Ibid.*, 96
29 *Ibid.*, 294–95
30 *Ibid.*, 63
31 Faÿ, letter to François Monahan, July 22, 1955, p. 13. Beinecke Library, Yale University
32 AT to Samuel Steward, April 8, 1949
33 W. G. Rogers to AT, July 6, 1948. Beinecke Library, Yale University
34 SOA, 184

NOTES

35 AT to W. G. Rogers, May 16, 1948. Beinecke Library, Yale University
36 SOA, 158
37 Naomi Barry, "Alice B. Toklas, An Appreciation"
38 AT to Sutherland, August 17, 1948. Beinecke Library, Yale University
39 SOA, 217
40 Conversation with Thornton Wilder, April 6, 1975
41 ABT, 165
42 Faÿ, *Les Précieux*, 146
43 Friedrich, 122–26
44 Lord, 168
45 *Ibid*
46 *Ibid*., 169–70
47 "They Who Came . . ."
48 Friedrich, 100
49 *Ibid*.
50 SOA, 180
51 Brinnin, 408
52 J. M. Brinnin to LS, February 17, 1975
53 J. M. Brinnin to LS, February 22, 1975
54 SOA, 204
55 *Ibid*., 210
56 *Ibid*., 157
57 *Ibid*., 221
58 Knapik, *Haute Cuisine*, xviii
59 ABTC, 273
60 SOA, 310
61 Dorothy Bowen to LS, March 13, 1975
62 SOA, 196
63 *Ibid*., 198
64 *Ibid*., 209
65 Sutherland to AT, September 21, 1951
66 SOA, 260
67 *Ibid*., 288
68 Knapik, "With Alice B. Toklas," 92
69 SOA, 291
70 Joseph Barry, *The People of Paris*, 254
71 SOA, 291
72 *Ibid*., 269
73 *Ibid*., 351
74 *Ibid*., 273
75 *Ibid*., 272
76 Katz dissertation
77 SOA, 273–74
78 *Ibid*., 301
79 *Ibid*., 219

80 *Ibid.*, 219
81 *Ibid.*, 281
82 *Ibid.*, 343
83 *Ibid.*, 327
84 *Ibid.*, 312
85 AT to Annette Rosenshine, April 14, 1956. The Bancroft Library, University of California at Berkeley
86 Harrison, "Gertrude Stein and the Nay-Sayers"
87 Harrison, "Alice B. Toklas," 38
88 Sprigge, *Gertrude Stein* . . . , 81
89 *Ibid.*, 158
90 *Ibid.*, 192
91 *Ibid.*, 83
92 AT to Sutherland, July 8, 1953. Beinecke Library, Yale University
93 SOA, 209
94 *Ibid.*, 323
95 Harrison, "Alice B. Toklas"
96 Cannon, in AT's *Aromas and Flavors* . . . , xii
97 *Ibid.*
98 *Ibid.*, xvii
99 SOA, 104
100 Sutherland, "The Conversion of Alice B. Toklas," 131
101 SOA, 354
102 *Ibid.*, 356
103 Balmain, 149
104 Gallup, *The Flowers of Friendship*, 386
105 Balmain, 89
106 SOA, 34
107 AT to Annette Rosenshine, May 1958. The Bancroft Library, University of California at Berkeley
108 EA, 269
109 Max White to GS, May 11, 1937
110 All material quoted in these pages comes from the following letters by Max White:
—draft of letter written to Liveright in November 1974, but not sent. Beinecke Library, Yale University
—Max White to his lawyer, June 29, 1958
—Max White to LS, April 10, 1976, and April 17, 1976; and from conversation with Max White, April 30, 1975
111 SOA, 361
112 AT to Samuel Steward, August 7, 1958. The Bancroft Library, University of California at Berkeley
113 SOA, 358
114 Duncan, 86
115 Sutherland, "Alice and Gertrude and Others"
116 SOA, 390

NOTES

117 Lord, 178
118 Conversation with Thornton Wilder, April 6, 1975
119 Joseph Barry, "Memories of Miss Toklas," New York *Post*, May 23, 1963
120 SOA, 414
121 *Ibid.*, 417
122 Sutherland, "Alice and Gertrude and Others," 295
123 Doda Conrad, letter in *Esquire*, April 1968, p. 188
124 Bernard Faÿ to AT, September 17, 1951. Beinecke Library, Yale University
125 Sutherland, "Alice and Gertrude and Others," 299

Bibliography

BY GERTRUDE STEIN

A&B   *Alphabets and Birthdays*. Introduction by Donald Gallup. New Haven: Yale University Press, 1957

ABT   (see SW, *below*)

AFAM   *As Fine as Melanctha*. Foreword by Natalie Clifford Barney. New Haven: Yale University Press, 1954

BTV   *Bee Time Vine and Other Pieces*. Preface and notes by Virgil Thomson. New Haven: Yale University Press, 1953

B&W   *Brewsie and Willie*. New York: Random House, 1946

EA   *Everybody's Autobiography*. New York: Random House, 1937

FIA   *Four in America*. Introduction by Thornton Wilder. New Haven: Yale University Press, 1947

GHA   *The Geographical History of America, or The Relation of Human Nature to the Human Mind*. Introduction by Thornton Wilder. New York: Random House, 1936

GMP   *Matisse, Picasso and Gertrude Stein*. New York: Something Else Press, 1972

G&P   *Geography and Plays*. Boston: Four Seas, 1922

BIBLIOGRAPHY

Haas, Vol. I   *Reflections on the Atomic Bomb*. Edited by Robert Bartlett Haas. Los Angeles: Black Sparrow Press, 1974

Haas, Vol. II   *How Writing Is Written*. Edited by Robert Bartlett Haas. Los Angeles: Black Sparrow Press, 1974

HTW   *How To Write*. Paris: Plain Edition, 1931

LCA   *Lucy Church Amiably*. New York: Something Else Press, 1969

LIA   *Lectures in America*. New York: Random House, 1935

LO&P   *Last Operas and Plays*. Edited and with an introduction by Carl Van Vechten. New York: Rinehart, 1949

Meyerowitz   *Gertrude Stein: Writings and Lectures 1909–1945*. Edited by Patricia Meyerowitz. Baltimore: Penguin, 1971

MOA   *The Making of Americans*. New York: Something Else Press, 1966. This is a photocopy of the original Contact Editions version (1925). An abridged version contains a preface by Bernard Faÿ (New York: Harcourt, Brace, 1934, 1966).

MR   *Mrs. Reynolds and Five Earlier Novelettes*. Foreword by Lloyd Frankenberg. New Haven: Yale University Press, 1952

             Narration: Four Lectures by Gertrude Stein. Introduction by Thornton Wilder. Chicago: University of Chicago Press, 1935

NOTY   *A Novel of Thank You*. Introduction by Carl Van Vechten. New Haven: Yale University Press, 1958

O&P   *Operas and Plays*. Paris: Plain Edition, 1932

PL   *Painted Lace and Other Pieces (1914–1937)*. Introduction by Daniel-Henry Kahnweiler. New Haven: Yale University Press, 1955

             Paris France. London: Batsford, 1940

BIBLIOGRAPHY

Picasso. Boston: Beacon, 1959

P&P   *Portraits and Prayers.* New York: Random House, 1934

QED   *Fernhurst, Q.E.D. and Other Early Writings by Gertrude Stein.* Edited and with an introduction by Leon Katz. Appendix by Donald Gallup. New York: Liveright, 1971

SIM   *Stanzas in Meditation and Other Poems.* Preface by Donald Sutherland. New Haven: Yale University Press, 1956

SO&P   *Selected Operas and Plays of Gertrude Stein.* Edited and with an introduction by John Malcolm Brinnin. Pittsburgh: University of Pittsburgh Press, 1970

SW   *Selected Writings of Gertrude Stein.* Edited by Carl Van Vechten. New York: Random House, 1946. Includes *The Autobiography of Alice B. Toklas* (ABT); *Tender Buttons*; *Composition as Explanation*; "Portrait of Mabel Dodge at the Villa Curonia"; *As a Wife Has a Cow: A Love Story*; *Four Saints in Three Acts*, and several short pieces.

Three Lives. New York: Grafton, 1909

TWO   *Two: Gertrude Stein and Her Brother and Other Early Portraits.* Foreword by Janet Flanner. New Haven: Yale University Press, 1951

UK   *Useful Knowledge.* London: Bodley Head, 1929

WAM   *What Are Masterpieces.* Los Angeles: Conference Press, 1940

WIHS   *Wars I Have Seen.* New York: Random House, 1945

BY LEO STEIN

ABC   *The ABC of Aesthetics.* New York: Boni & Liveright, 1927

APP   *Appreciation: Painting, Poetry and Prose.* New York: Crown, 1947

BIBLIOGRAPHY

JIS   *Journey into the Self*. Edited by Edmund Fuller; foreword by Mabel Weeks; introduction by Van Wyck Brooks. New York: Crown, 1950

Articles:
"Pablo Picasso," *The New Republic*, April 23, 1924

"Ritual and Reality," in *The American Scholar Reader*, eds., Hiram Haydn and Betsy Saunders. New York: Atheneum, 1960, pp. 149–56.

BY ALICE B. TOKLAS

ABTC   *The Alice B. Toklas Cook Book*. New York: Harper Brothers, 1954; Anchor, 1960

Aromas and Flavors of Past and Present. Introduction and notes by Poppy Cannon. New York: Harper Brothers, 1958

Duncan   Interview by Ronald E. Duncan, for Oral History Department, The Bancroft Library, University of California at Berkeley. Typescript of taped interview (8 reels), 116 pp.

SOA   *Staying on Alone: Letters of Alice B. Toklas*. Edited by Edward Burns; introduction by Gilbert Harrison. New York: Liveright, 1973. (Researchers should note the absence of ellipses throughout these edited letters.)

WIR   *What Is Remembered*. New York: Holt, Rinehart & Winston, 1963

Articles:
"Between Classics," review of *The Short Stories of F. Scott Fitzgerald*. *The New York Times Book Review*, March 4, 1951, p. 4.

"Fifty Years of French Fashions," *The Atlantic Monthly*, June 1958, pp. 55–57

"The Rue Dauphine Refuses the Revolution," *The New Republic*, August 18, 1958, p. 8

"Some Memories of Henri Matisse: 1907–1922." *The Yale Literary Magazine*, Fall 1955, pp. 15–16

"Sylvia and Her Friends," *The New Republic*, October 19, 1959, p. 24

BIBLIOGRAPHY

"They Who Came to Paris to Write," *The New York Times Book Review*, August 6, 1950, pp. 1, 25

Acosta, Mercedes de. *Here Lies the Heart*. New York: Reynal & Company, 1960

Acton, Harold. *Memoirs of an Aesthete*. London: Methuen, 1948

———. *Memoirs of an Aesthete (1939–69)*. New York: Viking, 1971

Aldington, Richard. *Life for Life's Sake*. New York: Viking, 1941

Aldrich, Mildred. *A Hilltop on the Marne*. Boston: Houghton, Mifflin, 1915

Anderson, Elizabeth, and Kelly, Gerald R. *Miss Elizabeth*. Boston: Little, Brown, 1969

Anderson, Margaret. *The Little Review Anthology*. New York: Horizon, 1953

———. *My Thirty Years' War*. New York: Covici, Friede, 1930

Anderson, Sherwood. *Letters of Sherwood Anderson*. Edited by Howard Mumford Jones and Walter B. Rideout. Boston: Little, Brown, 1953

———. *Sherwood Anderson's Memoirs*. New York: Harcourt, Brace, 1942

———. *Sherwood Anderson's Notebooks*. New York: Boni & Liveright, 1926

———. *The Portable Sherwood Anderson*. New York: Viking, 1949

———. *A Story-Teller's Story*. New York: Huebsch, 1924

Apollinaire, Guillaume. *The Cubist Painters*. Translated by Lionel Abel. New York: Wittenborn, 1944

Ashton, Dore. *Picasso on Art: A Selection of Views*. New York: Viking, 1972

Astre, Georges Albert. *Hemingway par Lui-Même*. Paris: Editions du Seuil, 1959

Atherton, Gertrude. *Adventures of a Novelist*. New York: Liveright, 1932

———. *California, An Intimate History*. New York: Harper Brothers, 1914

———. *Golden Gate Country*. New York: Duell, Sloan & Pearce, 1945

———. "San Francisco and Her Foes," *Harper's Weekly*, November 2, 1907; pp. 1590–93

———. "San Francisco's Tragic Dawn," *Harper's Weekly*, May 12, 1906; pp. 656–60

BIBLIOGRAPHY

Baker, Carlos. *Ernest Hemingway: A Life Story*. New York: Scribner's, 1969

Balmain, Pierre. *My Years and Seasons*. New York: Doubleday, 1965

Barlow, Samuel L. M. "Ave Dione a Tribute," 20 pp. typescript. Beinecke Library, Yale University

Barnes, Djuna. *The Ladies Almanack*. New York: Harper & Row, 1972

Barney, Natalie Clifford. *Traits et portraits*. Paris: Mercure de France, 1963

Barr, Alfred H. *Matisse*. New York: Museum of Modern Art, 1966

————. *Picasso: Fifty Years of His Art*. New York: Museum of Modern Art, 1946

Barr, Beryl, and Sachs, Barbara Turner. *The Artists' and Writers' Cookbook*. Introduction by Alice Toklas. Sausalito: Contact Editions, 1961

Barry, Joseph. *The People of Paris*. New York: Doubleday, 1966

————. "Alice B. Toklas," *Village Voice*, March 16, 1967, p. 8

————. "Miss Toklas on Her Own," *The New Republic*, March 30, 1963. (This piece is included in *The People of Paris*)

Barry, Naomi. "Alice B. Toklas, An Appreciation." Paris: *Herald Tribune*, March 8, 1967, p. 2

————. "Paris à table: A Memory of Alice B. Toklas," *Gourmet*. August 1967, pp. 13, 28, 30

Bashkirtseff, Marie. *The Journal of a Young Artist, 1860–1844*. Translated by Mary J. Serrano. New York: Cassell, 1889

————. *Letters of. . . .* Translated by Mary J. Serrano, New York: Cassell, 1891

Beach, Sylvia, and Le Centre Culturel Américain. *Les Écrivains américains à Paris et leurs amis, 1920–1930*. Exposition, March 11–April 25, 1959. Paris: Le Centre Culturel Américain

————. *Shakespeare and Company*. New York: Harcourt, Brace, 1956

Beaton, Cecil. *Photobiography*. New York: Doubleday, 1951.

————. *The Wandering Years: Diaries: 1922–39*. Boston: Little, Brown, 1961.

Beer, Thomas. *The Mauve Decade*. New York: Knopf, 1926

————. "Playboy," *American Mercury*, June 1934

Berenson, Bernard. *Sunset and Twilight*. Edited by Nicky Mariano. New York: Harcourt, Brace, 1963

Biddle, George. *An American Artist's Story*. Boston: Little, Brown, 1939

Bishop, John Peale. *The Collected Essays*. Edited by Edmund Wilson. New York: Scribner's, 1948

BIBLIOGRAPHY

Bloom, Ellen F. "Three Steins," *Texas Quarterly*, Summer 1970, pp. 15–22

Boas, George. *The Heaven of Invention*. Baltimore: Johns Hopkins Press, 1962

Bodart, Anne. *The Blue Dog, and Other Fables for the French*. Translated by Alice B. Toklas. Boston: Houghton, Mifflin, 1956

Bonner, Geraldine. "The Passing of the Argonauts' City," *The Reader*, August 1906, Vol. VII, No. 3

Bonney, Therese. "Gertrude Stein in France," *Vogue's First Reader*. New York: Halcyon House, 1944

Bowles, Paul. *Without Stopping*. New York: Putnam, 1972

Boyle, Kay, and McAlmon, Robert. *Being Geniuses Together*. New York: Doubleday, 1968

Brady, Henry J., "Bohemian Club of San Francisco," *Harper's Weekly*, September 22, 1894, p. 895

Braque, Georges, et al. "Testimony Against Gertrude Stein," *transition*, Supplement, February 1935

Brassai. *Picasso and Company*. Translated by Francis Price. New York: Doubleday, 1966

Bridgman, Richard. *The Colloquial Style in America*. New York: Oxford University Press, 1966

———. *Gertrude Stein in Pieces*. New York: Oxford University Press, 1970

Brinnin, John Malcolm. *The Third Rose*. New York: Grove Press, 1959

Brooks, Van Wyck. *The Confident Years, 1885–1915*. New York: Dutton, 1952

———. *Days of the Phoenix*. New York: Dutton, 1957

———. *The Dream of Arcadia: American Writers and Artists in Italy, 1760–1915*. New York: Dutton, 1958

Brown, Milton W. *The Story of the Armory Show*. New York: Joseph H. Hirshhorn Foundation, 1963

Bruml, Moses. "The Life Story of Moses Bruml (1823–1901) of Lockeford, California, as Related by Himself in 1900." Typescript at American Jewish Archives, Cincinnati, Ohio

Bryher. *The Heart to Artemis: A Writer's Memoirs*. New York: Harcourt, Brace, 1962

Burgess, Gelett. *Bayside Bohemia*. San Francisco: Book Club of California, 1954

———. "The Wild Men of Paris," *The Architectural Record*, May 1910, pp. 401–14

Burke, Kenneth. "Engineering with Words," *Dial*, April 1923, pp. 408–12

Callaghan, Morley. *That Summer in Paris*. New York: Coward-McCann, 1963

Cannell, Kathleen. "Alice Alone: A Voice Not an Echo," *C.S.M.* January 23, 1974

Cerf, Bennett. "Trade Winds," *Saturday Review*, July 14, 1946, p. 14

Church, Ralph. "A Note on the Writing of Gertrude Stein," *transition*, Fall 1928, pp. 164–68

Cloud, Roy Walter. *Education in California: Leaders, Organizations and Accomplishments*. Stanford, 1952

Coates, Robert M. *The View from Here*. New York: Harcourt, Brace, 1960

Coburn, Alvin Langdon. *The Life of Alvin Langdon Coburn*. Edited by Helmut and Alison Gernsheim. New York: Praeger, 1966

Cocteau, Jean. *My Contemporaries*. Edited by Margaret Crosland. Philadelphia: Chilton, 1968

————. *Professional Secrets: An Autobiography of Jean Cocteau*. Edited by Robert Phelps. New York: Farrar, Straus & Giroux, 1970

Cooper, Douglas, et al. *Four Americans in Paris*. New York: Museum of Modern Art, 1970

Cory, Donald Webster. *The Homosexual in America*. New York: Greenberg, 1951

Cowley, Malcolm. *Exile's Return*. New York: Viking, 1951

————. *A Second Flowering*. New York: Viking, 1973

Crosby, Caresse. *The Passionate Years*. New York: Dial, 1953

Davidson, Jo. *Between Sittings*. New York: Dial, 1951

Dos Passos, John. *The Best Times*. New York: New American Library, 1966

Downey, Fairfax. *Portrait of an Era as Drawn by C. D. Gibson*. New York: Scribner's, 1939

Draper, Muriel. *Music at Midnight*. New York: Harper's, 1929

Dupee, F. W. *Henry James*. New York: Morrow, 1974

Earnest, Ernest. *Expatriates and Patriots: American Artists, Scholars and Writers in Europe*. Durham, N.C.: Duke University Press, 1968

Eastman, Max. *Einstein, Trotsky, Hemingway, Freud and Other Great Companions*. New York: Colliers, 1962

Edel, Leon. *Henry James*. 5 vols. New York: Lippincott, 1953–72

Edstrom, David. *The Testament of Caliban*. New York: Funk & Wagnalls, 1937

Eglington, Laurie. "Gertrude Stein Reveals Reactions to Home Country," *Art News*, November 3, 1934, pp. 3–4

Eliot, T. S. "Composition as Explanation," unsigned review in *The Criterion*, January 1927, p. 162

Ellis, Havelock. *Studies in the Psychology of Sex: Sexual Inversion*. Philadelphia: Davis, 1901

Fabre, Michel. *The Unfinished Quest of Richard Wright*. Translated by Isabel Barzun. New York: Morrow, 1973

Fadiman, Clifton. *Party of One*. New York: World, 1955

Faÿ, Bernard. *De la Prison de ce monde: Journals prières et pensées, 1944–1952*. Paris: Editions du Sapin Vert, 1952

————. *Les Précieux*. Paris: Librarie Académique Perrin, 1966

————. "Portrait de Gertrude Stein," *La Revue européene*, May 1930, pp. 592–99

————. "Portrait de Picasso," *Transatlantic Review*, July 1924, pp. 489–91

————. "A Rose Is a Rose," *Saturday Review of Literature*, September 2, 1933

Fenton, Charles A. *The Apprenticeship of Ernest Hemingway*. New York: Viking, 1954

————. "Ambulance Drivers in France and Italy, 1914–1918." *American Quarterly*, Winter 1951

Ferrier, William Warren. *Ninety Years of Education in California, 1846–1936*. Berkeley: Sather Gate Book Shop, 1937

Fielding, Daphne. *Those Remarkable Cunards*. New York: Atheneum, 1968

Fitzgerald, F. Scott. *The Crack-Up*. Edited by Edmund Wilson. New York: New Directions, 1945

————. *The Letters of F. Scott Fitzgerald*. Edited by Andrew Trumbull. New York: Scribner's, 1963

FitzGibbon, Constantine. *Paradise Lost and More*. London: Cassell, 1959

Flanner, Janet. *An American in Paris*. New York: Simon & Schuster, 1940

————. *Men and Monuments*, New York: Harper Brothers, 1957

————. *Paris Journal, 1944–1965*. Edited by William Shawn. New York: Atheneum, 1965

————. *Paris Journal, 1965–1971*. Edited by William Shawn. New York: Atheneum, 1971

————. *Paris Was Yesterday*. Edited by Irving Drutman. New York: Viking, 1972

Ford, Ford Madox. *It Was the Nightingale*. New York: Lippincott, 1933

Ford, Hugh, ed. *The Left Bank Revisited: Selections from the Paris Tribune, 1917–34*. University Park: Pennsylvania State University Press, 1972

————. *Published in Paris*. New York: Macmillan, 1975

Friedrich, Otto. "The Grave of Alice B. Toklas," *Esquire*, January 1968, pp. 98–103, 121–24. See "The Sound and the Fury," letters column, *Esquire*, April 1968, p. 188, for a comment by Doda Conrad.

Gallup, Donald, ed. *The Flowers of Friendship*. New York: Knopf, 1953

————. "Always Gtrde Stein," *Southwest Review*, Summer 1949, pp. 254–58

BIBLIOGRAPHY

————. "Carl Van Vechten's Gertrude Stein" *Yale University Library Gazette*, October 1952, pp. 77–86

————. "Gertrude Stein and *The Atlantic*," *Yale University Library Gazette*. July 1953, pp. 109–28

————. "The Gertrude Stein Collection," *Yale University Library Gazette*. October 1947, pp. 21–32

————. "Picasso, Gris and Gertrude Stein," in *Picasso, Gris, Miro* in San Francisco Museum of Art, 1948, pp. 15–23

Gass, W. H. "Gertrude Stein: Her Escape from Protective Language," *Accent*, Autumn 1958, pp. 233–44

Genthe, Arnold. *As I Remember*. New York: Reynal & Hitchcock, 1936

Gervasi, Frank. "Liberation of Gertrude Stein," *Saturday Review*, August 21, 1971, pp. 13–14, 57

Gilot, Françoise, and Lake, Carlton. *Life with Picasso*. New York: McGraw-Hill, 1964

Gimpel, René. *Diary of an Art Dealer*. Translated by John Rosenberg. New York: Farrar, Straus & Giroux, 1966

Glanz, Rudolf. *The Jews of California, from the Discovery of Gold Until 1880*. New York: Ktav Publishing House, 1960

————. *Studies in Judaica Americana*. New York: Ktav Publishing House, 1970

Glasgow, Ellen. *Letters of Ellen Glasgow*. Edited by Blair Rouse. New York: Harcourt, Brace, 1958

Glassco, John. *Memoirs of Montparnasse*. New York: Oxford University Press, 1970

Goldstone, R. H. *Thornton Wilder*. New York: Saturday Review Press/Dutton, 1975

Gourmont, Rémy de. *Decadence and Other Essays on the Culture of Ideas*. Translated by William A. Bradley. New York: Harcourt, Brace, 1921

Gramont, Elizabeth de. *Pomp and Circumstance*. Translated by Brian W. Downs. New York: Jonathan Cape & Harrison Smith, 1929

Grant, Frederic James. *History of Seattle, Washington*. New York: American Publishing and Engraving Co., 1891

Grosser, Maurice. *The Painter's Eye*. New York: Rinehart, 1951

————. *Painting in Public*. New York: Knopf, 1948

Haas, Robert Bartlett. *A Primer for the Gradual Understanding of Gertrude Stein*. Los Angeles: Black Sparrow Press, 1971; includes Donald Sutherland, "Gertrude Stein and the Twentieth Century"

————. "Gertrude Stein Talking: A Transatlantic Interview," *Uclan Review 8*, Summer 1962, pp. 3–11; *9*, Spring 1963, pp. 40–48; *10*, Winter 1964, pp. 44–48.

————, and Gallup, Donald. *Catalogue of the Published and*

Unpublished Writings of Gertrude Stein. New Haven: Yale University Press, 1941

Hamnett, Nina. *Laughing Torso*. London: Constable, 1932

Hapgood, Hutchins. *A Victorian in the Modern World*. New York: Harcourt, Brace, 1939

Harriman, Margaret Case. *The Vicious Circle: The Story of the Algonquin Round Table*. New York: Rinehart, 1951

Harrison, Gilbert A. "Alice B. Toklas," *The New Republic*, March 18, 1967, pp. 24, 37–38

———. "Gertrude Stein and the Nay-Sayers," *The New Republic*, March 18, 1957, pp. 17–18

Hemingway, Ernest. *By-Line: Ernest Hemingway*. Edited by William White. New York: Scribner's, 1967

———. *The Green Hills of Africa*. New York: Scribner's, 1935

———. *The Hemingway Reader*. Edited by Charles Poore. New York: Scribner's, 1953

———. *A Moveable Feast*. New York: Scribner's, 1950

———. "The Farm," *Cahiers d'Art*, 1934, pp. 28–29

Hobhouse, Janet. *Everybody Who Was Anybody*. New York: Putnam, 1975

Hoffman, Frederick J. *Gertrude Stein*. Minneapolis: University of Minnesota Press, 1961

———. "The Color and Shape of the Thing Seen: Gertrude Stein," in *The Twenties*. New York: Viking, 1955, pp. 186–96

Holder, Alan. *Three Voyagers in Search of Europe: A Study of Henry James, Ezra Pound, and T. S. Eliot*. Philadelphia: University of Pennsylvania Press, 1966

Holroyd, Michael. *Lytton Strachey: The Years of Achievement, 1910–1932*. New York: Holt, Rinehart & Winston, 1968

Houseman, John. *Run-through: A Memoir*. New York: Simon & Schuster, 1972

Howe, Granville. *A Hundred Years of Music in America*. Chicago: Howe, 1889

Huddleston, Sisley. *Back to Montparnasse*. New York: Lippincott, 1931

Huebsch, B. W. "From a Publisher's Commonplace Book," *American Scholar*, Winter 1963–64, pp. 116–30

Hunt, Violet. *I Have This to Say: The Story of My Flurried Years*. New York: Boni & Liveright, 1926

Imbs, Bravig. *Confessions of Another Young Man*. New York: Henkle-Yewdale, 1936

Irwin, Will. "The City That Was," New York *Sun*, April 21, 1906

James, Henry. *The Novels and Tales*. New York Edition, Scribner's, 1908

BIBLIOGRAPHY

————. *Letters of Henry James*, Vol. I. Edited by Leon Edel. Cambridge, Mass.: Harvard University Press, 1974

————. *The Letters of Henry James*, Vols. I and II. Edited by Percy Lubbock. New York: Scribner's, 1920

James, William. "On Some Mental Effects of the Earthquake," in *Memories and Studies*. New York: Longmans, 1911, pp. 209–26

Jarry, Alfred. *Ubu Roi*. Translated by Barbara Wright. New York: New Directions, 1961

Jelenko, Therese. "Reminiscences," 10-page typescript of tape recording. The Bancroft Library, University of California at Berkeley

Jordan, David Starr. *The Call of the Twentieth Century*. Boston: American Unitarian Association, 1903

Josephson, Matthew. *Life Among the Surrealists*. New York: Holt, 1962

————. *Portrait of the Artist as American*. New York: Harcourt, Brace, 1930

Joy, Emmett P. *The Annals of Mokelumne Hill: The Story of a Veritable Gold Mountain*. Murphys, Calif.: Old Timer's Museum, 1968

Kahn, Albert. *Joys and Sorrows: Reflections by Pablo Casals*. New York: Simon & Schuster, 1970

Kahnweiler, Daniel-Henry. *Confessions esthétiques*. Paris: Gallimard, 1963

————. *Juan Gris*. Translated by Douglas Cooper. New York: Valentin, 1947

————. *The Rise of Cubism*. Translated by Henry Aronson. New York: Wittenborn, 1949

———— and Cremieux. *My Galleries and Painters*. Translated by Helen Weaver. New York: Viking, 1971

Kallen, Horace. "The Imagists: Gertrude Stein," *Art and Freedom*, Vol. II. New York: Duell, Sloan and Pearce, 1942, pp. 800–03

Katz, Leon. "The First Making of The Making of Americans." Ph.D. dissertation, Columbia University

Kazin, Alfred. "From an Italian Journal," *Partisan Review*, May 1948, pp. 550–67

————. "The Indignant Flesh," *The New Yorker*, September 9, 1950, p. 113

————. "The Mystery of Gertrude Stein," in *Contemporaries*. Boston: Little, Brown, 1962, pp. 99–104

Kirk, H. L. *Pablo Casals*. New York: Holt, Rinehart & Winston, 1974

Kirsch, Robert, and Murphy, William S. *West of the West*. New York: Dutton, 1967

Kellner, Bruce. *Carl Van Vechten and the Irreverent Decades*. Norman: University of Oklahoma Press, 1968

BIBLIOGRAPHY

Knapik, Harold. *Haute Cuisine Without Help*. New York: Liveright, 1971

————. "With Alice B. Toklas," *Gourmet*, March 1974, pp. 35–36, 90–95

Knoll, Robert E., ed. *McAlmon and the Lost Generation*. Lincoln: University of Nebraska Press, 1962

Kobler, J. F. "Hemingway's *The Sea Change:* A Sympathetic View of Homosexuality," *Arizona Quarterly*, Winter 1970, pp. 318–24

Lachman, Arthur. "Gertrude Stein As I Knew Her," 10-page typescript. Beinecke Library, Yale University

Levinson, Robert E. *Pioneer Jewish Cemeteries and Communities of the California Mother Lode*. Oakland: Commission for the Preservation of Pioneer Jewish Cemeteries and Landmarks, Magnes Memorial Museum, 1964

Levy, Harriet. *920 O'Farrell Street*. New York: Doubleday, 1947

————. "Recollections," unpaged typescript. The Bancroft Library, University of California at Berkeley

Lewis, Oscar. *Bay Window Bohemia*. New York: Doubleday, 1956

Leymarie, Jean. *Braque*. Translated by James Emmons. Paris: Skira, 1961

Lignian, Mildred. *Folks and Oaks of Olivet*. Olivet, Mich.: Olivet College, 1975

Lippard, Lucy, ed. *Dadas on Art*. Englewood Cliffs, N.J.: Prentice-Hall, 1971

————. *Surrealists on Art*. Englewood Cliffs, N.J.: Prentice-Hall, 1970

Lipschitz, Jacques. *My Life in Sculpture*. New York: Viking, 1972

Loeb, Harold. *The Way It Was*. New York: Criterion, 1959

Loos, Anita. *A Girl Like I*. New York: Viking, 1966

————. *Kiss Hollywood Good-bye*. New York: Viking, 1974

Lord, James. ". . . Where the Pictures Were: A Memoir . . . ," *Prose*, No. 7, 1973, pp. 133–87

Luce, Robert B., ed. *The Faces of Five Decades*. New York: Simon & Schuster, 1964

Lueders, Edward. *Carl Van Vechten*. New York: Twayne, 1965

Luhan, Mabel Dodge. *European Experiences*. New York: Harcourt, Brace, 1935

————. *Movers and Shakers*. New York: Harcourt, Brace, 1936

Lundell, William. Interview with Gertrude Stein on WJZ radio, New York, November 12, 1934; 9-page typescript at Beinecke Library, Yale University

Lynes, Russell. *Good Old Modern*. New York: Atheneum, 1973

Man Ray. *Self-Portrait*. Boston: Little, Brown, 1963

BIBLIOGRAPHY

Mayer, R. *San Francisco: A Chronological and Documentary History*. Dobbs Ferry, N.Y.: Oceana Publications, 1973

Mellow, James. *Charmed Circle*. New York: Praeger, 1974

Meyer, Martin A. *Western Jewry: An Account of the Achievements of the Jews and Judaism in California*. San Francisco: Emanu-El Pub., 1916

Miller, Rosalind S. *Gertrude Stein: Form and Intelligibility*. Jericho, N.Y.: Exposition Press, 1949

Monnier, Adrienne. *Les Gazettes d'Adrienne Monnier, 1925–1945*. Paris: René Julliard, 1953

————. *Rue de l'Odéon*. Paris: Albin Michel, 1960

Morrell, Lady Ottoline. *Memoirs: A Study in Friendship, 1873–1914*. Edited by Robert Gathorne-Hardy. New York: Knopf, 1964

Musée National d'Art Moderne. *Le Cubisme (1907–1914)*. Paris: Editions des Musées Nationaux, 1953

Norris, Kathleen. *My San Francisco*. New York: Doubleday, 1932

Olivier, Fernande. *Picasso and His Friends*. Translated by Jane Miller. London: Heinemann, 1964

Pach, Walter. *Queer Thing, Painting: Forty Years in the World of Art*. New York: Harper Brothers, 1938

Parmelin, Helene. *Picasso Says*. Cranbury, N.J.: A. S. Barnes, 1969

Paul, Elliot "Art and Camouflage," in *Vogue's First Reader*. New York: Halcyon, 1944, pp. 256–59

Paxton, Robert O. *Vichy France: Old Guard and New Order, 1940–1944*. New York: Knopf, 1972

Peixotto, Ernest. *Romantic California*. New York: Scribner's, 1910

Penrose, Roland. *Picasso: His Life and Work*. New York: Harper & Row, 1973

————. *Portrait of Picasso*. New York: Museum of Modern Art, 1956; rev. 1971

Phelan, J. D. "Rise of the New San Francisco," *Cosmopolitan*, October 1906, pp. 575–82

Pivano, Fernanda. "Alice B. Toklas a Roma," in *America Rossa e Nera*. Firenze: Vallechi Editore, 1964, pp. 103–08

Plimpton, George. "Hemingway," in *The Paris Review: Writers at Work*. New York: Viking, 1963, pp. 215–39

Pollack, Barbara. *The Collectors: Dr. Claribel and Miss Etta Cone*. New York: Bobbs-Merrill, 1962

Porter, Katherine Anne. "Gertrude Stein: Three Views," in *The Days Before*. New York: Harcourt, Brace, 1952, pp. 36–60

Pound, Ezra. "René Crevel," *The Criterion*, January 1939, p. 227

Preston, John Hyde. "A Conversation with Gertrude Stein," in *The Creative Process*. Edited by B. Ghiselin. New York: New American Library, 1952, pp. 159–67

Purrmann, Hans. "From the Workshop of Henry Matisse." Translated by Kenneth Burke. *The Dial*, July 1922, pp. 32–40

Putnam, Samuel. *Paris Was Our Mistress*. New York: Viking, 1948

Rago, Henry. "Gertrude Stein," *Poetry*, November 1946, pp. 93–97

Rahv, Philip, ed. *Discovery of Europe*. Boston: Houghton, Mifflin, 1947

Rather, Lois. *Gertrude Stein and California*. San Francisco: Rather Press, 1974

Reid, B. L. *Art by Subtraction: A Dissenting Opinion of Gertrude Stein*. Norman: University of Oklahoma Press, 1958

Riding, Laura. "The New Barbarism and Gertrude Stein," *transition*, June 1927, pp. 153–68

Rogers, W. G. *Ladies Bountiful*. New York: Harcourt, Brace, 1968

———. *When This You See Remember Me*. New York: Rinehart, 1948

Rose, Sir Francis. *Saying Life*. London: Cassell, 1961

———. "Gertrude Stein," *Vogue*, January 1, 1971, pp. 88–89, 133, 135

Rosenshine, Annette. "Life's Not a Paragraph," 267-page typescript, not dated [c. 1964]. The Bancroft Library, University of California at Berkeley

Ross, Lillian. "How Do You Like It Now, Gentlemen?" *The New Yorker*, May 13, 1950, pp. 36–56

Russell, Bertrand. *The Autobiography of Bertrand Russell, 1872–1914*. Boston: Little, Brown, 1967

Saarinen, Aline B. *The Proud Possessors*. New York: Random House, 1958

Sabartes, Jaime. *Picasso: An Intimate Portrait*. Englewood Cliffs, N.J.: Prentice-Hall, 1948

Salmon, André. *Souvenirs sans fin*, Vol. II. Paris: Gallimard, 1956

Salter, Elizabeth. *The Last Years of a Rebel: A Memoir of Edith Sitwell*. Boston: Houghton, Mifflin, 1967

Saroyan, William. *Places Where I've Done Time*. New York: Praeger, 1972

Schorer, Mark. "Gertrude Stein," in *The World We Imagine*. New York: Farrar, Straus & Giroux, 1968, pp. 299–305

Scudder, Janet. *Modeling My Life*. New York: Harcourt, Brace, 1925

Secrest, Meryle. *Between Me and Life*. New York: Doubleday, 1974

Sevareid, Eric. *Not So Wild a Dream*. New York: Knopf, 1946

Sharfman, I. Harold. *Nothing Left to Commemorate*. Glendale, Calif.: Clark, 1969

Shattuck, Roger. *The Banquet Years*. New York: Harcourt, Brace, 1955

Shaw, Barnett. "Encounter with Gertrude Stein, Paris, 1944," *Texas Quarterly*, Autumn 1966, pp. 21–23

Sitwell, Edith. *The Collected Poems*. New York: Vanguard, 1954

————. *Taken Care Of*. New York: Atheneum, 1965

————. "The Making of Americans," *The Criterion*, April 1926, pp. 390–92

————. "Notes on Innovations in Prose," in *Aspects of Modern Poetry*. Freeport, N.Y.: Books for Libraries, 1970, pp. 215–26

Sitwell, Osbert. *Laughter in the Next Room*. Boston: Little, Brown, 1948

Skinner, B. F. "Has Gertrude Stein a Secret," *The Atlantic Monthly*, January 1934, pp. 50–57

Skinner, Lloyd. "Alice and Gertrude Meet the Press," *San Francisco Magazine*, July 1970, pp. 20–22, 39–40

Smith, Logan Pearsall. *Unforgotten Years*. Boston: Little, Brown, 1939

Soby, James Thrall. *Juan Gris*. New York: Museum of Modern Art, 1958

————. *Modern Art and the New Past*. Norman: University of Oklahoma Press, 1957

Sokoloff, Alice Hunt. *Hadley, The First Mrs. Hemingway*. New York: Dodd, Mead, 1973

Sprigge, Elizabeth. *Gertrude Stein, Her Life and Work*. New York: Harper Brothers, 1957

————. "Gertrude Stein's American Years," *The Reporter*, August 11, 1955, pp. 46–52

Steegmuller, Francis. *Apollinaire, Poet Among the Painters*. New York: Farrar, Straus & Giroux, 1963

Steele, O. L. "Gertrude Stein and Ellen Glasgow: Memoir of a Meeting," *American Literature*, March 1961, pp. 76–77

Sterne, Maurice. *Shadow and Light*. New York: Harcourt, Brace, 1965

Stewart, Allegra. *Gertrude Stein and the Present*. Cambridge, Mass.: Harvard University Press, 1967

Stewart, Lawrence D. *Paul Bowles: The Illumination of North Africa*. Carbondale: Southern Illinois University Press, 1974

Sulzberger, Cyrus L. *A Long Row of Candles*. New York: Macmillan, 1969

Sutherland, Donald. *Gertrude Stein: A Biography of Her Work*. New Haven: Yale University Press, 1951

————. "Alice and Gertrude and Others," *Prairie Schooner*, Winter 1971–72, pp. 284–99

————. "The Conversion of Alice B. Toklas," *Colorado Quarterly*, Autumn 1968, pp. 129–41

————. "The Pleasures of Gertrude Stein," *New York Review of Books*, May 30, 1974, pp. 28–30

————. "Wicked Alice in Wonderland," *Denver Quarterly*, Spring 1974, pp. 80–83

Swift, Fletcher Harper. "Emma Marwedel, 1818–1893," *University of California Publications in Education*, Vol. VI, 1930–32. Berkeley: University of California Press, 1932, pp. 139–216

Tate, Allen. "Miss Toklas' American Cake," *Prose*, Fall 1971, pp. 137–61

Teresa of Jesus, St. *The Life of St. Teresa of Jesus.* Translated by David Lewis. London: Thomas Baker, 1916

Teriade, E. "Matisse Speaks," *Art News Annual 21*, 1952, pp. 40–71

Thomas, Gordon, and Witts, Max Morgan. *San Francisco Earthquake.* New York: Stein & Day, 1971

Thomson, Virgil. *Virgil Thomson.* New York: Knopf, 1966

————. "A Very Difficult Author," *New York Review of Books*, April 8, 1971, pp. 3–8

Tint, Herbert. *France Since 1918.* New York: Harper & Row, 1970

Tomkins, Calvin. *Living Well Is the Best Revenge.* New York: Viking, 1971

Troy, William. "A Note on Gertrude Stein," *The Nation*, September 6, 1933, pp. 274–75

Turgenev, Ivan. *Fathers and Sons.* Translated by Barbara Makanowitzsky. New York: Bantam, 1959

Tuttleton, James, moderator. New York University panel discussion on Gertrude Stein, with Perry Miller Adato, Edward Burns, Leon Katz, and W. G. Rogers, February 1973, 3 tapes. Beinecke Library, Yale University

Tyler, Parker. *The Divine Comedy of Pavel Tchelitchew: A Biography.* New York: Fleet Press, 1967

Valentin, Antonia. *Picasso.* New York: Doubleday, 1963

Van Vechten, Carl. *Peter Whiffle: His Life and Works.* New York: Knopf, 1922

————. *Sacred and Profane Memories.* New York: Knopf, 1932

————. "How to Read Gertrude Stein," *The Trend*, August 1914, pp. 553–57

————. "Some 'Literary Ladies' I Have Known," *Yale University Library Gazette 26*, January 1952, pp. 97–116

Vollard, Ambroise. *Souvenirs d'un marchand de tableaux.* Paris: Albin Michel, 1937

Warren, Lansing. "Gertrude Stein Views Life and Politics," *The New York Times Magazine*, May 6, 1934, p. 9

BIBLIOGRAPHY

Weil, Oscar. *Letters and Papers*. San Francisco: Book Club of California, 1923

Weininger, Otto. *Sex and Character*. New York: Putnam, 1906

Wells, Evelyn. *Champagne Days of San Francisco*. New York: Doubleday, 1947

White, Ray Lewis, ed. *Sherwood Anderson/Gertrude Stein*. Chapel Hill: University of North Carolina Press, 1972

Wickes, George. *Americans in Paris*. New York: Doubleday, 1969

————. "A Natalie Barney Garland," *The Paris Review*, Spring 1975, pp. 84–134

Wickham, Harvey. *The Impuritans*. New York: Dial, 1929

Williams, William Carlos. *The Autobiography of William Carlos Williams*. New York: Random House, 1951

————. *Selected Essays of William Carlos Williams*. New York: Random House, 1954

Wilson, Edmund. *Axel's Castle*. New York: Scribner's, 1952

————. *The Shores of Light*. New York: Farrar, Straus & Giroux, 1952

————. *The Wound and the Bow*. New York: Oxford University Press, 1947

Index

INDEX

INDEX

INDEX

INDEX

INDEX